IN SEARCH OF JYOTISH

24 JINENDRAMALA

SARAJIT PODDAR
AN EARNEST JYOTIṢA SEEKER

KINDLE DIRECT PUBLISHING
AUGUST 2023

FIRST EDITION
August 2023
ISBN: 979-8854501392

Published by
Kindle Direct Publishing

https://www.facebook.com/sarajit.poddar
https://www.facebook.com/srivarahamihira
https://www.facebook.com/insearchofjyotish
https://twitter.com/srivarahamihira

फलानि ग्रह चारेण सूचयन्ति मनीषिणः।
को वक्ता तारतम्यस्य तमेकं वेधसं विना॥
phalāni graha cāreṇa sūcayanti manīṣiṇaḥ।
ko vaktā tāratamyasya tamekaṃ vedhasaṃ vinā॥

For human beings, the fruits of their actions are indicated by the movement of Grahas. Except for the creator Brahmā, who can certainly tell what will happen!

01 AUGUST 2023

Dedicated to **Śrī Nīlakaṇṭha**
Who saved the Universe by
consuming Halāhala.

श्री नीलकंठ स्तोत्रम

विनियोग:

ॐ अस्य श्री भगवान नीलकंठ सदा-शिव-स्तोत्र मंत्रस्य श्री ब्रह्मा ऋषिः, अनुष्टुप छन्दः, श्री नीलकंठ सदाशिवो देवता, ब्रह्म बीजं, पार्वती शक्तिः, मम समस्त पाप क्षयार्थंक्षे म-स्थै-आर्यु-आरोग्य-अभिवृद्धयर्थं मोक्षादि-चतुर्वर्ग-साधनार्थं च श्री नीलकंठ-सदाशिव-प्रसाद-सिद्धयर्थे जपे विनियोगः।

ऋष्यादि न्यास:

श्री ब्रह्मा ऋषये नमः शिरसि। अनुष्टुप छन्दसेनमः मुखे। श्री नीलकंठ सदाशिव देवतायै नमः हृदि। ब्रह्म बीजाय नमः लिंगे। पार्वती शक्त्यैनमः नाभौ। मम समस्त पाप क्षयार्थंक्षेम-स्थै-आर्यु-आरोग्य-अभिवृद्धयर्थं मोक्षादि-चतुर्वर्ग-साधनार्थंच श्री नीलकंठ-सदाशिव-प्रसाद-सिद्धयर्थे जपे विनियोगाय नमः सर्वांगे।

स्तोत्रम्

ॐ नमो नीलकंठाय, श्वेत-शरीराय, सर्पालंकार भूषिताय, भुजंग परिकराय, नागयज्ञो पवीताय, अनेक मृत्यु विनाशाय नमः। युग युगांत काल प्रलय-प्रचंडाय, प्र ज्वाल-मुखाय नमः। दंष्ट्राकराल घोर रूपाय हूं हूं फट् स्वाहा। ज्वालामुखाय, मंत्र करालाय, प्रचंडार्क सहस्त्रांशु चंडाय नमः। कर्पूर मोद परिमलांगाय नमः।

ॐ इंद्र नील महानील वज्र वैलक्ष्य मणि माणिक्य मुकुट भूषणाय हन हन हन दहन दहनाय ह्रीं स्फुर स्फुर प्रस्फुर प्रस्फुर घोर घोर तनुरूप चट चट प्रचट प्रचट कह कह वम वम बंध बंध घातय घातय हूं फट् जरा मरण भय हूं हूं फट् स्वाहा। आत्म मंत्र संरक्षणाय नमः।

ॐ ह्रां ह्रीं ह्रीं स्फुर अघोर रूपाय रथ रथ तंत्र तंत्र चट् चट् कह कह मद मद दहन दाहनाय ह्रीं स्फुर स्फुर प्रस्फुर प्रस्फुर घोर घोर तनुरूप चट चट प्रचट प्रचट कह कह वम वम बंध बंध घातय घातय हूं फट् जरा मरण भय हूं हूं फट् स्वाहा।

अनंताघोर ज्वर मरण भय क्षय कुष्ठ व्याधि विनाशाय, शाकिनी डाकिनी ब्रह्मराक्षस दैत्य दानव बंधनाय, अपस्मार भूत बैताल डाकिनी शाकिनी सर्व ग्रह विनाशाय, मंत्र कोटि प्रकटाय पर विद्योच्छेदनाय, हूं हूं फट् स्वाहा। आत्म मंत्र संरक्षणाय नमः।

ॐ ह्रां ह्रीं ह्रौं नमो भूत डामरी ज्वालवश भूतानां द्वादश भू तानांत्रयो दश षोडश प्रेतानां पंच दश डाकिनी शाकिनीनां हन हन। दहन दारनाथ! एकाहिक द्वयाहिक त्र्याहिक चातुर्थिक पंचाहिक व्याध्य पादांत वातादि वात सरिक कफ पित्तक काश श्वास श्लेष्मादिकं दह दह छिन्धि छिन्धि श्रीमहादेव निर्मित स्तंभन मोहन वश्याकर्षणोच्चाटन कीलना द्वेषण इति षट् कर्माणि वृत्य हूं हूं फट् स्वाहा।

वात-ज्वर मरण-भय छिन्न छिन्न नेह नेह भूतज्वर प्रेतज्वर पिशाचज्वर रात्रिज्वर शीतज्वर तापज्वर बालज्वर कुमारज्वर अमितज्वर दहनज्वर ब्रह्मज्वर विष्णुज्वर रूद्रज्वर मारीज्वर प्रवेशज्वर कामादि विषमज्वर मारी ज्वर प्रचण्ड घराय प्रमथेश्वर! शीघ्रं हूं हूं फट् स्वाहा।

॥ॐ नमो नीलकंठाय, दक्षज्वर ध्वंसनाय श्री नीलकंठाय नमः॥

॥इतिश्री नीलकंठ स्तोत्रम संपूर्णः॥

ॐ गणानां त्वा गणपतिं हवामहे
कविं कवीनामुपमश्रवस्तमम् ।
ज्येष्ठराजं ब्रह्मणाम् ब्रह्मणस्पत
आ नः शृण्वन्नूतिभिःसीदसादनम् ॥
ॐ महागणाधिपतये नमः ॥

ॐ सह नाववतु। सह नौ भुनक्तु।
सह वीर्यं करवावहै।
तेजस्वि नावधीतमस्तु मा विद्विषावहै।
ॐ शान्तिः शान्तिः शान्तिः॥

om saha nāvavatu। saha nau bhunaktu।
saha vīryaṁ karavāvahai।
tejasvi nāvadhītamastu mā vidviṣāvahai।
om śāntiḥ śāntiḥ śāntiḥ॥

OM! May He protect us!
May He nourish us!
May we work together with great energy!
May our intellect be sharp and study effective!
Let there be no animosity between us!
OM! Let there be Peace in me!
Let there be Peace in the world!
Let there be Peace in the forces that act on me!

PREFACE

Jinendramāla, also called Jainendramāla, Jinendramālai or Jainendramālai, is an outstanding work on Praśna written in Tamil Language written by a Jain monk named Upendrācārya. This system makes extensive use of Udayalagna, Āruṛhalagna, and Chatralagna. In colloquial language, this is also called the Āruṛha system of predictions, or simply Āruṛham, due to the extensive use of Āruṛha. Among the Tamil Savants of Jyotiṣaśastra, this system is also called Sāmakkol Āruṛham or Jāmakkol Āruṛham. This is made up of two words, Sāma or Jāma, which is a Tamil short form of Jāmam or Yāma.

The term Yāma is used differently in different contexts. In the Patākiriṣṭa chapter, we notice that an Ahorātra has 8 Yāmas, and each Dina and Rātri has 4 Yāma each. The idea is also endorsed by Ācārya Harihara, who states in Praśnamārga 31.47, a night has four Yāmas. If the dream is seen in the 1st Yāma, the result is before the lapse of one full year; in the 2nd, before the lapse of 6 months; in the 3rd, before the lapse of 3 months; and in the 4th, before the lapse of one month.

If the dream occurs at dawn, the result takes place soon. According to this division, the duration of each Yāma is 7.5 Ghaṭi or 3 hours. In the same chapter of Patāki Riṣṭa, we note that a Yāma is divided into two parts, called Yamārdhas, which are of 3.75 Ghaṭi or 1.5 hours duration, and the 6th Vāreśa lords them from the previous yāmārdhapati. The yāmārdhapati reckoning starts from the Vāreśa at Sūryodaya. In the evening, however, the sequence changes to the 5th Vāreśa from the previous one.

In the context of Guḻika computation, however (vide Maharṣi Parāśara), each of Dina and Rātri is divided into 8 Yāmas each, making 16 Yāmas in an Ahorātra. In another context of Svaraśāstra, Ācārya Harihara states that are 16 Yāmas in an Ahorātra. He states in Praśnamārga 16.31 that of the eight Yāmas into which the daytime is divided, the odd ones begin in Pṛthvībhūta and end in Ākāśabhūta. The even ones rise in Ākāśabhūta and end in Pṛthvībhūta: the duration of the Bhūtas in a Yāma in terms of Vighaṭis being Pṛthvī 75, Apa 60, Agni 45, Vāyu 30 and Ākāśa 15. Similar is the case regarding the night.

The measure of Jāmam is also used in Pañcapakṣī Śāstra. However, in this Śāstra, the Jāmam used is of 2.4 hours, and there are 10 Jāmams in an Ahorātra, 5 each during the day and night, corresponding to the 5 Bhūtas. Therefore, the measure of Jāmam is used in different contexts where they mean different things. Coming to the topic of Jāmakkol Āruṛham, here, Jāmam is of 1.5 hours or 3.75 hours duration approx., and there are 16 Jāmams in an Ahorātra.

The Jāmams are, however, not of equal duration of the daytime and nighttime because that depends on the day length (Dinamāna) and night length (Rātrimāna). When the Dinamāna is divided into 8 parts, each of them is called Dina-Jāmam, and likewise, the night ones are called Rātri-Jāmam. The Dinamāna is the duration between Sūryāsta to Sūryodaya, and the Rātrimāna is the duration between Sūryāsta and the following Sūryodaya.

As per Jāmakkol Āruṛham, the Lord of the first Jāmam of either Day or Night is the Vāreśa (Vāra Lord), and the following are in the order of Sūrya → Maṅgala → Bṛhaspati → Budha → Śukra → Śani → Candra → Rāhu. Let us call this a Jāmamādhipati order for ease of reference. The order is almost like the Vāra order but with some differences: (1) Candra after Śani, and (2) there is an exchange of Budha and Bṛhaspati's order. This shall give rise to a fixed movement based on (1) Vāra and (2) Jāmam. The sequence of the Jāmamādhipati is the same for both Dina-Jāmam and Rātri-Jāmam, which always starts from the Vāreśa and ends with the 8th Graha in the Jāmamādhipati order.

Although this system is remarkably accurate, it is not much in use outside of the Tamil community, perhaps because of the lack of availability of literature in English. I had been searching for the text of Jinendramālai for several years, as I had heard about the remarkable accuracy of this system of Praśna; however, my search always eluded me, as I could not get much literature on this topic.

During my search, I came across the translation of the text by a Savant of Jyotiṣaśastra, Śrī Chidambaram Iyer, who had translated the text from Tamil to English, however, my ability to procure the book was not possible. It was, however, in my search of the text again, I realized that some part of the text is available in the form of Sāmakkol Āruṛham, and it was published by the Saptaṛṣi Publications, translated by Śrī Venkataraman. I found this is available in two parts, covering chapters 1 to 14, introducing the reader to the subject of drawing the Sāmakkol Āruṛham chart. This was exactly what I needed.

While studying the lessons presented by Śrī Venkataraman, I found the book on Archive.org by Śrī S Vaidyanāthan of Trichy. However, the book is in Tamil Language, which I always hoped I learnt. Tamil is such a beautiful Language, and the knowledge of this Language opens up the floodgate of not only myriads of Jyotiṣa literature but also several ancient sciences and disciplines, including medicine, music, spiritual sciences and numerous others. The inedible mark of Maharṣi Agathiyar cannot be eroded by the forces of time. I wish I would be born into a Tamil family in my next birth and surrounded by people adept in these ancient Śāstras. Nevertheless, I was disappointed that Tamil was the only available text.

However, the translation of Śrī Venkatraman and the yeoman work of Saptaṛṣi's Publications of Śrī Sunil John helped me immensely. Saptaṛṣi Publications also followed up with another article by Subramanian Venkataraman after the publication of the first part of 7 lessons, which clarifies some concepts of computation of Udayam from the Tamil Calendar. All these articles published by Saptaṛṣis are masterpieces. I am immensely indebted to the scholars of this ancient work, including Śrī Chidambaram Iyer, Śrī Vaidyanathan, Śrī Venkataraman, Śrī Subramanian Venkataraman and Saptaṛṣi Team. Eventually, I got hold of the translation of Śrī Chidambaram Iyer, which is the basis of my learning and this chapter. The book of Śrī Chidambaram was published in 1890.

The book by Śrī Chidambaram Iyer is divided into 24 chapters covering several areas of Praśna, which are (1) Definitions and Elementary Principles, (2) On Dhātu or Minerals, (3) On Mūla or Vegetables, (4) On Jīva or Animals, (5) On Naṣṭa, Muṣṭi Cintā, (6) On Good and Evil, (7) On Diseases, (8) On Death, (9) On Meals, (10) On Dreams, (11) On Omens, (12) On Marriage, (13) On Sexual Union, (14) On the Birth of Children, (15) On Daggers, (16) On Salya, (17) On Under-currents, (18) On the Approach of the Enemy, (19) On Travel, (20) On the Appearance of Freshes in the river, (21) On Rain, (22) On the Price of Commodities, (23) On the Return of Ships, (24) On Ceṣṭā or movements.

Regarding this system, glimpses of this are also found in the veritable text on Praśna, the Praśnamārga. In śloka 9.26-27, Ācārya Harihara states that "By Lagna or Āruṛha is meant the Udaya Rāśi at Praśna. Kṛṣṇīyam and other works say that results must be read either from one or both. A Rāśi Cakra is of two kinds, i.e., Sthira and Cara. The fixed circle (Sthira Cakra) is posited on the earth (all around the Daivajña). On the other hand, the Cara circle (Cara Cakra) moves in the sky. It is by a consideration of both the Cakras that predictions should be made." Even though the Sthira Cakra is translated normally as the Kālapuruṣa Kuṇḍalī, it can also be interpreted as the fixed Cakra that is determined by the Vāra and Jāmam and not by the movement of the Grahas through the Rāśi. The Cara Cakra, however, means the Cakra (Kuṇḍalī) that depicts the actual movements of the Grahas in the sky.

Praśnamārga also deals with the determination of Āruṛhalagna, Sūrya Vīthi and the Chatralagna. Āruṛhalagna is also called Āruṛharāśi, and Chatralagna, Chatrarāśi. They mean the same thing. Lagna is a generic term for any object used as the Pivot about which the entire Kuṇḍalī is seen.

Regarding the determination of Chatrarāśi, Ācārya Harihara states in śloka 9.34 that, "According as Sūrya occupies Vṛṣabha to Siṅha, Vṛścika to Kumbha and the remaining four Rāśis, Vīthi Rāśis are respectively Meṣa, Mithuna and Vṛṣabha. Chatrarāśi is the Rāśi arrived at by counting from the corresponding Vīthi Rāśi as many Rāśis as Lagna is removed from Āruṛha.

This Chatrarāśi applies to Āruṛha. Chatrarāśi of Udayalagna is its own Navāñśa." According to the text, Chatrarāśi of the Āruṛha is determined from Āruṛharāśi and the Sūrya Vīthi; however, Chatrarāśi of the Udayalagna is the Navāñśa Lagna. In Jinendramāla, however, Chatrarāśi exclusively means that of Āruṛharāśi.

As per Praśnamārga 8.1., there are 6 Rāśis in Praśna Kriya, the act of asking questions, which are **(1)** Āruṛha, **(2)** Udaya, **(3)** Navāñśa Lagna, **(4)** Chatra, **(5)** Spṛṣṭāṅga and **(6)** Janmalagna. All these Rāśis must be examined to determine good and bad to the Pṛcchaka. The six Rāśis should be strong by yutidṛṣṭi of a Saumya. If they are weak due to yutidṛṣṭi of a Krūra or have a Śatru/Nīca Graha, the Pṛcchaka shall be miserable in general conditions of life. The Daivajña's power of judgement should be fully utilized in determining the importance of several Lagnas from the subject of the Praśna and the characteristics of the Pṛcchaka when the Praśna is asked.

Regarding the efficacy of the Sāmakkol Āruṛham system, let me recount an episode narrated by Śrī Venkatraman in his first part translation of the Śrī Vaidyanathan's book in Saptaṛṣi's magazine. Śrī Venkatraman states, "When I was learning Sāmakkol Āruṛham from my late Guru Śrī Kalyana Rama Iyer. An incident happened which needs to be mentioned here.

One evening I went to meet him in a shop. The shopkeeper asked him, "Sir, I am considering disposing of this shop. Can you please tell me what the Āruṛham say?"

After remaining silent for about 5-6 minutes, my Guruji said, "Dispose of it, and you will get a profit of Rs. 40,000/- You are disposing of this shop to generate funds for your Daughter's marriage. A gentleman from a farmer community purchases the shop. He will open a medical shop here. It will run for six months, after which one sweet shop is opened, which will run for long. I will not be alive to see all those changes, but my disciple (pointing to me) will see it" Things happened as he said, and whenever I pass that sweet shop, it reminds me of my Gurudeva."

Śrī Venkatraman continues, "After his demise, I became a disciple of Śrī Alliyandal Arunachalam, and an incident connected with him needs to be mentioned here. One day while myself and my guru were discussing some subjects, one gentleman came for Āruṛham and asked, "What profession will suit me"? My guruji moved his hands like a coffee hotel server and said, you have already hired a shop to open a coffee hotel. The shop is south facing and in the street full of jewellers, most of whom belong to the Chettiyar community. The business is moderate, and income and expenditure are equal with little profit" The gentleman has been doing his coffee shop for the past 8 years without much of a profit."

I do not claim to be an expert on this system, and I am nothing more than a newbie compared to the outstanding exponents of this system. However, I would still like to try to elucidate my understanding and interpretation for the benefit of the non-Tamil speaking readers, which I believe will immensely benefit from this, as I did.

I am still on a journey, and hopefully, as my understanding matures, I can contribute even more to this subject. However, I would sincerely request my readers to forgive me for any mistakes I may have made. Let me start with sincere Pranāms to the Holy feet of my Guru, my Arādhya Devatās, Lord Śiva, Devī Durgā, Lord Subrahmaṇya and Lord Gaṇeśa.

Sarajit Poddar
(Varāhamihira)

ABOUT ME

I am an earnest seeker of Jyotiṣa, having an unquenching thirst for learning this discipline. I was born in Dhanu Lagna, Vṛścika Rāśi and Anurādhā Nakṣatra, on a Navamī Tithi, when Guru was in Kumbha, Śani, in Mithuna, and Sūrya, in Siṅha. In my thirteenth year, I stepped into the world of Jyotiṣa in 1988, and after that, guided by divine providence, to study it seriously. My paternal uncle and my first Jyotiṣa Guru, Śrī Manoj Kānti Poddar, an accomplished Jyotiṣaśastri and a Śakti Sādhaka guided me. My father was also a Śakti Sādhaka and an accomplished Palmist. Therefore, I was born into a family of Jyotiṣīs and Śakti Sādhakas, and Jyotiṣa runs down my family lineage.

I studied palmistry from 1988 to 1993, and eventually, in 1993, I got introduced to Jyotiṣa through Dr BV Raman's astrological magazine. I commenced my learning through the astrological magazine for months. After that, it continued through a Bengali edition of Bṛhatparāśara and Sarvārtha Cintāmaṇi that my uncle gave me. During my initial years, I learned immensely from Dr Raman's books, Hindu Predictive Astrology and How to Judge a Kuṇḍalī Vol I and II. In 1999, Pt Sanjay Rath accepted me as his student, an event I will always cherish. It was the beginning of learning advanced Jyotiṣa. From him, I learned several advanced topics, including Āruṛhas, Argalās, Vargas, Tithi Praveśa Cakra, etc. His books, Crux of Vedic Astrology: Timing of Events and Jaimini Maharṣi's Upadeśa Sūtras, remained my constant companion for several years.

In my studies over thirty-three years, I always endeavoured to uncover the hidden meaning behind the ślokas and sūtras and reconcile the principles across several classical texts. My search slowly took the shape of this book, so I named it "In Search of Jyotiṣa". I started penning down my thoughts and experiences in a blog, "http://varahamihira.blogspot.com/" in 2004 and later continued to write in other mediums such as Facebook.com, Medium.com, and LinkedIn.com. I kept my pen name as Varāhamihira in honour of the great Jyotiṣaśastri, who adorned the court of King Vikramāditya as one of his Navaratnas (nine jewels).

Who am I? It is difficult to say who I am. Different people see me in so many different ways. From my viewpoint, I am a soul trapped inside the world of illusion! I am not a Paṇḍita, Ācārya, or Guru who claims to be a master of this discipline. I am a seeker who wishes to share his observations and experiences with like-minded seekers. I encountered numerous challenges navigating the arduous path of Jyotiṣa. In this book, I am narrating my reflections with a sincere prayer so it could be of some help to others in their journey.

Sarajit Poddar
(Varāhamihira)

Contents

24 JINENDRAMĀLA **1**

24.1 THE CORE PRINCIPLES 12
24.1.1 Jāmam *13*
24.1.2 Udayarāśi *13*
24.1.3 Āruṛhalagna *14*
24.1.4 Sūrya Vīthi *15*
24.1.5 Chatralagna *16*
24.1.6 Jāmakkol *16*
24.1.7 Cara and Sthira Cakra *17*
24.1.8 Illustration *20*
24.2 THE ADHYĀYAS 23
24.2.1 Adhyāya 1: Definitions and Elementary Principles *23*
24.2.2 Adhyāya 2: On Dhātu Matters *35*
24.2.3 Adhyāya 3: On Mūla Matters *38*
24.2.4 Adhyāya 4: On Jīva Matters *40*
24.2.5 Adhyāya 5: Naṣṭa and Manomuṣṭi Cintā *42*
24.2.6 Adhyāya 6: On Good and Evil *48*
24.2.7 Adhyāya 7: On Diseases *52*
24.2.8 Adhyāya 8: On Death *55*
24.2.9 Adhyāya 9: On Meals *57*
24.2.10 Adhyāya 10: On Dreams *59*
24.2.11 Adhyāya 11: On Omens *61*
24.2.12 Adhyāya 12: On Marriage *62*
24.2.13 Adhyāya 13: On Sexual Love *64*
24.2.14 Adhyāya 14: On the Birth of Children *66*
24.2.15 Adhyāya 15: On Dagger *74*
24.2.16 Adhyāya 16: On Salya *75*
24.2.17 Adhyāya 17: On undercurrents *79*
24.2.18 Adhyāya 18: On the Invasion of Enemy *82*
24.2.19 Adhyāya 19: On Travel *86*
24.2.20 Adhyāya 20: On the appearance of freshes in the river *88*
24.2.21 Adhyāya 21: On Rain *89*
24.2.22 Adhyāya 22: On the Price of Commodities *90*
24.2.23 Adhyāya 23: On the Return or Ships *91*
24.2.24 Adhyāya 24: On Ceṣṭā *92*
24.3 THE DISCOURSE 98
24.4 ABOUT "IN SEARCH OF JYOTIṢA" 292

24.1
THE CORE PRINCIPLES

Let us review this system's core principles; these are critical for understanding and applying this system. There are 3 significant entities in this method, called Udayarāśi, Āruṛharāśi and Chatrarāśi. They are also called Udayalagna, Āruṛhalagna, and Chatralagna because they are treated as a Lagna or a pivotal point. Udayarāśi is the Rāśi rising at the horizon at Praśna, and the Āruṛha is determined from several methods, including placing a gold coin or asking for a number to the Pṛcchaka etc. Chatrarāśi is determined from Udayarāśi, Āruṛharāśi, and the Sūrya Vīthi Rāśi. Sūrya Vīthi Rāśi means the lane travelled by Sūrya and is determined from Sūrya's Rāśi in the Kuṇḍalī. The Chatralagna denotes an umbrella, which conceals important matters known by studying the Graha placements from this Lagna.

This Praśna involves dividing a day into two cycles of 8 parts called Yāma or Jāmam, and 8 Grahas are assigned to each part in the order Sūrya → Rāhu → Candra → Śani → Śukra → Budha → Bṛhaspati → Maṅgala. These fixed sequences of Grahas are called Yāmagrahas or Jāmakkol or Sāmakkol, and an entire Praśna system is based on this, called the Sāmakkol Āruṛham or Jāmakkol Āruṛham. Each Jāmam is lorded by a Graha, which starts from the Vāreśa.

For instance, for Ravivāra, the 1st Jāmam of the day or night is ruled by Sūrya, for Maṅgalavāra, it is Maṅgala and so on. Rāhu governs the 2nd Jāmam of Ravivāra because, in the sequence mentioned above, Rāhu comes 2nd to Sūrya, the 1st Jāmam Lord of Ravivāra. The Jāmam Lord is always assigned to Mīna Rāśi, and 2nd from the Jāmam Lord in the sequence is assigned to the next Rāśi from Mīna in Vyutkrama (Anti-zodiacal) order, i.e., Makara. Notice that the Sthirarāśis are skipped for the Yāmagrahas assignment to the Rāśis. The assignment of the Grahas to the Rāśis is in the order Sūrya → Maṅgala → Bṛhaspati → Budha → Śukra → Śani → Candra → Rāhu. This order is the reverse of the order in which the Jāmam Lord is determined.

The 8 Yāmagrahas are assigned to the 8 Rāśis (Dvisva and Cara Rāśis). Therefore, a Rāśi has two kinds of Grahas, the Grahas as per the Praśna and the Grahas as per the Yāmagrahas or Jāmakkol. It is from the interaction of the regular Grahas and the Yāmagrahas that the details of a Praśna are deciphered.

Now coming to the topic of Chatralagna, there are two prevalent views. According to Praśnamārga and the translation of Jinendramāla by Śrī Chidambaram Iyer, Udayarāśi is the Rāśi same as Praśnalagna, i.e., the Rāśi of the horizon. However, according to Śrī Vaidyanathan, the erudite author of Sāmakkol Āruṛham in Tamil, Udayarāśi travels 1 Rāśi per hour, which is the definition of

Horālagna as per Maharṣi Parāśara. To distinguish between Udayarāśi of Jinendramāla/Praśnamārga and Sāmakkol Āruṛham, I refer to the one defined by the Jinendramāla/Praśnamārga as **Udayarāśi**, and the one defined in Sāmakkol Āruṛham as **Udayam**. Further details of this system are as follows:

24.1.1 JĀMAM

There are 8 Jāmams in a day and as many Jāmams in the night. This makes 16 Jāmams in an Ahorātra, each of mean duration of 1.5 hrs or 3.75 Ghaṭi. The precise duration of Jāmam is dependent on the precise duration of Dinamāna and Rātrimāna. The Dinamāna is the day duration and the period between Sūryodaya and Sūryāsta. On the other hand, the Rātrimāna is the duration of the night and is the period between Sūryāsta and the following Sūryodaya.

Let us take an example. Today is 15th January 2021, and the time is 14:15 SGT (14.25). The Sūryodaya today is 7:15:56 (7.266), and Sūryāsta is 19:12:07 (19.202). The Lagna rising at the time, called the Udayalagna, is in Meṣa 16:06:49. The time elapsed from Sūryodaya is 14.25 - 7.266 = 6.984, and the Dinamāna is 19.202 - 7.266 = 11.936. The Jāmam is 6.984 / 11.936 * 8 = 4.68, meaning that 68% of the 5th Jāmam continues.

The information of Jāmam can also be found in Local Pañcāṅga or ephemeris or can be readily computed using the Sūryodaya and Sūryāsta time stated there. Today is Śukravāra, and on today's Vāra, the Jāmam are lorded by Grahas in order Śukra → Śani → Candra → Rāhu → Sūrya → Maṅgala → Bṛhaspati → Budha. We notice that Sūrya governs the 5th Jāmam. We shall see later that the assignment of Grahas as per Jāmakkol is from Sūrya, starting in the Anti-zodiacal direction from the Mīna Rāśi.

24.1.2 UDAYARĀŚI

The Udayalagna normally means the Lagna rising at a time or the Rāśi on the horizon; however, a different rising Rāśi is used in Jāmakkol Āruṛham. It is called Udayam in the Jāmakkol Āruṛham system. However, as per the translation presented by Śrī Venkatraman, according to Śrī Vaidyanāthan, the Lagna covers 24 Rāśis during an Ahorātra, i.e., 12 Rāśis in the day and 12 Rāśis in the night. This concept is identical to the Horālagna.

Horālagna may be meant with the term Udayam in the text. However, instead of questioning what the erudite author presents, let us accept that and see how to find the Udayam at the moment. For the sake of unambiguity, let us call this Udayam or Udayarāśi, whereas the Praśnalagna is the Udayalagna, which is the Rāśi rising at the Horizon.

The average speed of Sūrya is 0.9856° per day. Therefore, in half a day, Sūrya's motion is 0.4928°. In Half day, from Sūryodaya to Sūryāsta, the Udayam moves 360° of the zodiac from the Sūryasphuṭa at Sūryodaya and meets Sūrya at the Sūryāsta. However, by the time Lagna moves to the original spot where it started at Sūryodaya, Sūrya would have moved by 0.4928°. Therefore, during the duration of Dinamāna or Rātrimāna, the Lagna moves 360.4928°.

Therefore, the Sphuṭa of Udayam should be determined using the formula, Udayam Sphuṭa = Sūryasphuṭa at Sūryodaya + Time elapsed from Sūryodaya / Dinamāna * 360.4928. Let us say that today (15 Jan 2021), Sūryasphuṭa at Sūryodaya is Makara 0:46:39.19 (270.778). Therefore, Udayam is 270.778 + 6.984/11.936 * 360.4928 = 481.710 = 121.710. This falls in Siṅha 1:42:35.2.

Let us use our formula on the example given by Śrī Venkatraman in the Saptaṛṣi article. The given time is 11:00 hrs IST on 6th August 1993 at Tiruchirappalli. The Udayam worked out to be Dhanu in the given an example. The Sūryodaya is at 6.073, and Sūryāsta is at 18.627.

The Dinamāna is 12.554 hours, and the time elapsed from Sūryodaya is 4.927 hours. The Sūryasphuṭa at Sūryodaya is 109.692. Udayam Sphuṭa = Sūryasphuṭa at Sūryodaya + Time elapsed from Sūryodaya / Dinamāna * 360.4928 = 109.692 + 4.927/12.554 * 360.4928 = 251.175. This equates to Dhanu 11:10:26, which is the Udayam.

24.1.3 ĀRUṚHALAGNA

There are several methods of finding the Āruṛhalagna or Āruṛharāśi, and a detailed exposition of this is given in the Praśna Adhyāya of this book. However, for the sake of reference, I am giving here some common methods:

(1) Position of the Pṛcchaka method: The Āruṛha can be known from the direction occupied by the Pṛcchaka about the Daivajña's position. Considering that the Daivajña is facing towards Meṣa, the direction of the Pṛcchaka can be known.

(2) Gold coin method: The Pṛcchaka can be asked to place a gold coin in a Rāśi drawn on the table or a place where the Praśna is being performed.

(3) Cowrie method: The Daivajña can find out the Āruṛha using his cowries that are energised by Mantra and devotion to the Iṣṭa Devatā or consecrated in a temple.

(4) Number method: The Daivajña can ask the Pṛcchaka to provide a number between 1 to 108, and from the number, by expunging multiples of 12, one can determine Āruṛharāśi.

(5) Spṛṣṭāṅga method: The Daivajña can take the Rāśi indicated by the body part touched by the Pṛcchaka while putting the Praśna.

(6) Praśna Akṣara method: The Daivajña can take the Rāśi indicated by the first Akṣara uttered by the Pṛcchaka. For this method, the knowledge of Kaṭapayādi varga is necessary.

(7) Minutes method: One can merely take the minutes when asking the Praśna, divide it by 5, and take the quotient. The quotient with decimals should always be rounded "up". For instance, if a Praśna is put at 8:21 pm, then the Āruṛha is 21/5 = 4.2 = 5 = Siṅha Rāśi.

(8) Book method: One can use a notebook or a book with 108 pages and can randomly draw out a page at the time of Praśna after duly remembering one's Iṣṭa Devatā. The number should be divided by 12, and the remainder should be considered. If a book with 108 pages is not available, one can take a book with any number of pages, draw out a page, and do the same procedure of dividing by 12 and finding the remainder.

24.1.4
SŪRYA VĪTHI

Vīthi means alley, and there are three of them depending on the Rāśi occupied by Sūrya at Praśna. It is unclear why the term Vīthi or alley designates these Rāśis. Perhaps there is some hidden meaning behind them, waiting to be discovered. The Sūrya Vīthi Rāśis are needed to determine Chatrarāśi.

(1) When Sūrya is in Vṛṣabha, Mithuna, Karka or Siṅha, Meṣa becomes the Vīthi Rāśi.

(2) When Sūrya is in Tulā, Kanyā, Mīna or Meṣa, Vṛṣabha becomes the Vīthi.

(3) When Sūrya is in Vṛścika, Dhanu, Makara or Kumbha, Mithuna becomes the Vīthi.

The Sūrya Vīthi Rāśi can be easily determined from the Indian Solar Calendar, where the months are based on Sūrya's position in the Rāśi. In the northern parts of India, Sūrya in Mīna Rāśi correspond to Caitra Māsa and in Meṣa, Vaisakha Māsa, and so on. Whereas, in Tamil Nadu and a few other parts, Sūrya in Meṣa Rāśi corresponds to Caitra Māsa and so on.

The names of the months are (1) Caitra (Mīna), (2) Vaiśākha (Meṣa), (3) Jyeṣṭhā (Vṛṣabha), (4) Āṣāṛhā (Mithuna), (5) Śravaṇa (Karka), (6) Bhadrā (Siṅha), (7) Aśvina (Kanyā), (8) Kārtika (Tulā), (9) Mārgaśīrṣa (Vṛścika), (10) Pauṣa (Dhanu), (11) Maghā (Makara) and (12) Phālguna (Kumbha).

The Tamil names are(1) Chittarai (Meṣa), (2) Vaikāsi (Vṛṣabha), (3) Āni (Mithuna), (4) Ādi (Karka), (5) Avaṇi (Siṅha), (6) Puṭṭarāsi (Kanyā), (7) Aippasi (Tulā), (8) Kārttikai (Vṛścika), (9) Mārkazhi (Dhanu), (10) Tai (Makara), (11) Māsi (Kumbha) and (12) Paṅkuni (Mīna).

24.1.5
CHATRALAGNA

Chatralagna, also called Chatrarāśi, is a special Rāśi that is specifically useful for finding the hidden aspects of a Praśna. Chatra means umbrella in Sanskrit. It is called **Kavippu** in Tamil, which means the same, i.e., an umbrella. The term signifies that something is hidden under the umbrella and is uncovered using the Kavippu Rāśi.

Regarding the computation of Chatrarāśi, Praśnamārga 9.34. states, Depending on Sūrya in Vṛṣabha to Siṅha, Vṛścika to Kumbha and the remaining four Rāśis, Vīthi Rāśis are respectively Meṣa, Mithuna and Vṛṣabha. Chatrarāśi is the Rāśi arrived at by counting from the corresponding Vīthi Rāśi as many Rāśis as Lagna is removed from Āruṛha. This Chatrarāśi applies to Āruṛha. Chatrarāśi of Udayalagna is its own Navāñśa.

Let us focus on determining Chatrarāśi of the Āruṛha. This involves two steps, (1) Count Āruṛharāśi from the Udayalagna, and (2) Count as many Rāśis from the Sūrya Vīthi Rāśi. For instance, in the Praśna example given above, the Praśna Sūrya is in Makara, and Udayarāśi is Siṅha and let us take the Āruṛha as Mithuna Rāśi. Sūrya Vīthi for Makara Sūrya is Mithuna. Step (1) From Udayarāśi, Āruṛha is 11th Rāśi, and Step (2) Counting 11 Rāśis from Sūrya Vīthi in Mithuna, we arrive at Meṣa. Therefore, Meṣa is the Kavippu or Chatrarāśi.

Note that there are differences in opinion among the Savants. As per Ācārya Harihara of Praśnamārga, the Udayalagna is to be considered for determination of Chatrarāśi; however, as per Śrī Vaidyanathan, the Tamil author of Sāmakkol Āruṛham, the Udayam or Udayarāśi must be reckoned. To remain unambiguous, the Udayam determined above is referred to us Udayam or Udayarāśi, whereas the Lagna rising at the moment is referred to as Udayalagna or Praśnalagna.

24.1.6
JĀMAKKOL

Jāmakkol is the most unique aspect of this system. In this system, there are 8 Jāmams in the day and as many Jāmam at night. In these 8 Jāmams, the Grahas move around the zodiac in a fixed sequence. The movement commences with Mīna Rāśi as the first Jāmam and the Vāreśa as the Graha commencing the sequence.

The sequence of the Grahas is in order, **Sūrya → Maṅgala → Bṛhaspati → Budha → Śukra → Śani → Candra → Rāhu**. This sequence is unique to Jāmakkol, and this is the sequence of the Kālacakra (Praśnamārga 16.81-84). As the day progresses, the Grahas move from Mīna to Makara in order and move in anti-zodiacal order from Mīna to Meṣa. This sequence is called Jāmakkol, where Jama stands for Jāmam, and Kol stands for Grahas.

In the translation provided by Śrī Venkatraman, the names of the Grahas mentioned in Śrī Vaidyanathan's book are **Kadir → Sei → Pon → Mal → Pugar → Mandan → Madi → Pambu**. Candra or *Madi* is missed out in the translation, but the sequence can be seen elsewhere.

24.1.7
CARA AND STHIRA CAKRA

Praśnamārga 9.26-27. States that "By Lagna or Āruṛha is meant the Udaya Rāśi at Praśna. Kṛṣṇīyam and other works say that results must be read either from one or both. A Rāśi Cakra is of two kinds, i.e., Sthira and Cara. The fixed circle (Sthira Cakra) is posited on the earth (all around the Daivajña). On the other hand, the Cara circle (Cara Cakra) moves in the sky. It is by a consideration of both the Cakras that predictions should be made."

The text mentions that the Praśna utilizes two kinds of Cakras, the Cara Cakra and the Sthira Cakra. The Cara Cakra is the zodiac, in which the Grahas move in the sky, but the Sthira Cakra is constructed on the Ground. It is, however, not clear what is meant by the Sthira Cakra. It could mean the Kālapuruṣa Kuṇḍalī, but it can also mean another Cakra that is not revealed in Praśnamārga. The Sthira Cakra could is the Cakra used in Jāmakkol Āruṛham.

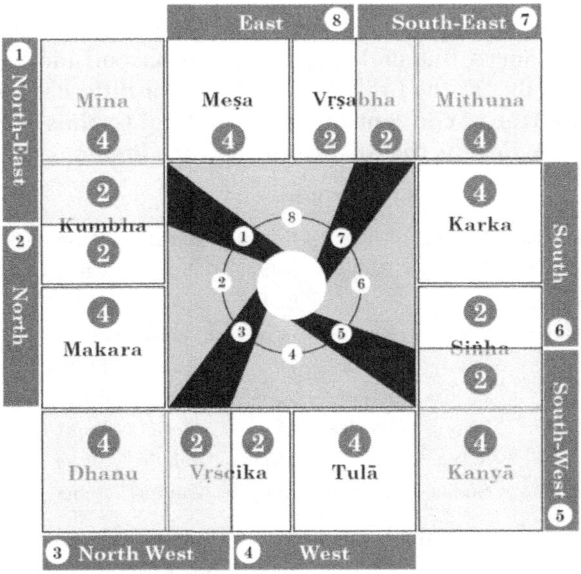

In the Jāmakkol Āruṛham, the Jāmam Grahas move in a fixed pattern right from Sūryodaya, corresponding to the Mīna Rāśi and Vāreśa Graha. After the expiry of the first Jāmam, the Vāreśa moves from Mīna to Makara, in the sequence of Mīna → Makara → Dhanu → Tulā → Kanyā → Karka → Mithuna - Meṣa. We notice that the Sthirarāśis are left out. There are 12 Rāśis, and 8

Jāmams, which means that 4 Rāśis are in excess. Therefore, the 4 Rāśis are removed from the picture, leaving behind the Cara and Dvisva Rāśis. Therefore, each of these 8 Rāśis corresponds to 8 Jāmams, which is of about 3.375 Ghaṭis or 1.5 hours duration approx.

In the following diagram, the movement of the Jāmam Grahas from Mīna to Meṣa is indicated. The 9 Jāmams and the 8 Rāśis also correspond to the 8 directions, as the diagram below indicates. Now, if four Sthirarāśis are removed from the scene, what happens to them? To explain this, Śrī Vaidyanathan explains that each Rāśi is divided into 4 parts, giving rise to 48 parts (for 12 Rāśis). The Sthirarāśis contribute half of their parts to Cara and another half to Dvisva. Therefore, each of the Cara and Dvisva Rāśis becomes 6 parts.

Regarding the Sthirarāśis, Śrī Vaidyanathan states that the Sthirarāśis are powerful by themselves, and there is no need for any Graha to be present in them. Whenever these Rāśis become Udayarāśi, it is beneficial in all cases except Praśnas regarding disease. Because when Udayarāśi falls in the Sthirarāśis, they indicate prolongation of diseases.

Below are seven tables showing the Grahas movement through the eight Rāśis in different Jāmams. For instance, in the 1st Jāmam of Ravivāra (Dina or Rātri), Sūrya is in Mīna, Maṅgala is in Makara, Bṛhaspati is in Dhanu and so on. In the 2nd Jāmam, Sūrya moves to Māraka, and the last Graha, Rāhu, who is behind Sūrya, moves to Mīna, and in this manner, the order continues.

Therefore, in the 2nd Jāmam of Ravivāra, the Grahas allotted to the Rāśis are Mīna- Rāhu, Makara- Sūrya, Dhanu- Maṅgala, Tulā- Bṛhaspati and so on. Using these tables, one can easily put the Grahas in the Rāśis for different Jāmams on different Vāras. **As a matter of convention, the Jāmakkol Grahas are written outside the Rāśicakra, whereas the Gocara Grahas are inside.**

Table 1: Ravivāra

Jāmam	Mīna	Makara	Dhanu	Tulā	Kanyā	Karka	Mithuna	Meṣa
1st	Sūrya	Kuja	Guru	Budha	Śukra	Śani	Candra	Rāhu
2nd	Rāhu	Sūrya	Kuja	Guru	Budha	Śukra	Śani	Candra
3rd	Candra	Rāhu	Sūrya	Kuja	Guru	Budha	Śukra	Śani
4th	Śani	Candra	Rāhu	Sūrya	Kuja	Guru	Budha	Śukra
5th	Śukra	Śani	Candra	Rāhu	Sūrya	Kuja	Guru	Budha
6th	Budha	Śukra	Śani	Candra	Rāhu	Sūrya	Kuja	Guru
7th	Guru	Budha	Śukra	Śani	Candra	Rāhu	Sūrya	Kuja
8th	Kuja	Guru	Budha	Śukra	Śani	Candra	Rāhu	Sūrya

Table 2: Somavāra

Jāmam	Mīna	Makara	Dhanu	Tulā	Kanyā	Karka	Mithuna	Meṣa
1st	Candra	Rāhu	Sūrya	Kuja	Guru	Budha	Śukra	Śani
2nd	Śani	Candra	Rāhu	Sūrya	Kuja	Guru	Budha	Śukra
3rd	Śukra	Śani	Candra	Rāhu	Sūrya	Kuja	Guru	Budha
4th	Budha	Śukra	Śani	Candra	Rāhu	Sūrya	Kuja	Guru
5th	Guru	Budha	Śukra	Śani	Candra	Rāhu	Sūrya	Kuja

Jāmam	Mīna	Makara	Dhanu	Tulā	Kanyā	Karka	Mithuna	Meṣa
6th	Kuja	Guru	Budha	Śukra	Śani	Candra	Rāhu	Sūrya
7th	Sūrya	Kuja	Guru	Budha	Śukra	Śani	Candra	Rāhu
8th	Rāhu	Sūrya	Kuja	Guru	Budha	Śukra	Śani	Candra

Table 3: Maṅgalavāra

Jāmam	Mīna	Makara	Dhanu	Tulā	Kanyā	Karka	Mithuna	Meṣa
1st	Kuja	Guru	Budha	Śukra	Śani	Candra	Rāhu	Sūrya
2nd	Sūrya	Kuja	Guru	Budha	Śukra	Śani	Candra	Rāhu
3rd	Rāhu	Sūrya	Kuja	Guru	Budha	Śukra	Śani	Candra
4th	Candra	Rāhu	Sūrya	Kuja	Guru	Budha	Śukra	Śani
5th	Śani	Candra	Rāhu	Sūrya	Kuja	Guru	Budha	Śukra
6th	Śukra	Śani	Candra	Rāhu	Sūrya	Kuja	Guru	Budha
7th	Budha	Śukra	Śani	Candra	Rāhu	Sūrya	Kuja	Guru
8th	Guru	Budha	Śukra	Śani	Candra	Rāhu	Sūrya	Kuja

Table 4: Budhavāra

Jāmam	Mīna	Makara	Dhanu	Tulā	Kanyā	Karka	Mithuna	Meṣa
1st	Budha	Śukra	Śani	Candra	Rāhu	Sūrya	Kuja	Guru
2nd	Guru	Budha	Śukra	Śani	Candra	Rāhu	Sūrya	Kuja
3rd	Kuja	Guru	Budha	Śukra	Śani	Candra	Rāhu	Sūrya
4th	Sūrya	Kuja	Guru	Budha	Śukra	Śani	Candra	Rāhu
5th	Rāhu	Sūrya	Kuja	Guru	Budha	Śukra	Śani	Candra
6th	Candra	Rāhu	Sūrya	Kuja	Guru	Budha	Śukra	Śani
7th	Śani	Candra	Rāhu	Sūrya	Kuja	Guru	Budha	Śukra
8th	Śukra	Śani	Candra	Rāhu	Sūrya	Kuja	Guru	Budha

Table 5: Śukravāra

Jāmam	Mīna	Makara	Dhanu	Tulā	Kanyā	Karka	Mithuna	Meṣa
1st	Guru	Budha	Śukra	Śani	Candra	Rāhu	Sūrya	Kuja
2nd	Kuja	Guru	Budha	Śukra	Śani	Candra	Rāhu	Sūrya
3rd	Sūrya	Kuja	Guru	Budha	Śukra	Śani	Candra	Rāhu
4th	Rāhu	Sūrya	Kuja	Guru	Budha	Śukra	Śani	Candra
5th	Candra	Rāhu	Sūrya	Kuja	Guru	Budha	Śukra	Śani
6th	Śani	Candra	Rāhu	Sūrya	Kuja	Guru	Budha	Śukra
7th	Śukra	Śani	Candra	Rāhu	Sūrya	Kuja	Guru	Budha
8th	Budha	Śukra	Śani	Candra	Rāhu	Sūrya	Kuja	Guru

Table 6: Śanivāra

Jāmam	Mīna	Makara	Dhanu	Tulā	Kanyā	Karka	Mithuna	Meṣa
1st	Śukra	Śani	Candra	Rāhu	Sūrya	Kuja	Guru	Budha
2nd	Budha	Śukra	Śani	Candra	Rāhu	Sūrya	Kuja	Guru
3rd	Guru	Budha	Śukra	Śani	Candra	Rāhu	Sūrya	Kuja
4th	Kuja	Guru	Budha	Śukra	Śani	Candra	Rāhu	Sūrya
5th	Sūrya	Kuja	Guru	Budha	Śukra	Śani	Candra	Rāhu

Jāmam	Mīna	Makara	Dhanu	Tulā	Kanyā	Karka	Mithuna	Meṣa
6th	Rāhu	Sūrya	Kuja	Guru	Budha	Śukra	Śani	Candra
7th	Candra	Rāhu	Sūrya	Kuja	Guru	Budha	Śukra	Śani
8th	Śani	Candra	Rāhu	Sūrya	Kuja	Guru	Budha	Śukra

Table 7: Śanivāra

Jāmam	Mīna	Makara	Dhanu	Tulā	Kanyā	Karka	Mithuna	Meṣa
1st	Śani	Candra	Rāhu	Sūrya	Kuja	Guru	Budha	Śukra
2nd	Śukra	Śani	Candra	Rāhu	Sūrya	Kuja	Guru	Budha
3rd	Budha	Śukra	Śani	Candra	Rāhu	Sūrya	Kuja	Guru
4th	Guru	Budha	Śukra	Śani	Candra	Rāhu	Sūrya	Kuja
5th	Kuja	Guru	Budha	Śukra	Śani	Candra	Rāhu	Sūrya
6th	Sūrya	Kuja	Guru	Budha	Śukra	Śani	Candra	Rāhu
7th	Rāhu	Sūrya	Kuja	Guru	Budha	Śukra	Śani	Candra
8th	Candra	Rāhu	Sūrya	Kuja	Guru	Budha	Śukra	Śani

24.1.8 ILLUSTRATION

This is a Praśna asked by one of my close acquaintances, asking a generic question regarding what is happening in his life. The Praśna was put on 9th January 2021, 10:32 am SGT, in Singapore, a Śanivāra. The Sūryodaya is at 7.172, and Sūryāsta 19.214. The Dinamāna is 12.043, and the Time elapsed from Sūryodaya is 10.533 - 7.172 = 3.361.

The Sūryasphuṭa at Sūryodaya was 264.633. The Jāmam was 3.361 / 12.043 * 8 = 2.23 = 3rd Jāmam. The Udayalagna was Kumbha and Udayam was 264.633 + Time elapsed / Dinamāna * 360.4928 = 264.633 + 3.361 / 12.043 * 360.4928 = Meṣa 5:14:25. Therefore, Udayam is in Meṣa. The Āruṛha based on the minutes is (32/5=6.4) 7, which is Tulā Rāśi.

At Praśna, Sūrya was in Dhanu Rāśi, and therefore Sūrya Vīthi is Mithuna. Āruṛham is in Tulā, and Udayam is in Meṣa. Counting Āruṛham from Udayam, we have 7. Counting 7 from Sūrya Vīthi in Mithuna, we arrive at Chatra or Kavippu in Dhanu Rāśi. For the 3rd Jāmam on a Śanivāra, the Jāmakkol Grahas are:

Table 8

Jāmam	Mīna	Makara	Dhanu	Tulā	Kanyā	Karka	Mithuna	Meṣa
3rd	Budha	Śukra	Śani	Candra	Rāhu	Sūrya	Maṅgala	Bṛhaspati

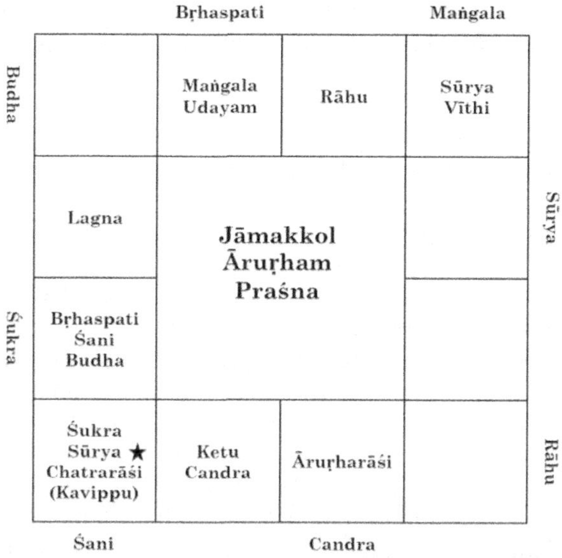

The Jāmakkol Praśna Kuṇḍalī is given here. As per regular Praśna assessment, Lagneśa Śani is in the 12th House of loss, with the 5th Lord Budha. 5th Lord shows the state of mind, and his presence with Śani in the 12th House indicates sadness and mild depression. The depression is mild because Budha is with the Lagneśa, in a Mitrarāśi, and with a Mitragraha.

However, Śani does give dejection and detachment from life. The native confirmed that he was not interested in doing anything and was passing his time not doing anything productive. However, he was unsure what was troubling him and what he could solve. The problems were deeply psychological and were not apparent in the conscious mind. This is indicated by Budha's conjunction with Śani in the 12th House.

Moving further, since I thought of focusing on the nature of the problems, I moved my focus to the 6th House. I noticed that the 6th House is empty, but the 6th Lord Candra is with Ketu in the 10th House. Ketu's nature is to cause chaos and a situation that is not under control. I enquired whether he was doing something at work from which he felt disconnected and could not control the outcome. Is his work getting impacted by others? He confirmed that this is true, as the work given to him was not purely in his area, and he feels that his work has not been very productive.

Then, I checked the condition of the 9th House and the Lord. Normally, affliction to 9H/9L gives a sense of helplessness. I noticed that the 9th House is where Āruṛharāśi is, which is not bad because Āruṛha in the Kendrakoṇa from the Praśnalagna is always favourable. 9th House is otherwise vacant, but the 9th Lord Śukra is in Dhanu Rāśi, with Śatru Sūrya and Pāpakartari yoga caused by Rāhu and Śani. The results are mixed.

It is favourable because the presence of the 9th Lord in the Naisargika Bhāgya Bhāva, i.e., Dhanu Rāśi, is favourable, and with Kāraka Sūrya is also good. This shows blessings of Iṣṭa Devatā; however, the Pāpakartari yoga is concerning. The Pāpakartari yoga and conjunction with Śatrugraha indicate temporary unhappiness from the Iṣṭadevatā. I enquired whether he had recently asked for some Divine Grace, but the problem was not solved.

He later recounted that he asked his Iṣṭadevatā to help resolve a longstanding misunderstanding with his mother and sister. Still, he didn't see improvement in such matter, which worsened his psychological battle – albeit at a subconscious level. Delving further, I noticed that Rāhu is afflicting Śukra by being in his Rāśi. Rāhu is in the 4th House, indicating House, mother, vehicles etc.

I enquired whether he has issues with his home or land-related challenges. Or whether he wanted to visit his hometown and could not do so due to the Covid19 Pandemic. It was not entirely the case, but an element was troubling him. However, what was more problematic was that large rats spoiled his car and made a mess of the interior due to prolonged keeping it locked. But the main issue was that of the mother and sister, which bothered him without realizing it. Mother is Candra, the 6th Lord, Nīca, and Sister is Śukra, the 4th and 9th Lord, in Pāpakartari.

Now, from a Jāmakkol standpoint, Kavippu is in Dhanu containing Śukra and Sūrya, indicating issues related to sister (Śukra) and work (Sūrya). Even from Kavippu, the 9th Lord Sūrya is in Pāpakartari, in the Lagna, indicating the trouble is serious and confirming the earlier observation regarding the Iṣṭadevatā. Outer Śani is in Dhanu, afflicting Sūrya and Śukra, causing delays in resolving the problem. Outer Candra is aspecting the 3rd House and Maṅgala, indicating the issues with the younger sibling.

However, outer Bṛhaspati on inner Maṅgala in the 3rd House indicates that the younger sister is doing well. However, the presence of outer Śukra on inner Śani and Budha, the 5th Lord, indicate the thoughts of the sister prevailing on the mind. Chatrarāśi and the Jāmakkol Graha confirmed several previous observations, and the native confirmed that.

24.2 THE ADHYĀYAS

24.2.1 ADHYĀYA 1: DEFINITIONS AND ELEMENTARY PRINCIPLES

SALUTATIONS

0.1. Salutation to the Gracious Lord whose greatness can neither be conceived nor expressed by the three worlds and by sages freed from the trammels of re-birth and who is full of love to all sentient beings.

0.2. I purpose to write this sacred science invoking to my aid the grace of those eminent astrologers who are well-read in and observant of the rules of life and possess full knowledge of the events of the three worlds-past, present and future.

0.3. I name this work Jinendramāla. In it, I lay down rules for predicting life's good and evil events, past, present and future.

0.4-6. He that makes predictions on duly ascertaining the Āruṛha (a), the Chatra (6) and the Udaya Rāśis (c), the Trikoṇa and the Kendra Rāśis, the aspect (d), positions (e), strength, dik (direction), sex, the odd or even character, caste, colour, legs, shape, horns race, size, distance, age, taste, moles and scars, sides, light, the movable, fixed and double character, the walking, flying and creeping character, the places of resort, the day and night and the periods of the Rāśis and Grahas may be said to be possessed of a divine character.

0.7-9. In this work, I mean to treat of prediction of questions relating to objects of the mineral vegetable and animal kingdoms, to things lost, hidden or thought of, to good and evil in general (a), to diseases, deaths, meals, dreams and omens, to married women, sexual love and the birth of children, to the dagger, to Salya (b), to under-currents, to the approach of the enemy, to travels, to the appearance of freshes in the river, to rain, to the price of food grains, to the return of ships and Ceṣṭā (c).

SŪRYA VĪTHI

1.1. (1) If the months when Sūrya passes through Vṛṣabha, Mithuna, Karka and Siṅha, Meṣa is the Sūrya Vīthi; **(2)** in the months when Sūrya passes through Vṛścika, Dhanu, Makara and Kumbha, Mithuna is the Sūrya Vīthi and **(3)** in the months when Sūrya passes through Meṣa, Kanyā, Tulā and Mīna, Vṛṣabha is the Sūrya Vīthi.

CHATRARĀŚI:

1.2. Count the Rāśis from Āruṛharāśi to Sūrya Vīthi, both inclusive; count as many Rāśis from Udayarāśi which must be carefully ascertained- the Rāśi thus obtained is said to hide or cover Āruṛharāśi and is therefore known as Chatrarāśi.

1.3. Count the number of Rāśis from Āruṛha to Sūrya Vīthi. Take half the number and count as many Rāśis from Udayarāśi. The Rāśi thus determined is also known as Chatrarāśi.

1.4-5. If Udayarāśi is Meṣa, its Chatrarāśi is Vṛṣabha; if Udayarāśi is Vṛṣabha, Mithuna, Karka or Siṅha, its Chatrarāśi is Meṣa; if Udayarāśi is Kanyā or Tulā, its Chatrarāśi is Vṛṣabha; if Udayarāśi is Vṛścika, Dhanu, Makara or Kumbha, its Chatrarāśi is Mithuna, and if Udayarāśi is Mīna, its Chatrarāśi is Vṛṣabha.

Notes: This śloka aims at determining Chatrarāśi of Udayarāśi. These Chatrarāśi of Āruṛharāśi is found from Sūrya Vīthis. However, the method of delineating Chatrarāśi of the Udayalagna is presented here.

ŚĪRṢODAYA, PṚṢṬODAYA AND UBHAYODAYA:

1.6. (1) Mithuna, Siṅha, Kanyā, Tulā, Vṛścika and Kumbha are Śīrṣodaya Rāśis. **(2)** Meṣa, Vṛṣabha, Karka, Dhanu and Makara are Pṛṣṭodaya Rāśis. And **(3)** Mīna is the only Ubhayodaya Rāśi.

1.7. (1) Budha, Bṛhaspati, Śukra and Rāhu are Śīrṣodaya. **(2)** Sūrya, Maṅgala and Śani are Pṛṣṭodaya. And **(3)** Candra and Ketu are Ubhayodaya Grahas.

1.8. The Śīrṣodaya Rāśis and Grahas are awake during the daytime. The Pṛṣṭodaya Rāśis and Grahas are awake at nighttime. The Ubhayodaya Rāśi and Grahas are awake both day and night.

DṚṢṬI OF RĀŚI AND GRAHAS:

1.9. The Manuṣya Rāśis look straight as men; the Catuṣpāda Rāśis look sideways like animals; the Pakṣi Rāśis look upward like the birds; and the Kīṭa Rāśis look downward like the reptiles.

1.10. Candra and Bṛhaspati look straight; Maṅgala looks sideways; Sūrya looks upward, Budha and Śukra look downward, and Śani and Rāhu look obliquely.

1.11. Rāśis and Grahas aspect themselves and the 7th Rāśis fully; the 4th and the 10th Rāśis with three-quarters of a sight; the 5th and the 9th Rāśis with half a sight, the 3rd and the 11th Rāśis with quarter sight and the 8th Rāśi with one-eighth of a sight.

FRIENDLY GRAHAS AND RĀŚIS:

1.12-13. (1) Bṛhaspati is friendly to **Sūrya**; **(2)** Budha and Bṛhaspati are friendly to **Candra**; **(3)** Budha and Śukra are friendly to **Maṅgala**; **(4)** Candra, Maṅgala, Bṛhaspati, Śukra and Śani are friendly to **Budha**; **(5)** Sūrya, Candra, Budha and Śukra are friendly to **Bṛhaspati**; **(6)** Maṅgala, Budha, Bṛhaspati and Śani are friendly to **Śukra**; **(7)** Budha, Bṛhaspati and Śukra are friendly to **Śani**.

1.14-15. (1) Dhanu and Mīna are friendly to **Sūrya**; **(2)** Mithuna, Kanyā, Dhanu and Mīna are friendly to **Candra**; **(3)** Vṛṣabha, Mithuna, Kanyā and Tulā are friendly to **Maṅgala**; **(4)** Meṣa, Vṛṣabha, Karka, Tulā, Vṛścika, Dhanu, Makara and Kumbha are friendly to **Budha**; **(5)** Vṛṣabha, Mithuna, Siṅha, Kanyā, Tulā and Kumbha are friendly to **Bṛhaspati**; **(6)** Meṣa, Mithuna, Vṛścika, Dhanu, Makara and Kumbha are friendly to **Śukra**; **(7)** Vṛṣabha, Mithuna, Kanyā, Dhanu and Mīna are friendly to **Śani**.

SVAKṢETRA AND UCCA:

1.16. (1) Sūrya is the Lord of Siṅha, **(2)** Candra of Karka, **(3)** Maṅgala of Meṣa and Vṛścika, **(4)** Budha of Mithuna and Kanyā, **(5)** Bṛhaspati of Dhanu and Mīna, **(6)** Śukra of Vṛṣabha and Tulā and **(7)** Śani of Makara and Kumbha.

1.17. (1) Meṣa is the Uccarāśi of Sūrya, **(2)** Vṛṣabha that of Candra, **(3)** Mithuna of the Graha Pariveṣa, **(4)** Karka of Bṛhaspati, **(5)** Siṅha of Dhūma **(6)**, Kanyā of Budha, **(7)** Tulā of Śani, **(8)** Vṛścika of Rāhu, **(9)** Dhanu of Indradhanuṣa, **(10)** Makara of Maṅgala, **(11)** Kumbha of Sukṣma, and **(12)** Mīna of Śukra.

Notes: The Uccarāśis of four Upagrahas are also mentioned here. The Upagrahas are Dhūma, Sukṣma, Indradhanuṣa, and Pariveṣa. These four are known as minor Grahas. The details about them are found in śloka 1.84. According to Maharṣi Parāśara, there are five Aprakāśa Grahas. In Śloka 3.61-64, the Maharṣi Parāśara states, "Add 4 Rāśis 13°20' to Sūrya to get the position Dhūma. Reduce Dhūma from 12 Rāśis to arrive at Vyatipāta. Add six Rāśis to Vyatipāta to determine Pariveṣa. Deduct Pariveṣa from 12 Rāśis to determine Indradhanuṣa. Add 16°40' to Indradhanuṣa, to get Upaketu. By adding a Rāśi to Upaketu, we arrive at Sūryasphuṭa. These are the Aprakāśa Grahas, devoid of splendour, highly inauspicious (Krūra) in nature and cause affliction." We do not see Sukṣma in the list, and Upaketu may be called Sukṣma here because Ketu is small, and Upaketu is smaller.

1.18. (1) The 10th degree of Meṣa, **(2)** the 3rd of Vṛṣabha, **(3)** the 5th of Karka, **(4)** the 15th of Kanyā, **(5)** the 20th of Tulā, **(6)** the 28th of Makara and **(7)** the 27th of Mīna are the Uccāñśa of the respective Grahas.

HOSTILE GRAHAS:

1.19-20. (1) Candra, Maṅgala, Budha, Śukra and Śani are hostile to **Sūrya**. **(2)** Sūrya, Maṅgala, Śukra and Śani are hostile to **Candra**. **(3)** Sūrya, Candra, Bṛhaspati and Śani are hostile to **Maṅgala**. **(4)** Sūrya is hostile to **Budha**. **(5)** Maṅgala and Śani are hostile to **Bṛhaspati**. **(6)** Sūrya and Candra are hostile to **Śukra**. **(7)** Sūrya, Candra and Maṅgala are hostile to **Śani**. The Rāśis of the hostile Grahas are the Śatrurāśis of the Grahas.

Notes: Notice that the relationships stated here are different from the normally accepted ones as per Parāśarī Jyotiṣa. For instance, Candra and Maṅgala are friendly to Sūrya, and likewise, Bṛhaspati is friendly to Maṅgala and so on.

NĪCA RĀŚI AND THE NĪCĀÑŚA:

1.21-22. **(1)** Tulā is the Nīcarāśi of Sūrya, **(2)** Vṛścika of Candra; **(3)** Karka of Maṅgala; **(4)** Mīna of Budha; **(5)** Makara of Bṛhaspati; **(6)** Kanyā of Śukra; **(7)** Meṣa of Śani; **(8)** Mithuna of Indradhanuṣa; **(9)** Kumbha of Dhūma; **(10)** Dhanu of Pariveṣa; and **(11)** Siṅha of Sukṣma. The depression degrees of the several Grahas are the same as their exaltation degrees (a).

THE MITRARĀŚI, SVAKṢETRA, UCCA, ŚATRU AND NĪCA RĀŚIS OF RĀHU:

1.23. **(1)** Mithuna, Kanyā, Tulā, Dhanu, Makara and Mīna are Mitra Rāśis to Rāhu; **(2)** Kumbha is his Svarāśi; **(3)** Vṛścika is his Uccarāśi; **(4)** Meṣa, Karka and Siṅha are his Śatrurāśis; and **(5)** Vṛṣabha is his Nīcarāśi.

Notes: Normally, Vṛṣabha is considered the Uccarāśi for Rāhu, and Vṛścika is his Nīcarāśi. However, here it is reversed.

THE KENDRA AND TRIKOṆA RĀŚIS:

1.24. Udayarāśi and the 5th and the 9th Rāśis from it are the Trikoṇa Rāśis.

1.25-26. Udayarāśi and the 4th, 7th, and 10th Rāśis from it are the Kendra Rāśis. They are respectively known as **(1)** the Udaya Kendra, **(2)** the Jala Kendra, **(3)** the Asta Kendra and **(4)** the Svarga Kendra.

THE PERIODICAL STRENGTHS:

1.27. **(1)** The Śīrṣodaya Rāśis and Grahas are powerful by day; **(2)** the Pṛṣṭodaya Rāśis and Grahas are powerful at night. **(3)** The Ubhayodaya Rāśis and Grahas are powerful both by day and at night.

GRAHA ASPECTS:

1.28. **(1)** Sūrya, Candra, Budha and Śukra powerfully aspect the 7th House; **(2)** Maṅgala, the 4th and 8th Houses; **(3)** Śani, the 3rd and 10th Houses; **(4)** Bṛhaspati the 5th and 9th Houses; and **(5)** Rāhu the 3rd and 11th Houses.

THE STHĀNABALA:

1.29-30. **(1)** An Uccagraha possesses ten times its ordinary strength; **(2)** a Svakṣetra Graha double its ordinary strength. **(3)** A Graha in a Mitrarāśi possesses just its ordinary strength. **(4)** A Graha in its Śatrurāśi possesses one-half of its ordinary strength, and **(5)** a Graha in its Nīcarāśi possesses a fourth of its ordinary strength.

Notes: Furthermore, Cararāśis possess their ordinary strength, Sthirarāśis twice and Dvisvarāśis three times such strength.

THE KENDRABALA:

1.31. **(1)** The Manuṣya Rāśis are powerful in the Lagna; **(2)** the Catuṣpāda Rāśis in the 10th House; **(3)** the Kīṭa Rāśis in the 7th House and the **(4)** Sarīsṛpa Rāśis in the 4th House.

Notes: For the division of Rāśis into Manuṣya, Catuṣpāda, Kīṭa and Sarīsṛpa is explained in śloka 1.48.

1.32. **(1)** Budha and Bṛhaspati are powerful in the Lagna; **(2)** Candra and Śukra are powerful in the 4th House; **(3)** Śani and Rāhu in the 7th House and **(4)** Sūrya and Maṅgala in the 10th House.

Notes: This is also known as the Dikbala.

OTHER STRENGTHS:

1.33. **(1)** If the Rāśis and Grahas are not found powerful in any of the Kendras from Udayarāśi, **(2)** examine whether they are powerful in any of the Kendras from Āruṛharāśi, then **(3)** from Chatrarāśi, then, **(4)** from the Rāśi occupied by Bṛhaspati, **(5)** then from the Rāśi occupied by Budha, **(6)** then from the Rāśi occupied by the Lord of Udayarāśi in the order stated.

Notes: In the solution to a Praśna, the most powerful Rāśi and Graha play a prominent role.

THE NAISARGIKA STRENGTH OF GRAHAS:

1.34-35. Budha, Maṅgala, Śani, Bṛhaspati, Śukra, the Candra, Sūrya and Rāhu are each more powerful than the preceding Grahas.

Notes: As per this sequence, Rāhu is the most powerful, and Budha is the least, in the natural order of strength.

DIRECTIONS:

1.36. **(1)** Meṣa is East; **(2)** Siṅha and Dhanu, South-East; **(3)** Vṛṣabha is South; **(4)** Kanyā and Makara South-West; **(5)** Mithuna is West; **(6)** Tulā and Kumbha North-West; **(7)** Karka is North; **(8)** Vṛścika and Mīna North-East.

1. **1.37.** **(1)** Sūrya is East; **(2)** Śukra, South-East; **(3)** Maṅgala, South; **(4)** Rāhu, South-West; **(5)** Śani, West; **(6)** Candra North-West; **(7)** Budha, North; **(8)** Bṛhaspati, North-East.

GENDER:

1.38. **(1)** Meṣa, Mithuna, Siṅha, Tulā, Dhanu and Kumbha are Puruṣa Rāśis, and **(2)** Vṛṣabha, Karka, Kanyā, Vṛścika, Makara and Mīna are Strī Rāśis.

1.39. **(1)** Sūrya, Maṅgala and Bṛhaspati are Puruṣa Grahas; **(2)** Candra, Śukra and Rāhu are female Grahas; **(3)** Budha, Śani and Ketu are Napuṅśaka Grahas.

SINGULAR AND DUAL:

1.40. (1) Meṣa and Siṅha are singular Puruṣa Rāśis. **(2)** Mithuna, Tulā, Dhanu and Kumbha are dual Puruṣa Rāśis. **(3)** Vṛṣabha, Karka, Kanyā and Vṛścika are singular Strī Rāśis, **(4)** Makara and Mīna are dual Yugmarāśis.

Notes: The singular Rāśi indicate one object, whereas the dual Rāśis denote two objects.

1.41. (1) Sūrya and Maṅgala are singular Puruṣa Grahas. **(2)** Bṛhaspati is a dual Puruṣa Graha. **(3)** Candra is a singular Strī Graha. **(4)** Śukra and Rāhu are dual Strī Grahas. **(3)** Budha, Śani and Ketu are dual Napuṅśaka Grahas.

Notes: There are no Napuṅśaka Rāśis and singular Napuṅśaka Grahas.

VARṆA:

1.42. (1) Dhanu and Mīna are Brāhmaṇas; **(2)** Meṣa and Siṅha are Kṣatriyas; **(3)** Karka and Vṛścika are Vaiśya; **(4)** Mithuna, Tulā and Kumbha are Śudras; and **(5)** Vṛṣabha, Kanyā and Makara are Mlecchas.

Notes: This classification is different from the Tattva-based classification, where Agnitattva Rāśis are Kṣatriyas, Pṛthvītattva Rāśis are Vaiśyas, Vāyuttatva Rāśis are Śudras, and Jalatattva Rāśis are Brāhmaṇas. This classification is, however, based on the Lordship of the Rāśis.

1.43-44. (1) Candra and Bṛhaspati are Brāhmaṇas; **(2)** Sūrya and Maṅgala are Kṣatriyas; **(3)** Budha is a Vaiśya; **(4)** Śukra is a Śudra; **(5)** Śani and Rāhu are Mlecchās.

Notes: According to Maharṣi Parāśara, Bṛhaspati and Śukra are Brāhmaṇas, Sūrya and Maṅgala are Kṣatriyas; Candra and Budha are Vaiśyas, and Śani is Śudra.

COLOUR:

1.45. (1) Meṣa, Siṅha, and Dhanu are red; **(2)** Vṛṣabha, Karka and Tulā are white; **(3)** Vṛścika, Kumbha and Mīna are green; **(4)** Mithuna, Kanyā and Makara are black.

Notes: This classification is different from that of Maharṣi Parāśara, Maharṣi Nārada, and Ācārya Varāhamihira.

1.46. (1) Bṛhaspati is of golden colour; **(2)** Sūrya, Maṅgala and Ketu are red; **(3)** Candra and Śukra are white; **(4)** Budha is green; **(5)** Śani and Rāhu are black.

1.47. (1) Bṛhaspati is of the colour of gold; **(2)** Sūrya, of the colour of fire, **(3)** Maṅgala is of the colour of blood; **(4)** Candra is of the colour of crystal; **(5)** Śukra is of the colour of milk; **(6)** Budha is green and **(7)** Śani and Rāhu are black.

LEGS OR PĀDAS:

1.48. (1) Mithuna, Kanyā, Tulā and Kumbha are Manuṣya Rāśis (2 legs). **(2)** Meṣa, Vṛṣabha, Siṅha and Dhanu are Catuṣpāda Rāśis (4 legs); **(3)** Makara and

Mīna are Sarīsṛpa Rāśis (no legs). **(4)** Karka and Vṛścika are Kīṭa Rāśis (6 or more legs).

1.49. (1) Budha, Bṛhaspati and Śukra are Manuṣya Grahas, **(2)** Sūrya, Maṅgala and Śani are Catuṣpāda Grahas; **(3)** Candra and Rāhu are Kīṭa Grahas.

ZODIACAL FORMS:

1.50. (1) Mithuna is in the form of a man and a woman, the former with a club in his hand and the latter with a lyre in her band; **(2)** Kanyā is in the form of a virgin holding crops and a lamp in her bands and travelling in a boat; **(3)** Tulā is of the form of a man holding a balance in his hand; **(4)** Dhanu is of the form of a man holding a bow in his band with the lower parts of a horse; **(5)** Makara is of the form of a crocodile with the face of a deer; **(6)** Kumbha is of the form of a man holding a pitcher; and **(7)** Mīna is of the form of two fish (8); the other Rāśis are of the form of the creatures whose names they bear.

GRAHA SHAPES:

1.51. (1) Sūrya is quadrangular in shape; **(2)** Candra is of the shape of a small circle; **(3)** Maṅgala is of the shape of a Ḍamaru; **(4)** Budha is triangular; **(5)** Bṛhaspati is elliptical; **(6)** Śukra is octagonal; **(7)** Śani is of the shape of a winnow and **(8)** Rāhu is of the shape of a line.

Notes: Ḍamaru: a small drum shaped like an hourglass, held by Lord Śiva and indicates the universe's heartbeat.

GRAHA HORNS:

1.52. (1) Sūrya and Budha have bent horns; **(2)** Candra has a flat one; **(3)** Maṅgala a short one; **(4)** Bṛhaspati and Śukra a long one; **(5)** Śani a broken one and **(6)** Rāhu has a horn partly cut away.

Notes: The horns of the Rāśis are the same as those of their lords.

RAŚMIS:

1.53. (1) Meṣa has 7 Raśmis; **(2)** Vṛṣabha 8; **(3)** Mithuna 5; **(4)** Karka 8; **(5)** Siṅha 7; **(6)** Kanyā 11; **(7)** Tulā 2; **(8)** Vṛścika 4; **(9)** Dhanu 6; **(10)** Makara 8; **(11)** Kumbha 8; **(12)** Mīna 27.

2. **1.54. (1)** Sūrya has 5 Raśmis; **(2)** Candra 21; **(3)** Maṅgala 7; **(4)** Budha 9; **(5)** Bṛhaspati 10; **(6)** Śukra 16; **(7)** Śani 4; **(8)** Rāhu 4.

GRAHA SIZE:

1.55. (1) Candra, Maṅgala and Śani are short; **(2)** Budha, Bṛhaspati and Rāhu are long; **(3)** Sūrya and Śukra are of middle length.

Notes:: The size of a Rāśi follows that of its Lord.

GRAHA YOJANAS:

1.56. (1) Sūrya and Budha are each 8 yojanas; **(2)** Candra is a yojana; **(3)** Maṅgala is 7 yojanas; **(4)** Bṛhaspati 9; **(5)** Śukra 16; and **(6)** Śani 20.

Notes: The yojanas of the Rāśis follow those of their lords. A Yojana is about 9 English miles. Śani is 20 yojanas, according to some and more than 20, according to others. In Hanumāna Cālisā, it is written जुग सहस्त्र योजन पर भानु, लील्यो ताहिमधुर फल जानू". This means Lord Hanumāna tried to grab Sūrya in the sky, thinking that is a sweet fruit. To explain the difference, Śrī Tulasīdāsa states that Sūrya is 1000 yugas away. The value of Yuga Sahasra is 12000 * 1000. Sūrya's Aphelion distance is 152,097,700 km, Perihelion distance is 147,091,144 km, and the mean distance is 149,597,870.7 km, called an astronomical unit. If we consider that Śrī Tulasīdāsa referred to the mean distance as the astronomical unit, then 1 yojana = 149,597,870.7 / 12E6 = 12.46649 km, or 7.746 miles. This is nearly 8 miles or 13 km. The precise measure is 12.5 km or 7.77 miles.

GRAHA AGE:

1.57. (1) The age of Sūrya is 50; **(2)** that of Candra is 70; **(3)** that of Maṅgala is 16 **(4)** that of Budha is 20; **(5)** that of Bṛhaspati 30; **(6)** that of Śukra is 7; **(7)** of Śani and Rāhu, each 100.

Notes: The age of a Rāśi follows that of its Lord.

GRAHA TASTE:

1.58. (1) Sūrya presides over the pungent taste; **(2)** Candra over astringent taste; **(3)** Maṅgala over sharp taste; **(4)** Budha over saline taste; **(5)** Bṛhaspati over sweet taste; **(6)** Śukra over sour taste; **(7)** Śani and Rāhu over bitter taste.

Notes: The taste of a Rāśi follows that of its Lord.

MOLES AND SCARS:

1.59. Place: (1) Sūrya presides over moles and scars in the hip; **(2)** Candra over those in the head; **(3)** Maṅgala over those in the back; **(4)** Budha under the arms and in the armpits; **(5)** Bṛhaspati in the arms; **(6)** Śukra in the face; **(7)** Śani in the thighs; and **(8)** Rāhu in the legs.

Notes: The scar of a Rāśi follows that of its Lord.

1.60. Side: (1) Sūrya, Maṅgala, Budha and Bṛhaspati have moles and scars on the **right side**; **(2)** and Candra, Śukra, Śani and Rāhu on the **left side**.

Notes: The sides of the scar of a Rāśi follow that of its Lord.

1.61. Shape: (1) The mole or scar of Sūrya is of the shape of the flower of the Sida Populifolia or Sida cordifolia; **(2)** that of Candra is of the shape of the flower of Asclepias gigantea (Calotropis); **(3)** that of Maṅgala is of the shape of broken dal; **(4)** that of Budha is of the shape of the leaf of Coronilla grandiflora (a yellow flower); **(5)** that of Bṛhaspati is of the shape of the leaf of Palma christi (Ricinus); **(6)** that of Śukra is of the shape of the leaf of the tamarind; **(7)** that of Śani is of the shape of the leaf of Datura Metel (Dhatura); **(8)** that of Rāhu is of the shape of the leaf of Cassia Anriculata (Senna).

Notes: The Rāśis follow their lords in the shape of moles and scars.

LIGHTS:

1.62. (1) The light of Meṣa, Karka, Tulā and Kumbha are 8 each; **(2)** of Vṛṣabha, Mithuna, and Makara 6 each; **(3)** of Siṅha 7; **(4)** of Kanyā and Dhanu, 11 each; **(5)** of Vṛścika 4; **(6)** of Mīna 27.

1.63. (1) The light of Sūrya is 5; **(2)** of Candra 21; **(3)** of Maṅgala 14; **(4)** of Budha 9; **(5)** of Bṛhaspati 10; **(6)** of Śukra 11; **(7)** of Śani and Rāhu 4 each.

Notes: Śrī Chidambaram Iyer states that, according to another reading, the light of Sūrya is 7 and that of Śukra is 16.

CARA, STHIRA AND DVISVA:

1.64. (1) Vṛṣabha, Siṅha, Vṛścika, and Kumbha are Sthirarāśis. **(2)** Meṣa, Karka, Tulā, and Makara are Cararāśis. **(3)** Mithuna, Kanyā, Dhanu and Mīna are Dvisvarāśis.

1.65. (1) Sūrya and Śukra are Sthira Grahas; **(2)** Candra, Maṅgala and Rāhu are Cara Grahas; **(3)** Budha, Bṛhaspati and Śani are Dvisva Grahas.

WALKING, CREEPING AND FLYING:

1.66. (1) Karka and Vṛścika are creeping Rāśis; **(2)** Makara and Mīna are flying Rāśis; **(3)** and the rest are walking Rāśis. **(1)** Candra and Rāhu are creeping Grahas; **(2)** Budha is a flying Graha; **(3)** Śani is a limping Graha; **(4)** and the rest (Sūrya, Maṅgala, Bṛhaspati, Śukra) are walking Grahas.

RĀŚI PLACES:

1.67. (1) Meṣa and Dhanu are jungles; **(2)** Vṛṣabha is a rice field; **(3)** Mithuna and Kanyā are villages; **(4)** Karka is a water course; **(5)** Siṅha is a mountain; **(6)** Tulā, Makara and Mīna are rivers; **(7)** Vṛścika is well; **(8)** Kumbha is a water pot. These are employed in the discovery of the places of stolen property.

1.68. According to some, **(1)** Meṣa is a forest; **(2)** Vṛṣabha is a rice field; **(3)** Mithuna is a village; **(4)** Karka is a water canal; **(5)** Siṅha is a mountain; **(6)** Kanyā is water; **(7)** Tulā is a village; **(8)** Vṛścika, a well; **(9)** Dhanu, a garden; **(10)** Makara, a dry river or salt pan; **(11)** Kumbha, a lake; and **(12)** Mīna, the sea.

1.69. According to some again, **(1)** Meṣa is a forest; **(2)** Vṛṣabha is a rice field; **(3)** Mithuna is a garden; **(4)** Karka is a water canal; **(5)** Siṅha is a mountain; **(6)** Kanyā is water; **(7)** Tulā, a riverbank or tank; **(8)** Vṛścika, a well; and **(9)** Dhanu, Makara, Kumbha and Mīna are each a well, a tank, or a ditch.

1.70. According to others, **(1)** Meṣa is a forest; **(2)** Vṛṣabha a rice field; **(3)** Mithuna a village; **(4)** Karka is water; **(5)** Siṅha is a mountain; **(6)** Kanyā, a village; **(7)** Tulā, a river; **(8)** Vṛścika, a well or a pit; **(9)** Dhanu a garden; **(10)** Makara, a ditch; **(11)** Kumbha the Sea; and **(12)** Mīna a spring or the sea.

1.71. According to others again, **(1)** Meṣa, Siṅha, Vṛścika and Dhanu are forests; **(2)** Vṛṣabha, Karka, Makara and Mīna are waters; **(3)** Mithuna, Kanyā, Tulā and Kumbha are Villages.

GRAHA PLACES:

1.72. **(1)** Sūrya, Maṅgala and Śani preside over forests; **(2)** Candra and Śukra over water; **(3)** Budha and Bṛhaspati over villages and **(4)** Rāhu over hollow places.

Notes: According to Śrī Chidambaram Iyer, if the Grahas occupy Mitrarāśis, the stolen property is likely to be found within the House; if they occupy their Svakṣetra Rāśis the stolen property is found within the village; if they occupy their Uccarāśis, then near the village; and if they occupy Nīca/Śatru Rāśis, then far away from the village. According to some, the above rule applies to the Lord of Āruṛharāśi and, according to others, to Sūrya.

1.73. According to some, **(1)** Sūrya and Bṛhaspati preside ever places of worship or high-rise places; **(2)** Candra and Śukra preside over water; **(3)** Maṅgala over the earth; **(4)** Budha over bedroom; **(5)** Śani over places where offerings are burnt or the hearth, and **(6)** Rāhu over tree-holes.

Notes: According to Śrī Chidambaram Iyer, further to what mentioned, Sūrya presides over the dinner table and kitchen utensils; Candra over the vinegar pot; Maṅgala over a small pot; Budha over a wall; Bṛhaspati over a corn-measure; Śukra over a water-pot; Śani over battlefields and Rāhu over snake-holes or anthills.

DIVISIONS OF DAY:

1.74. **(1)** The Pṛṣṭodaya Rāśis and Grahas preside over the night-time; **(2)** Śīrṣodaya Rāśis and Grahas preside over the daytime, and the **(3)** Ubhayodaya Rāśis and Grahas preside over the twilight hours.

1.75. According to some, **(1)** the Cararāśis and Grahas preside over the night; **(2)** the Sthirarāśis and Grahas preside over the day; and **(3)** the Dvisvarāśis and Grahas preside over the twilight hours.

ON DETERMINATION OF DAY, NIGHT AND VĀRA:

1.76. **(1)** Divide the nighttime of 30 Ghaṭis into parts of 3.75 Ghaṭis each; the time of Praśna indicates night or day as it falls in an odd or an even part (odd = night, and even = day). **(2)** Again, divide the daytime of 30 Ghaṭis into parts of 3.75 Ghaṭis each; the time of Praśna indicates day or night according as it falls in an odd or an even part (odd = day and even = night). **(3)** Again, divide the 60 Ghaṭis of the day of Praśna into parts of 3.75 Ghaṭis each. Name the parts after the Vāras beginning from the Vāra of Praśna. The Vāra pointed out by the time of Praśna is Vāra required.

Notes: When the daytime or nighttime is divided into parts of 3.75 Ghaṭis each, each part is called a Jāmam. If the Praśna is put on an Oja Jāmam, then a Night Praśna denotes the Nighttime of occurrence of the event, and Yugma Jāmam indicates the daytime event. This is reversed for Day Praśna. For Vāra, count the Jāmam from the Praśna Vāreśa in Vāra order (Sūrya, Candra, Maṅgala, Budha, Bṛhaspati, Śukra and Śani), and the resultant denote the Vāra. Suppose a Praśna is put on the 3rd Jāmam in the evening, on a Ravivāra. This corresponds to Maṅgalavāra Nighttime when the object of the Praśna is to occur or has occurred.

GRAHA PERIODS:

1.77. (1) The period of Śani and Rāhu is a year each; **(2)** that of Sūrya is 6 months or an Āyana; **(3)** that of Budha is 2 months, a Ṛtu or a season; **(4)** that of Bṛhaspati is one month; **(5)** that of Śukra is a fortnight or Pakṣa; **(6)** that of Maṅgala is a day; **(7)** and that of Candra is a Muhūrta.

Notes: A Muhūrta is of 48 minutes. The periods of the Rāśis are the same as those of their lords.

1.78. According to some, **(1)** the periods of Grahas occupying Śatru and Nīcarāśis are as many "Varṣas" as the number of their Raśmis; **(2)** those of Grahas occupying Mitrarāśis are as many "Māsas" as the number of their Raśmis; **(3)** those of Grahas occupying their Svarāśis are as many "Dinas" as their Raśmis; **(4)** those of Grahas occupying Uccarāśis are as many "Ghaṭis" as their Raśmis.

PREDICTION OF DAYS:

1.79. An event may be predicted to occur in as many days as the number of Nakṣatras obtained from the Nakṣatra occupied by Candra at the time of Praśna to the rising (Udaya or Lagna) Nakṣatra at the time.

RULE OF PREDICTION OF PERIOD:

1.80. In the prediction of the period of occurrence of an event, the Daivajña shall be guided **(1)** by the Vṛṣabhodaya Rāśi, **(2)** by the Grahas occupying such Rāśi, or **(3)** by the most powerful Graha in the Praśnakuṇḍalī.

Notes: Vṛṣabhodaya Rāśi determined for the Praśna, counting from Vṛṣabha, and assigning 2.5 Ghaṭis (1 Horā) for each Rāśi from Sūryodaya. Suppose, for example, the 20th Ghaṭi or 8th Horā from Sūryodaya to the time of Praśna. The 8th Rāśi from Vṛṣabha is Dhanu, and therefore Dhanu is the Vṛṣabhodaya Rāśi. According to some, instead of the Vṛṣabhodaya Rāśi, the Sūryodaya Rāśi and the Grahas occupying it should be considered. The Sūryodaya Rāśi is determined by counting from the Rāśi occupied by Sūrya, assigning 2.5 Ghaṭis (1 Horā) for each Rāśi from Sūryodaya. This is also called the Horā Lagna.

THE ĀRUṚHA CAKRA:

1.81. Draw a circle with two pairs of parallel lines cutting each other at right angles. Draw lines dividing into two halves each of the four quarters thus formed-thus dividing the circle of the horizon into 12 equal parts corresponding to the 12 Rāśis of Zodiac: Vṛṣabha is due east; and the other Rāśis are named in the order of the Rāśis of Zodiac from Vṛṣabha all round, from left to right.

THE OPPOSITE RĀŚIS:

1.82. The mutually opposite Rāśis are **(1)** Meṣa and Tulā; **(2)** Vṛṣabha and Vṛścika; **(3)** Mithuna and Dhanu; **(4)** Karka and Makara; **(5)** Siṅha and Kumbha; and **(6)** Kanyā and Mīna.

THE ĀRUṚHAGRAHAS OR YĀMAGRAHAS, JĀMAKKOL OR SĀMAKKOL:

1.83. The 8 Āruṛhagrahas are **(1)** Sūrya, **(2)** Maṅgala, **(3)** Bṛhaspati, **(4)** Budha, **(5)** Śukra, **(6)** Śani, **(7)** Candra, and **(8)** Rāhu, supposed to move in a circle, with an interval of a Rāśi and a half between every two adjacent Grahas. Sūrya being at the first point of Meṣa at every Sūryodaya, and the Grahas move from left to right.

Notes: The interval of a Rāśi and a half between every two Grahas remains the same, and the time taken for one complete revolution is from Sūryodaya to Sūryodaya, that is, 60 Ghaṭis. Each Graha takes, therefore, 5 Ghaṭis to go over a Rāśi. It is found that the process gives us 24 different Cakras for each day, at the rate of a Cakra for every hour from Sūryodaya. The 8 Āruṛhagrahas are known as Yāmagrahas (Jāmakkol or Sāmakkol), and they are employed nearly throughout this work. Śrī Chidambaram Iyer clarifies that a Yāma is 3 hours corresponding to the interval between two adjacent Grahas. The Tables of Yāmagrahas are stated in the principles section of this chapter.

THE INVISIBLE GRAHAS:

1.84. The 12 invisible Grahas are **(1)** Sūrya, **(2)** Dhūma, **(3)** Rāhu, **(4)** Candra, **(5)** Śani, **(6)** Sukṣma, **(7)** Śukra, **(8)** Indradhanuṣa, **(9)** Budha, **(10)** Bṛhaspati, **(11)** Maṅgala, and **(12)** Pariveṣa, supposed to more in the circle of the horizon from right to left with ah interval of a Rāśi or 30° between every two adjacent Grahas, Sūrya occupying the last point of Vṛṣabha at Sūryodaya every day, the time for a complete revolution being also a day.

Notes: The Cakras differ only every two hours, and there are 12 such Cakras in all, and every Graha takes two hours to go over a Rāśi. These Grahas are employed in **śloka 8.23, on the Return of Ships**.

THE VĀRA GRAHAS:

1.85. The Vāra Grahas are the same as the Āruṛhagrahas (Yāmagrahas). They move from right to left, and the Graha presiding over the Vāra is at the first point of Meṣa at Sūryodaya on the particular Vāra, and the time taken for a complete revolution is 12 hours.

Notes: (a). These are Sūrya, Maṅgala, Bṛhaspati, Budha, Śukra, Śani, Candra, and Rāhu moving from right to left in the order stated, that is, Maṅgala beings to the left of Sūrya, Bṛhaspati to the left of Maṅgala, and so on. In as much as each Graha takes an hour to go over a Rāśi, it is found that for every half hour, the Cakra is different, and there are 24 Cakras on the whole. The same Cakras are also the Cakras for the night.

THE MUTUALLY OPPOSITE GRAHAS:

1.86. The several pairs of mutually opposite Grahas are **(1)** Sūrya and Śukra; **(2)** Maṅgala and Śani; **(3)** Budha and Rāhu; **(4)** Bṛhaspati and Candra; **(5)** Dhūma and Indradhanuṣa; **(6)** Sukṣma and Pariveṣa.

Notes: This is the case in every Cakra of the day.

24.2.2 ADHYĀYA 2: ON DHĀTU MATTERS

DIVISION OF DHĀTU, MŪLA, AND JĪVA:

2.1. (1) Meṣa, Karka, Tulā, and Makara are Dhātu; **(2)** Vṛṣabha, Siṅha, Vṛścika, and Kumbha are Mūla; **(2)** Mithuna, Kanyā, Dhanu and Mīna are Jīva Rāśis.

Notes: Cararāśis are Dhātu, Sthirarāśis are Mūla and Dvisvarāśis are Jīva.

2.2. (1) Candra, Maṅgala, Śani and Rāhu are Dhātu; **(2)** Sūrya and Śukra are Mūla and **(3)** Budha and Bṛhaspati are Jīva.

2.3. (1) Sūrya and Candra are Dhātu when in Svarāśi, **(2)** and they are Mūla when in other Rāśis. **(3)** Śani is a Mūla when in Svarāśi, and **(4)** Budha is a Dhātu when in Svarāśi.

Notes: Śani is Dhātu when in other Rāśis, and Budha is Jīva when in other Rāśis. These special rules apply to Sūrya, Candra, Śani and Budha and do not apply to the remaining 4 Grahas.

THE DISCOVERY OF THE CHARACTER OF THE OBJECT OF PRAŚNA:

2.4. If Āruṛharāśi is a Dhātu Rāśi and its Chatrarāśi is also a Dhātu Rāśi, the Praśna refers to Dhātu matters. Likewise, if Āruṛharāśi is a Dhātu Rāśi and is dṛṣṭied by a Dhātu Graha, then also the Praśna pertains to Dhātu matters. The Mūla or Jīva character of the object of Praśna shall be similarly determined.

Notes: When Āruṛharāśi is a Mūla Rāśi, it is Chatrarāśi be also a Mūla Rāśi, or if such Āruṛharāśi is dṛṣṭied by a Mūla Graha, the Praśna relates to Mūla. If Āruṛharāśi is a Jīva Rāśi, it is Chatrarāśi be also a Jīva Rāśi, or if such Āruṛharāśi is dṛṣṭied by a Jīva Graha, the Praśna relates to Jīva.

2.5. (1) Dhātu and Mūla, when combined, give Jīva; (1) Jīva and Dhātu, when combined, give Mūla; (3) Mūla and Jīva when combined, give Dhātu. (4) When Dhātu, Mūla and Jīva are combined, the object of the Praśna shall be determined from their strength.

Notes: When Āruṛharāśi is a Dhātu Rāśi, its Chatrarāśi be a Mūla Rāśi, and if such Āruṛharāśi is dṛṣṭied by a Mūla Graha, the Praśna relates to Jīva. If Āruṛharāśi is a Mūla Rāśi, its Chatrarāśi is a Dhātu Rāśi, and if such Āruṛharāśi is dṛṣṭied by a Dhātu Graha, then also the Praśna relates to Jīva. The object of the Praśna is determined from Āruṛharāśi, its Chatrarāśi, and the Graha aspecting Āruṛharāśi. If these three belong to three different kinds, the object of the Praśna is determined by the stronger two among them in this manner:

If Āruṛharāśi is a Dhātu Rāśi, it is dṛṣṭied by a powerful Mūla Graha; the Praśna refers to Mūlajīva, i.e., it is Jīva but of Mūla kind.

If Āruṛharāśi is a Dhātu Rāśi, and it is dṛṣṭied by a powerful Jīva Graha, the Praśna refers to Jīvamūla, i.e., it is Mūla but of Jīva kind.

If Āruṛharāśi is a Mūla Rāśi, and it is dṛṣṭied by a powerful Jīva Graha, the Praśna relates to Jīvadhātu, and

If dṛṣṭied by a powerful Dhātu Graha, the Praśna refers to Dhātujīva.

If Āruṛharāśi is a Jīva Rāśi, it is dṛṣṭied by a powerful Dhātu Graha, the Praśna refers to Dhātumūla, and

if dṛṣṭied by a powerful Mūla Graha, the Praśna refers to Mūladhātu.

Also, according to the commentator, if when Udayarāśi is a Dhātu Rāśi, it is dṛṣṭied by a Dhātu Graha occupying:

A Dhātu Rāśi, the object of the Praśna, refers to Dhātu matters.

A Mūla Rāśi, the object refers to Mūla matters.

A Jīva Rāśi, the object refers to Jīva matters.

Again, if, when Udayarāśi is a Mūla Rāśi, it is dṛṣṭied by a Mūla Graha occupying:

A Mūla Rāśi, the object of the Praśna, refers to Mūla matters.

Other than a Mūla Rāśi, the object refers to Jīva matters.

Again, if, when Udayarāśi is a Jīva Rāśi, it is dṛṣṭied by a Jīva Graha occupying:

A Jīva Rāśi, the object of the Praśna, refers to Jīva matters.

Other than a Jīva Rāśi, the object refers to Mūla matters.

Again, If at Praśna, Candra should occupy or aspect Udayarāśi, the character of the object of Praśna, if already determined to be:

Dhātu shall be construed into Mūla.

Mūla shall be construed into Jīva.

Jīva shall be construed into Dhātu.

The indication of Pure Dhātu, Mūla, and Jīva matters are:

Dhātu: This term includes earth, stone, gold and the like.

Mūla: This term includes grass, plants, trees and the like.

Jīva: This term includes worms, birds, animals and the like.

The indications of mixed Dhātu, Mūla, and Jīva matters are:

Mūladhātu: decayed remains and the bark, roots, and flowers of grass, plants, trees and the like.

Jīvadhātu: decayed remains as well as the skin, claws, flesh and the like of worms, birds and animals.

Dhātumūla: objects and figures in the representation of grass, plants and trees made of Mūladhātu or Jīvadhātu.

Jīvamūla: the same as Mūla and includes growing grass, plants and trees.

Dhātujīva: figures in the representation of worms, birds, and animals made of *Mūladhātu and Jīvadhātu*.

Mūlajīva: figures in the representation of worms, birds, and animals made of *Mūladhātu*.

GRAHA METALS:

2.6. (1) Sūrya is brass; **(2)** Candra is bronze; **(3)** Maṅgala is copper; **(4)** Budha is a mixture of copper and spelter or zinc; **(5)** Bṛhaspati is gold; **(6)** Śukra is silver; and **(7)** Śani and Rāhu are iron.

Notes: These are applied when the object of the Praśna is found to be metal. According to some, Sūrya is a mixture of the 5 metals gold, silver, copper, iron and lead. Candra is the lead.

Notes: The metals of the Rāśis follow that of their lords.

GRAHA WEAPONS:

2.7. (1) Sūrya, Maṅgala, Śukra, and Śani are single-edged weapons; **(2)** Candra, Budha and Bṛhaspati are double-edged weapons. **(3)** When a Graha occupies his Svarāśi, the weapon is of his shape, **(4)** if otherwise, it is of the shape of the Rāśi occupied by the Graha.

Notes: Rāhu's weapon is the same as that of the Lord of the Rāśi occupied by him.

GRAHA MINERALS:

2.8. (1) Sūrya is stone; **(2)** Candra is brackish soil; **(3)** Maṅgala is artificial coral; **(4)** Budha is loose soil; **(5)** Bṛhaspati is golden sand; **(6)** Śukra is crystal and artificial pearls; **(7)** Śani is iron sand, and **(8)** Rāhu is arsenic.

Notes: According to some, Bṛhaspati is brick, Śani is stone and clay, and Rāhu is stone in general.

GRAHA GEMSTONES:

2.9. (1) Sūrya is Sūryakānta; **(2)** Candra is Candrakānta; **(3)** Budha is emerald; **(4)** Śukra is Vaidurya; and **(5)** Śani is blue stone.

Notes: Sūrya's gemstone is ruby, Candra's pearl or moonstone, Maṅgala's red coral, Bṛhaspati's yellow sapphire, Śukra's is Diamond, Śani's blue sapphire, Rāhu's hessonite, and Ketu's cat's eye.

2.10. (1) Sūrya is ruby; **(2)** Candra is pearl; **(3)** Maṅgala is coral; **(4)** Budha is emerald; **(5)** Bṛhaspati is Padmarāga; **(6)** Śukra is Vaidūrya; **(7)** Śani is blue stone, **(8)** Rāhu is diamond; **(9)** Ketu is Gomeda.

Notes: Normally, Śukra's stone is diamond, Rāhu's is hessonite (Gomeda), and Ketu's is Vaidurya (Cat's eye).

JEWELS AND ORNAMENTS:

2.11. If the Praśnalagna is a Manuṣya Rāśi and if a Manuṣya Graha occupies it, the Praśna refers to ornaments, and these are of the colour of the Graha.

2.12. (1) Sūrya, Maṅgala, and Bṛhaspati are neck ornaments; **(2)** Candra and Budha are ear ornaments; **(3)** Śukra is a head ornament; and **(4)** Śani and Rāhu are ornaments of the hands and feet.

2.13. Again, **(5)** Bṛhaspati is gold beads; **(6)** Candra is an ornament set with brilliants; **(7)** Śani is an ornament set with blue stones, wool, nails, bones and iron.

Notes: Likewise, Śukra and the other Grahas are ornaments set with their respective stones.

2.14. (1) If at Praśna, Bṛhaspati and Rāhu occupies together a Rāśi, the ornament is a gold thready and the like; **(2)** if Bṛhaspati and Śukra occupy together a Rāśi, the ornament is one set with pearls and crystals; and **(3)** if Bṛhaspati and Candra occupies together a Rāśi, it is an amulet.

Notes: If Bṛhaspati be one of the Grahas occupying together a Rāśi, the ornament is one of daily use; otherwise, it is one of occasional use. If Maṅgala is one of the Grahas occupying together a Rāśi, the ornament is a borrowed one; otherwise, it is the person's property.

24.2.3
ADHYĀYA 3:
ON MŪLA MATTERS

DIVISION OF MŪLA:

3.1-2. (1) Sūrya is a tree; **(2)** Candra is a creeping plant; **(3)** Maṅgala is dry crops; **(4)** Budha and Śukra are wet crops; **(5)** Bṛhaspati is sugarcane; **(6)** Śani and Rabu are thorny plants. Also, **(7)** Budha is a plant without thorns, and **(8)** Śukra is a sugarcane and the like.

3.3-4. (1) Siṅha and Dhanu are trees; **(2)** Vṛṣabha, Karka, and Tulā are creeping plants and wet crops; **(3)** Meṣa and Vṛścika are dry crops like millet; **(4)** Mīna is sugarcane and the like reeds; **(5)** Mithuna and Kanyā are plants without thorns. **(6)** Makara and Kumbha are thorny plants. Again, **(1)** Sūrya, Maṅgala, Śani and Rāhu are thorny and poisonous plants; and **(2)** Candra, Budha, Bṛhaspati and Śukra are plants which are neither thorny nor poisonous.

3.5-6. According to some, **(1)** Sūrya is a mountain tree; **(2)** Candra, a plantain tree; **(3)** Bṛhaspati, a cocoa tree; **(4)** Śani and Rāhu are both palmyras; **(5)** Budha and Śukra are both plantains; and **(6)** Maṅgala is a plant. The same remarks apply to the Rāśis of the several Grahas.

Notes: Candra is a flowering tree; Budha is a creeping plant; Bṛhaspati is the Campaka tree; Śukra is a flowering tree, a creeping plant and roots, and Śani is a ginger, turmeric and the like.

3.7. (1) Sūrya is bark, **(2)** Candra is the fleshy root; **(3)** Maṅgala is the flower; **(4)** Budha is the leaf; **(5)** Bṛhaspati is the ripe fruit; **(6)** Śukra is the unripe fruit; **(7)** Śani is the root; and **(8)** Rāhu is the creeper. These remarks also apply to the Rāśis of the several Grahas.

3.8. (1) Meṣa and Vṛścika are flowers; **(2)** Vṛṣabha and Tulā are unripe fruits; **(3)** Mithuna and Kanyā are leaves; **(4)** Dhanu and Mīna are ripe fruits; **(5)** Makara and Kumbha are roots; **(6)** Siṁha is bark; and **(7)** Karka is fleshy root.

Notes: It is found that the above are identical to the parts of the lords of the Rāśis.

THORNS:

3.9. (1) Śani and Rāhu are bent thorns; **(2)** Sūrya is a large straight thorn; **(3)** Maṅgala is a small straight thorn. Also, **(1)** Makara and Kumbha are bent thorns; **(2)** Siṁha is a large straight thorn and **(3)** Meṣa and Vṛścika are small straight thorns.

FRUITS:

3.10. (1) Sūrya, Candra and Śani are barren plants, and **(2)** the other Grahas are fruit plants: of these **(2a)** Bṛhaspati and Śukra are inner fruits; **(2b)** Maṅgala, Budha and Rāhu are outer fruits. **(3)** The fruits are of the colour of the Grahas. **(4)** The same remarks apply to several Svakṣetra Rāśis.

RICE AND BEANS:

3.11. (1) Candra is white paddy; **(2)** Maṅgala is millet; **(3)** Śukra is white sesamum seed; **(4)** Budha, Bṛhaspati and Śani are beans of their respective colour. **(5)** Also, the four Saumyas and Śani are hard grains, and **(6)** the three-remaining Krūras are pod grains (pulses, such as peas, dal etc., which grow inside pods).

3.12. (1) Sūrya is a bean; **(2)** Candra is white sesamum; **(3)** Maṅgala is Bengal gram; **(4)** Budha is a small species of pulse; **(5)** Bṛhaspati is gram; **(6)** Śukra is white gram; **(7)** Śani is sesamum, and **(1)** Rāhu is black gram.

GROWING FIELDS:

3.13. (1) Sūrya and Budha are high grounds; **(2)** Candra and Śukra are watery places; **(3)** Maṅgala and Bṛhaspati are stony places; **(4)** Śani is an arid tract, and **(5)** Rāhu is a place full of snake-holes or anthills.

Notes: According to some, Maṅgala is high ground; Budha is a watery place, while according to others, Budha is a place full of snake-holes.

THE SHAPE AND THE LIKE OF DHĀTU, MŪLA, AND MŪLADHĀTU:

3.14. The shape, flavour and family **(1)** of gems, weapons and the like Dhātus, **(2)** of trees, plants and the like Mūlas, **(3)** of the bark, root and the like Mūladhātus are the same as those of the Grahas and Rāśis.

24.2.4
ADHYĀYA 4:
ON JĪVA MATTERS

MAHĀBHŪTA AND SENSES:

4.1-2. **(1)** Sūrya is the father, and **(2)** Candra is the mother. Of the 5 Grahas, **(3)** Bṛhaspati is earth (Pṛthvī), **(4)** Śukra is water (Jala), **(5)** Maṅgala is fire (Agni), **(6)** Budha is air (Vāyu), and **(7)** Śani is ether (Ākāśa). **(1)** Śani, therefore, presides over the sense of touch; **(2)** Budha over touch and taste; **(3)** Maṅgala over touchy taste and sight; **(4)** Śukra over touch, taste, sight and smell; and **(5)** Bṛhaspati over touch, taste, sight, smell and bearing.

GRAHAS AND ANIMALS:

4.3. Accordingly, **(1)** Budha is a conch, a cowry, an oyster and the like possessed of the two senses of touch and taste; **(2)** Maṅgala is an ant, a louse, a fly, and the like possessed of the three senses of touch, taste and sight; **(3)** Śukra is a wasp, a beetle, and the like possessed of the four senses of touch, taste, sight, and smell.

Notes: The object possessed of the single sense of touch is a Mūla or plant.

4.4. **(4)** Bṛhaspati is a Deva, a man, an animal, a bird, and the like possessed of the 5 senses of touch, taste, sight, smell and hearing.

THE FOURFOLD DIVISION OF ANIMALS:

4.5. Living creatures may be divided into four classes; **(1)** Those that walk, **(2)** Those that fly, **(3)** Those that creep, **(4)** Those that live in water.

OF THE BIRDS:

4.6. If at Praśna, Mīna or Makara is **(1)** dṛṣṭied by Candra, the Praśna refers to a peacock; **(2)** if Dṛṣṭied by Maṅgala or Śani, the Praśna refers to a fowl; **(3)** if by Budha, then to a parrot; **(4)** if by Śukra, then to a swan.

4.7. If at Praśna, Mīna or Makara is **(1)** dṛṣṭied by Sūrya, the Praśna refers to the Brahminy kite; **(2)** if dṛṣṭied by Bṛhaspati, then to a heron; and **(3)** if dṛṣṭied by Rāhu, then to a crow. **(1)** If the Praśna be about other birds, these shall be determined by the colour of the aspecting Grahas

OF ANIMALS:

4.8. If at Praśna, Meṣa **(1)** is occupied by Sūrya, the Praśna refers to a tiger; **(2)** if occupied by Candra, then to a bullock; **(3)** if occupied by Maṅgala, then to a sheep; **(4)** if by Budha then to a rabbit; **(5)** if by Bṛhaspati then to a horse; **(6)** if by Śukra then to a cow; **(7)** if by Śani then to a bull; and **(8)** if by Rāhu then to a buffalo.

4.9. If at Praśna, Vṛṣabha **(1)** is occupied by Sūrya, the Praśna refers to a bull; **(2)** if occupied by Candra or Śukra then to a cow; **(3)** if occupied by Maṅgala then to a deer; **(4)** if occupied by Budha then to a monkey; **(5)** if occupied by Bṛhaspati then to a horse; **(6)** if by Śani then to a buffalo; and **(7)** if by Rāhu, then to a male buffalo.

4.10. If at Praśna, Siṅha **(1)** is occupied by Sūrya or Candra, the Praśna refers to a lion; **(2)** if occupied by Maṅgala then to a tiger; **(3)** if by Budha, to a monkey; **(4)** if by Bṛhaspati, to a horse; **(5)** if by Śukra to a dog; **(6)** if by Śani to a buffalo; **(7)** and if by Rāhu then to a male buffalo.

4.11. If at Praśna, Dhanu **(1)** is occupied by Sūrya or Śani, then the Praśna refers to an elephant; **(2)** if occupied by Candra, Maṅgala or Śukra, then to a horse; **(3)** if occupied by Budha or Bṛhaspati then to a monkey; **(4)** and if occupied by Rāhu, then to a male buffalo.

4.12. If at Praśna, Maṅgala **(1)** occupies Karka; the Praśna refers to an ass; **(2)** if he occupies Makara, then to a buffalo; **(3)** if Mīna then to a bullock; **(4)** if Mithuna, Kanyā, Tulā or Kumbha, then to a mongoose, a jackal or a dog. The same remarks apply to Sūrya and Śani.

4.13. If at the time of Praśna Tulā **(1)** is occupied by Candra, then the Praśna refers to a cow; **(2)** and if occupied by Śukra, then to a calf. **(3)** The number of animals is that of the Grahas aspecting Candra or Śukra, as the case may be.

Notes: The colour, horn and age shall also be ascertained from the aspecting Grahas.

FEMALE OF ANIMALS:

4.14. If the Graha from which the female animal involved in the Praśna is determined, **(1)** is dṛṣṭied by Budha, the animal is young; **(2)** if the Graha is dṛṣṭied by Sūrya or Bṛhaspati, the animal is pregnant; **(3)** if dṛṣṭied by Candra or Śukra, the animal is wet; **(4)** if dṛṣṭied by Śani, or Rāhu, the animal is barren; **(5)** and if dṛṣṭied by Maṅgala it is dry (ceased to yield milk).

MEN:

4.15. Depending on Sūrya in **(1)** an Uccarāśi, **(2)** his Svarāśi, or **(3)** a Mitrarāśi, **(4)** a Śatru/Nīca Rāśi at Praśna, the person referred to in the Praśna is respectively **(1)** a king, **(2)** a commander of an army, **(3)** a soldier, or **(4)** a spy. Depending on Maṅgala in **(1)** an Uccarāśi, **(2)** his Svarāśi, **(3)** a Mitrarāśi, **(4)** a Śatrurāśi or his Nīcarāśi, the person is **(1)** a smith, **(2)** a potter, **(3)** an oil monger, or **(4)** a painter.

4.16. If at the time of Praśna Bṛhaspati occupies **(1)** an Uccarāśi, the person referred to in the Praśna, is a Brāhmaṇa; **(2)** if he occupies his Svarāśi, the person is a minister and **(3)** if he occupies a Mitrarāśi then the person is a Jain. If Budha occupies **(1)** an Uccarāśi, the person is a dancing master; **(2)** if he occupies his Svarāśi, the person is a priest; **(3)** if he occupies a Mitrarāśi, he is a tradesman. If Śukra occupies **(1)** his Uccarāśi, the person is an agriculturist; **(2)** if he occupies his Svarāśi, he is a shepherd; and **(3)** if he occupies a Mitrarāśi, the person is a Vaiśya.

4.17. If at Praśna, Śani occupies **(1)** his Uccarāśi, the person is one of a low caste; **(2)** if he occupies his Svarāśi, the person is a Caṇḍāla; **(3)** if he occupies a Mitrarāśi, he is a shoemaker. If Candra occupies **(1)** an Uccarāśi, the person is a physician; **(2)** if he occupies his Svarāśi, he is an actor; **(3)** if he occupies a Mitrarāśi, he is a Daivajña. If Rāhu occupies **(1)** an Uccarāśi, the person is a snake charmer; **(2)** if he occupies his Svarāśi, he is a ballad singer; and **(3)** if he occupies a Mitrarāśi, the person is one of the obeying class (serving class).

4.18. **(1)** If Sūrya, Maṅgala, Budha, or Bṛhaspati occupies a Śatru/Nīca Rāśi, the person is one of a class of filthy people. **(2)** If Candra occupies a Śatru/Nīca Rāśi, the person is a lime burner. **(3)** If Śukra occupies a Śatru/Nīca Rāśi, the person is a washerman; **(4)** if Śani occupies a Śatru/Nīca Rāśi, the person is a vegetable seller; **(5)** if Rāhu occupies a Śatru/Nīca Rāśi, the person is a fisherman.

MEN AND ANIMALS:

4.19. Where the **Praśna refers to a Manuṣya**, **(1)** if Candra is in his Svarāśi, the person referred to in the Praśna is a Daivajña; **(2)** if Budha is in his Svarāśi, the person is a dancing-master; **(3)** if Bṛhaspati is in his Svarāśi, the person is a singer or a poet; **(4)** if Śukra is in his Svarāśi, the person is a wearer. Also, where the **Praśna refers to a Catuṣpāda**, **(1)** if Sūrya is in his Svarāśi, the animal referred to in the Praśna is a lion or a tiger; **(2)** if Maṅgala is in his Svarāśi, the animal is a sheep; **(3)** if Śani or Rāhu is in his Svarāśi the animal is an elephant.

4.20. If at Praśna, **(1)** Bṛhaspati occupies Kumbha, while Candra occupies the 5th, 7th or the 9th House, the person is a king; and **(2)** if other Saumyas occupy such 5th, 7th or 9th House, the Praśna refers to an elephant. **(3)** If, in the same Yoga, Bṛhaspati occupies Dhanu, or Mīna instead of Kumbha, the Praśna refers to a monkey.

24.2.5
ADHYĀYA 5:
NAṢṬA AND MANOMUṢṬI CINTĀ

THE NATURE OF THE PRAŚNA 1:

5.1. The thought of the Pṛcchaka is determined from the Grahas aspecting Āruṛharāśi, and where the thought refers to living creatures, whether such creature is Manuṣya, Catuṣpāda, Sarīsṛpa or Kīṭa or Jalacara class, is determined from such aspecting Grahas.

5.2. **(1)** The **Pṛcchaka's thought (Cintā)** is determined from the strength of Āruṛharāśi and the Grahas aspecting it. **(2)** **Property lost (Naṣṭa)** is determined from the strength of Udayarāśi and the Grahas aspecting it. **(3)**

Concealed object (Muṣṭi) shall be determined from the strength of Chatrarāśi and the Grahas aspecting it.

Notes: The aspecting Graha is effective only when strong; else, the Rāśi holding Āruṛharāśi, Udayarāśi, or Chatrarāśi shall be effective.

5.3. Find out the Graha possessing Kendrabala (Dikbala, from stronger of Āruṛharāśi, Udayarāśi or Chatrarāśi). **(1)** If such Graha occupies a **Mitrarāśi**, the character of **concealed object (Muṣṭi)** is determined from it; **(2)** if it occupies a **Svarāśi**, the character of **property lost (Naṣṭa)** is determined from it, **(3)** and if the Graha occupy an **Uccarāśi**, the **Pṛcchaka's thought (Cintā)** is determined from the same.

5.4. The character of **(1) Naṣṭa (lost objects), (2) Muṣṭi (concealed object),** and **(3) Cintā (Pṛcchaka's thoughts)** is also determined respectively from the Dhātu, Mūla or Jīva characteristics of Udayarāśi, Āruṛharāśi or Chatrarāśi and the Grahas occupying such Rāśi.

5.5. Also, **(1) Cintā or thought** shall be determined from the 10th House, **(2) dreams** from the 4th House, **(3) Muṣṭi or concealed object** from Chatrarāśi, **(4) past events** from the 7th House, **(5) future events** from Udayarāśi, and **(5) Naṣṭa** or stolen property from Āruṛharāśi.

PERSONS REFERRED TO IN THE PRAŚNA:

5.6. (1) Udayarāśi refers to the Pṛcchaka; **(2)** the 2nd House to his family; **(3)** the 3rd to his brothers; **(4)** the 4th to his mother; **(5)** the 5th to his father; **(6)** the 6th to his enemy; **(7)** the 7th to his wife; **(8)** the 8th to his length of life; **(9)** the 9th to his paternal grandfather; **(10)** the 10th to his avocation; **(11)** the 11th to his gain; **(12)** and the 12th to his loss.

THE NATURE OF THE PRAŚNA 2:

5.7. (1) If Āruṛharāśi is a Manuṣya Rāśi and if it is occupied by Sūrya, Candra, Budha, Bṛhaspati or Śukra, the Praśna refers to a Manuṣya (human being); **(2)** and if such Grahas are accompanied by Śani or Rāhu, the Praśna refers to a thief or a person stolen away (abducted, kidnapped or lost).

5.8. If at Praśna, **(1)** the Udaya Graha is Sūrya, the Praśna refers to fear from the king; **(2)** if it is Candra, Budha, Bṛhaspati, or Śukra, the Praśna refers to prosperity; **(3)** if it is Maṅgala, it refers to quarrel; **(4)** if it is Śani, it refers to property lost or stolen; **(5)** if it is Rāhu, the Praśna refers to disease or poison.

Notes: The Udaya Graha that is rising, i.e., present in the Praśnalagna.

5.9. If at Praśna, **(1)** the Krūras occupy Udayarāśi, the Praśna refers to death; **(2)** if they occupy Āruṛharāśi, it refers to disease; and **(3)** if they occupy the 2nd House from Udayarāśi or Āruṛharāśi, the Praśna refers to property lost or stolen.

5.10. If at Praśna, **(4)** Krūras occupy the 8th House, the Praśna refers to property lost or stolen; **(5)** if they occupy the 6th House, the Praśna refers to reverses; **(3)** if they occupy the 12th House, the Praśna refers to diseases. **(4)** If

Saumyas occupy the 8th, 6th, or 12th House, the Praśna will refer to gain, success and health, respectively.

TIME.

5.11. **(1)** If Āruṛharāśi is the 3rd, 6th, 9th or 12th House, the Praśna refers to past events; **(2)** if it is Udayarāśi, the 4th, 7th or 10th House, the Praśna refers to future events; **(3)** and if it is the 2nd, 5th, 8th or 11th House, the Praśna refers to present events.

THE RECOVERY OF STOLEN PROPERTY:

5.12. **(1a)** If Tulā is Udayarāśi and Meṣa Āruṛharāśi, there is a recovery of stolen property; **(1b)** but if Meṣa is Udayarāśi and Tulā Āruṛharāśi, there is no recovery. Again, **(2a)** if Vṛṣabha is Udayarāśi and Vṛścika Āruṛharāśi, there is no recovery; but if **(2b)** Vṛścika is Udayarāśi and Vṛṣabha Āruṛharāśi, there is recovery. Again, **(3a)** if Dhanu is Udayarāśi and Mithuna Āruṛharāśi, there is no recovery; but **(3b)** if Mithuna is Udayarāśi and Dhanu Āruṛharāśi, there is recovery.

5.13. **(4a)** If Makara is Udayarāśi and Karka Āruṛharāśi, there is recovery but **(4b)** if Karka is Udayarāśi, and Makara Āruṛharāśi, there is no recovery. Again, **(5a)** if Siṅha is Udayarāśi and Kumbha Āruṛharāśi, there is recovery; but **(5b)** if Kumbha is Udayarāśi and Siṅha Āruṛharāśi, there is no recovery. Again, **(6a)** if Kanyā is Udayarāśi and Mīna Āruṛharāśi, there is recovery; but **(6b)** if Mīna is Udayarāśi and Kanyā Āruṛharāśi, there is no recovery.

5.14. **(1)** If Udayarāśi is a Śīrṣodaya Rāśi and Āruṛharāśi, a Pṛṣṭodaya Rāśi, there is recovery of stolen property; but **(2)** if Udayarāśi is a Pṛṣṭodaya Rāśi and Āruṛharāśi, a Śīrṣodaya Rāśi, there is no recovery. Again, **(3)** if Saumyas occupy Udayarāśi and Āruṛharāśi, there is an immediate recovery of stolen property.

5.15. **(1)** If at Praśna, Krūras occupy the 3rd House from Udayarāśi, Āruṛharāśi or Chatrarāśi, and if they are dṛṣṭied by Krūras, there is a recovery of the stolen property; **(2)** but if such Krūras are dṛṣṭied by Saumyas, there is no recovery.

5.16. **(1)** If at Praśna, Meṣa, Kanyā, or Makara is the Astarāśi, there is no recovery of stolen property; **(2)** but if Vṛṣabha, Tulā, Dhanu or Kumbha, is the Astarāśi, there is recovery; **(3)** and if any of the other Rāśis is the Astarāśi, there is recovery of property after a time. Again, **(4)** if Bṛhaspati occupies the Astarāśi, there is recovery of property, and **(5)** if any of the other Grahas occupy the 7th House, there is no recovery.

5.17. **(1)** If at Praśna, Candra occupies or aspects a Pṛṣṭodaya Rāśi, there is recovery; **(2)** if such Candra is dṛṣṭied by Śani, there is no recovery; **(3)** but if Maṅgala occupies the 10th House from such Candra, there is recovery.

5.18. If at Praśna, either **(1)** Sūrya and Candra or **(2)** Budha and Bṛhaspati occupy the 7th House, there is recovery.

5.19. If at Praśna, **(1)** Saumyas occupy the 5th, 7th and 9th Houses, there is recovery of stolen property; **(2)** but if Krūras occupy these Rāśis, there is no recovery of property.

PLACE OF STOLEN PROPERTY:

5.20. If at Praśna, **(1)** Saumyas occupy the 3rd, 5th, and 9th Houses from Udayarāśi or Āruṛharāśi, there is recovery of property; **(2)** but if Krūras occupy such Houses, there is no recovery of property. Property stolen would have been removed in the direction of the Grahas.

5.21. Suppose at Praśna, the Indradhanuṣa, Pariveṣa, Dhūma or Sukṣma occupy Udayarāśi or Āruṛharāśi. In that case, there is recovery of property lost, which would have been carried in the direction of the Grahas.

MODE OF RECOVERY:

5.22. If at Praśna, Krūras occupy the 3rd House from Udayarāśi or Āruṛharāśi, and if Saumyas occupy the 4th or 5th House from such Krūras, the property lost is brought and delivered by a person of his own accord.

THE RETURN OF A CATUṢPĀDA LOST:

5.23. If at Praśna, Sūrya, Maṅgala, and Śani occupies the 10th House from Udayarāśi or Āruṛharāśi, a Catuṣpāda lost returns home of itself.

CONDITION OF CATUṢPĀDA AND MANUṢYA LOST:

5.24. If at Praśna, Rāhu occupies a Catuṣpāda Astarāśi; the Praśna refers to the loss of a Catuṣpāda. If Rāhu occupies Udayarāśi while a Catuṣpāda Rāśi is the Astarāśi, a Catuṣpāda lost remains shut or bound with cords. If Rāhu occupies Udayarāśi while a Manuṣya Rāśi is the Astarāśi, a person lost remains bound or confined.

Notes: The 7th Rāśi from Udayarāśi is the Astarāśi, also called the Astarāśi or the descendant. The kind of creature lost is seen from the characteristics of the Astarāśi, whereas whether the creature is bound or confined is seen from the presence of Rāhu in the Lagna.

METALS LOST:

5.25. **(1)** If at Praśna, Bṛhaspati occupies Udayarāśi, gold lost is not destroyed; **(2)** if Śukra occupies the 4th House, silver lost is not destroyed; **(3)** if Śani occupies the 7th House, iron lost is not destroyed; and **(4)** if Maṅgala occupies the 10th House, copper lost is not destroyed.

Notes: If the Praśna is about some metal items, we must identify the Graha governing the metal. If the Graha is in Dikbala, then the lost article is not destroyed or melted into something else. In this regard, Bṛhaspati governs gold, Śukra, silver, Śani, iron, Maṅgala, copper, Budha, black copper, Candra, bronze, Rāhu, lead and Sūrya, brass. The Dikbala Bhāvas of the Grahas are Budha/Bṛhaspati: Lagna, Candra/Śukra: 4th, Śani/Rāhu: 7th and Sūrya/Maṅgala: 10th. Nothing is assigned to Ketu.

5.26. **(5)** If at Praśna, Budha occupies Udayarāśi, black-copper lost is not destroyed; **(6)** if Candra occupies the 4th House, bronze lost is not destroyed; **(7)** if Rāhu occupies the 7th House, lead lost is not destroyed; and **(8)** if Sūrya occupies the 10th House, brass lost is not destroyed.

PLACE OF STOLEN PROPERTY FROM RĀŚI:

5.27. **(1)** If Udayarāśi is Karka or Vṛścika, the property lost is concealed within a House; **(2)** if it is Makara or Mīna, the place of concealment is to the outer veranda or wall; and **(3)** if it is any other Rāśi, the place is a crossbeam or the eaves of a House.

Notes: The place where the lost object is kept can be known from Udayarāśi. Karka and Vṛścika are the Kīṭa Rāśi, and they signify concealment in a house. Makara and Mīna are Sarīsṛpa or Jalacara Rāśi, and they indicate an outer veranda or wall.

PLACE OF STOLEN PROPERTY FROM GRAHA:

5.28. **(1)** If the Udaya Graha is Sūrya or Budha, the property lost is concealed on the top of a wall; **(2)** if it is Candra or Śukra, the place of concealment is a water pot; **(3)** if it is Maṅgala, the place is close to a wall or the outer veranda of a House; **(4)** if it is Bṛhaspati, the place is the kitchen; **(5)** if it is Śani, the place is the hearth (fire place, stove), and **(6)** if it is Rāhu, the place of concealment is a hole.

Notes: If a Graha is in Udayarāśi, then the placement of concealment should be judged from the Graha; else, it should be from the Rāśi. The Grahas govern different places.

PLACE OF STOLEN PROPERTY FROM NAKṢATRA:

5.29. If at Praśna, **(1)** the Udaya Nakṣatra is Aśvinī, the place of concealment of the lost object is within a village or town; **(2)** if the Udaya Nakṣatra is Bharaṇī, the place of concealment is a street; **(3)** if it is Kṛttikā, the place is a forest; **(4)** if it is Rohini, the place is a vinegar pot; **(5)** if it is Mṛgaśirā, the place is under a cot; **(6)** if it is Ārdrā, the place is a temple; **(7)** if it is Punarvasu, the place is a granary; **(8)** if it is Puṣya, the place is a House; and **(9)** if it is Aśleṣā, the place is a dust-heap.

Notes: The place of concealment can also be known from the Udaya Nakṣatra or the Nakṣatra of the Praśnalagna. Regarding this, the Nakṣatras are assigned several places.

5.30. If at Praśna, **(10)** the Udaya Nakṣatra is Magha, the place of concealment of property lost is a receptacle for paddy; **(11)** if it is Pūrvāphālgunī, the place of concealment is an uninhabited House; **(12)** if it is Uttarāphālgunī, the place is a piece of water; **(13)** if it is Hasta, the place is a tank; **(14)** if it is Citrā, the place is a water bank; **(15)** if it is Swati, the place is a rice-field; **(16)** if it is Viśākhā, the place is a cotton-field; **(17)** if it is Anurādhā, the place is one overgrown with the gloriosa or fire lilies, and **(18)** if it is Jyeṣṭhā, the place is a desert.

5.31. If at Praśna, **(19)** the Udaya Nakṣatra is Mūla, the object is concealed in a stable; **(20)** if it is Pūrvāṣāṛhā, the place of concealment is a thatched House; **(21)** if it is Uttarāṣāṛhā, the place is the dhobi's washing spot; **(22)** if it is Śravana, the place is a parade ground; **(23)** if it is Sraviṣṭhā, the place is near a mill; **(24)** if it is Śatabhiṣā, the place is a street; **(25)** if it is Pūrvābhādra the place is the south-east House-ground; **(26)** if it is Uttarābhādra, the place is a swamp; **(27)** and if it is Revatī, the place is a flower garden.

THE EARTHEN VESSEL OF CONCEALMENT:

5.32. In determining the nature of the vessel in which stolen property is hidden, **(1)** Maṅgala represents a little pot; **(2)** Budha a sugar boiler or caldron; **(3)** Bṛhaspati a large water pot; **(4)** Śukra a water pot; **(5)** Śani a large pot; Rāhu, **(6)** a vessel with a hole; **(6)** Sūrya a vinegar pot; and **(7)** Candra a fine vessel.

Notes: The kind of vessel in which the lost article is kept should be seen from the Graha in Udayarāśi.

THE DIRECTION OF THE PLACE WHERE PROPERTY WAS KEPT BEFORE IT WAS STOLEN:

5.33. The direction of the place where the property was kept before it was stolen is the Rāśi, which is occupied by Udayarāśi Lord, Vṛṣabha representing the east.

Notes: Vṛṣabha is east; Siṅha south; Vṛścika west; Kumbha north; and the several pairs of intermediate Rāśis represent respectively south-east, southwest, north-west, and north-east.

THE DIRECTION OF THE PLACE TO WHICH STOLEN PROPERTY IS CARRIED TO 1:

5.34a. The direction of the place to which stolen property is carried is that of the Rāśi aspecting the Āruṛha and Chatrarāśi

THE NUMBER OF THINGS STOLEN:

5.34b. The number of things stolen is known from the Raśmis of such aspecting Rāśi and the Raśmis of the number of aspecting Grahas.

Notes: Notice that in the case of Grahas, we are not taking the Raśmis of the Grahas, but instead taking the number of Grahas.

THE SEX OF THE THIEF:

5.35. If the Udaya and Āruṛha Rāśis are Ojarāśis, the thief is a man; and if they are Yugmarāśis, the thief is a woman.

Notes: When one of them is Ojarāśi, and the other Yugmarāśi, then the stronger between the two should determine the sex of the thief. Note that the gender is seen from the Udaya and Āruṛha Rāśis, and Chatrarāśi is not resorted to here.

THE DIRECTION OF THE PLACE TO WHICH STOLEN PROPERTY IS CARRIED TO 2:

5.36a. The direction of the place to which stolen property has been carried is that dṛṣṭied by the most powerful Graha.

THE COLOUR OF THE STOLEN PROPERTY AND THE COLOUR, CASTE, AND MARKS OF THE BODY OF THE THIEF:

5.36b. The colour of the stolen property is that of the Graha dṛṣṭied by the most powerful Graha. The colour, caste, marks of body and the like of the thief is also those of the Graha dṛṣṭied by the most powerful Graha.

TIME OF RECOVERY:

5.37. The period of recovery of stolen property is that of the most powerful Graha, as stated already.

Notes: The periods ruled by the Grahas, i.e., Candra- a Muhūrta, Maṅgala- a Dina etc., should be used here.

24.2.6
ADHYĀYA 6:
ON GOOD AND EVIL

MATTERS COVERED:

6.1. In this Chapter, I propose to treat the effects of the several matters referred to and omitted in the Adhyāya on 'Married women', 'Sexual love', 'Travels' and other Adhyāyas.

Notes: The Adhyāyas referred to here are 12, 13 and 19. This Adhyāya covers the general success or failure of an attempt. This is also called Kāryasiddhi Praśna.

THE EFFECT OF UDAYARĀŚI:

6.2. (1) If at Praśna, Udayarāśi is Śīrṣodaya, there is the success of an attempt; **(2)** if it is a Pṛṣṭodaya one, there is a failure; and **(3)** if it is a Ubhayodaya, there is success after attempts.

6.3. If Udayarāśi is a Cararāśi, there is no recovery of stolen property; there is recovery from illness, approach of the enemy and peace with him.

Notes: Cararāśi in Udayarāśi in a theft Praśna indicates that the article is carried over a long distance, whereas Sthirarāśi indicates that the article is located somewhere nearby. On the other hand, in an illness-related Praśna, Cararāśi indicates that the situation is improving quickly, whereas Sthirarāśi indicates that the situation is not changing. In an enemy or invasion Praśna,

Cararāśi indicate movement or that the invasion is likely. This also indicates changes to the situation, i.e., the negotiation etc., is not standstill but moving in a positive direction. Cararāśi indicates the movement, but whether it is in a positive or negative direction is to be seen from Śubha or Krūra Graha influences on Udayarāśi.

6.4. If Udayarāśi is a Sthirarāśi, there is the recovery of stolen property, no approach of the enemy, no death, success of an attempt, no recovery from illness, and there is the gain of presents.

Notes: In the translation of Śrī Chidambaram Iyer, there is a misprint, which states this as Cararāśi instead of Sthirarāśi. Sthirarāśi indicates the gain of gifts etc., because the possibility of the gifts being diverted to something else is not there.

6.5. If Udayarāśi is a Dvisvarāśi, there is no recovery of stolen property, no travel, no recovery from illness, no peace with the enemy, no completion of learning, and there is failure of all attempts.

Notes: Dvisvarāśi is not good for any Praśna, which indicates an undecided state, neither Cara nor Sthira.

THE CHANGE IS IN POSITIVE OR NEGATIVE DIRECTION:

6.6. Even though Udayarāśi is a Cararāśi or a Dvisvarāśi, if it is occupied by Saumyas in their Mitrarāśi, Svakṣetra or Uccarāśis, all evils disappear, and there is a success. Still, if each Udayarāśi is occupied by Krūras in their Śatru/Nīca Rāśi, there is an increase in evil.

Notes: Cararāśi, along with dignified Saumyas, indicate success. Krūras in their Sva/Ucca/Mitra etc. Rāśi indicates success after initial difficulties. If the Saumyas are in their Śatru/Nīca Rāśi, then even though it may appear positive but the situation worsens. Krūras in the Śatru/Nīca Rāśi indicate a fast worsening situation.

EFFECTS OF ĀRUṚHARĀŚI FROM UDAYARĀŚI:

6.7 If Āruṛharāśi is Udayarāśi, there is a recovery of stolen property and also recovery from illness; if it is the 4th House, there is also recovery of stolen property and success of attempts; if it is the 7th House, there not only be no recovery of the lost object but also further loss of property; and if it is the 10th House, there is an increase of wealth.

Notes: The recovery of the lost object is affected by the placement of Āruṛharāśi from Udayarāśi. It is favourable to have Āruṛharāśi in 1st/4th/10th from Udayarāśi. If Āruṛharāśi is in opposition with Udayarāśi, then the chances of recovering the lost object become bleaker.

6.8. If Āruṛharāśi is the 2nd, 6th, 8th or 12th House, there is a failure of attempts and loss of property and the enemy triumphs.

Notes: If Āruṛharāśi is in the remaining houses, i.e., the 3rd, 5th, 9th or 11th House, the effects are those described for the same Houses when they happen to be Chatrarāśis. The effects of Chatrarāśis are given below.

EFFECTS OF CHATRARĀŚI FROM UDAYARĀŚI:

6.9. If Chatrarāśi is the 2nd or 4th House, there is no peace with the enemy, but if Bṛhaspati occupies such Chatrarāśi, the enemy submits after some difficulty.

6.10. If Chatrarāśi is the 3rd House, there is continued success and prosperity; and if Saumyas occupy such Rāśi, there is much success, and if Krūras occupy it, there is a little evil. Again, if Chatrarāśi is the 11th House, there is continued evil and failure; if Krūras occupy such Rāśi, there is much misery; but if Saumyas occupy it, there is little success.

6.11. If Chatrarāśi is the 5th or the 9th House, there is a traveller's return and success of attempts; the enemy comes to terms, and there is success and prosperity.

6.12. If Chatrarāśi is in the 1st, 6th, 8th, or 12th from Udayarāśi, there is no recovery of stolen property, no recovery from illness, and no success. But if Saumyas occupy such Chatrarāśi, there is a slight success.

6.13. If Chatrarāśi is the 7th or 10th House, there is a success; and if Saumyas occupy such Rāśi in their Mitrai, Sva or Ucca Rāśis, there is much success.

EFFECTS OF GRAHAS IN THE UDAYA/ĀRUṚHA/CHATRA RĀŚI:

6.14. If Bṛhaspati occupies Udayarāśi, Āruṛharāśi or Chatrarāśi, there is a gain of wealth and the successful return of persons who have gone abroad for the acquisition of wealth. There is also recovery from illness, and the enemy comes to terms.

Notes: The effect is greatest when the Graha occupies Udayarāśi and less so when it is in the Āruṛha or Chatrarāśi.

6.15. If Candra occupies Udayarāśi, Āruṛharāśi, or Chatrarāśi, there is a gain of wealth and rare objects from a distant land, and also the success of all attempts.

6.16. Suppose Śukra occupies Udayarāśi, Āruṛharāśi, or Chatrarāśi. In that case, there is glory, a gain of wealth, triumph over enemies, recovery from illness, gain of a woman, and prosperity of every kind.

6.17. Suppose Budha occupies Udayarāśi, Āruṛharāśi or Chatrarāśi. In that case, the enemy will fail in his attempts, and there will be no trouble from him. There is recovery from illness, the enemy will come to terms, and attempts will succeed.

6.18. If Sūrya, Maṅgala or Śani occupies Udayarāśi, Āruṛharāśi or Chatrarāśi, there is a waste of wealth, illness, death and misery.

6.19. If Rāhu occupies Udayarāśi, Āruṛharāśi, or Chatrarāśi, there is murder, theft, suffering from poison and fire, and there also death and numerous miseries.

DṚṢṬI OF GRAHAS FROM DIGNITY:

6.20. If Uccagrahas Udayarāśi, Āruṛharāśi, or Chatrarāśi, there is the success of attempts and gain of rare objects. But if Grahas occupies Śatru/Nīca Rāśi aspect the same Rāśis, there is a failure of attempts and neither gain of rare objects nor that of a woman.

6.21a. If Grahas in their Mitrarāśi, Svakṣetra or Uccarāśis aspect Udayarāśi, Āruṛharāśi or Chatrarāśi, the enemies come to terms

DṚṢṬI OF GRAHAS TO THEIR DIGNIFIED PLACES:

6.21b. If such Rāśis (**Udaya/Āruṛha/Chatra**) is the Mitrarāśi, Svakṣetra, or Uccarāśis of the aspecting Grahas, the enemies become friends; there is a gain of women and all manner of prosperity.

GRAHAS IN THEIR ŚATRURĀŚI IN UDAYA/ĀRUṚHA/CHATRA:

6.22. Suppose Grahas in their Śatrurāśis occupy Udayarāśi, Āruṛharāśi, or Chatrarāśi. In that case, there is death, imprisonment from the enemy, no return of a traveller, no recovery of property lost or stolen, and failure of all objects questioned.

ŚUBHA OR KRŪRA GRAHAS IN THE KENDRAS:

6.23. If Candra and Bṛhaspati occupy the Kendras, there is no death and recovery of lost or stolen property; if Krūras occupies the Kendras, there is death, no recovery of stolen property, and suffering from misery.

6.24. If the Krūras occupy all the Kendras, or if the Saumyas occupy the 10th or 11th House, there is the success of all attempts.

Notes: This is a counterintuitive śloka. Normally, Saumyas in the Kendras and Krūras in Triṣaḍāyas give success. This appears to be a misprint because 6.23 states that Krūras in the Kendras cause suffering.

6.25. If Rāhu occupies one of the Kendras, there is suffering from fetters, no return of a traveller and no gain of wealth; death from poison or illness, no journey, and failure of attempts.

DIKBALI GRAHAS GIVE SUCCESS:

6.26. If at Praśna, Candra occupies Udayarāśi and Śukra the 10th House, or if Bṛhaspati occupies Udayarāśi and Sūrya the 10th House, there is complete success of all attempts.

SAUMYAS IN KENDRAS ARE GOOD:

6.27. If at Praśna, Śukra occupies the 7th or the 10th House, there is a gain of a woman, wealth, and the king's favour. If Candra occupies such House, there is a gain of a woman.

KRŪRAS IN KENDRAS ARE DETRIMENTAL:

6.28. If at Praśna, the Saumyas occupy the Kendras, a person enjoys the pleasures of royalty and is happy. Still, if the Krūras occupy the Kendras, the property is lost and suffering from the enemy, diseases, and other miseries.

RĀŚIS OCCUPIED BY THE GRAHAS IN UDAYA/ĀRUṚHA/CHATRA:

6.29. Grahas occupying Mitra or Svakṣetra Rāśi bring friendship and prosperity; Grahas occupying Uccarāśis bring, in addition, the gain of wealth and the like. Grahas occupying Śatrurāśis bring enmity and misery, and Grahas occupying depression Rāśis bring, in addition, loss of property and the like.

SUMMARY:

6.30. In short, if at Praśna, Saumyas occupy Āruṛharāśi, Chatrarāśi, and the Kendras, there is success and prosperity; if such Saumyas are powerful, there is an increase of prosperity; and if such powerful Saumyas occupy, at the same time, their Mitrarāśi, Svakṣetra or Uccarāśis, there is a vast increase of success and prosperity.

6.31. Again, If at Praśna, Krūras occupy Āruṛharāśi, Chatrarāśi, and the Kendras, there is misery; if such Krūras are powerful, there is an increase of adversity; and if such powerful Krūras occupy their Śatru/Nīca Rāśi, there is a vast increase of misery.

24.2.7
ADHYĀYA 7:
ON DISEASES

THE HOUSES OF DISEASE AND DEATH:

7.1. The 6th House from Udayarāśi is known as the House of Disease, and the 8th House from Udayarāśi is known as the House of Death according to the science of the Devas.

Notes: The 6th House from the 6th House, i.e., the 11th House from Udayarāśi, is also the House of disease and the 8th House from the 8th House, i.e., the 3rd House from Udayarāśi is also known as the House of death.

AGGRAVATION OF DISEASE:

7.2. If Āruṛharāśi falls in the house of diseases (from Udayarāśi), or if the House of disease is dṛṣṭied by Krūras occupying Śatru/Nīca Rāśi, there is no recovery from illness.

Notes: Krūras in their Śatru/Nīca Rāśi indicate an aggravation of diseases, whereas, in their Ucca/Śatru/Mitra Rāśi, they indicate only slight improvement.

7.3. If Rāhu, Dhūma or the Indradhanuṣa occupies either the House of disease or Āruṛharāśi, there is no recovery from illness, and there is no escape from the attacks of the enemy or injury from fire and poison.

Notes: Simultaneous affliction to 6th from Udayarāśi and 1st from Āruṛharāśi indicate aggravation of sickness. Among the Krūras, Rāhu, Dhūma and Indradhanuṣa are the most sinister.

7.4. If the Āruṛha or Chatrarāśi be one of the down-looking Rāśis or if such Rāśi is occupied or dṛṣṭied either by down-looking Grahas or by Krūras, there is no recovery from illness.

Notes: As per śloka 1.9-10, the Adhomukhi Rāśis are Karka and Vṛścika, and the Adhomukhi Grahas are Budha and Śukra. Adhomukhi Rāśi and Grahas cause health to go down.

7.5. If Krūras occupy the House of Disease or the 7th House from it or if Candra occupies the 6th House from the House of Disease, or if Krūras aspect Candra there is no recovery from illness.

Notes: Krūras in the 6th/7th from the house of disease, i.e., the 6th house, does not indicate recovery. These are the 11th and 12th houses from Udayarāśi. Candra, in the 11th from Udayarāśi, afflicted by Krūras, is highly detrimental.

RECOVERY FROM THE DISEASE:

7.6. If Saumyas occupy Udayarāśi, the 9th House and the 10th House, there is recovery from illness. If such Saumyas occupy at the same time their Śatru/Nīca Rāśi, there is an appearance of recovery but no complete recovery. Again, if Maṅgala occupies the 10th House and if such House is its Śatru/Nīca Rāśi, there is recovery from illness. Still, if such is its Mitrarāśi, Svakṣetra or Uccarāśi, there is an appearance of recovery but no complete recovery.

Notes: Maṅgala, in his Dikbali Rāśi in Śatru/Nīca Rāśi, indicates recovery of illnesses, but in good dignity, indicates no recovery and only appearance of recovery.

EFFECTS OF INDRADHANUṢA AND PARIVEṢA:

7.7. If at Praśna, the Indradhanuṣa or Pariveṣa occupy the 10th House, there is no recovery from illness; but if either of these Grahas are dṛṣṭied by Candra, Budha, Bṛhaspati or Śukra occupying a Mitra, a Svakṣetra or an Uccarāśi, there is complete recovery after an appearance of non-recovery.

EFFECTS OF ŚUBHA VS KRŪRAS IN 6TH OR 8TH:

7.8. Generally, if the House of disease or death is occupied or dṛṣṭied by Krūras, there is no recovery from illness; and if it is occupied or dṛṣṭied by Saumyas, there is recovery.

PERIOD OF RECOVERY:

7.9. If either the House of Disease or the Rāśi occupied by Candra is occupied or dṛṣṭied by Krūras in their Mitrarāśi, Svakṣetra or Uccarāśis, recovery from illness occurs after the years or months, of the most powerful Graha.

Notes: Refer to ślokas 1.77-78 for the periods associated with the Grahas.

7.10. If either the House of Disease or the Rāśi occupied by Candra is occupied or dṛṣṭied by Saumyas in their Mitrarāśi, Svakṣetra or Uccarāśis, recovery from illness occurs after the days and Ghaṭis, of the Graha.

RĀŚIS AND THE HUMAN BODY:

7.11. Rāśi Meṣa represents the head, Vṛṣabha the face, Mithuna the shoulders, Karka the breast, Siṅha the nipples, Kanyā the belly, Tulā the armpits, Vṛścika the back, Dhanu the thighs, Makara the knees, Kumbha the ankles and Mīna the feet.

GRAHAS AND THE HUMAN BODY:

7.12. Maṅgala represents the head, Śukra the face, Budha the neck and shoulders, Candra the breast, Sūrya the belly, Bṛhaspati the hip, Śani the thighs and Rāhu the legs.

Notes: According to some, Budha represents the face and Śukra the shoulders.

Notes: The Grahas rule the same body part as their Rāśis rule. For instance, Maṅgala rules Meṣa and Vṛścika, and therefore, Maṅgala rules the head and rectum. Śukra: face and genital, Budha: Budha respiratory organ, lungs, shoulders, lower belly, Candra: lungs, and breast, Sūrya: belly, Bṛhaspati: Hip and foot, Śani: thigh, knee, and Rāhu: shanks. Rāhu rules Kumbha, which is associated with the shanks or calves. Ketu should govern the rectum, as he is co-owner of Vṛścika.

PARTS OF THE BODY AFFECTED:

7.13. The disease affects body parts corresponding to Udayarāśi and the Udaya Graha. If such Graha or the Lord of such Udayarāśi occupy Śatru/Nīca Rāśi, the disease is severe. Still, if such Graha occupies its Mitrarāśi, Svakṣetra or Uccarāśi, the disease is mild.

NAKṢATRAS AND THE HUMAN BODY:

7.14. The Nakṣatra of Kṛttikā represents the head; that of Rohini the forehead; that of Mṛgaśirā the brows; that of Ārdrā the eyes; of Punarvasu the nose; of Puṣya the face; Aśleṣā the ears; Magha the lips and the upper mouth; Pūrvāphālgunī the right arms; Uttarāphālgunī the left arms; Hasta the fingers.

Notes: According to some, Punarvasu represents the face; that of Puṣya the upper lip, and that of Aśleṣā represents the lower lip.

7.15. The Nakṣatra of Citrā represents the neck; that of Swati the breast; of Viśākhā the nipples; of Anurādhā the belly; of Jyeṣṭhā the right side; of Mūla the left side; of Pūrvāṣāṛhā the back; of Uttarāṣāṛhā the hip; of Śravana the privities; of Sraviṣṭhā the anus; of Śatabhiṣā the right thigh; of Pūrvābhādra the left thigh.

7.16a. The Nakṣatra of Uttarābhādra represents the knees; that of Revatī represents the ankles; that of Aśvinī the upper part of the feet; and that of Bharaṇī the soles of the feet.

UDAYA NAKṢATRA AFFECTING THE BODY PARTS:

7.16b. The part of the body corresponding to the Udaya Nakṣatra is affected by disease. If the Lord of the Rāśi containing the Nakṣatra (i.e., Udayarāśi Lord) occupies his Śatru/Nīca Rāśi, the disease is severe. Still, if he occupies the Mitrarāśi, Svakṣetra or Uccarāśi, the disease is mild.

GRAHA AND DISEASES:

7.17. Maṅgala presides over headache and frothy diarrhoea; Candra presides over chest pain and cold; Budha over pain in the armpit; Sūrya over stomachache.

7.18. Śani presides over flatulence and lameness; Rāhu over pulmonary consumption and sufferings from poison; Śukra over the diseases of the eye, and Bṛhaspati over piles.

Notes: The Rāśis preside over the same diseases as those over which their lords preside.

7.19. Pariveṣa presides over leprosy; Dhūma over atrophy and wasting disease of children; Rāhu over spasms; Sūrya over the devil (Preta, Piśāca etc.); Śani over consumption and Maṅgala over the barking disease (Klazomania[1]).

24.2.8
ADHYĀYA 8:
ON DEATH

DEATH OR NO DEATH:

8.1. (1) If Āruṛharāśi and Chatrarāśis are both Sthirarāśi, there is no death. **(2a)** If Tulā is Āruṛharāśi and Dhanu its Chatrarāśi, there is suffering from serious illness; **(2b)** but if Dhanu is Āruṛharāśi and Tulā, its Chatrarāśi there is death.

Notes: For death matters, the conditions about the 3-11 mutual position of Āruṛharāśi and Chatrarāśi are given. If the 3rd from Āruṛharāśi is its

[1] Klazomania refers to compulsive shouting; it has features resembling the complex tics such as echolalia, palilalia and coprolalia seen in tic disorders, but has been seen in people with encephalitis lethargica, alcohol abuse and carbon monoxide poisoning.

Chatrarāśi, there is suffering from serious illness; but if the 11th House is its Chatrarāśi, there is death.

8.2. **(3a)** If Meṣa is Āruṛharāśi and Mithuna, its Chatrarāśi, there is suffering from serious illness; **(3b)** but if Mithuna is Āruṛharāśi and Meṣa, its Chatrarāśi, there is death. **(4a)** If Karka is Āruṛharāśi and Kanyā its Chatrarāśi, there is suffering from serious illness; **(4b)** but if Kanyā is Āruṛharāśi and Karka, its Chatrarāśi, there is death. **(5a)** Again, if Makara is Āruṛharāśi and Mīna its Chatrarāśi, there is suffering from serious illness; **(5b)** but if Mīna is Āruṛharāśi and Makara its Chatrarāśi, there is death.

8.3. **(1)** If at Praśna, the House of Death is Āruṛharāśi and Candra occupies the 8th House from it or **(2a)** if either the House of Death or **(2b)** the Rāśi occupied by Candra or **(2c)** the Rāśi indicated by the part of the body touched, is dṛṣṭied only by Krūras, there is no recovery from illness.

TIMING OF DEMISE:

8.4. Death occurs after a period equal to the years, months and days of the Grahas aspecting the House of Death and Āruṛharāśi.

8.5. If at Praśna, **(1)** Candra occupies Udayarāśi and is in yuti with Krūras or **(2)** if Candra occupies the 6th or 8th House from Udayarāśi while Krūras occupy the 7th House, death occurs after a period equal to the years, months and days of the **Grahas aspecting Candra** in either case.

8.6. If, while Krūras occupy the 10th House from Udayarāśi, the 3rd House is occupied by Sūrya, death occurs within 10 days and if such 3rd House is occupied by Bṛhaspati or Śukra, death occurs within 7 days.

Notes: The 3rd House from the 10th House, according to some.

8.7. If at Praśna, Sūrya, Maṅgala, Śani, or Rāhu occupies the 8th House from Āruṛharāśi, death occurs within 8 days; but if one of these Grahas occupies Udayarāśi or Āruṛharāśi, death occurs within 14 days.

8.8. If at Praśna, the 2nd House, the 7th House or the 10th House is occupied by Sūrya, Maṅgala, Śani or Rāhu, death occurs within 8 days. Again, if Sūrya or Rāhu occupies the 10th House and if Maṅgala or Śani occupies the 7th House from such Graha, death occurs on the day of Praśna.

CAUSE OF DEATH:

8.9. Sūrya causes death by fire; the Candra by water; Maṅgala by weapons; Budha by diarrhoea; Bṛhaspati by stomach-ache; Śukra by the wind, by the dew or by cold; Śani by starvation and Rāhu by poison.

Notes: The cause of death is indicated by the Graha occupying the house of death, i.e., the 8th from Udayarāśi.

PLACE OF DEATH:

8.10. If the House of Death is a Sthirarāśi, death occurs in one's native land; if it is a Cararāśi, death occurs in a foreign land; and if it is a Dvisvarāśi, death occurs in a neighbouring country.

THE FUTURE STATE:

8.11. If the most powerful Graha occupy its Uccarāśi, a person after death is born a Deva; if such powerful Graha occupy its Svakṣetra or Mitrarāśi, he is born a human being. Again, if such Graha occupies its Śatrurāśi, the person is born an animal, and if such Graha occupies its Nīcarāśi, he is born a bird or a worm or a creature of water.

24.2.9 ADHYĀYA 9: ON MEALS

MATTERS COVERED:

9.1. When the Praśna refers to the meals a person has eaten, we shall treat the following: **(1)** the time of cooking, **(2)** the nature of rice and curry, **(3)** their flavour, **(4)** the person that dined together, **(5)** the vessels in which food was served, **(6)** the persons that served the food and the like. Curry.

THE NATURE OF THE DISH:

9.2. (1) If Udayarāśi is Meṣa or Vṛṣabha, there is a preparation of leaves, milk and buttermilk; **(2)** if Udayarāśi is Mithuna, Dhanu or Siṅha, there is a curry of fish; **(3)** if Udayarāśi is Karka, Vṛścika, Makara or Mīna there is fruits; **(4)** if Udayarāśi is Tulā, there are vegetable curries, and if it is Kanyā or Kumbha, there is no curries.

Notes: According to some, Meṣa indicates a preparation of leaves and Vṛṣabha of milk and buttermilk.

EFFECTS OF GRAHAS IN UDAYARĀŚI:

9.3. (1) If Sūrya occupies Udayarāśi, the flavour is bitter and sour; **(2)** if it is Budha, there is cold rice or parboiled rice; **(3)** if it is Bṛhaspati, there is good rice; **(4)** if it is Rāhu, the rice is over-cooked; **(5)** if it is Śani, there is a curry of leaves and oil, and **(6)** if it is Maṅgala, there is meat.

Notes: According to some, Budha presides over fruits, Bṛhaspati over rice, Śani over gruel, and Maṅgala over hot or fried curry. Generally, the flavour of food is the flavour presided over by the Graha (śloka 1.58). The food is grains of the respective colour of the Grahas. The predictions are also made from the most powerful Grahas occupying the Lagna if there is more than one Graha so placed. If there is no one in the Lagna, then the dṛṣṭi of the most powerful Graha must be judged. In all cases, it is Udayarāśi (not Āruṛha or Chatra) that should be judged for the food preparation.

SŪRYA'S YUTIDṚṢṬI ON A GRAHA IN UDAYARĀŚI:

9.4. (1) If Udayarāśi is occupied by Sūrya and Maṅgala, the food eaten is meat and rice. **(2)** If Candra, Śukra and Rāhu occupy together a Rāśi aspect or accompany Sūrya, the food eaten is rice mixed with curd, milk and ghee.

Notes: This śloka tells us the effects of Sūrya's yutidṛṣṭi on a Graha in Udayarāśi. If Maṅgala is in Udayarāśi, having Sūrya's yutidṛṣṭi, the food is meat and rice. If Candra has Sūrya's yutidṛṣṭi, then it is curd and rice. Likewise, Śukra and Sūrya indicate milk rice, and Rāhu and Sūrya indicate Ghee rice.

DṚṢṬI OF GRAHAS ON UDAYARĀŚI:

9.5. (1) If the Graha aspecting Udayarāśi is Bṛhaspati, the food eaten consists of black gram, leaves, fish, and beans; **(2)** if the aspecting Graha is Candra, the food consists of vegetables, roots and fish; **(3)** if the Graha is Śukra, the food is honey, milk, and tamarind broth. **(4)** If the Graha is Śani, it is cold rice.

Notes: According to some, the same remarks apply to the Grahas, which occupy either Kumbha or Mīna.

EFFECTS OF OJARĀŚI AND YUGMARĀŚI:

9.6. (1) If Udayarāśi at the time of Praśna is an Ojarāśi, the food eaten is simple rice; **(2)** if it is Yugmarāśi, the food eaten is rice and curry; Likewise, **(3)** if the Graha occupying Udayarāśi is Puruṣa (Ojagraha), the food is mere rice; **(4)** and if it is Strī (Yugmagraha), it is rice with curry. **(4)** Also, if Śani and Rāhu either occupy an Ojarāśi or are in yuti with an Ojagraha, the food is rice with curry; **(5)** but if Śani and Rāhu either occupy a Yugmarāśi or is in yuti with a Yugmagraha, the food is mere rice.

Notes: Mere rice includes old rice, i.e., rice cooked the day before and soaked in water.

OILY FOOD:

9.7. (1) If one of the Jalacara Rāśis, Karka, Tulā, Makara, Kumbha or Mīna is occupied by Sūrya, Maṅgala, Budha, Śani or Rāhu, the food eaten is rice mixed with oil. **(2)** If one of the said Rāśis is occupied by Candra or Bṛhaspati, the food is rice mixed with ghee; and **(3)** if Śukra occupies such Rāśi, it is rice mixed with butter.

Notes: Jalacara Rāśi indicate watery substances like oil, ghee etc. Sūrya, Maṅgala, Budha, Śani or Rāhu indicate oil, Candra and Bṛhaspati, ghee and Śukra, butter. Krūras denote oil, Saumyas, ghee and butter. According to some, the same remarks apply to the Cararāśis as to the Jalacara Rāśis.

FOOD VESSELS AND SERVERS:

9.8. (1) If the most powerful Graha is Krūra, the food is rice mixed with oil; and the vessel in which it was served is a broken one; **(2)** but if such Graha is Śubha, the food is rice mixed with ghee, and the vessel is whole. **(3)** The colour of the server is that of the Graha.

Notes: According to the commentator, if the most powerful Graha is Krūra, the eaters are bad people, the servers are not a relative, and the food eaten is not palatable; but if such Graha is Śubha, the reverse of these is the case. Also, according to some, if the most powerful Graha occupy Ojarāśis, the food is rice with ghee and curry, and if such Grahas occupy the Yugmarāśis, the food is mere rice with no curry. It must have been taken during the daytime.

FOOD VESSELS:

9.9. (1) If the most powerful Graha is Sūrya, Maṅgala, Śani or Rāhu, the food vessel is old and broken. **(2)** The vessel is new if such Graha is Candra, Budha, Bṛhaspati or Śukra.

Notes: The metals of the Graha, i.e., Sūrya brass, Maṅgala copper, Śani iron, Rāhu lead etc., can also be deciphered from the most powerful Graha.

24.2.10 ADHYĀYA 10: ON DREAMS

The matters dreamt by a person can be deciphered using Praśna. The four Kendras are intimately connected with the matters of the dream. **(1)** Future dreams should be predicted from the Praśnalagna and from the Grahas occupying it; **(2)** past dreams should be predicted from the fourth House and the Grahas occupying it; **(3)** dreams long past and forgotten should be predicted from the 7th House, and from the Grahas occupying it; **(4)** and dreams dreamt in a waking state should be predicted from the 10th House, and the Grahas occupying it. Normally, Lagna denotes standing state, 4th, sleeping; 7th, sitting and 10th, walking. Therefore, the dream one has recently experienced should be seen from the 4th house of sleeping.

MATTERS DREAMT OF FROM UDAYARĀŚI:

10.1. (1) If the Praśnalagna is Meṣa, the dream is the sight of Devas, of their buildings, and of the palaces of kings; **(2)** if it is Vṛṣabha, the dream is moving in such places; and **(3)** if it is Mithuna, the dream is the sight of Devas, of Brāhmaṇas, and of persons practising austerities.

Notes: The matters concerning the dream should be known from the Praśnalagna or Udayarāśi. In śloka 10.4, it is mentioned that the Āruṛha and Chatra Rāśis can also be used.

10.2. If the Praśnalagna is **(4)** Karka, the dream is the sight of dry and wet crops and then getting into the marsh and plucking branches of trees; **(5)** if it is Siṅha, the dream is the sight of hill-men, of rocks and stones; **(6)** if it is Kanyā, the dream is that of drinking and playing with a woman of the shaven head; and **(7)** if it is Tulā, the dream is the sight of gold, of a king and of tradesmen.

Notes: According to some, Siṅha indicates battles, buffaloes, and Tulā, the sight of girls.

10.3. (8) If the Praśnalagna is Vṛścika, the dream is the sight of bullocks, horses and foot-soldiers; **(9)** if it is Dhanu, the dream is the sight of flowers, perfumes, sandal paste, fragrant powder, and jewels; **(10)** if it is Makara, the dream is the sight of men and gold; **(11)** if it is Kumbha, the dream is the sight of rivers; **(12)** and if it is Mīna, the dream is the sight of looking glasses.

Notes: According to some, Vṛścika indicates the sight of animals and scorpions; Dhanu, the sight of widows and men; and Mīna, the sight of fish.

MATTERS DREAMT OF FROM THE GRAHAS IN UDAYARĀŚI:

10.4. (1) If the Graha occupying Udayarāśi is Śukra, the dream is the sight of white buildings; and **(2)** if such Graha is Budha, the dream is the sight of Devas. Dreams may be similarly predicted from Āruṛha and Chatra Rāśis and the Grahas occupying the same.

Notes: Budha indicates the dream is the sight of public officials and Rākṣasas. Also, if any of the Grahas, other than Śukra and Budha, occupy the Praśnalagna, the prediction is the same as that given for the Svakṣetra Rāśis of the Grahas when they happen to be the rising Rāśis. For instance, if it is Sūrya, then the indications of Siṅha Rāśi shall prevail, which is the sight of hill-men, of rocks and stones.

DREAMS DREAMT AND TO LE DREAMT OF:

10.5. In the case of predictions of dreams from Udayarāśi and from the Grahas occupying it, such dreams also apply to dreams dreamt, as to dreams to be dreamt of.

Notes: What is mentioned about the dreams also applies to the Praśna dealing with "what will I dream of".

PREDICTION OF DREAMS FROM THE GRAHAS IN THE 4TH HOUSE:

10.6. (1) If the Graha occupying the fourth House from Udayarāśi is Śukra, the dream is the sight of ornaments of silver. **(2)** If such Graha is Rāhu or Maṅgala, the dream refers to meat; **(3)** if the Graha is Bṛhaspati, it refers to fruits and public officers; **(4)** if the Graha is Śani, it refers to animals; **(5)** if it is Budha, the dream refers to swimming in a flood, tree holes or fasting.

Notes: The other articles governed by the Graha, like Śukra, diamond, pearl, ornaments, jewels etc., should also be deciphered from the Graha in the 4th from Udayarāśi. The same results apply when the Grahas are in their Svakṣetra besides the 4th.

10.7. (6) If the Graha occupying the fourth House from the Praśnalagna be Sūrya, the dream refers to the fall of a dead tree on the person and may also be the sight of dead men returned to life and weeping before them; **(7)** if the Graha is Candra, the dream refers to the death of the person himself, to his suffering from thirst, or to his sleep. Also, in the case of Sūrya and Candra occupying the fourth House, the dreams stated for their Svakṣetra Rāśis shall also be predicted.

Notes: This means that when Sūrya is in the 4th house, what is said about Siṅha Rāśi can also be said about the dream, i.e., a fort, jungle, rocks and stones etc. Likewise, if Candra is in the 4th, the matters related to Karka can be said.

24.2.11 ADHYĀYA 11: ON OMENS

GOOD AND BAD OMENS:

11.1. **(1)** If the Praśnalagna is a Dvisvarāśi, there is no meeting with omens; **(2)** if it is a Sthirarāśi, the omen is an adverse one; **(3)** and if it is a Cararāśi, the omen is a favourable one. Also, if the Praśnalagna is a Sthirarāśi, there is no travel.

Notes: If the Praśnalagna be a Cararāśi, there is long-distance travel, and if it is a Dvisvarāśi, there is travel for a short distance and then return, according to the commentator. Sthirarāśi denotes no travel. The omens are seen on the way.

PREDICTION OF OMENS FROM THE STRONGEST GRAHA:

11.2. **(1)** If the most powerful Graha is Sūrya, the omen is the appearance of a black-kite and a Brahminy kite; **(2)** if the Graha is Candra, the omen is the appearance of an owl, a dove, or a glede (kite); **(3)** if it is Budha, the omen is a mungo (?), a monkey, a cat, a rabbit, a hog, a deer, a wagtail, a crow, the nightingale, a mainate/mynah, or a parrot; **(4)** if it is Śani or Rāhu, the omen is a crow, a red-snake, a mungo, a monkey, a jackal, a dog, a cat, a rabbit, a hog, a deer, an ass, a horse, a tiger, or a wagtail.

11.3. **(5)** If the most powerful Graha is Maṅgala, the omen is the appearance of the red-bird or wagtail; **(6)** if it is Bṛhaspati, the omen is a partridge, a kingfisher, or a dove; and if it is 'Śukra, the omen is a partridge, a heron or a kingfisher.

PREDICTION OF OMENS FROM THE GRAHA OCCUPYING THE LAGNA:

11.4. **(1)** If the Graha occupying the Praśnalagna is Sūrya, the omen is the appearance of red-birds; **(2)** if it is Candra, the omen is a fish; **(3)** if it is Maṅgala, the omen is a jackal; **(4)** if it is Budha, it is the appearance of a pot of uncurdled milk; **(5)** if it is Bṛhaspati, it is the appearance of a pot of ghee; **(6)** if it is Śukra, it is the appearance of a pot of milk; **(7)** if it is Śani, it is the appearance of fire and enemies, and **(8)** if it is Rāhu, it is the appearance of a Napuṅśaka or a snake.

Notes: According to some, **(1)** Candra indicates Kākabali (rice ball offered to the crow); **(2)** if it is Bṛhaspati, birds of gold colour; **(3)** if it is Śani, thieves, low-caste men, or oil mongers; and **(4)** if it is Rāhu, House lizard or a dog.

OMENS ON THE RIGHT OR LEFT SIDE:

11.5. The Grahas from which omens are predicted are the **(1)** most powerful Grahas at the time of Praśna, **(2)** those aspecting them, those occupying the Praśnalagna, and **(3)** those aspecting the Praśnalagna. **(a)** If the Grahas have moles on the right side, the omens appear on the right side, and **(b)** if the Grahas have moles on the left side, the omens appear on the left side.

Notes: Check for moles in śloka 1.60. According to the commentator, the omens thought of (imagined but didn't happen) shall be predicted from Āruṛharāśi, and the omens that are about to appear are to be predicted from Udayarāśi.

24.2.12
ADHYĀYA 12:
ON MARRIAGE

EFFECTS OF GRAHAS ON THE GIRL FOR WHOM MARRIAGE IS BEING SOUGHT:

12.1. (1) If Sūrya or Maṅgala occupies the Praśnalagna, the woman questioned about becomes a widow; **(2)** if Candra occupies it, she dies when young; **(3)** if Budha, Bṛhaspati, or Śukra occupy it, she prospers well as a Sumangali; **(4)** if by Śani, she is barren; **(5)** and if by Rāhu, she bears children and loses them.

Notes: Sumangali means having a live husband. According to some, if Śani or Rāhu occupies the Praśnalagna, a woman bears children after continuing barren for a long time and then loses them.

GRAHAS IN THE 2ND HOUSE:

12.2. (1) If the 2nd House from Praśnalagna is occupied by Sūrya, Maṅgala, Śani, or Rāhu, the woman suffers miseries; **(2)** if Candra occupies it, she bears many children; **(3)** if Budha, Bṛhaspati or Śukra occupy it, she prospers well in every way.

GRAHAS IN THE 3RD HOUSE:

12.3. (1) If Sūrya or Rāhu occupies the 3rd House from Praśnalagna, the woman is poor and barren; **(2)** if it is occupied by any one of the remaining six Grahas, she prospers in every way; **(3)** she prospers more so, especially in the case of Maṅgala, Budha, Bṛhaspati and Śukra.

GRAHAS IN THE 4TH HOUSE:

12.4. (1) If Sūrya or Candra occupies the 4th House from Praśnalagna, the woman commits sinful deeds; **(2)** if it is occupied by Maṅgala, Budha, Bṛhaspati or Śukra, she prospers well in every way; **(3)** if Śani occupies it, she is without milk, i.e., unable to breastfeed her child; **(4)** if Rāhu occupies it, her husband marries an additional wife.

Notes: Rāhu in the 4th indicates extramarital affairs, having a second wife, or concubine.

GRAHAS IN THE 5TH HOUSE:

12.5. (1) If the 5th House from Praśnalagna has Sūrya or Candra, she does not enjoy the company of her husband; **(2)** if Maṅgala occupies it, she bears children only to lose them eventually; **(3)** if Budha, Bṛhaspati or Śukra occupy it, she bears several children; **(4)** if Śani occupies it, she suffers from diseases; and **(5)** if Rāhu occupies it she dies young, prematurely.

GRAHAS IN THE 6TH HOUSE:

12.6. (1) If the 6th House from Praśnalagna is occupied by Sūrya, Maṅgala, Bṛhaspati, Śani or Rāhu, the woman gains wealth and is happy; **(2)** if Candra occupies it, she becomes a widow; **(3)** if Budha occupies it, she is quarrelsome; and **(4)** if Śukra occupies it, she lives long and continues a Sumangali (husband lives long).

GRAHAS IN THE 7TH HOUSE:

12.7. (1) If Sūrya or Candra occupies the 7th House from Praśnalagna, the woman suffers from diseases; **(2)** if Maṅgala occupies it, she suffers imprisonment (or bondage of some kind); **(3)** if Budha and Bṛhaspati occupy it, she lives in prosperity; **(4)** if Śukra occupies it, she dies young; and **(5)** if Śani or Rāhu occupies it, she becomes a widow.

GRAHAS IN THE 8TH HOUSE:

12.8. (1) If Sūrya or Maṅgala occupies the 8th House from Praśnalagna, the woman becomes a widow; **(2)** if Candra occupies it, she dies young; **(3)** if Budha or Śani occupies it, she has an increasing family; **(4)** and if Bṛhaspati, Śukra or Rāhu occupy it, she loses her children.

GRAHAS IN THE 9TH HOUSE:

12.9. (1) If Sūrya or Maṅgala occupies the 9th House from Praśnalagna, the woman is without milk, i.e., can't breastfeed her child; **(2)** if Candra or Bṛhaspati occupies it, she begets both sons and daughters; **(3)** if Budha occupies it, she suffers from diseases; **(4)** if Śukra occupies it, she bears sons; and **(5)** if Śani or Rāhu occupies it, she is barren.

GRAHAS IN THE 10TH HOUSE:

12.10. (1) If Sūrya or Budha occupies the 10th House from Praśnalagna, the woman prospers in every way; **(2)** if Candra occupies it, she is barren; **(3)** if Maṅgala, Śani or Rāhu occupy it, she becomes a widow; **(4)** if Bṛhaspati occupies it, she is poor; **(5)** and if Śukra occupies it, she becomes a prostitute.

GRAHAS IN THE 11TH HOUSE:

12.11. (1) If Sūrya occupies the 11th House from Praśnalagna, the woman prospers well; **(2)** if it is occupied by Candra, Bṛhaspati, Śukra, Śani or Rāhu, she lives in prosperity and plenty with sons and daughters; and **(3)** if Maṅgala or Budha occupies it, she lives a Sumangali for a long time (i.e., husband lives long).

GRAHAS IN THE 12TH HOUSE:

12.12. (1) If Sūrya or Rāhu occupies the 12th House from Praśnalagna, the woman remains barren; **(2)** if Candra occupies it, she dies early; **(3)** if Maṅgala or Śani occupies it, she indulges in liquor; **(4)** if Budha occupies it, she bears sons; **(5)** if Bṛhaspati occupies it, she is wealthy; and **(5)** if Śukra occupies it, she prospers in every way.

Notes: In making predictions concerning marriage, greater importance is attached to the Rāśi that contains Āruṛha.

24.2.13
ADHYĀYA 13:
ON SEXUAL LOVE

MATTERS TREATED HERE:

13.1. We shall now proceed to state **(1)** mutual love or want of love between husband and wife, **(2)** the chastity or the want of chastity of the wife, and **(3) the** good and evil connected with married life.

AN UNCHASTE WIFE:

13.2. When the Pṛcchaka questions his wife's character, (1) Rāhu occupies one of the Kendras, the woman may be declared unchaste, though she may belong to the class of Devatās.

Notes: Dṛṣṭi of Rāhu should also be considered according to the commentator.

13.3. If at Praśna, Candra has yutidṛṣṭi from Puruṣa Grahas, the wife joins other men as stated by the sages.

Notes: Here, Bṛhaspati is exempted, and only Sūrya and Maṅgala are considered. Candra in the Rāśi of Puruṣa Grahas, except that of Bṛhaspati, also indicates similar things as per śloka 13.7.

A CHASTE WIFE:

13.4. If at Praśna, Candra occupies the 3rd, 7th, 10th or 11th House from the Praśnalagna and is dṛṣṭied by Bṛhaspati, the wife is chaste.

Notes: Candra in the Praśna Lagna is also included, according to the commentator.

EXCEEDINGLY CHASTE OR UNCHASTE WIFE:

13.3. (1) If, in the Aśubha yogas stated above, Candra occupies a Śatru/Nīca Rāśi and is dṛṣṭied by Grahas occupying Śatru/Nīca Rāśi, the wife is exceedingly unchaste. **(2)** Again if, in the Śubha Yogas stated above, Candra occupies a Mitra, a Svakṣetra, or an Uccarāśi, and is dṛṣṭied by Grahas occupying their Mitrarāśi, Svakṣetra or Uccarāśis, the wife is exceedingly chaste.

A LOVING AND AN UNLOVING WIFE:

13.6. (1) If at Praśna, Krūras have yutidṛṣṭi with Candra, the lady does not love her husband; **(2)** but if Saumyas have yutidṛṣṭi with Candra, the wife loves her husband; **(3)** and if such Saumyas occupy their Mitrarāśi, Svakṣetra or Uccarāśis, her love for her husband is exceedingly great.

Notes: But if such Krūras occupy Śatru/Nīca Rāśi, indicate no love at all, whereas, in Ucca/Sva/Mitra Rāśi, some love is indicated.

13.7. If at Praśna, Candra occupies one of the Rāśis of Bṛhaspati or of the female Grahas, the lady loves her husband.

Notes: If Candra occupies the Rāśis of other male Grahas (Sūrya or Maṅgala), she does not love her husband.

THE CASTE AND THE LIKE OF THE HUSBAND AND WIFE:

13.8. (1) If Āruṛharāśi is either the 12th or the 6th from the Praśnalagna, the wife is questioned about is a widow; **(2)** and the husband is questioned about is the son of a widow. **(3)** If Śukra owns Āruṛharāśi or the 7th House from it, the person is a Śudra; **(4)** if Budha owns the Rāśi, the person is a Vaisya.

Notes: If the Praśna is about a man, and Āruṛha is in the 6th/12th from the Praśnalagna, then the man is the son of a widow. However, if the Praśna is put for a lady, the lady is the widow. If Āruṛha or the 7th, whichever is stronger, is in the Rāśi of other Grahas, the persons belong to the respective Varṇas of the Grahas, vide śloka 1.48.

DESCRIPTION OF A WOMAN ENJOYED BY THE PṚCCHAKA:

13.9. (1) If at Praśna, Śukra and Maṅgala occupy a Rāśi together, the Pṛcchaka would have sexually united with a widow of his class of people and suffered; **(2)** but if Śukra and Sūrya occupy a Rāśi together, he would have sexually united with a lady of the king's family (royal lady or one from nobility) and suffered from it.

13.10. (3) If at Praśna, Candra occupies a Śatrurāśi, the Pṛcchaka would have joined a woman belonging to his enemies; **(4)** if Candra occupies a Mitrarāśi, he would have joined a woman belonging to his friend; **(5)** and if Candra occupies its Nīcarāśi, the Pṛcchaka would have joined a woman belonging to a lowly class.

13.11. (6) If at Praśna, Candra occupies her Svarāśi, the Pṛcchaka would have sexually united a woman of his own family; **(7)** if Candra occupies her Uccarāśi, he would have united with a woman of a higher family; and **(8)** if Candra occupies a Śatru/Nīca Rāśi, he would have joined a prostitute.

Notes: Candra, in his Svarāśi, can indicate union with his wife.

NUMBER OF TIMES OF SEXUAL UNION:

13.12. (1) If Udayarāśi or the Graha occupying it is Oja, the Pṛcchaka would have had sexual intercourse only once; **(2)** if such Rāśi or Graha is yugma, he would have had the intercourse twice. **(3)** Again, the intercourse will have occurred as many times as the number of Grahas occupying Udayarāśi or the number of Raśmis of the most powerful of such Grahas.

Notes: Where there are no Grahas in Udayarāśi, the intercourse would have occurred the number of times represented by the Raśmis of Udayarāśi.

EMOTIONS PREVAILING AT THE TIME OF SEXUAL UNION:

13.13. (1) If Candra and Maṅgala occupy Udayarāśi, the Pṛcchaka would have united and quarrelled with a prostitute; **(2)** but if the Candra is in yuti with either Śukra or Śani in Udayarāśi, the Pṛcchaka would have united and quarrelled with his wife.

13.14. If at Praśna, the 1st, 3rd, 4th or 7th from Udayarāśi is occupied by Candra and Śukra, the Pṛcchaka would have quarrelled with his wife and torn her clothes.

Notes: According to some, the 5th House from Udayarāśi is also included.

UNION IN THE DREAM:

13.15. If at Praśna, the 1st, 5th, 7th or 9th from Udayarāśi has yutidṛṣṭi of Candra and Śani, the Pṛcchaka should have united with a woman in his dream.

A SLEEPLESS NIGHT:

13.16. If at Praśna, Candra occupies Udayarāśi, and Maṅgala the 2nd House, or if Maṅgala aspect Candra in Udayarāśi/2nd House, the Pṛcchaka may be declared to have had a sleepless night owing to his fear of robbers.

13.17. If at Praśna, the 7th House is occupied by Krūras, the 10th House by Maṅgala, and the 3rd House by Budha, the Pṛcchaka may be declared to have slept on bare ground with disgust of mind after arguing at length a disputed question.

Notes: There is a possibility of two yogas here, (1) Krūras in the 7th and Maṅgala in the 10th, or (2) Krūras in the 7th and Budha in the 3rd.

24.2.14
ADHYĀYA 14:
ON THE BIRTH OF CHILDREN

PREGNANCY PREDICTED:

14.1. If, when a woman questions whether she should have a son, Udayarāśi or Āruṛharāśi (a) is occupied by Rāhu, she may be declared to be then pregnant, even though the conception may have taken place on the night previous.

Notes: According to the commentator Rāhu in the 4th, 5th or 9th from Udayarāśi/Āruṛharāśi confirm pregnancy. According to some writers, if the said Rāhu is in yuti with Sūrya, the woman becomes pregnant in future; if Rāhu is in yuti with Maṅgala, she does not become pregnant till Maṅgala should have passed through such Rāśis but only after that.

CHILD OR NO CHILD:

14.2. If at Praśna, Candra occupies Udayarāśi, yuti with Saumyas, there is childbirth; but if Candra occupies the 3rd, 5th or 9th House from Udayarāśi and is in yuti with Sūrya or Śukra, there is no birth of a child.

Notes: Candra in Udayarāśi or Āruṛharāśi (or 3/5/9 from there), according to the commentator.

14.3. If at Praśna, Bṛhaspati occupies Udayarāśi, Āruṛharāśi, the 5th or 7th House, there is the birth of a child. If Bṛhaspati occupies, at the same time, a Mitrarāśi, his Svakṣetra or Uccarāśi, the child is of long life; but if Bṛhaspati occupies a Śatru/Nīca Rāśi, the child dies when young.

Notes: Bṛhaspati, in 1/5/7 from the Udaya/Āruṛha Rāśi, promises pregnancy. The health and longevity of the child is known from the dignity of such Bṛhaspati.

THE SEX OF THE CHILD:

14.4. If at Praśna, Udayarāśi (or Āruṛharāśi) is occupied by the Graha Pariveṣa, accompanied by one of the child's Yogagrahas (Rāhu, Candra and Bṛhaspati) there is the birth of a child. If such accompanying Graha is a male Graha, the child is a male; and if it is a female Graha, the child is a female.

Notes: The children's number, complexion and other peculiarities shall also be determined from such Grahas.

14.5. If at Praśna, Sūrya occupies the 3rd, 6th, 7th, 10th or 11th House from Udayarāśi, there is birth of a male child (female child if it is Candra). If the 7th house is occupied by a Saumya (excepting Candra), there is the birth of a male child; but if the 7th House is occupied by a Krūra (excepting Sūrya), there is the birth of a female child.

Notes: Also, if an Ojarāśi is occupied by a Saumya or by an Ojagraha, there is the birth of a male child; but if a Yugmarāśi is occupied by a Krūra or by a Yugmagraha, there is the birth of a female child.

14.6. If at Praśna, an Oja Nakṣatra rises above the horizon, a male child is born; if a Yugma Nakṣatra rises, there is a female child. The alternate Nakṣatras of Aśvinī, Kṛttikā, Mṛgaśirā and the like are known as Oja Nakṣatras, and the alternate Nakṣatras of Bharaṇī, Rohini, Ārdrā, and the like are known as Yugma Nakṣatras.

Notes: According to some, if the Lord of Udayarāśi, Candra and Śani occupies Ojarāśis, the birth is a male child, and if they occupy Yugmarāśis, the birth is a female child.

TIME OF BIRTH:

14.7. The birth of a child occurs on the day, the hour and minute when Candra begins to enter the 7th House from Āruṛharāśi.

Notes: This refers to a Praśna in the child's birth month.

MISCARRIAGE OF PREGNANCY AND DEATH OF THE PREGNANT WOMAN:

14.8. (1) If at Praśna by a pregnant woman, Udayarāśi or Āruṛharāśi is occupied by the Graha Pariveṣa, there is a miscarriage of pregnancy; **(2)** and if the 8th House from Udayarāśi or Āruṛharāśi so occupied (by Pariveṣa) is occupied by Candra, the pregnant woman dies (probably during labour)

Notes: According to the commentator, the woman dies only if Candra occupies a Śatru/Nīca Rāśi, but if Candra occupies a Mitrarāśi, her Svakṣetra or Uccarāśi, the mother suffers from labour but shall escape death.

ON THE DEATH OF THE CHILD:

14.9. If at Praśna, Krūras are in 1st/7th/8th/10th/12th from Udayarāśi devoid of Bṛhaspati's dṛṣṭi and the presence of other Saumyas in the Kendras, the infant dies at birth.

Notes: According to the commentator, the Krūras should be in their Śatru/Nīca Rāśi. Powerful Saumyas in the Kendra and Bṛhaspati's dṛṣṭi on the Krūras protect the child.

14.10. If, at the time of birth or Praśna, **(1)** Sūrya occupies the 8th House and Maṅgala or Śani occupies the 7th from Sūrya (i.e., 2nd House), **(2)** or if Maṅgala or Śani occupies the 7th House from Udayarāśi, in either case, the infant dies at birth, provided the Yogagrahas are not dṛṣṭied by powerful Saumyas.

Notes: The Yoga involves the presence of Sūrya in the 8th and Śani/Maṅgala in the 2nd, or Sūrya in the 8th and Śani/Maṅgala in the 7th.

DEATH ON THE DAY OF BIRTH:

14.11. If Candra occupies Udayarāśi, Maṅgala the 8th House from such Candra and Śukra or Śani the 9th House from such Candra, the infant dies on the day of birth, provided the Yogagrahas are not dṛṣṭied by powerful Saumyas.

DEATH WITHIN 4 DAYS FROM BIRTH:

14.12. If Candra is dṛṣṭied by Krūras, and if the 6th or 8th House from Udayarāśi or Āruṛharāśi (or Candra's Rāśi) is occupied by Śani, the infant will die within 4 days from birth.

Notes: Śani can be in the 6th/8th from the Udaya/Āruṛha/Candra's Rāśi.

DEATH IN 4 OR 8 DAYS FROM BIRTH:

14.13. If Candra occupies Udayarāśi, Budha, the 8th House and the Krūras, the 4th and 8th Houses, the infant dies within 4 or 8 days, even though the fates try to prevent such death.

Notes: Even when the Yogagrahas are dṛṣṭied by Saumyas, death inevitably occurs. According to the commentator, the text "death occurs in 4, 8 days" may also be interpreted as 4 times 8 or 32 days.

DEATH WITHIN A MONTH:

14.14. If the Krūras occupy the 8th and 12th Houses and are not dṛṣṭied by Śukra or Budha, the infant dies within a month.

Notes: According to the commentator, the 6th House is also included, which I don't think is correct because Krūras in the 6th does not harm longevity. Regarding the dṛṣṭi of Saumyas, Bṛhaspati is also included.

DEATH WITHIN A YEAR:

14.15. If Krūras occupy the 8th and 12th Houses from Udayarāśi and are not dṛṣṭied by Saumyas, the child dies within a year, and the parents and kinsmen also suffer miseries.

Notes: Why are the ślokas 14.14 and 14.15 repeated? Perhaps for the child to live for a year, there must be some protection from the Saumyas.

14.16. If, when Candra occupies Udayarāśi, the Krūras occupy either the Kendras or the 2nd and 8th Houses, the child inevitably dies in a year.

14.17. When the Saumyas do not aspect Candra, and if the Krūras occupy Udayarāśi and the 7th House or are in yuti with Candra, the child dies within a year.

DEATH WITHIN TWO YEARS:

14.18. If the 8th House from Udayarāśi is occupied by Maṅgala, the 9th House by Sūrya, or the 12th House by Śani, each in his Śatru/Nīca Rāśi, the child born will die within two years.

Notes: Provided the Krūras are not dṛṣṭied by Saumyas.

EARLY DEATH IN GENERAL:

14.19. If three Krūras occupy the 2nd House, and if such House be at the same time their Śatru/Nīca Rāśi, the child dies, even if the Yogagrahas are dṛṣṭied by Saumyas.

14.20. The child dies if Krūras occupies the 3rd and 8th Houses from Udayarāśi. Also, if these Grahas aspect Candra occupying the 6th or 8th House from Udayarāśi, the child dies.

THE DEATH OF FATHER AND MOTHER:

14.21. (1) If Maṅgala or Śani aspect Sūrya, the father dies or falls ill. **(2)** If Maṅgala or Śani dṛṣṭies Candra, the mother dies. **(3)** If Bṛhaspati aspect Sūrya, the father escapes death; and **(4)** if he aspect Candra, the mother escapes death.

Notes: The father falls ill if Sūrya occupies a Mitrarāśi, his Svakṣetra or Uccarāśi. Likewise, the mother falls ill if Candra occupies a Mitrarāśi or her Svakṣetra or Uccarāśi, according to the commentator.

THE DEATH OF THE FATHER, MOTHER, CHILD AND RELATIVES:

14.22. If the 5th House from Udayarāśi at the time of birth (or Praśna) is occupied by Sūrya, the father dies; if Candra occupies it, the mother dies; and if Śani occupies it, the child dies; and if it is occupied by Śukra (or Maṅgala?), the relatives (maternal) of the child die.

Notes: According to this Brahmaśrī Sitarama Josier, if the 5th House from Udayarāśi is not occupied, the 5th House from Āruṛharāśi should be considered, and if Grahas do not occupy the latter, the 5th House from Chatrarāśi should be considered. According to Śrī Sitarama, most of the yogas of this chapter apply both at Praśna and birth.

THE DEATH OF THE FATHER, MOTHER, CHILD AND BROTHER:

14.23. (2) If the 6th House or the 10th House from Udayarāśi is occupied by the Krūra Candra, the child's mother dies; **(2)** if such House is occupied by Sūrya, the child's father dies; **(3)** if Śani occupies it, the child dies; and **(4)** if it is occupied by Maṅgala, the child's brothers die.

Notes: Krūra Candra is either the Kṛṣṇapakṣi Candra or Candra occupying his Śatru/Nīca Rāśi. The Grahas Sūrya, Śani or Maṅgala should be in his Śatru/Nīca Rāśi.

THE DEATH OF THE FATHER, MOTHER AND CHILD:

14.24. (1) If Maṅgala and Śani occupy the 7th House from Candra, the mother dies; **(2)** if they occupy the 7th House from Sūrya, the child's father dies; and **(3)** if Maṅgala, Śani and Rāhu occupy the 2nd and 12th Houses from Udayarāśi the child dies.

14.25. (1) If Maṅgala and Śani occupy the 7th House from Candra, the mother falls ill; **(2)** if they occupy the 7th House from Sūrya, the father falls ill; **(3)** if Maṅgala and Śani occupy the 2nd and 12th Houses from Candra, the mother dies: and **(4)** if they occupy the 2nd and 12th Houses from Sūrya, the father dies.

Notes: This śloka is the same as 14.24, but here illness is indicated for the Śani-Maṅgala's placement in the 7th from Candra or Sūrya. We should interpret this way- if both Śani and Maṅgala are in the 7th and the Kāraka, Candra or Sūrya is also weak/afflicted, death is imminent. However, if only one among Śani and Maṅgala is in the 7th, and the Kāraka Candra or Sūrya is in Śubharāśi, then illness is indicated. What is said about the mother from Candra and the father from Sūrya must be said about the child from Udayarāśi.

14.26. If, at the time of birth (or Praśna), **(1)** the 2nd or 3rd Caraṇa of Nakṣatra, Puṣya or Pūrvāṣāṛhā rise above the horizon, the father dies; and **(2)** if the 1st or 2nd Caraṇa of Nakṣatra, Uttarāphālgunī or Citrā rise above the horizon, the mother dies. **(3)** If Sūrya, Śukra, or Śani aspect the Nakṣatra, Puṣya or Pūrvāṣāṛhā, the child dies before the father; and **(4)** if the Grahas aspect Uttarāphālgunī or Chitra, the child dies before the mother

Notes: According to the commentator, if the 1st Caraṇa of the 4 Nakṣatras mentioned in the text rise above the horizon, the child's father dies; if the 2nd Caraṇa of the 4 Nakṣatras rise above the horizon, the child's mother dies; if the 3rd Caraṇa rises above the horizon the child dies; and if he 4th Caraṇa rise the child's kinsmen dies.

14.27. If, at the time of birth (or Praśna), **(1)** Puṣya or Pūrvāṣāṛhā Nakṣatra rise above the horizon, and if such Nakṣatra is dṛṣṭied by Sūrya, the child's father dies; **(2)** if such Nakṣatra is dṛṣṭied by Budha, the child's mother dies; **(3)** if the Nakṣatra is dṛṣṭied by Śukra, the child dies; and **(4)** if it is dṛṣṭied by Maṅgala, the child's kinsmen (maternal uncles) die

Notes: (h). That is maternal uncles. According to the commentator, if Sūrya's Rāśi rises, and if it is dṛṣṭied by Sūrya, the father dies. If Budha's Rāśi rises, and it is dṛṣṭied by Budha, the mother dies. If the Śukra's Rāśi rises and it is dṛṣṭied by Śukra, the child dies. If Maṅgala's Rāśi rises, and it is dṛṣṭied Maṅgala, the child's kinsmen die.

14.28. **(1)** If Rāhu, not dṛṣṭied by Bṛhaspati, occupy Udayarāśi, the child dies; **(1)** if Candra, not dṛṣṭied by Bṛhaspati, occupies the 2nd, 6th, 8th or 12th House from Udayarāśi, and if, at the same time, the 7th from Candra is occupied by Krūras, both the mother and child die.

Notes: According to the commentator, if Sūrya, not being dṛṣṭied by Bṛhaspati, occupies the 2nd, 6th, 8th or 12th House from Udayarāśi and if, at the same time, the 7th from Sūrya is occupied by Krūras, both the father and the child die.

THE DEATH OF THE MOTHER AND THE CHILD:

14.29. If Candra occupies Udayarāśi and Maṅgala, the Astarāśi, or if Maṅgala occupies Udayarāśi and Candra, the Astarāśi or if Candra occupies Udayarāśi and Śukra the Astarāśi, or if Śukra occupies Udayarāśi and Candra the Astarāśi, both the mother and the child die, provided the Yogagrahas are not dṛṣṭied by Bṛhaspati or other Saumyas.

Notes: The presence of Candra-Maṅgala or Candra-Śukra yogas in the 1-7 axis, which is devoid of Bṛhaspati's dṛṣṭi, causes the death of the child and the mother. The Astarāśi is the 7th Rāśi from Udayarāśi.

THE DEATH OF THE FATHER AND THE CHILD:

14.30. If Sūrya occupies Udayarāśi and Śani, the Astarāśi, or if Śani occupies Udayarāśi and Sūrya the Astarāśi, or if Sūrya occupies Udayarāśi and

Śukra the Astarāśi or if Śukra occupies Udayarāśi and Sūrya the Astarāśi, both the father and the child die, provided the Yogagrahas are not dṛṣṭied by Bṛhaspati.

Notes: The presence of Sūrya-Śani or Sūrya-Śukra yogas in the 1-7 axis that is devoid of Bṛhaspati's dṛṣṭi cause the death of the child and the father.

14.31. If Candra occupies Udayarāśi in yuti with 3 Krūras in their Śatru/Nīca Rāśi, both the mother and the child die.

Notes: According to the commentator, if Sūrya occupies Udayarāśi in yuti with 3 Krūras in their Śatru/Nīca Rāśi, both the father and the child will die. The Śatru/Nīca Rāśi should be that of Candra or Sūrya and need not be of the other Grahas. Sūrya is excluded from the list of Krūras here because he is the Kāraka for father. Instead Śani, Maṅgala, Rāhu and Ketu are considered.

14.32. If Candra occupies the 6th House from Udayarāśi and if Krūras occupy the 7th House from such Candra (12th from Udayarāśi), both the mother and the child die. Again, if Candra (or Sūrya) occupies the 6th House from the Lagna and if Krūras occupy the 5th House from such Candra (10th from Udayarāśi), the child is disabled in its arm. Again, if the 12th House from the Lagna is occupied by Candra (and Sūrya, also in their Śatru/Nīca Rāśi), the child is blind.

Notes: According to the commentator, if Sūrya occupies the 6th House from Udayarāśi and if Krūras occupy the 7th House from such Sūrya, both the father and the child die.

BLIND CHILD AGAIN:

14.33. If Sūrya occupies the 12th House from Udayarāśi, the child is blind in its right eye; if the Candra occupies the 12th House from Udayarāśi, the child is blind in its left eye; and if both Sūrya and Candra occupy the 12th House, the child is blind of both eyes.

Notes: The yoga also refers to lameness, according to the commentator.

BIRTH OF A DWARF AND A CHILD WITH DEFECTIVE LIMBS:

14.34. (1) If Śani occupies Udayarāśi and Maṅgala, the Astarāśi or **(2)** if Budha occupies Udayarāśi and Śani, the Astarāśi, the child born is a dwarf. **(3)** If the above Yogagrahas are dṛṣṭied by Krūras, the child born is of a defective organ (disabled).

Notes: Eight personal defects are enumerated, shortness, blindness, lameness, crookedness, deafness; dumbness; inability of limbs; and abortion. A dwarf (shortness) is a person whose height does not exceed 2 cubits.

BIRTH OF AN ILLEGITIMATE CHILD:

14.35. If either Udayarāśi or Āruṛharāśi is not dṛṣṭied by Śukra or Bṛhaspati, and if Candra is in yuti with Sūrya, Maṅgala, Śani, or Rāhu, the child born is illegitimate.

Notes: According to the commentator, if Udayarāśi or Āruṛharāśi is dṛṣṭied by Śukra or Bṛhaspati, the child is legitimate regardless of whether or not

Candra is in yuti with Sūrya, Maṅgala, Śani, or Rāhu. Again, if the Graha in yuti with Candra is Sūrya, the illegitimate father is a Brāhmaṇa or a Kṣatriya; if Maṅgala, the illegitimate father is a Vaiśya or a Śudra; if Śani, such father belong to a lower caste than the Śudras; and if Rāhu, the father is a Caṇḍāla.

YOGA AND AVAYOGA:

14.36. (1) If Saumyas in their Uccarāśis occupy both sides of Udayarāśi, or **(2)** if they occupy the 4th, 7th or 10th House, or **(3)** if Krūras in their Svakṣetra Rāśis occupy Chatrarāśi or **(4)** if Saumyas in their Uccarāśi or Svakṣetra occupy Udayarāśi, the child born is a prosperous one. If otherwise, the child will suffer misery.

Notes: The birth is Aśubha if Krūras, in their Śatru/Nīca Rāśis, have Pāpakartari on Udayarāśi, or if they occupy the 4th, 7th or 10th, or if Saumyas in their Śatru/Nīca Rāśis occupy Chatrarāśi, or if Krūras in their Śatru/Nīca Rāśis occupy Udayarāśi. What is said about Udayarāśi also applies to Candra and Āruṛharāśi.

THE BIRTH OF A WEALTHY PERSON:

14.37. If a Saumya in its Uccarāśi is before (2nd) Candra, the person born is rich; and if such Grahas occupy the Rāśis both before (2nd) and behind (12th) Candra (Durdharā), the person born is immensely rich.

Notes: In the first case, the amount of wealth, however vast, is limited; in the second case, it is unlimited.

THE RULER OF A VILLAGE AND A PROVINCE:

14.38. (1) If a Saumya in its Uccarāśi occupies the Rāśi before (2nd) Āruṛharāśi, the person born becomes the chief of a village; **(2)** but if such Grahas occupy the Rāśis both before (2nd) and behind (12th) Āruṛharāśi, the person born becomes the chief of a province. **(3)** But if the child born under either yoga is a female child, she becomes the wife of such chief.

THE GOVERNOR OF A PROVINCE AND A COMMANDER OF ARMIES:

14.39. (1) If three Grahas occupy their Uccarāśis, or if three Saumyas occupy Udayarāśi, the person born becomes a commander of armies. **(2)** Again, if four Grahas occupy their Uccarāśis or if four Saumyas occupy Udayarāśi, the person born under the yoga becomes the Governor of a province.

TO DISCOVER THE NAKṢATRA OF THE CHILD BORN:

14.40. Find the number of Rāśis from Āruṛharāśi to Udayarāśi; double the number; add to it the number of Rāśis from the 2nd House (from Udayarāśi) to Meṣa Rāśi, and also the number of Rāśis from Vṛṣabha Rāśi to the 12th House from Āruṛharāśi. Divide the sum by 27. The remainder calculated from the Aśvinī is the Nakṣatra occupied by Candra during childbirth.

Notes: According to the commentator, the Nakṣatra thus discovered leads to the determination of the various Daśā periods in the life of the person, and the effects of the various yogas would come to pass in the Daśā and Antardaśā periods of the several Grahas. Here is a Praśna that is put to determine the Nakṣatra of the Pṛcchaka. The Lagna is Meṣa, and the Āruṛha number is 48, denoting 12 (Mīna). **Step1:** Āruṛha to Udayarāśi = Mīna to Meṣa = 2. **Step2:** Double the number = 2 * 2 = 4. **Step3:** Add to it the number of Rāśis from the 2nd House to Meṣa = Count from Vṛṣabha to Meṣa = 12. Sum = 4 + 12 = 16. **Step4:** Add the number of Rāśis from Vṛṣabha to the 12th House from Āruṛharāśi = 12th from Mīna is Kumbha and counting from Vṛṣabha to Kumbha is 10. Sum = 16 + 10 = 26. Divide the sum by 27, and the remainder denotes the Nakṣatra occupied by Candra at birth. Here the remainder is 26, which is Uttarābhādra, which Śani rules. The Pṛcchaka is born in Anurādhā, which Śani rules. Therefore, we should accept the Nakṣatra arrived or its Trikoṇa to arrive at the Janma Nakṣatra.

24.2.15
ADHYĀYA 15:
ON DAGGER

THE BREAKING OF THE DAGGER:

15.1. If at Praśna, Candra is in yuti with Rāhu, or if Candra is dṛṣṭied either by Krūras or by Grahas in their Śatru/Nīca Rāśi, the dagger break.

THE PLACE OF BREAKING:

15.2. (1) If Candra (afflicted as per śloka 15.1) is either in Udayarāśi or the Astarāśi, the dagger breaks at the hilt; **(2)** if it is the 5th or the 9th House, the dagger breaks just below the hilt; **(3)** if it is the 4th or the 10th House, the dagger breaks in the middle; and **(4)** if it is the 3rd or the 11th House, the dagger breaks at the end.

Notes: According to the commentator, if Candra is in the 2nd, 6th, 8th or 12th House, the dagger does not break.

THE LOSS OF THE DAGGER:

15.3. (1) If Udayarāśi or Āruṛharāśi is dṛṣṭied by Krūras from their Śatru/Nīca Rāśi, the dagger is lost from the hand; and **(2)** if such Rāśi is dṛṣṭied by Saumyas from their Mitrarāśi, Svakṣetra or Uccarāśis, the dagger is not lost.

TO WHOM THE DAGGER BELONGS:

15.4. (1) If Udayarāśi or Āruṛharāśi is dṛṣṭied by Candra or Bṛhaspati (or Sūrya, according to the commentator), the dagger belongs to the Pṛcchaka himself; **(2)** if such Rāśi is dṛṣṭied by Maṅgala (or Śani or Rāhu, according to the commentator), the dagger belongs to another; **(3)** if such Rāśi is dṛṣṭied by Budha or Śukra it is common property, or the possessor of it meets with death.

Notes: Also, the commentator adds that if the aspecting Grahas are in their Mitrarāśis, the dagger belongs to a friend; if they are in their Svakṣetra Rāśis, the dagger belongs to the person himself; if they occupy their Uccarāśis, the dagger belongs to one of superior rank; if they occupy their Śatrurāśis, the dagger belongs to the person's enemy; and if the Grahas occupy their Nīcarāśis, the dagger belongs to a person of inferior rank.

WOUND OR NO WOUND:

15.5. If Krūras occupy Āruṛharāśi, the person gets wounded; but if such Rāśi is occupied by Saumyas alone, the person does not get wounded.

Notes: (a). According to the commentator, if both Saumya and Krūras occupy Āruṛharāśi, the wound is superficial.

24.2.16
ADHYĀYA 16:
ON SALYA

CALCULATION FOR DISCOVERING SALYA:

16.1. Find out the length of a man's shadow in Sūrya at the time of Praśna; add to it 28 and the number of Rāśis from Meṣa to Udayarāśi; multiply the sum by 12. Divide the product by 16. The remainder gives the particular Salya underground.

Notes: The length of the shadow is obtained by measuring it with one's foot. Salya is an object found underground; 16 are enumerated in śloka 16.2.

SALYAS:

16.2. The Salya substances are (1) human skull; (2) bones; (3) brickbats; (4) pot-shred; (5) wood; (6) images; (7) ashes; (8) charcoal; (9) dead-bodies; (10) grain; (11) gold; (12) stone; (13) frog; (14) horn; (15) a dead dog; (16) human hair.

DETERMINATION OF SALYA:

16.3. The Salya questioned by a person is given by the number representing the remainder resulting from the calculation of the shadow. Of the 16 Salyas, 10-grain, 11-gold and 14-horn are Śubha, and the others are Krūra.

Notes: If, for instance, the remainder is 5, the Salya is wood and so on. If the remainder is zero, it should be considered as 16.

THE SALYA CAKRA:

16.4. The Salya Cakra consists of 28 squares for the 28 Nakṣatras (including Abhijit), 7 in each of the north to the south lines, and 4 in each of the east to the west lines. The square of the ground containing Candra at Praśna denotes the Salya.

THE 1ST OF THE FORENOON CAKRAS:

16.5. Dividing the period from Sūryodaya to the following Sūryodaya into 28 equal parts, the 1st diagram for the forenoon is as follows: the 3 Nakṣatras from Kṛttikā to Mṛgaśirā occupy the three central squares in the easternmost row from north to south. Then beginning from the square just below the last of these three, the four squares from south to north of the 2nd line are occupied by the next four Nakṣatras, from Ārdrā to Aśleṣā. Then beginning from the square just below the last of these four, the 5 squares from north to south are occupied by the next 5 Nakṣatras, from Maghā to Citra. Then the two squares above the last of these 5 are occupied by the next two Nakṣatras, Swati and Viśākhā. The remaining 14 Nakṣatras occupy the remaining 14 squares of the diagram, beginning from the square next to the right of the square occupied by Viśākhā and going around.

Notes: The reader should refer to the explanation of **Candragupti Cakra** in the Kūpa Praśna section narrated in volume 23B of this book series.

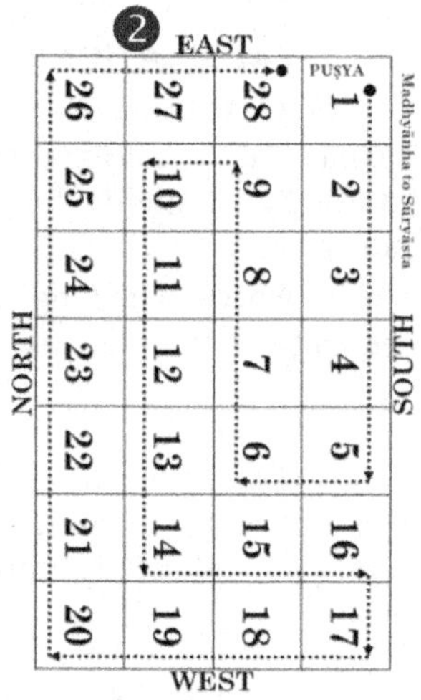

THE OTHER DIAGRAMS:

16.7. The Nakṣatras move backwards at the rate of 60/28 or 2 1/7 Ghaṭis, equal to 51 minutes and 26 seconds for each square. Put down the diagram for the time of Praśna; the square relating to Candra's Nakṣatra denotes the Salya.

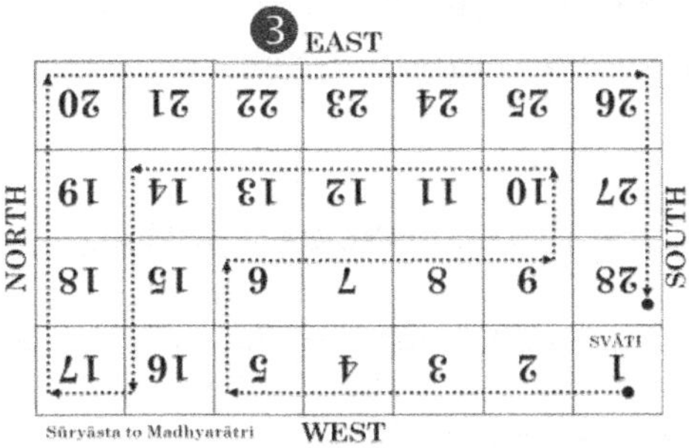

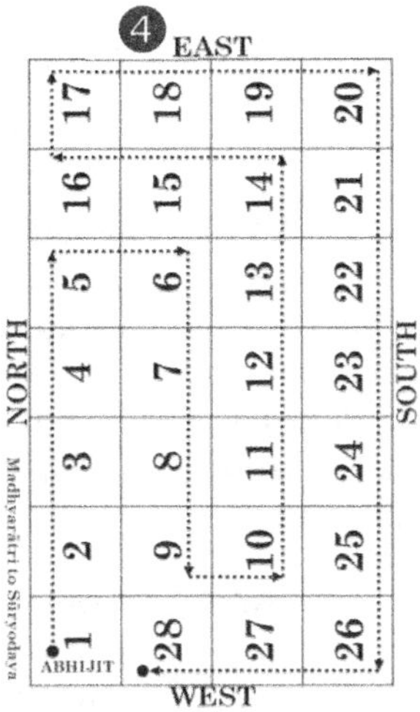

ANOTHER PROCESS FOR DISCOVERING SALYA:

16.8. Find the Udaya Nakṣatra at the time of Praśna and begin from it as from the Nakṣatra of Kṛttikā in the 1st of the 28 diagrams, and you get the diagram required. The square of the Nakṣatra occupied by Candra will contain the Salya.

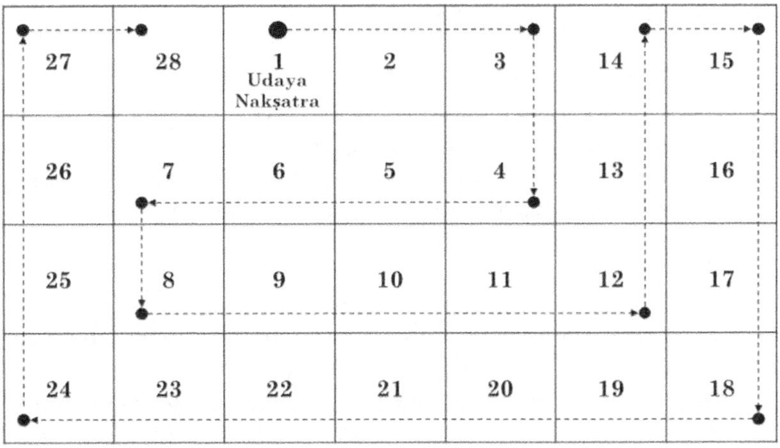

SALYA OR NO SALYA:

16.9. If at Praśna, Saumyas occupying the Kendras is having yutidṛṣṭi of Krūras, there is Salya underground. Again, if Candra occupying a Kendra is having Maṅgala yutidṛṣṭi, there is the bone of a sheep in the square of the Nakṣatra occupied by Maṅgala.

Notes: If the Saumyas in the Kendras are not having yutidṛṣṭi from Krūras, there is no Salya underground. Maṅgala's yutidṛṣṭi indicates the leg of the sheep, according to some.

THE BONE OF A BRĀHMAṆA OR A COW, BRICKBAT OR GOLD:

16.10. If at Praśna, Candra occupying a Kendra is having yutidṛṣṭi of Bṛhaspati, there is the bone of a Brāhmaṇa or a cow, or a brickbat or a piece of gold in the square of the Nakṣatra occupied by Bṛhaspati.

THE STATUE OF A DEVA AND THE BONE OF A BUFFALO:

16.11. If at Praśna, Candra, occupying a Kendra is having yutidṛṣṭi of Sūrya, there is the statue of a Deva in the square of the Nakṣatra occupied by Sūrya. But if such Candra is accompanied or dṛṣṭied by Śani, there is the bone of a buffalo in the square of the Nakṣatra occupied by Śani.

Notes: According to the commentator, Sūrya's yutidṛṣṭi also indicate a human skull.

SNAKE, SNAKE-HOLE OR THE BONE OF A SNAKE:

16.12. If at Praśna, Candra occupying a Kendra is having yutidṛṣṭi of Rāhu, there is a snake, its bone, or a snake hole in the place of the Nakṣatra occupied by such Rāhu (a).

Notes: According to some, the bone is located in the square of the Nakṣatra occupied by Candra.

THE BONE OF A DOG OR A PIECE OF SILVER:

16.13. If at Praśna, Candra occupying a Kendra is having yutidṛṣṭi of Budha, there is the bone of a dog in the square of the Nakṣatra occupied by Budha. If Candra occupying a Kendra is either accompanied or dṛṣṭied by Śukra, there is a piece of silver in the square of the Nakṣatra occupied by Śukra.

THE FORTUNES OF THE OWNER OF A HOUSE SITE:

16.14. If at Praśna, the Saumyas occupying the Kendras are having yutidṛṣṭi of Krūras, the owner of the House-site questioned about meets with failure, does not enjoy the ground, and suffers poverty.

16.15. If at Praśna, the Kendras are having yutidṛṣṭi of Krūras alone, i.e., that of Rāhu, Maṅgala, Sūrya and Śani, there is misery. Still, there is prosperity if the Kendras are having yutidṛṣṭi of Saumyas alone.

Notes: According to the commentator, if the Kendras are having yutidṛṣṭi of both Krūra and Śubha Grahas, there is both misery and happiness.

16.16. If at Praśna, the Kendras are having yutidṛṣṭi of Candra, Śukra, Bṛhaspati and Budha; there is an increase of wealth and prosperity and enjoyment of House-site.

16.17. If at Praśna, the 10th House from Praśnalagna has yutidṛṣṭi of Saumyas, the owner himself enjoys the House site. Still, if such 10th House has yutidṛṣṭi of Krūras, the House site is occupied by the Devas, the Piśācas or the Rākṣasas (by entities besides the owner).

THE DEPTH OF SALYA:

16.18. The Raśmi of the Graha indicating the Salya is the depth at which such Salya lies, the depth being taken in spans.

Notes: Refer to śloka 1.54 for Graha Raśmis. According to the commentator, if the Graha occupies its Uccarāśi, the number of its Raśmis represents a depth of so many spans. If the Graha occupies its Svarāśi, the number represents the depth in as many cubits. If the Graha occupies its Mitrarāśi, the number given is the depth of so many men. If the Graha occupies its Śatru/Nīca Rāśi, the number of its Raśmis shall be taken to indicate simply great depth. One cubit = 2 spans. One cubit = measure from the elbow to the end of the ring finger.

16.19-20. Measure the length and breadth of the House-site with the measuring rod (of 2-cubit length). Multiply the numbers representing the length and breadth. Divide the product by 28; the quotient gives the depth in cubits; multiply the remainder by 2[2], and divide the product by 28; the quotient gives the depth in spans; multiply the remainder by 4 and divide the product by 28; the quotient gives the depth in inches.

24.2.17
ADHYĀYA 17:
ON UNDERCURRENTS

PREDICTION OF UNDERCURRENTS:

17.1. If Udayarāśi, Āruṛharāśi or the 4th House from Praśnalagna is Vṛṣabha, Karka, Tulā, Vṛścika, Makara, Kumbha, or Mīna, undercurrents may be predicted. If such Udayarāśi, Āruṛharāśi or 4th House is having yutidṛṣṭi from Candra or Śukra, the supply of water is inexhaustible, but if such Rāśi is having yutidṛṣṭi from Budha or Bṛhaspati, the supply of water is limited in its nature.

DEEP CURRENTS AND SUPERFICIAL CURRENTS:

17.2. If Udayarāśi, Āruṛharāśi, or the 4th House, is having yutidṛṣṭi from Sūrya, Maṅgala or Śani, there is no water underground; but if Āruṛharāśi is having yutidṛṣṭi from Rāhu, the supply of water is unlimited. Again, if the Jalatattva Grahas (Candra/Śukra) occupy Āruṛharāśi, the current is deep underground, and if they occupy Chatrarāśi, the current is close to the surface.

Notes: The nature of the current is determined by the character of the Rāśi occupied by the Yogagraha, and the direction of the current is that of the Yogagraha.

17.3. (1) If, when Rāhu occupies Udayarāśi, **(2)** the Jalatattva Grahas occupy Āruṛharāśi, or **(3)** the other Grahas occupy Chatrarāśi, the current is superficial; but if the reverse is the case, the current is deep underground.

---

[2] 12, as mentioned in the text, which is evidently an error according to Śrī Chidambaram Iyer.

Notes: If the Jalatattva Grahas occupy Chatrarāśi and the other Grahas occupy Āruṛharāśi, the current is deep underground.

17.4. (1) If Udayarāśi, Āruṛharāśi, and the 4th House be Jalacara Rāśis and if Jalatattva Grahas occupy them, the current is superficial; but **(2)** if such Rāśis are occupied by other than Jalatattva Grahas, the current lie deep underground.

QUANTIFY OF WATER SUPPLY:

17.5. If, when Candra occupies a Kendra, Bṛhaspati has yutidṛṣṭi on the Rāśi occupied by Candra, the supply of water is unlimited; but if Śukra has yutidṛṣṭi on the said Rāśi, the supply is limited.

Notes: The current lie under the square of the Nakṣatra (as per Candragupti Cakra) occupied by Bṛhaspati or Śukra at the time of Praśna.

17.6. (1) When Candra occupies a Kendra, and Pariveṣa is having yutidṛṣṭi on such House (Candra's Rāśi), there is an unlimited supply of water; but **(2)** if such Kendra is having yutidṛṣṭi from Budha or Bṛhaspati, there is an old and unused well in the place.

17.7. (1) If the Kendras have yutidṛṣṭi from Candra or Śukra, the supply of water is abundant; **(2)** and if each House has yutidṛṣṭi from Indradhanuṣa, Pariveṣa, Dhūma, or Sukṣma, there is an old ditch or pond in the ground.

CHARACTER OF THE SOIL AND WATER:

17.8. (1) If a Kendra has yutidṛṣṭi of Sūrya, there is a layer of salt earth; **(2)** if such House has yutidṛṣṭi from Pariveṣa, the ground is hard; **(3)** if it is having yutidṛṣṭi from Candra or Śukra, the water is clear; and **(4)** if such Houses are having yutidṛṣṭi from other Grahas, the water is muddy.

17.9. (5) If a Kendras have yutidṛṣṭi of Maṅgala, there is a layer of white soil; **(6)** if such Houses have yutidṛṣṭi of Budha, the bank gives way. **(7)** If the Kendras are Mithuna, Kanyā or Siṅha, lateral springs or breaches are underground.

Notes: According to the commentator, the bank is firm if the Kendras are having yutidṛṣṭi of other Grahas. The flavour of the water follows the flavour of the Grahas.

17.10. (8) If the Kendras have yutidṛṣṭi of Śani or Rāhu, there is a breach yielding an abundant supply of water; **(9)** if having yutidṛṣṭi of Bṛhaspati, there are stones; **(10)** and if by the other Grahas, there are bones.

THE DEPTH OF THE WATER:

17.11. Dividing the depth (as per next śloka) to the surface of the undercurrent into three parts, Candra gives the water in the first part and Budha in the last part (other Grahas middle part). Also, Sūrya gives it below 8 cubits, Rāhu occupying Kanyā gives it below a rock, and Śani gives it below a hillock.

17.12. The number of Raśmis of the Grahas by which the undercurrent is determined, together with the number of Raśmis of the Rāśis occupied by such

Grahas, gives the depth of the surface of the water in spans. These may be converted into cubits.

Notes: If the Grahas occupy their Uccarāśis, the number denotes the depth in spans; if they occupy their Svakṣetra Rāśis, the number is in cubits; if they occupy their Mitrarāśis, the number is in so many men; and if they occupy their Śatru/Nīca Rāśi, the current lies deep underground. The depth of Salya shall also be similarly determined.

THE CHARACTER OF THE GROUND:

17.13. (1) If the Yogagraha is Sūrya, the ground in which a well is intended to be dug is forest land; **(2)** if such Graha is Maṅgala or Śani, the ground is covered with thorns; **(3)** if it is Rāhu, the ground is covered with snake-holes and ant-bills; **(4)** if it is Candra, the ground contains plantain crops; **(5)** if it is Budha, there is jackfruit trees; **(6)** if Bṛhaspati, there is cocoa, palm, areca-nut, and mango trees, and **(7)** if it is Śukra, the ground is covered with creepers.

THE ENJOYER OF THE WELL:

17.14. (1) If the Rāśis by which the spring or undercurrent is determined is occupied or dṛṣṭied by Saumyas in their Mitrarāśi, Svakṣetra, or Uccarāśis, the well continues in the enjoyment of the owner; **(2)** but if such Rāśis are occupied or dṛṣṭied by Krūras in their Śatru/Nīca Rāśi, the enjoyment of the good pass to other men.

17.15. (1) If the Rāśis mentioned above are either Cara or Dvisva Rāśis, the owner of the well is happy and enjoys it only if such Rāśis are dṛṣṭied by Saumyas in their Mitrarāśi, Svakṣetra or Uccarāśis; **(2)** but if such Rāśis are not so dṛṣṭied, the person is unhappy, and other men enjoy the well.

Notes: If the Rāśis are Sthirarāśis, the owner is happy.

EFFECTS OF THE POSITION OF THE WELL (VĀSTU EFFECTS):

17.16-17. (1) If the well is to the East (Sūrya), Southeast (Śukra) or South (Maṅgala) of the residence of the owner, his children die; **(2)** if it is to the Southwest (Rāhu), there is a gain of servants; **(3)** if it is to the West (Śani), the crops suffer, **(4)** if it is to the Northwest (Candra), the family prosper; **(5)** if it is to the North (Budha), there is an increase of grain; **(6)** if it is to the Northeast (Bṛhaspati), there is acquisition of wealth and **(7)** if it is in the centre of the House, there is immense prosperity and happiness.

Notes: The same remarks apply to the village tank. The effects are based on the Graha dik or directions. It is best to have the tank, well or waterbody (Jalatattva/prosperity) in the direction denoted by Candra (NW), Budha (N), and Bṛhaspati (NE). Incidentally, Śukra's direction is not considered favourable, even though he is a Saumya. Besides that, Rāhu's direction of SW is favourable, as that shows a gain of servants.

EFFECTS OF MARKING THE GROUND:

17.18. (1) If the Pṛcchaka, when asked to mark out the shape of the ground, should do so with his little finger, he begets daughters; **(2)** if with his ring finger, he gets wealth; **(3)** if with his middle finger, there is wandering, and **(4)** if with his pointer or thumb, there is misery.

Notes: The fingers are related to Tattvas, whereby the thumb (Aṅguṣṭhā) is Ākāśatattva, the index finger is Jalatattva, the middle finger (Madhyamā) is Pṛthvītattva, ring finger (Anāmikā) is Agnitattva, and little finger (Kaniṣṭhā) is Vāyuttatva.

TIME OF DIGGING A WELL:

17.19. (1) If the digging of the well is commenced in the month of Meṣa, Vṛṣabha, or Mithuna, water is abundant, and prosperity in addition to that; **(2)** if it is commenced in the month of Karka, or Siṅha, the supply of water is small; and **(3)** if the digging be commenced in the other months, there is little water and misery in addition to that. **(4)** Graha positions shall also be considered in making the prediction.

Notes: The months denote the presence of Sūrya in those Rāśis.

24.2.18
ADHYĀYA 18:
ON THE INVASION OF ENEMY

THE ARRIVAL OR NON-ARRIVAL OF THE ENEMY:

18.1. When the 5th House from Udayarāśi is having Krūrayutidṛṣṭi; **(1)** if Udayarāśi is a Cararāśi, the enemy arrives; **(2)** if it is a Sthirarāśi, the enemy does not leave his place; and **(3)** if it is a Dvisvarāśi and if the 5th House is dṛṣṭied by Maṅgala the enemy returns to its place after coming halfway.

Notes: Affliction to the 5th house is necessary for the Prāṇa on invasion by an enemy.

18.2. (1) If Udayarāśi is a Cararāśi and it has yutidṛṣṭi from Sūrya, Maṅgala, Bṛhaspati, or Śani, or again, if the 6th or 7th House from Udayarāśi is Āruṛharāśi the enemy arrives; **(2)** but if Karka, Vṛścika, Kumbha, or Mīna, is Udayarāśi, or the 4th House, the enemy returns to its place after coming halfway.

18.3. (1) If Sūrya or Budha occupies the 6th House from Udayarāśi or Āruṛharāśi, the enemy arrives, **(2)** but if Bṛhaspati occupies the 4th or the 6th House from Udayarāśi or Āruṛharāśi the enemy does not arrive.

THE ARRIVAL AND RETURN OF THE ENEMY:

18.4. (1) If at Praśna, Śani occupies the 2nd House from Udayarāśi or Āruṛharāśi, the enemy arrives; and **(2)** if Śani occupies the 3rd, 5th, 6th, 11th or

12th House from such Rāśi the enemy returns to its place loaded with booty and carrying away women as enslaved people.

18.5. **(1)** If Śukra occupies the 4th or 5th House from Udayarāśi or Āruṛharāśi, the enemy returns to its place with the loss of property and leaving its women as prisoners; **(2)** if he occupies the 6th House from such Rāśi there is peace; and **(2)** if Śukra occupies the 7th House there is no reason for fear.

18.6. If at Praśna, **(1)** Śani occupies the 2nd, 3rd, 4th or 8th House from Udayarāśi or Āruṛharāśi, the enemy does not arrive; **(2)** if he occupies the 10th, 11th or 12th House from such Rāśi, the enemy returns to its place loaded with booty and carrying away women as enslaved people; **(3)** and if Śani occupies the 5th House the enemy becomes (or is) powerful.

THE DEFEAT AND DEATH OF THE ENEMY:

18.7. If at Praśna, **(1)** Sūrya occupies the 11th House from Udayarāśi or Āruṛharāśi, the enemy returns to its place with the loss of his kinsmen and army and leaving its women as enslaved people; and **(2)** if Sūrya occupies Udayarāśi and if such Rāśi be his Śatru/Nīca Rāśi, the chief of the enemy is slain in the battle.

PEACE, BATTLE, THE ARRIVAL AND NON-ARRIVAL OF THE ENEMY:

18.8: If at Praśna, **(1)** Sūrya and Śukra occupy the 6th House from Udayarāśi or Āruṛharāśi, the enemy arrives, and **(2)** if the Rāśis are their Mitrarāśis there is peace (battle if Śatrurāśi). **(3)** If Bṛhaspati occupies the 4th or 6th House from Udayarāśi or Āruṛharāśi, the enemy does not arrive.

THE MOVEMENTS OF THE ENEMY:

18.9: If at Praśna, **(1)** Candra is in a Cararāśi in Udayarāśi, the enemy appears to be friendly and secretly endeavours to take possession of the country. **(2)** If Candra occupies a Dvisvarāśi in Udayarāśi, the enemy returns to his place after coming halfway.

SUCCESS AND DEFEAT:

18.10. If at Praśna, **(1)** Grahas in their Mitrarāśi, Svakṣetra or Uccarāśis occupy Āruṛharāśi, the chief of the place attacked wins the battle; **(2)** but if such Grahas occupy Chatrarāśi, the enemy, making the attack, wins.

18.11. If at Praśna, **(3)** Grahas in their Śatru/Nīca Rāśi occupy Āruṛharāśi, the enemy making the attack wins the battle; but **(4)** if such Grahas occupy Chatrarāśi, the chief of the place attacked wins the battle.

18.12. If at Praśna, **(5)** the Grahas occupying Āruṛharāśi (or its Lord) are powerful, the chief attacked wins the battle; **(6)** but if the Grahas occupying Chatrarāśi (or its Lord) are powerful, the enemy, making the attack, wins.

18.13. If at Praśna, **(7)** Budha occupies one of the front Rāśis (6 Rāśis from Āruṛharāśi), and Sūrya one of the back Rāśis (the remaining 6 Rāśis), the chief attacked wins the battle; but if the reverse is the case (Budha back Rāśi, and Sūrya front Rāśis), the enemy making the attack wins the battle.

SUCCESS AND DEFEAT, BATTLE AND PEACE:

18.14. If at Praśna, **(1)** Udayarāśi is a Śīrṣodaya Rāśi, and if Saumyas occupy it, the chief attacked wins the battle; **(2)** but if Udayarāśi is a Pṛṣṭodaya Rāśi and if it is occupied by Saumyas the enemy making the attack wins the battle. Again, **(3)** if Udayarāśi is a Manuṣya Rāśi and if Krūras occupy it, there is a fight; **(4)** and if Saumyas occupy such Manuṣya Rāśi, there is peace.

18.15. If at Praśna, **(5)** Udayarāśi is either a Pṛṣṭodaya Rāśi (Kīṭa Rāśi according to some) or a Catuṣpāda Rāśi, and if Krūras occupy such Rāśi there is a fight; **(6)** but if Saumyas occupy such Rāśi there is peace.

TRIBUTE:

18.16. If at Praśna, **(1)** Maṅgala occupies the 3rd, 7th, 8th or 9th House, the enemy making the attack pays tribute; but **(2)** if Maṅgala occupies any remaining places, the chief attacked pays tribute.

FIGHT, PEACE, AND TRIBUTE:

18.17. (1) If Sūrya occupies the 3rd or 5th House from Udayarāśi or Āruṛharāśi, the chief of the place suffers defeat in battle; **(2)** if such Sūrya occupies a Mitrarāśi, the chief sues for peace; **(3)** but if Sūrya occupies a Śatrurāśi he offers fight; **(4)** if Sūrya occupies the 4th House be pays tribute, and if Sūrya occupies the 12th House the enemy is despoiled of his arms.

FATE OF THE ENEMY:

18.18. If at Praśna, **(1)** Udayarāśi is occupied (or dṛṣṭied) by Sūrya, Maṅgala or Śani, the enemy making the attack wins the battle; **(2)** if Udayarāśi is occupied (or dṛṣṭied) by Budha or Śukra, the enemy sues for peace; **(3)** if Udayarāśi is occupied (or dṛṣṭied) by Bṛhaspati, the enemy suffers defeat and flee.

18.19. If at Praśna, **(4)** Bṛhaspati occupies the 3rd, 5th, 10th or 12th House from Udayarāśi or Āruṛharāśi the enemy loses its strength; **(5)** if Bṛhaspati occupies the 2nd House, he sues for peace. **(6)** If Candra and Budha occupy the 11th House, he loses all and flees from the battlefield.

TRIBUTE, SUCCESS AND FAILURE:

18.20. If at Praśna, **(1)** Budha occupies the 5th House, the chief of the place attacked pays tribute to the enemy; **(2)** if Budha occupies the 2nd or 3rd House, the enemy pays tribute; **(3)** if Budha occupies the 12th House the chief of the place attacked wins the battle; and **(4)** if Budha occupies the 11th House the enemy wins.

NEWS OF THE APPROACH OF THE ENEMY:

18.21. If at Praśna, **(1)** Candra occupies the 6th House from Udayarāśi or Āruṛharāśi, there is news of the approach of the enemy; **(2)** if he occupies the 4th or the 5th House, no danger need be apprehended; **(3)** if in the former case, Candra occupies his Mitrarāśi, Svakṣetra or Uccarāśi the enemy does not arrive despite his rumoured approach; but **(4)** if, in the latter case, Candra occupies his Śatru/Nīca Rāśi there is some slight loss or injury.

FATE OF THE CHIEF ATTACK:

18.22. If at Praśna, **(1)** Sūrya and Candra occupy Ojarāśis, the chief of the place attacked wins the battle; **(2)** but if they occupy Yugmarāśis, he suffers defeat. Again, **(3)** the chief wins if Sūrya occupies Udayarāśi and Candra the 12th House.

Notes: If Candra occupies Udayarāśi and Sūrya the 12th House, the place's chief suffers defeat.

FATE OF THE CHIEF AND THE ENEMY:

18.28. The 6 Houses beginning from the 4th House from Udayarāśi, are those of the Yāyi (the enemy making the attack), and the remaining 6 Houses are those of the Poura (the chief of the town attacked); so that the party represented by the Houses occupied by Saumyas in their Mitrarāśi, Svakṣetra, or Uccarāśis wins the battle; and the party represented by the Houses occupied by Krūras in their Śatru/Nīca Rāśi loses it.

WHO COMMENCES THE FIGHT:

18.24. If at Praśna, **(1)** Krūras occupying the Poura and Yāyi Houses are of equal strength, both parties commence the fight; **(2)** but if such Grahas are not of equal strength, the fight is commenced by the party whose Houses are occupied by the more powerful Grahas.

THE SOLAR AND LUNAR NAKṢATRAS:

18.25. The thirteen and a half Nakṣatras from the 2nd half of Dhaniṣṭhā to the end of Aśleṣā (Nakṣatras from Kumbha to Karka) are known as lunar Nakṣatras, and the thirteen and a half Nakṣatras from Magha to the end of the first half of Dhaniṣṭhā (Siṅha to Makara), are known as solar Nakṣatras.

RESULT OF THE FIGHT:

18.26. If the fight is commenced when Candra occupies a lunar Nakṣatra and Sūrya a solar Nakṣatra, there is peace before the fight (else there is a fight). If it is commenced when Sūrya occupies a lunar Nakṣatra, the Poura (defender) wins; and if it is commenced when Candra occupies a solar Nakṣatra, the Yāyi (attacking party) wins.

24.2.19 ADHYĀYA 19: ON TRAVEL

MATTERS COVERED:

19.1. We purpose to speak of the **(1)** return (or non-return) of a traveller, **(2)** of the wealth acquired by him, **(3)** of the persons who meet him in his travel, and **(4)** of the good and evil which befall him.

PEOPLE MET:

19.2. If the Grahas aspecting Udayarāśi, Āruṛharāśi or the 10th House is in their Mitrarāśis, the traveller meets with friends or kinsmen; if such Grahas are in their Nīcarāśis the traveller meets with his inferiors or with men of low birth; and if the Grahas are in their Uccarāśis, the traveller meets with his superiors or with men of high birth.

Notes: (a). If such Grahas are in their Svarāśis, the traveller meets with his people; and if the Grahas are in their Śatrurāśis, the traveller meets with his enemies.

19.3. If Udayarāśi, Āruṛharāśi or the 10th House are Ojarāśis, and if they are dṛṣṭied by Ojagrahas, the traveller meets with men **(2)** if such Houses are Yugmarāśis and if they are dṛṣṭied by Yugmagrahas, the traveller meets with women. **(3)** The object of the travel shall be determined from the Rāśis and Houses mentioned above and from the Grahas aspecting them.

DIRECTION OF TRAVEL:

19.4. If Udayarāśi is a Cararāśi, or if the Udaya Graha is a Cara Graha or if the Lord of Udayarāśi (or the Lord of Āruṛharāśi or 10th House) occupy a Cararāśi, the direction taken by the traveller is that of such powerful Rāśi or Graha.

TRAVEL OR NO TRAVEL:

19.5. If Udayarāśi, Āruṛharāśi or the 10th House is a Cararāśi and if such Rāśi is occupied (or dṛṣṭied) by Candra, Budha, Bṛhaspati or Śukra, there is travel; if such Rāśi is a Dvisvarāśi, and if Krūras then occupy it the traveller returns after proceeding halfway.

19.6. If at Praśna, Udayarāśi, Āruṛharāśi or the 10th House is a Sthirarāśi and if such Rāśi is occupied (or dṛṣṭied) by Sūrya, Maṅgala or Śani (or Rāhu), there is no travel and a journey in a particular direction, though already commenced, is given up.

CONDITION OF TRAVELLER:

19.7. If at Praśna, Udayarāśi is a Śīrṣodaya Rāśi, the traveller is happy in his place (a); and if such Rāśi is a Pṛṣṭodaya Rāśi, he is happy in the place to which he travels (b).

Notes: (a). And miserable in the place to which he travels. (b). And miserable in his place. If the concerned Rāśi is Ubhayodaya, the traveller is both happy and miserable in both places.

NEWS OF RETURN OF TRAVELLER:

19.8. If the 2nd or 3rd House from Udayarāśi/Āruṛharāśi/10th House from Udayarāśi is a Manuṣya Rāśi and if such Rāśi is occupied by Manuṣya Grahas (a), there is received a written or verbal message before the return of the traveller relating to such return.

Notes: (a). If such House is occupied by other than Manuṣya Grahas, such a message is received either after the traveller's return or after the expected time.

IMMEDIATE RETURN OF TRAVELLER:

19.9. If the 1st, 2nd, 3rd and 10th are occupied by Candra, Budha, Bṛhaspati and Śukra, the traveller immediately returns.

HEALTH OF THE TRAVELLER:

19.10. If the 5th or 6th House from Udayarāśi/Āruṛharāśi/10th House from Udayarāśi is occupied by Saumyas, the traveller returns healthy. Still, if Krūras occupy such Houses, the traveller returns ill.

IMMEDIATE OR SLOW RETURN OF TRAVELLER.

19.11. If at Praśna, Candra occupies Vṛṣabha, Karka, Siṅha or Dhanu; the traveller returns immediately. If Candra and Bṛhaspati occupy the 4th House, the traveller returns that day with a young woman.

Notes: If Candra occupies any of the remaining Rāśis, the traveller will return after a time.

TIME OF TRAVEL AND RETURN:

19.12. If the 10th House is occupied by Candra, Budha, Bṛhaspati or Śukra, there is travel after the period assigned to the Grahas occupying the 10th House; if the 7th House is occupied by Candra, Budha, Bṛhaspati or Śukra, the traveller returns after the period assigned to the Grahas occupying the 7th House.

Notes: For Graha periods, refer to śloka 1.77.

ILL HEALTH OF THE TRAVELLER:

19.13. If at Praśna, Saumyas occupy the 10th House, and if such House be at the same time their Śatru/Nīca Rāśi, there is both success of object and suffering from diseases and wounds. But if Krūras occupy the 10th House, the traveller will fail in his object; and if such House be at the same time as their Śatru/Nīca Rāśi, there is also suffering from diseases and wounds.

IMPORTANCE OF THE 10TH HOUSE:

19.14. There will be a success if Saumyas occupy the 10th and other Houses mentioned in the various yogas above. Generally, all travel-related matters should be determined from the 10th House and the Grahas occupying it.

NON-RETURN AND SLOW RETURN OF TRAVELLER:

19.15. If the 1st and 2nd from Udayarāśi were occupied by Krūras, the traveller would have lost his wealth and could not return because of his poverty. If Krūras occupies the 4th House, he suffers from his enemies and returns after a while.

24.2.20
ADHYĀYA 20:
ON THE APPEARANCE OF FRESHES IN THE RIVER

The Praśna about water, rain etc., employs the classification of Rāśis and Grahas into Sajala and Nirjala designations. Sajala means endowed with water, and Nirjala is without water. Nirjala also means Śuṣka (dry). According to Phalita Mārtaṇḍa 2.13, Candra and Śukra are the Sajala Grahas. Śani, Sūrya and Maṅgala are the Śuṣka Graha. Budha and Bṛhaspati's characteristics depend on the Rāśis occupied by them. If they occupy a Sajala Rāśi, they are Sajala, and in Śuṣka Rāśi, they are Śuṣka.

The designations are also used to determine the size of someone's physical body, which is known from the influence of the Jalatattva on the Lagna, Navāñśa Lagna, and their lords are judged. In this regard, the Grahas and Rāśis are classified as Sajala, Nirjala, Ardhajala and Pādajala. Sajala is also called Purṇajala, means one that is endowed with 100% water; Nirjala is also known as Śuṣka and means dry, i.e., devoid of water (0% water); whereas the Ardhajala means one that is partly endowed with water.

Among the Rāśis, **Karka, Makara and Mīna** are **Sajala** Rāśis; **Mithuna, Siṅha and Kanyā** are **Nirjala** Rāśis; **Vṛṣabha, Dhanu and Kumbha** are **Ardhajala** Rāśis; and, **Meṣa, Tulā are Vṛścika** are Pādajala Rāśis. Notice that Vṛścika is only Pādajala, even though it is a Jalatattva Rāśi. Furthermore, Makara is a Pṛthvītattva Rāśi, but it is Sajala because a swamp or a shallow river symbolizes it. The Ardhajala Rāśis has 50% water, and Pādajala Rāśis, 25% water. The principle that is used in the determination of body type, i.e., whether someone is plump or not, the same principle is used in the determination of the amount of rain.

There is another classification: the Rāśis are classified into five Groups. They are classified into four groups, viz, **(1) Purṇajala:** Karka/Mīna, **(2)**

Tripādajala: Makara/Kumbha, **(3) Ardhajala:** Tulā, and **(4) Pādajala:** Vṛṣabha/Vṛścika, and **(5) Nirjala:** Mithuna/Siṅha/Kanyā. From the Rāśi standpoint, the %age of water in the Rāśis are **(1) Meṣa** 25%, **(2) Vṛṣabha** 25%, **(3) Mithuna** 0%, **(4) Karka** 100%, **(5) Siṅha** 0%, **(6) Kanyā** 0%, **(7) Tulā*** 50%, **(8) Vṛścika** 25%, **(9) Dhanu*** 0%, **(10) Makara*** 75%, **(11) Kumbha*** 75%, **(12) Mīna** 100%.

There are some differences in opinion about Makara, Dhanu, Tulā and Kumbha. According to some scholars, Dhanu is 50% water, whereas according to others, it is 0%. Likewise, some believe that Makara is 100%, whereas others believe it to be 75%. Tulā, according to some, is 50%, whereas according to others is 25%. According to some, Kumbha is 75%, and according to others, it is 50%. Generally, Karka, Mīna, Makara and Kumbha are considered Sajala Rāśis to judge well, water-streams and rain.

FRESHES[3] IN THE RIVER:

20.1. If the Astarāśi from Udayarāśi is a Sajala Rāśi, freshes soon appear in the river (a); if Sajala Grahas occupy such Astarāśi, the flood is excessive and overflows the banks (b). If Krūras occupy such Astarāśi, the freshes appear after a time.

Notes: (a) If such Astarāśi is other than a Sajala Rāśi, freshes do not appear. (b) If such Grahas are other than Sajala Grahas, the flood is moderate. Again, if Āruṛharāśi is powerful, the river is one flowing from West to East; and if Chatrarāśi is powerful, the river is one flowing from East to West.

QUANTITY OF FRESHES:

20.2. If the (Sajala) Astarāśi is either Karka or Mīna, there is a full flood in the river; if such Rāśi is either Makara or Kumbha, the river is three-fourths full; if such Rāśi is Tulā, the river is half-full; and if it is either Vṛṣabha or Vṛścika, the river is one-fourth full.

24.2.21
ADHYĀYA 21:
ON RAIN

RAIN OR NO RAIN:

21.1. If Udayarāśi is a Sajala Rāśi or if it is occupied or dṛṣṭied by Sajala Grahas, there is rain; but if Udayarāśi is not a Sajala Rāśi or if it is occupied or dṛṣṭied by other than Sajala Grahas, there is no rain.

---

[3] Freshes are short-duration flow events that submerge the lower parts of the river channel. They are important for plants that grow low on the banks and provide opportunities for fish and other animals to move more easily along the river. High flows are larger and last longer than freshes.

QUANTITY OF RAIN:

21.2. If Udayarāśi is occupied or dṛṣṭied by **Candra or Śukra**, there is abundant rain; but if such Rāśi is occupied or dṛṣṭied by **Budha or Bṛhaspati,** there is slight rain. A similar remark applies to Udayarāśi itself.

Notes: (a) If Udayarāśi is either Karka, Makara, Kumbha or Mīna, there is abundant rain; and if such Rāśi be either Vṛṣabha, Tulā or Vṛścika, there is slight rain. If Udayarāśi is a Nirjala Rāśi, i.e., Mithuna, Kanyā and Siṅha, there is no rain. Candra and Śukra are Purṇajala Grahas, whereas Budha and Bṛhaspati are Pādajala Grahas. Budha and Bṛhaspati in Purṇajala Rāśis become Purṇajala Grahas.

HEAVY RAIN:

21.3. If Chatrarāśi is Pṛṣṭodayi, or if Āruṛharāśi is dṛṣṭied by a Pṛṣṭodayi Graha, or if it is occupied by the Graha Pariveṣa, Sukṣma, or Indradhanuṣa, there is heavy rain.

TIME OF RAINFALL:

21.4. If the Grahas (Candra, Budha, Bṛhaspati or Śukra) is in their Svakṣetra, Mitrarāśi or Uccarāśi or if they are the lords of the Kendras (or Trikoṇas), there is immediate rain[4]. If Śukra occupies the 4th House, there is rain on the day of Praśna; if Budha (or Bṛhaspati) occupies the 2nd House, there is rain within two days; and if he occupies the 3rd House, there is rain within three days.

INDICATIONS OF RAIN:

21.5. If Sūrya, Maṅgala, Śani or Rāhu occupies Udayarāśi (a), there is no rain; but if Udayarāśi so occupied be a Sajala Rāśi, cold and moist winds will blow; and if a Sajala Graha accompanies such Grahas there is a slight drizzle.

Notes: (a). Or aspect it, according to the commentator.

24.2.22
ADHYĀYA 22:
ON THE PRICE OF COMMODITIES

FLUCTUATIONS IN THE PRICE:

22.1. (1) If Udayarāśi and the 10th House are dṛṣṭied by Grahas in their Uccarāśis, the price of commodities fall; (2) if such Houses are dṛṣṭied by Grahas in their Śatru/Nīca Rāśi, the price rise; (3) and if such House is dṛṣṭied by Grahas in their Mitra or Svakṣetra Rāśis, the price neither rises nor falls.

---

[4] But if the Grahas are in their Śatru/Nīca Rāśi, or if they be lords of the 6tb, 8th or 12th House there is rain after a time

22.2. (4) If Saumyas occupy Udayarāśi and the 10th House, the price of commodities falls; (5) if the Grahas occupy the 7th House, the price rises. (6) Again, if Krūras occupy Udayarāśi and the 10th House and be at the same time in their Śatru/Nīca Rāśi, the price rise (a).

Notes: If the Krūras, occupying Udayarāśi and the 10th House in their Svakṣetra, Mitrarāśi or Uccarāśis at the same time, the price neither rises nor falls. Likewise, if the Saumyas occupying Udayarāśi and the 10th House is in their Śatru/Nīca Rāśi, then also the price neither rises nor falls. The commodities referred to are those of the respective Grahas as per 3.11-12.

24.2.23
ADHYĀYA 23:
ON THE RETURN OR SHIPS

PREDICTION OF RETURN:

23.1. If Udayarāśi or Āruṛharāśi (a) is a Sajala Rāśi and if such Rāśi is occupied by Candra, Bṛhaspati or Śukra (Sajala Grahas), the return of a ship may be predicted as follows: If such Sajala Rāśi is a Sthira or Dvisva Rāśi, the ship returns direct; but if such Rāśi is a Cararāśi, the ship returns after stopping on its way or having been away from its course.

Notes: (a) Or the 3rd, 5th or 9th House, according to other writers. It follows from the text that if Udayarāśi or Āruṛharāśi are other than a Sajala Rāśi, and if those besides the Sajala Grahas occupy such Rāśi, it should be predicted that the ship which has gone out on a voyage does not return.

FATE OF THE SHIP:

23.2. (1) If Udayarāśi or Āruṛharāśi is occupied by Krūras (in their Sva/Ucca/Mitra Rāśis), the ship is driven away from its course on a foreign shore; but **(2)** if the Krūras are at the same time in their Śatrurāśis, the ship never returns; **(3)** and if the Krūras are in their depression Rāśis, the vessel is wrecked and return disabled (for sinking, refer to the next śloka).

23.3. (4) If either Udayarāśi or Āruṛharāśi is occupied by one of the invisible Grahas, the vessel may be declared to have sank. **(5)** But, If at Praśna, one of such Grahas is visible in the sky, the ship loses its way and returns after a time.

Notes: The invisible Grahas are Pariveṣa, Indradhanuṣa and the like, per śloka 1.84. The invisible Grahas are visible in the sky in the form of portents such as halo, rainbow etc.

23.4. (6) If Āruṛharāśi and Chatrarāśi be both Cararāśis, the ship is driven away from its course and does not return; **(7)** but if the 3rd House from either Rāśi is occupied by Śukra, the ship, though driven away from its course, return soon.

24.2.24
ADHYĀYA 24:
ON CEṢṬĀ

MATTERS COVERED:

24.1. In this chapter, **(1)** the persons (before the Daivajña) shall be treated as Grahas, **(2)** their words as Āruṛha and **(3)** Udayarāśi, their senses as the Rāśis of Zodiac and their acts as the Mitrarāśi, Svakṣetra, exaltation, Śatru/Nīca places of the Grahas.

Notes: By a due interpretation of the words and acts of the persons around as indicated in this chapter, a Daivajña can make all predictions which can be made by the help of the Grahas, the Rāśis of Zodiac, Āruṛharāśi, Udayarāśi, and the Mitrarāśi, the Svakṣetra, the Uccarāśi, the Śatrurāśi and Nīcarāśi of the Grahas as indicated in the preceding chapters. Varāhamihira, in chapter 51 of the Bṛhatsamhitā, says that "a Daivajña must examine and interpretation of casual words, gestures, and the like. Note down indications connected with the dik (direction), Sthāna (place) and Ahrita (anything carried), as well as the Ceṣṭā (motion of the body) of the Pṛcchaka or of any other person and time. For the all-knowing, universal intelligence pervading all Cara and Sthira objects indicates coming events by motions and casual words to devout souls who have faith in Him."

THE HISTORY OF THE SCIENCE:

24.2, The science of Ceṣṭā originally proceeded from Brihaspati, the Daivajña of the Devas in the court of Indra and is, therefore, an important one. Though I cannot treat it fully, I shall try to say what I have learned from books and teachers.

PREDICTION OF CASTE:

24.3. When the caste of a person is required in a Praśna, **(1)** if the part of body touched be from the top of the head to the neck, the person is a Brāhmaṇa; **(2)** if it is from below the neck to the navel, the person is a Kṣatriya; **(3)** if it is from below the navel to the knees, the person is a Vaiśya; **(4)** if it is from below the knees to the ankles, the person is a Śudra; and **(5)** if it is the feet or hair, the person is a Caṇḍāla or a Mlecchā.

COLOUR:

24.4. When colour is required in a Praśna of any sort, if the part scratched or touched (spontaneously and naturally) **(1)** is the leg or the privities, the colour is green (Budha); **(2)** if it is the hands or the face, the colour is red (Maṅgala); **(3)** if it is the hair or the belly, the colour is black (Śani); **(4)** if it is the hip, the colour is that of gold (Bṛhaspati/Sūrya); and if it is any other organ, the colour is white (Candra/Śukra).

TIME:

24.5-6. When the number of years, months, days or Ghaṭis are required in a Praśna, **(1)** if the part touched is the head, the number is 100 (Meṣa); **(2)** if it is the face, the number is 90 (Vṛṣabha); **(3)** if it is the neck, shoulders or the breast, the number is 80 (Mithuna/Karka); **(4)** if it is the belly, the number is 70 (Siṁha); **(5)** if it is the navel or the hip, the number is 60 (Kanyā); **(6)** if it is from below the hip to the arms, the number is 50 (Tulā/Vṛścika); **(7)** if it is the thigh, the number is 40 (Dhanu); **(8)** if it is the knees, the number is 30 (Makara); **(9)** and if it is from below the knees to the soles of the feet, the number is 10 (Kumbha/Mīna).

Notes: The other numbers shall be determined by proportion.

DHĀTU, MŪLA, OR JĪVA:

24.7. If at Praśna, **(1)** the arm be stretched out with anything taken up in hand, Dhātu is indicated; **(2)** if it is kept bent up, Mūla is indicated; **(3)** if it is neither stretched out nor bent up, Jīva is indicated. Again, if the Praśna begins with a word whose **(4)** first letter is a, ā, ai, au, Dhātu is indicated; **(5)** if such letter is i, ī, e, Mūla is indicated; **(6)** if it is u, ū, o, Jīva is indicated.

Notes: Words beginning with vowel consonants follow the rule of the vowels. Of the two rules to determine the Dhātu, Mūla and Jīva of the object of Praśna, the first refers to Muṣṭi alone, and the 2nd to Naṣṭa, Muṣṭi and Cintā.

CERTAIN PREDICTIONS:

24.8. (1) If the part touched is the forehead, Patta (crown plate) and the like are meant; **(2)** if it is the ears, ear-rings, ear-pendants, and the like are meant; **(3)** if it is the teeth, eatables are meant; **(4)** if it is the neck, the marriage Tali (corresponding to the marriage ring) and sometimes marriage itself is meant; **(5)** if it is the hand, then bracelets and the like are meant; **(6)** if it is the belly, pregnancy and the like are meant; **(7)** and if it is the thighs then clothes and the like are meant.

24.9. (8) If the part touched is the genital organ, the Praśna refers to marriage connections; **(9)** if it is the throat, the Praśna refers to learning; **(10)** if it is the nose, the Praśna refers to marriage, learning and rights in general; **(11)** if it is the feet, the Praśna refers to anger or quarrel; **(12)** and if the substance touched is the lamp or flower, the Praśna refers to a business of importance.

GOOD AND EVIL IN GENERAL:

24.10. If the Pṛcchaka is in the direction of the Śubha (Āruṛha) Grahas, (a) there is success and prosperity; if he is in the direction of the Krūra (Āruṛha) Grahas there is failure and misery. Again, if the Saumyas occupy Śatru/Nīca Rāśi, they bring evil (b); and if the Krūras are in their Svakṣetra, friendly or Uccarāśis, they bring success (e).

Notes: (a) Refer śloka 1.88. (b) There is success at first and failure immediately. (c) There is a failure at first and success after that. It also follows that if Saumyas are in their Svakṣetra, friendly or Uccarāśis, there is continued success and prosperity, and that if Krūras are in their Śatru/Nīca Rāśi, there is continued failure and misery.

SEATING POSITION:

24.11. (1) If the Pṛcchaka takes his seat on the right side of the Daivajña, there is success; **(2)** if he takes his seat on the left side, there is failure. **(3)** Again, there is a failure if the Pṛcchaka sits too close to the Daivajña. **(4)** If the Pṛcchaka is near, he succeeds, **(5)** and fails if he is too far.

24.12. (1) If the Pṛcchaka touches the right side of his head, the right brow, the right eye or the right shoulder, or if he touches the ears, the month, the nipples, the belly, or the right leg, he succeeds in his object; **(2)** and if be touch any other part of his body he fails.

24.13. (1) If the Pṛcchaka looks straight in the face, there is an immediate success; **(2)** if he looks down, there is success after a time; **(3)** and if he looks up, he fails in his object. **(4)** Again, if the Pṛcchaka looks leaning on anything, there is success if the attempt is in a good cause and failure if the attempt is in a bad cause.

24.14. (1) If the Pṛcchaka be found tying his cloth round his neck, there is success or acquisition of wealth; **(2)** if he is found to tie it round his waist or legs, there is loss. Again, **(1)** if the Pṛcchaka be seated on a high ground, there is a success; and **(2)** if he is found to come down from a high ground, there is a failure. Also, **(3)** if the Pṛcchaka be found to slip or fall from high ground, there is a failure.

24.15. (1) If a person be found to enlarge anything at the time of Praśna, there is wealth and enjoyment; if this is seen at the time of marriage, sexual union, or meals eaten by a person, there is a great success. **(2)** If, on the other hand, a person is seen to reduce, break, or make holes in any substance, there is loss and failure.

24.16. (1) If the Pṛcchaka be found to look vacantly in space or to rub his hands or bend down and hold the feet of the Daivajña, or remain long with his hands united, there is no recovery of stolen property, no birth of a child and there is also loss of property.

24.17. (2) If the Pṛcchaka be found to be throwing pebbles at the time or to look at a thing obliquely, or to speak with a hoarse throat, or to loosen his hairs, or to crack his finger joints, or draw lines on the ground with his toes, he has already lost the object of his Praśna.

24.18. (3) If cattle or men are found to pass between the Pṛcchaka and the Daivajña at the time of Praśna, or if a weight of wood he carried at the time or if the Pṛcchaka be found to speak harsh language at the time, or if he is found to question with his head covered, he will fail in his object.

24.19. (4) If at Praśna, a sword, a knife, a bow, and the like are found brought, or if a wild or poisonous plant is brought in at the time, or if cotton or fire are dropped on the ground, or if the Daivajña is questioned when he is in an angry mood, there is loss and failure.

24.20. If at Praśna, the Pṛcchaka or any of the persons present is found to blow through the nose, to contract the face, to sigh, to stammer, or to yawn, there is no recovery from illness; no recovery of stolen property and there is loss of even the property on hand.

24.21. If at Praśna, the left knee is touched, the Pṛcchaka fails in his object; there is no acquisition of property, no recovery of stolen property, and there is loss of object gained; there is also an increase of illness and no recovery from it.

24.22. If at Praśna, the left side of the waist or the left buttock is touched, married life, marriage, and enjoyment suffer, or the Pṛcchaka loses his wife. But no such loss occurs if the right side of the head, breast, or right leg is touched.

RECOVERY OF LOST ARTICLES:

24.23. If at Praśna, a person is found to **(1)** draw a circle on the ground or **(2)** touch his face, **(3)** month, **(4)** shoulders or **(5)** belly, there is a recovery of lost articles, but if he touches the **(1)** back of the neck, **(2)** the armpits, **(3)** the back, **(4)** the waist, **(5)** the buttock or **(6)** the legs, there is no recovery of lost articles.

RECOVERY FROM ILLNESS:

24.24. If the Praśna is in such terms as **(1)**, what a sad sight! O, it is insufferable! What karma is this? Will he move about again! and the like? There is no recovery from illness.

Notes: If, on the other hand, the Praśna begin in such terms as; **(2)** I hope there is recovery; I suppose he is all right in a day or two, and the like, there is recovery from illness. Therefore, the tone of asking the Praśna is significant. The outcome is negative if the Praśna is laden with hopelessness and destitution (denoted by Śani). The outcome is positive if the Praśna is full of hope and optimism (denoted by Bṛhaspati).

DEATH:

24.25. When the Praśna refers to death, if there appear, at the time of Praśna, **(1)** a snake charmer (Rāhu), **(2)** a lame man (Śani), **(3)** shameless persons (Śani/Maṅgala), **(4)** a grieving person (Śani), **(5)** persons carrying weapons (Maṅgala), **(6)** ascetics (Śani/Maṅgala), **(7)** widows (Rāhu), **(8)** or one's enemies (Maṅgala), there is certain death.

Notes: The omens about Krūras, such as Rāhu, Śani and Maṅgala, indicate death.

24.26. If at Praśna, a person be found **(1)** to twist a piece of yarn or make it into a string or **(2)** to hold his legs with his hands, or **(3)** to rub his eyes or to take up a bundle of sticks, or wood on the head, or **(4)** to question while lying down, or **(5)** to question and then fall asleep, there is death.

Notes: All these omens are related to the effects of Śani. For instance, the clothes mill is denoted by Śani. Śani denotes legs held by someone with his hands, which Maṅgala denotes.

24.27. **(1)** If the Praśna be put while the Pṛcchaka is rubbing oil on his body, or **(2)** cleaning his teeth, **(3)** or getting shaved, **(4)** or with his eyes closed, **(4)** or shutting the doors at the time, **(5)** or if a cow be found to run, or a herd of cattle be found to disperse, there is death.

Notes: These omens are related to the effects of Krūras. For instance, rubbing oil is related to Śani; cleaning teeth is Śani; shaving is Śani etc.

RĀJAYOGA:

24.28. If at Praśna, **(1)** lines are drawn on the ground with powdered rice or the like substance, **(2)** or an umbrella is spread over a person, **(2)** or the hairs be tied up, **(3)** or flower wreaths worn, the Pṛcchaka or the person referred to in the Praśna becomes a king.

Notes: The person may become an authority, such as the governor of a province or the chief of a town or village.

Notes: These omens relate to Saumyas, mainly Śukra.

ACQUISITION OF WEALTH:

24.29. If at Praśna, **(1)** the ground is tilled, **(2)** or pictures are drawn or held in hand, **(3)** or if the Pṛcchaka is in a cheerful mood of mind, **(4)** or if he is found to embrace anything, **(5)** or speak the sweet language, there is an acquisition of wealth.

Notes: These omens relate to Saumyas, mainly Candra.

UNDER-CURRENTS:

24.30. If at Praśna, **(1)** there appears milk, butter, **(2)** a Brāhmaṇa, **(3)** a horse, an ox, a buffalo, **(4)** a pregnant cow, a pregnant woman, **(5)** a full water pot, **(6)** or a young woman in her menses, there is an abundant supply of water.

Notes: These omens relate to Saumyas, mainly Candra and Bṛhaspati. These also relate to watery substances, which flows, or articles in which water or watery substance is kept. If there is a pitcher that is full of water, that means there shall be an abundant water supply. If the pitcher is half full, then the water is half.

PEACE OR NO PEACE:

24.31. If at Praśna, **(1)** two substances be found joined together, there is peace; **(2)** if one of several united substances is separated from the rest, there is no peace. Again, **(3)** if torn or broken substances are re-united, there is peace; (2) if a substance is torn or split up at the time, there is no peace.

Notes: Peace is related to Ākāśatattva, which binds. The splitting or breaking is done by either Agnitattva or Vāyuttatva, which does not indicate peace. Splitting of breaking, of the impact of Agnitattva, indicates conflict instead.

TRAVEL OR NO TRAVEL:

24.32. If at Praśna, there appear **(1)** a bull, **(2)** a monkey, **(3)** a man on horseback or **(4)** girls or men of liberal gift, **(5)** or a king, **(6)** or a traveller, there is travel.

24.33. If at Praśna, there appear men **(1)** suffering from grief or **(2)** from irremediable diseases, **(3)** or haughty men or a murderer, **(4)** an injured man, **(5)** an idler, **(6)** or a quarrelsome man, there is no travel.

IMMEDIATE RAIN:

24.34. When the Praśna is about rain, **(1)** if a person be found to spit or throw out saliva from the mouth, **(2)** or if saliva be found to run out at the month corner, **(3)** or if a person be found to wink his eyes or **(4)** lower his eyelid **(5)** or shed tears, there is immediate rain.

24.3 THE DISCOURSE

This is a hypothetical discourse between Ācārya Svarajit and his disciples Jayanta, Kailaśa and Sunidhi on Praśna. It took place at Vaidyanātha Dhāma at Deoghar in Śravaṇa Māsa.

Ācārya: We are in such a sacred place. Let us discuss something important.

Jayanta: Guruji, we look forward to discussing the Praśnaśāstra of the Jain Monks.

Ācārya: The Jain Ācāryas made significant contributions to Jyotiṣa, including Praśnaśāstra. Jinendramāla is a great example, and the other one is Jñānapradīpikā.

Jayanta: Shall we explain about Jñānapradīpikā? You have already covered the principles of Jinendramāla. So, discussing the principles from another great Praśna text will be helpful.

Ācārya: Absolutely! However, why not start our discussion with this sacred place?

Kailāśa: Guruji, kindly tell us about the Mahima of the Vaidyanātha Dhāma.

Ācārya: The Baba Vaidyanātha Dhāma is dedicated to Śrī Śiva. It is located in Deoghar, in the Santhal Parganas division of Jharkhand. It is one of the twelve Jyotirlingas and is considered the most revered of Śiva Mandirs.

The temple complex comprises the central Mandir of Baba Vaidyanath, housing the revered Jyotirlinga and 21 other temples.

According to Paurāṇic legends, Rākṣasa Rāja Śrī Rāvaṇa worshipped Śrī Śiva at this location to gain divine blessings, which he used to cause chaos and destruction in the world. Śrī Rāvaṇa offered his ten heads as a symbol of sacrifice to Śrī Śiva. Pleased with this gesture, Śrī Śiva recovered Rāvaṇa from his injuries. As Śrī Śiva acted as a doctor, he is also called Vaidya ("doctor"). The temple is named after this aspect of Śrī Śiva.

According to Paurāṇic legends, Śrī Rāvaṇa was performing penance in the Himalayan region to appease Śrī Śiva. He offered nine of his heads as an offering to Śrī Śiva. As he was to sacrifice his tenth head, Śrī Śiva appeared before him and expressed satisfaction with the offering; then, Śrī Śiva asked what boon he desired. Ravana asked to take the "Kamna Liṅga" to the island of Lanka and expressed his desire to take Śrī Śiva from Kailaśa to Śrī Lanka.

Lord Shiva agreed to Śrī Rāvaṇa's request but with a condition. He said that if the Liṅgam was placed en route, it would become the permanent abode of the Devatā and could never be moved.

Celestial Devatās became worried upon hearing that Śrī Śiva had departed from his abode on Kailaśa Parvata. They sought a resolution from Śrī Viṣṇu. Then, Śrī Viṣṇu asked Śrī Varuṇa, the Devatā of the waters, to enter Śrī Rāvaṇa 's stomach through ācamana, a ritual which involves sipping water from the palm of one's hand. As a consequence of performing ācamana, Śrī Rāvaṇa departed for Śrī Lanka with the lingam and felt the need to urinate in the vicinity of Deoghar.

The story goes that Śrī Viṣṇu took the form of a cowherd named Baiju. While Rāvaṇa was off to urinate, he gave a Liṅgam to this cowherd. Baiju positioned the Liṅgam on the ground. Upon Ravana's return, he attempted to displace the Liṅgam, but he was unsuccessful in his endeavour. He became upset and proceeded to press his thumb onto the Liṅgam before departing. Śrī Brahmā, Śrī Viṣṇu, and other Devatās then worshiped the Śivaliṅgam. Since then, Śrī Mahādeva has taken up residence in Deoghar as the embodiment of the Kamna Liṅga.

Kailāśa: Dhanyavād Guruji, for the enlightening legend of Śrī Śiva.

Jayanta: Guruji, we are in Śravaṇa Māsa now. Kindly tell us the glory of this Māsa.

Ācārya: Do you know when this Māsa starts?

Jayanta: Guruji, kindly elaborate on the commencement of this Māsa.

Ācārya: The commencement depends on the calendar used. We have three calendars in Bhāratavarṣa, (1) Saura, (2) Candra Amānta and (3) Candra Śuklānta. Candra Śuklānta is also called Candra Pūrṇimānta, and Candra Amānta is called Candra Amāvasyānta.

Candra Amānta and Śuklānta are the Candra calendars based on tithis or synodic months of Candra. The Amānta calendar is called Mukyamāna (main reckoning), and Pūrṇimānta is called Gauṇamāna (subsidiary reckoning).

Jayanta: Why do we have three calendars?

Ācārya: These three calendars are necessary to keep track of time using Sūrya and Sūrya-Candra. Different communities follow them. Bengalis, Punjabis, Odiyas, Tamilians, Malayalis, and others follow Saura. The Amānta calendar is followed mostly in the south, and the Śuklānta one is followed mostly in the north.

The Saura Māsas correspond to the 12 Rāśis.

Mīna - Caitra, Meṣa - Vaiśākha, Vṛṣabha - Jyeṣṭhā, Mithuna - Āṣāṛhā, Karka - Śravaṇa, Siṅha - Bhadrā, Kanyā - Aśvina, Tulā - Kārtika, Vṛścika - Mārgaśīrṣa, Dhanu - Pauṣa, Makara - Maghā, Kumbha - Phālguna.

Jayanta: I suppose the Māsa commences with Sūrya's entry into the Rāśi. Isn't it?

Ācārya: That is right.

Jayanta: How about the Candra Māsa?

Ācārya: The Amānta Māsa commences with the Amāvasyā in the associated Rāśi.

Jayanta: Can you elaborate?

Ācārya: Suppose we know that Caitra Māsa commences with Mīna Rāśi. This means Amānta Caitra commences with Amāvasyā in Mīna. This also gives rise to Caitra Śukla Pratipada. Every month commences with Śukla Pratipada. Therefore after Caitra Śukla Pratipada, we have Vaiśākha Śukla Pratipada, Jyeṣṭhā Śukla Pratipada, corresponding to Amāvasyā in Meṣa, Vṛṣabha etc.

Jayanta: How about the Pūrṇimānta Māsa?

Ācārya: The Pūrṇimānta Māsa a Pakṣa before the commencement of the Amānta Māsa. Suppose Caitra Amānta commenced on March 21, 2023 (Śukla Pratipada). Then Pūrṇimānta would commence on March 7, 2023, coinciding with Kṛṣṇa Pratipada and the mid of the previous month.

Jayanta: This means that the order of precedence for the commencement of a Māsa is Saura → Pūrṇimānta → Amānta.

Ācārya: It is not always the case. We should first determine the Amānta based Saura → Amānta. This is step 1. In step 2, we identify Pūrṇimānta, which is Amānta – 1 Pakṣa.

Let us consider Caitra Māsa of 2023.

Saura = March 15

Amānta = March 21

Pūrṇimānta = March 7

Jayanta: It is crystal clear now, Guruji!

Ācārya: Now that you know that, you can identify when the Śravaṇa Māsa commences in different regions. But you need to remember that Śravaṇa = Karka Rāśi.

Jayanta: Let me look up the dates

Saura = July 17: Sūrya moved into Karka 0°

Amānta = July 18: S.Pratipada (S1) in Karka

Pūrṇimānta = July 3: K.Pratipada (K1) before Amānta Śravaṇa

Kailāśa: Guruji, why was the Kāvaḍa Yātrā held from 4-15 July? Is this because the Pūrṇimānta Śravaṇa Māsa commenced on July 3?

Ācārya: That is indeed the case. The Kāvaḍa Yātrā starts from Pūrṇimānta Śravaṇa Kṛṣṇa Pratipada, and therefore, it started from 4 to 15 July.

Jayanta: Guruji, a day (Ahorātra) commences with Sūryodaya; how do we identify the first day or month and year?

Ācārya: For that, you must understand the Udaya (rising) of Tithi, Nakṣatra, Karaṇa and Yoga.

Jayanta: What is the Udaya of the mentioned Pañcāṅga elements?

Ācārya: Udaya means Sūrya rising on the Eastern Horizon, or the Lagna coinciding with Sūrya. That causes the Udaya of the five Pañcāṅga elements for the Ahorātra. This is a fundamental principle of Jyotiṣa and reckoning time.

Jayanta: Does this mean we must identify the day Pratipada rises at Sūryodaya to commence the month?

Ācārya: Yes, the same principle is used for the commencement of a Dina, Māsa and Varṣa. The Horā is also computed based on Sūryodaya. The Horā, Dina, Māsa and Varṣa form a continuous time-element aggregation.

Jayanta: Now I understand. I suppose we use Ujjain for India time. Isn't it?

Ācārya: The Sūryodaya at different places are different. We must consider the Udaya in the country's capital for the entire country. For the world, we should consider Ujjain, the ancient prime meridian.

Sunidhi: Guruji, why must we do that?

Ācārya: Suppose we wish to know when Śravaṇa Māsa commenced for the whole world; we need to find the centre (meridian) which applies to the whole world. It is GMT (Greenwich Meridian); however, the True Meridian of the world is Ujjain, the seat of Mahākāleśvara (time personified).

Sunidhi: Thank you for explaining this, Guruji!

Jayanta: I suppose, for Bhāratavarṣa, we should use New Delhi. Right?

Ācārya: Yes, that is right.

Jayanta: On July 3, Sūryodaya was at 5:27:46. The Pañcāṅga at that moment was Somavāra, Mūla Nakṣatra, Pūrṇimā Tithi, Viṣṭi Karaṇa, Brahmā Yoga.

Ācārya: You notice that Pūrṇimā prevailed on July 3, and therefore, it was a Pūrṇimā day.

Jayanta: Alright, if I check July 4, with Sūryodaya at the same time, the Pañcāṅga elements were Maṅgalavāra, Pūrvāṣāṛhā, Kṛṣṇa Pratipada, Kaulava Karaṇa and Indra Yoga.

Ācārya: Now, you see that July 4 was a Kṛṣṇa Pratipada, and therefore, the Pūrṇimānta Śravaṇa began on that day. That is why the Kāvaḍa Yātrā was from July 4 to July 15, which coincided with K13 (Kṛṣṇa Trayodaśī).

Jayanta: Guruji, is this the basis for selecting the day for festivals like Janmāṣṭami, Gaṇeśa Chaturthi etc?

Ācārya: Yes, that is the basis. However, there are some exceptions to the rule.

Some festivals are Prātaḥ Vyāpini, some are Madhyānha Vyāpani, Sandhyā Vyāpani and Madhyarātri Vyāpini. In that case, the Tithi prevailing during the Madhyānha (Noon), Sāyaṁ Sandhyā (evening twilight), and Madhyarātri (midnight) is seen.

Jayanta: Can you give some examples?

Ācārya: Let us consider Mahā Śivarātri. It is celebrated on ***Amānta Phālguna Kṛṣṇa Caturdaśī***. Since it is Madhyarātri Vyāpini Pujā, the Caturdaśī must prevail at midnight. Therefore, if it rises at Sūryodaya and ends before

Madhyarātri, that day is not celebrated. But instead, it is celebrated the previous day when the Tithi prevails at Madhyarātri.

Jayanta: Dhanyavād, Guruji!

Sunidhi: Guruji, how about Kālī Pujā?

Ācārya: Even Kālī Pujā is Madhyarātri Vyāpini. It occurs on ***Amānta Aśvina Amāvasyā***. In 2023, it will occur during the midnight of Nov 12, 2023, since the Tithis starts at 14:45 and ends at 14:57 (Nov 13).

Sunidhi: Thank you for clarifying.

Ācārya: For other Pujas, most of them are Prātaḥ Vyāpini; you should study from a local Pañcāṅga.

Kailāśa: You briefly mentioned Kāvaḍa Yātrā before. Kindly elaborate on it.

Ācārya: Kāvaḍa Yātrā (कांवड़ यात्रा) is an annual pilgrimage of devotees of Śrī Śiva, known as Kāvaḍiyā to Hindu pilgrimage places of Haridwar, Gaumukh and Gangotri in Uttarakhand and Sultanganj in Bhagalpur, Bihar to fetch holy waters of Gaṅgā River.

Millions of pilgrims fetch the holy Gaṅgājala and carry it on their shoulders for hundreds of miles to offer it in their local Śiva Mandirs, or important Mandirs such as Pura Mahādeva in Baghpat, Augharnath in Meerut, Kāśi Viśvanātha in Vārāṇasī and Vaidyanātha in Deoghar.

The pilgrimage derives its name from a sacred water-carrying apparatus called Kāvaḍa, and the source of the water is often Gaṅgā. The offering is dedicated to Śrī Śiva.

In particular, the Kāvaḍa pilgrimage to Haridwar has grown to be India's largest annual religious gathering, with an estimated 12 million participants in the 2010 and 2011 events.

The devotees come from Delhi, Uttar Pradesh, Haryana, Rajasthan, Punjab, and Bihar and some from Jharkhand, Chhattisgarh, Odisha and Madhya Pradesh.

Outside of India, the tradition has led to the annual Maha Shivaratri pilgrimage, where around half a million Hindus in Mauritius go on a pilgrimage to Gaṅgā Talao, many walking bare feet from their homes carrying Kāvaḍas.

Kāvaḍa Yātrā is named after the Kāvaḍa, a single pole (usually made of bamboo) with two roughly equal loads fastened or dangling from opposite ends. The Kāvaḍa is carried by balancing the middle of the pole on one or both shoulders.

The Hindi word Kāvaḍa is derived from the Sanskrit Kāvaḍarathi (काँवाँरथी). Kāvaḍa-carrying pilgrims, called Kāvaḍiyās, carry covered water-pots in Kāvaḍas slung across their shoulders. This practice of carrying Kāvaḍa as a part of religious pilgrimage, especially by devotees of Śrī Śiva, is widely followed throughout India (see Kavadi). Yātrā means a journey or procession.

Kāvaḍa Yātrā is related to the churning of the Kṣīra Samudra in the Purāṇas. When the poison "Halāhala" came out before "Amṛta" and the world started burning from its heat, Śrī Śiva consumed the poison. But, after consuming it, his body started burning due to the negative energy of the poison. In Treta Yuga, Śrī Śiva's devout follower Rāvaṇa brought Gaṅgājala by using Kāvaḍa and poured it on Śrī Śiva's Mandir in Puramhādeva (in Bagpat). Thus releasing Śiva from the negative energy of the poison.

The festivals run during the Śravaṇa Māsa. After taking water from the Gaṅgā Nadi (or its tributaries), the Kāvaḍiyās (Śiva Bhaktas) travel barefooted and in saffron robes with their Kāvaḍa (walking sticks used to hang the urns of water) for 105 km by various routes and usually in groups made of family, friends and or neighbours, and return to their own local or other more important Śiva Mandirs to pour the Gaṅgājala on Śrī Śivaliṅga.

The Śravaṇa Māsa is dedicated to Śrī Śiva, and most devotees observe a fast on Somavāras during the month, as it also falls during Caturmāsa. Caturmāsa is traditionally set aside for religious pilgrimages, bathing in holy rivers and penance.

Most travel the distance on foot; a few travel on bicycles, motor cycles, scooters, mini trucks or jeeps. Numerous Hindu organizations and other voluntary organizations like local Kāvaḍa Sanghs, the Rashtriya Swayamsevak Sangh and the Vishwa Hindu Parishad setup camps along the National Highways during the Yātrā, where food, shelter, medical-aid and stand to hang the Kāvaḍas, holding the Gaṅgājala is provided.

Smaller pilgrimages are also undertaken to places like Allahabad and Vārāṇasī. Śravaṇi Mela is a major festival at Deoghar in Jharkhand, where thousands of saffron-clad pilgrims bring holy water from the Gaṅgā at Sultanganj, covering a distance of 105 kilometres on foot and offer it to Śrī Vaidyanātha. Once the pilgrims reach their hometown, the Gaṅgājala is used to bathe the Śivaliṅgas on Śravaṇa Trayodaśī.

Kailāśa: Dhanyavād for this enlightening details on Kāvaḍa Yātrā. Kindly also tell us about the significance of Śravaṇa Māsa.

Ācārya: Śrāvaṇa Māsa is the fifth month of Cāndramāna calendar (Caitra, Vaiśākha, Jyeṣṭhā, Āṣāṛhā, Śravaṇa). In the Sauramāna calendar that starts with Vaiśākha (Bengal, Orissa, Punjab etc.), it is the fourth month, coinciding with Sūrya in Karka.

In the Sauramāsa, the months are also numbered in numeric order, i.e., Prathama, Dvitīya, Tṛtīya, Caturtha, Pañcama, Ṣaṣtha, Saptama, Aṣṭama, Navama, Daśama, Ekādaśa and Dvādasa. For instance, Maharṣi Vālmīki states that Śrī Rāma was born in Dvādasa Māsa, i.e., Sūrya was in Mīna.

Kailāśa: Is Śravaṇa Māsa coincide with the rainy season? As that is what I find in most places?

Ācārya: That is the most misleading thing, as people hardly know about the calendar of Sanātana Dharma and mix it with the Gregorian calendar, mostly followed by the west.

Kailāśa: Kindly explain the difference between them, Guruji.

Ācārya: Gregorian calendar is a Tropical calendar, and therefore, it is aligned to the seasons. However, Sanātana Calendars (Sauramāna or Cāndramāna) are Sidereal (Nirāyana) and therefore aligned to the Nakṣatras instead of seasons.

Kailāśa: But Śravaṇa falls in the rainy season. Isn't it?

Ācārya: Can you tell me Śravaṇa fell in which season in Ācārya Varāhamihira's time? Jayanta, can you check?

Jayanta: Guruji, his epoch is 505 AD. Sūrya entered Karka on July 26, 505. Sūrya was in Karka 3:10 as per Sāyana Calendar. The following chart maps the season with Rāśi.

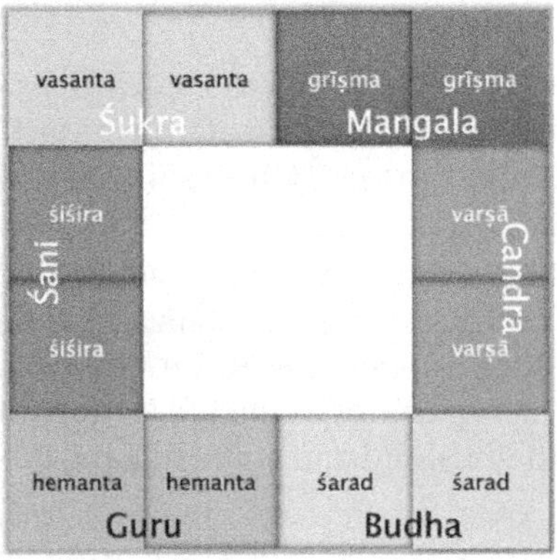

Every season (Ṛtu) is of 60 days, of which 30 are ascending, and the remaining 30 are descending. It shows that during Varāhamihira's time, Śravaṇa coincided with the initial 3 days of the rainy season (Varṣa ṛtu).

Ācārya: How about now?

Jayanta: In 2023, Sūrya entered Karka on July 17th. This coincided with Karka 24:16 Sāyana. This means now; it is near the mid of the rainy season.

Ācārya: How about the beginning of Kaliyuga?

Jayanta: Kaliyuga commenced on Jan 23, -3101 (proleptic Gregorian), with Caitra Śukla Pratipada. Sūrya entered Karka on May 6. This coincided with Vṛṣabha 13:28. This is equivalent to the 14th day of Grīṣma (summer - ascending). Therefore it was summer instead of the rainy season.

Ācārya: Absolutely! Over time, the Saura and Candra Māsa would align to different seasons. It slowly changes, with 2147.62 years per Rāśi. In the future, Śravaṇa Māsa would fall in Sharad (Autumn) and then Hemanta (pre-winter). It is slow; after 2577 years, Śravaṇa Māsa would fall in Sharad (autumn).

For many Sanātanis, Śravaṇa Māsa is a fasting month. People fast every Somavāra to Śrī Śiva and every Maṅgalavāra to Devī Pārvati. Fasting on Maṅgalavāra of this month is known as ***Maṅgala Gauri Vrata***.

Śravaṇa is considered a holy month due to the numerous festivals celebrated. Some of the important festivals are:

Nāga Pañcamī: Amānta Śravaṇa Śukla Pañcamī

Rakṣa Bandhan: Amānta Śravaṇa Pūrṇimā

Kṛṣṇa Janmashtami: Amānta Śravaṇa Kṛṣṇa Aṣṭamī

Kailāśa: Dhanyavād, Guruji, for the enlightening discussion.

Sunidhi: Dhanyavād, Guruji, we learnt a lot about Śravaṇa Māsa.

Ācārya: Alright, let us focus on Jyotiṣa now.

Jayanta: Guruji, kindly tell us about this Praśna method called Jāmakkol Āruṛham, which uses Āruṛha, Chatra and Yāmagrahas.

Ācārya: This is a specialized branch of Praśna that finds its source in Jinendramālai, a text written by a Jain Monk Ācārya Upendrācārya. It uses almost the same methods of a regular Praśna, as stated in classical texts such as Praśnamārga, Daivajñavallabha, Kṛṣṇīyam and Ṣaṭpañcāśikā. However, the focus here is on some special parameters, including Āruṛha, Chatra and Yāmagrahas.

Kailāśa: Guruji, kindly explain these parameters.

Ācārya: I will explain them and their use in due course. In this deliberation, I will use the Praśna text *"Jñānapradīpikā"* (ज्ञानप्रदीपिका) as the basis so that we have a structure to our discussion. I will refer to the book "Praśna Āruṛhaphala" by Rev. Pandit Kadalangudi Natesa Sastri.

Jayanta: That sounds fantastic.

Ācārya: It is also my reverence to Śāstrīji for his yeoman service to the cause of Jyotiṣa. He wrote several books on Jyotiṣa and Hindu Śāstras, which you should study.

The text started with the invocation of Lord Viṣṇu "शुक्लाम्बरधरं विष्णुं शशिवर्णं चतुर्भुजम् । प्रसन्नवदनं ध्यायेत् सर्वविघ्नोपशान्तये ॥"

It means, "May we meditate upon Lord Viṣṇu, the one adorned in white garments, whose complexion resembles Candra (resplendent with a cooling aura), and who possesses four arms. Let us focus on his benevolent and radiant face as we seek to pacify all obstacles and disturbances." **1.1**

An invocation of Lord Gaṇeśa follows it. "श्रीमद्गङ्गाधरसुतं चन्द्रलेखावतंसकम् । सिद्धिदं सर्वविद्यानां वन्दे दन्तावळाननम् ॥२॥ "I bow to the one with the radiant face resembling a moonbeam, the beloved son of Lord Śiva, who beholds Devī Gaṅgā in his matted locks. He bestows success to all seekers of knowledge. I offer my salutations to the one with shining teeth." **1.2**

Kailāśa: Why do the Hindu Śāstras always commence with an invocation of a Devatā?

Ācārya: The reasons are manifold. Firstly, this is to invoke the blessings of the Devatā. Secondly, it is for dedication to one's Iṣṭa Devatā, who has guided the person in advancing in the world of knowledge. And thirdly, it is for acknowledging that one is only a medium through which the divine will manifests knowledge. Without the divine will, we are merely empty vessels!

It also ensures that we do not develop an ego that we are the beholder of knowledge, which is dangerous. Not only does it make you falter, but it also makes you lose it eventually! So, always be humble, and consider yourself a servant of divinity. Arrogance makes one lose one's head or intellect (Ketu)!

1.3. I now narrate the Śāstra of Praśna entitled Jñānapradīpikā which, like a mirror, reflects the truth and a knowledge of which is beneficial to the world "ज्ञानप्रदीपकं नाम शास्त्रं लोकोपकारकम् । प्रश्नादर्श प्रवक्ष्यामि सर्वशास्त्रानुसारतः ॥३॥"

Kailāśa: Guruji, who is the author of the text Jñānapradīpikā?

Ācārya: It is unclear who is the original author. However, in his Hindi translation Acharya Ashok Sahejanand of the text, the author mentions that even though the original author is unknown, it is likely written by a Jain monk.

1.4-6. Past, future, present, auspicious and inauspicious sight, five paths, four Kendras, strength and weakness, Āruṛha, Chatra, Varga, the strength of rising, combustion, Kṣetra, dṛṣṭi, male, female, eunuch, complexion, animal and human forms, Raśmi, distance in Yojana, age, taste, rising, etc., by examining them, an intelligent should predict the outcome. भूत, भविष्य, वर्तमान, शुभाशुभ दृष्टि, पाँच मार्ग, चार केन्द्र, बलाबल, आरुढ़, छत्र, वर्ग, उदय बल, अस्तबल, क्षेत्र, दृष्टि, नर, नारी, नपुंसक, वर्ण, मृग तथा नर आदि रूप, किरण, योजन, आयु, रस, उदय आदि की परीक्षा करके बुद्धिमान् को फल कहना चाहिये ॥५॥"

चरस्थिरोभयान् राशीन् तत्प्रदेशस्थलानि च । निशादिवससंध्याश्च कालदेशस्वभावतः ॥७॥ धातुमूलं च जीवं च नष्टं मुष्टिं च चिन्तनम् । लाभालाभं गदं मृत्युं भुक्तं स्वप्नं च शाकुनम् ॥८॥ जातकर्मायुधं शल्यं कोपं सेनागमं तथा । सरिदागमनं वृष्टिमध्यं नौसिद्धिमादितः ॥६॥ क्रमेण कथयिष्यामि शास्त्रे ज्ञानप्रदीपके ।

1.7-10. I will explain cara, sthira, dvisvabhāva Rāśis, their countries, predictions from day, night and twilight, and the characteristics of the Rāśis. (7) I will describe the rules about dhātu, mūla, jīva, naṣṭa, muṣṭi, lābha, hāni, roga, mṛtyu, eating, sleeping and omens (8). I will also provide the rules for deciphering janma, karma, weapons, śalya (bones), anger, marching of armies, flow of rivers, rains, commodity prices, state of ships etc. (9)

चर, स्थिर, द्विस्वभाव राशियाँ, उनके प्रदेश, दिन, रात, सन्ध्या का कालादेश, राशियों का स्वमावः (7) धातु, मूल, जीव, नष्ट, मुष्टि, लाभ, हानि, रोग, मृत्यु, भोजन, शयन और शकुन सम्बन्धी प्रश्न (8), जन्म, कर्म, अस्त्र, शल्य (हड्डी), कोप, सेना का आगमन, नदियों की बाट, वर्षा, अवर्षण, नौकासिद्धि आदि (9)। इन बातों को इस ज्ञानप्रदीपक शास्त्र में क्रमश कहूंगा।

Jayanta: Guruji, let us focus on the 2nd Adhyāya.
Ācārya: This Adhyāya deals with the friendship and hostility between the Grahas.

Ācārya: The friendship of the Grahas explained below as per the Śāstra

1.10. Maṅgala: Śukra and Budha are friends.

1.11. Śukra: Budha, Maṅgala, Sūrya and Guru are friends.

1.12. Guru: All Grahas except Maṅgala are friends. **Sūrya**: Guru is friend. **Śani**: Budha, Guru and Śukra are friends.

1.13. Budha: all are friends except Sūrya. **Candra:** Guru and Budha are friends.

Kailāśa: Guruji, this looks odd. How can Maṅgala and Budha be friends?

Ācārya: Indeed, there are some differences in opinion about this between the author and the principles of Maharṣi Parāśara.

Sunidhi: What are the principles of Maharṣi Parāśara?

Table 9

	Meṣ	Vṛṣ	Mit	Kar	Siṅ	Kan	Tul	Vṛś	Dha	Mak	Kum	Mīn
Sūr	♥	⚔	⚔	♥	⌂	♥	⚔	♥	♥	⚔	⚔	♥
Can	♥	⌂	♥	♥*	♥	♥	⚔	⚔	♥	♥	⚔	⚔
Maṅ	⌂	♥	⚔	♥	♥	⚔	⚔	♥	♥	♥*	⚔	♥
Bud	♥	♥	⚔	⚔	♥	⌂	♥	⚔	♥	♥	⚔	⚔
Gur	♥	⚔	⚔	♥	♥	⚔	⚔	♥	⌂	♥*	⚔	♥
Śuk	⚔	♥	♥	⚔	⚔	♥	⌂	♥	⚔	♥	♥	⚔
Śan	⚔	♥	♥	⚔	⚔	♥	♥	⚔	⚔	♥	⌂	♥

Ācārya: In this table ⌂ represents the Mūlatrikoṇa of the Grahas (on the left-hand side). A Graha is hostile to Rāśis in Upacayas and 7 from its Mūlatrikoṇa. There is some exception to it. A Graha is not hostile to its own Rāśi (Candra-Karka) and Uccarāśi (Maṅgala-Makara). They are denoted by ♥* symbol. In the rest of the places, the friendly is indicated by ♥ and the hostile Rāśis are indicated by ⚔.

When a Graha is both friendly and hostile to a Graha, it becomes Sama (neutral). For instance, Budha is friendly to Meṣa and hostile to Vṛścika, and therefore, he is neutral to Maṅgala.

Sunidhi: Is Maṅgala neutral to Budha also?

Ācārya: From Maṅgala's Mūlatrikoṇa, Meṣa, he is hostile to Mithuna and Kanyā, and therefore, Maṅgala is hostile to Budha.

Sunidhi: What is the relationship between Budha and Guru?

Ācārya: Budha is neutral to Guru, but Guru is hostile to Budha. Check this in the table.

Sunidhi: How about Candra?

Ācārya: Candra is only friendly to Budha and Sūrya and neutral to the remaining Grahas. He is hostile to no one.

Kailāśa: Should we follow the above rule given by the author?

Ācārya: You can try that. That appears to amplify certain characteristics of the Grahas.

2.14-15. The lords of the Rāśis are the following: Maṅgala for Meṣa and Vṛścika; Śukra for Vṛṣabha and Tulā; Guru for Dhanu and Mīna; Budha for Mithuna and Kanyā; Śani for Makara and Kumbha; Sūrya for Siṅha; Candra for Karka.

Jayanta: Guruji, should we consider Rāhu and Ketu as the lords of Kumbha and Vṛścika?

Ācārya: No, that has limited applicability, and therefore, we must use them in those places, such as Daśāvarṣa computation in Rāśidaśā.

Kailāśa: Guruji, some scholars even consider Grahas to be the lord of their Mūlatrikoṇa Rāśis also. Should we do that?

Ācārya: There is no Śāstraic basis for that. The best is to stick to the Śāstras and avoid the Kaliyuga innovations. The Yuga tends to corrupt everything, including Jyotiṣa knowledge.

Jayanta: Now the author provides his views regarding the Rāśis that are friendly to the Grahas.

2.16. Śani is friendly to Dhanu and Mithuna, Mīna, Kanyā, and Vṛṣabha; Sūrya is friendly to Dhanu and Mīna; Maṅgala to Tulā, Mithuna, Vṛṣabha, and Kanyā.

2.17. Candra is friendly to Dhanu, Mīna, Mithuna and Kanyā. Budha is friendly to Dhanu, Makara, Vṛścika, Karka, Meṣa, Vṛṣabha, Tulā and Kumbha.

2.18. Śukra is friendly to Meṣa, Mithuna, Dhanu, Kumbha, Vṛścika and Makara. Guru is friendly to Karka, Tulā, Kumbha, Mithuna, Vṛṣabha and Siṅha. In this Śāstra, not only Graha relations but the relationship between Grahas and Rāśis are emphasized.

Ācārya: There is some pattern to it. Let us understand them:

Here, the Sva/Ucca/Mūlatrikoṇa Rāśis are not mentioned as they have special dignities. What is not mentioned is the Grahas' hostile Rāśis.

Sūrya: Dhanu/Mīna. Sūrya is friendly to only Guru's Rāśis.

Candra: Dhanu/Mīna, Mithuna/Kanyā. Candra is friendly to Guru's and Budha's Rāśis.

Maṅgala: Vṛṣabha/Tulā, Mithuna/Kanyā. Maṅgala is friendly to Śukra's and Budha's Rāśis.

Budha: Dhanu, Makara/Kumbha, Meṣa/Vṛścika, Karka, Vṛṣabha/Tulā. Budha is friendly to all Rāśis except his Nīcarāśi, Mīna.

Guru: Karka, Siṅha, Vṛṣabha/Tulā, Kumbha, Mithuna. Guru is friendly towards his friend's Rāśis Karka/Siṅha. Normally Guru is friendly towards Kanyā; however, here, Mithuna is mentioned. Guru is also generally considered good in Kumbha (like his Uccarāśi).

Śukra: Meṣa/Vṛścika, Mithuna, Dhanu, Makara/Kumbha. Śukra is friendly to Maṅgala's and Śani's Rāśi. He is also friendly to his friend, Budha's Rāśi, except his Nīcarāśi (Kanyā).

Śani: Dhanu/Mīna, Mithuna/Kanyā, Vṛṣabha. Śani is friendly to Guru's Budha's Rāśis and his friend, Śukra's Rāśi, Vṛṣabha.

Jayanta: The author describes the Uccarāśis of the Grahas

2.19. The Uccarāśis of the Grahas are the following: Meṣa for Sūrya; Vṛṣabha for Candra; Mithuna for *Paridhi*; Karka for Guru; Siṅha for *Dhūma*; Kanyā for Budha; Tulā for Śani; Vṛścika for Rāhu; Dhanu for *Indracāpa*; Makara for Maṅgala; Kumbha for Ketu; and Mīna for Śukra. सूर्येन्द्रोः परिधेर्जीवा धूमज्ञशनभोगिनाम् ॥८॥ शक्रचापकुजेणानां शुक्रस्योच्चास्त्वजादयः ।

Ācārya: The author gives the Uccarāśi of the Aprakāśa Grahas, Dhūma etc. They are environmental portents that depend on Sūrya's position.

Sunidhi: Guruji, how to find them?

Ācārya: They are found from Sūrya's position. **Dhūma** = Sūrya + 133°20'. **Vyatipāta** = 360 - Dhūma. **Pariveṣa** = Vyatipāta + 180. **Indracāpa** = 360 - Pariveṣa. **Upaketu** = Indracāpa + 16°40'. Sūrya = Upaketu + 30.

Kailāśa: Even here, we have differences in opinion. Rāhu's Uccarāśi is considered Vṛścika and Ketu's Kumbha.

Ācārya: Yes, normally, Rāhu's Uccarāśi is considered Mithuna and Ketu's Dhanu. Also, Indracāpa is called Śakracāpa here. Ketu is called "Aṇa". The Uccarāśi for Vyatipāta and Upaketu are not mentioned, but Vyatipāta can attain Ucca in Makara (same as Maṅgala) and Upaketu in Kumbha (same as Ketu).

Jayanta: Now, the Uccāñśa of the Grahas are described.

2.20. The Uccāñśa for these Grahas are 10° for Sūrya; 3° for Candra; 28° for Maṅgala; 15° for Budha; 5° for Guru; 27° for Śukra; and 20° for Śani.

Ācārya: This is the same as standard Jyotiṣa works.

The Uccarāśi and Uccāñśa of the Grahas are Sūrya Meṣa 10°, Candra Vṛṣabha 3°, Maṅgala Makara 28°, Budha Kanyā 15°, Bṛhaspati Karka 5°, Śukra Mīna 27° and Śani Tulā 20°. The seventh Rāśi/Añśa from the said Uccarāśi the Grahas have their Nīca Rāśi/Añśa.

Sunidhi: What is the basis for deriving these Añśas, Guruji?

Ācārya: There is no astronomical basis identified for them. Some scholars think they represent the Graha's Mandocca, but that is not true, as you can see from my Siddhānta book.

Besides, the Añśas have a tremendous astrological significance. The years equivalent to the Añśas indicate important events in a person's life. For instance, Sūrya's Uccāñśa is 10°; therefore, in 10y, a significant event (good or bad) of Sūrya is likely in everyone's life. These are certain natural trends that apply to all.

Jayanta: Now, the hostility between the Grahas are described.

2.21. Sūrya is hostile to Budha; Sūrya and Candra to Śukra; Maṅgala to Guru; and Sūrya, Candra, Guru and Śani are all hostile to Maṅgala.

2.22. Except for Guru, all are hostile to Sūrya, i.e. Candra, Maṅgala, Budha, Śukra and Śani. All Grahas are hostile to Śani, as also the Rāśis of these Grahas.

2.23. The various Grahas are Nīca in the following houses: Sūrya in Tulā; Candra in Vṛścika; Maṅgala in Karka; Budha in Mīna; Śani in Meṣa; Śukra in Kanyā, and Guru in Makara.

Sunidhi: Guruji, even here, there are differences with the standard texts.

Ācārya: That is right. The author is trying to amplify certain attributes of the Grahas based on his experiences. For instance, it is said that Sūrya is hostile to Budha, but Sūrya is Sama to him. Also, Candra is hostile to Śukra. In actual fact, Candra is hostile to none, but Śukra is hostile to Candra.

Jayanta: Now, the dignity of Rāhu, Ketu, Indracāpa, Pariveṣa and Dhūma are explained.

Ācārya: It appears that the author does not use the other two Aprakāśa Grahas, Vyatipāta and Upaketu, and therefore, has left out their designations.

2.24. Rāhu in Vṛṣabha, Indracāpa in Mithuna, Ketu in Siṅha, Pariveṣa in Dhanu, and Dhūma in Kumbha are Nīca.

2.25. Rāhu's Mitra Rāśis are Tulā, Makara, Kanyā, Mithuna, Dhanu and Vṛṣabha, Rāhu's own house is Kumbha; his Śatrurāśi is Karka; he is Nīca in Vṛṣabha.

Jayanta: Now, the special designations of the Kendras are explained.

2.26. The fourth place from Udaya is called "Jalakendra"; the 4th from that (i.e. 7H) is "Astamaya"; the 4th from that again (i.e. 10H) is "Turya" or Ākāśa; the 4th from that (i.e. 1H) is called "Udaya". These are the four Kendras.

उदयादिचतुष्कं तु जलकेन्द्रमुदाहृतम् ॥१५॥ तच्चतुर्थं चास्तमयं तत्तुर्यं वियदुच्यते तत्तुर्यमुदयं चैव चतुष्केन्द्रमुदाहृतम् ॥१६॥

Ācārya: Indeed! The four Kendras, Jala, Asta, Turya and Udaya, are the pivotal points in a Kuṇḍalī. The Kuṇḍalī stands and remains steady on these pivots. Various dṛṣṭies of a Praśna are judged from these Kendras.

2.27. One must investigate thoughts from 10H, dreams from 4H; closed fists from Chatrarāśi (Kavippu) and about loss of property in 7H. One has also to consider the "Āruṛha" Lagna.

चिन्तनायां तु दशमे हिबुके स्वप्नचिन्तनम् | छत्रे मुष्टिं चयं नष्टमात्येश्चारुढतोऽपि वा ॥ १७॥

2.28. As Dhanu, Vṛṣabha, Karka, Makara, and Meṣa rise by their hinder parts, they are designated "Pṛṣṭodaya"; Mīna is designated "Tiryak". The rest, i.e. Mithuna, Siṅha, Kanyā, Tulā, Vṛścika and Kumbha, are designated "Śīrṣodaya" as they rise by their heads. Mīna and Makara are designated "Ubhayodaya"; the rest rise naturally.

2.29. Among Grahas, Sūrya, Maṅgala and Śani are "Pṛṣṭodaya" Grahas. Rāhu, Guru, Śukra and Budha are "Śīrṣodaya" Grahas. Candra and Ketu are "Tiryag" Grahas.

अर्काङ्गारकमन्दास्तु सन्ति पृष्ठोदया ग्रहाः। राहुजीवभृगुज्ञाश्च ग्रहाः स्युर्मस्त-कोदयाः॥१६॥ उद्यतस्तिवर्गेवेन्दुः केतुस्तत्र प्रकीर्तितः।

2.30-31. Guru, Budha are Puruṣa and they are strong in Udayarāśi. Sūrya and Maṅgala are Catuṣpāda and they are strong in 10H (Anta). The Śukra and Candra are Jalacara and they are strong in 4H in Jalarāśis (Karka/Mīna). Śani and Rāhu are Kīṭa and they are powerful in 7H.

उदये बलिनौ जीवबुधौ तु पुरुषौ स्मृतौ ॥३०॥ अन्ते चतुष्पदो भानुभूमिजौ बलिनौ ततः ।
चतुर्थे शुक्रशशिनौ जलराशौ बलोत्तरी ॥३१॥ अही बलिनौ चास्ते कीटकाश्च भवन्ति हि ।

Jayanta: Guruji, kindly elaborate on this.

Ācārya: You must have already heard about Dikbala. Guru/Budha attain Dikbala in Lagna, Candra/Śukra in 4H, Śani in 7H and Sūrya/Maṅgala in 10H. These are Graha Dikbala.

Similarly, there are Rāśi Dikbala. For this purpose, the Rāśis are classed into four categories, Jalacara, Manuṣya, Catuṣpāda and Kīṭa. This classification is based on the number of legs. Jalacara have no legs, like fishes, Manuṣya has 2 legs, Catuṣpāda has four legs, and Kīṭa has 6 or more legs.

The Jalacara Rāśis, also called Sarīsṛpa, includes snakes and reptiles. Manuṣya Rāśis are also called Dvipāda, and they represent all hominids and creatures that stand on two legs, such as monkeys, chimpanzees and orangutans. Catuṣpāda includes all cattle and animals that walk on four legs. The Kīṭa Rāśi includes all creatures that have 6 or more legs, including crabs, shrimps, scorpions, centipedes and millipedes.

The Rāśi Dikbala is as follows: 1H – Manuṣya, as they are known for intellect; 4H – Jalacara, as they are known for their swimming abilities; 7H – Kīṭa as they are known for their reach to all corners of the world, and 10H – Catuṣpāda as they are known for their muscle power and action.

Sunidhi: Guruji, is that the reason why Guru/Budha are classified as Manuṣya, Candra/Śukra as Jalacara, Śani as Kīṭa and Sūrya/Maṅgala as Catuṣpāda?

Ācārya: Well! That is one of the opinions.

Jātakapārijāta 2.12 states it differently. It states that Sūrya and Budha are in the form of Birds (Vihaga), Candra reptile (Sarīsṛpa), Bṛhaspati and Śukra Biped (Dvipāda) and Śani and Maṅgala Quadruped (Catuṣpada).

Kailāśa: So, what to accept?

Ācārya: Let as accept the following Dikbala conditions: 1H - Guru/Budha + Manuṣya Rāśi; 4H – Śukra/Candra + Jalacara; 7H – Śani + Kīṭa; and, 10H – Sūrya/Maṅgala + Catuṣpāda.

Jayanta: Now, the author enumerates the different classes of Rāśis.

2.32-33. Mithuna, Kanyā, Dhanu-1, Kumbha and Tulā are Manuṣya Rāśis. Makara and Mīna are Antyodaya Rāśis. The remaining are based on their nomenclature (Svabhāva). Meṣa, Vṛṣabha, and Siṅha are Catuṣpāda, Karka and Vṛścika are Bahupāda (multipede or multiple legs), Makara and Mīna are Kṣīṇapāda (weak legs, like those of birds) and Kumbha, Mithuna, Tulā and Kanyā are Dvipāda (two-legged) Rāśis.

Kailāśa: Guruji, what is the basis of this assignment?

Ācārya: That is based on the symbols of these Rāśis.

Let us take Manuṣya Rāśis.

Mithuna = two people having a dialogue

Kanyā = a girl in a garden or a boat

Dhanu-1 = a centaur with a human head

Kumbha = a man holding a pot

Tulā = several people having transactions in a market

Now, let us see the Jalacara Rāśis.

Makara-2 = a crocodile in a swamp with a deer's head (Mṛga)

Mīna = fishes swimming in an ocean

These Rāśis also indicate birds since bids rely solely on wings; therefore, their legs are relatively weak.

Now, let us focus on the Kīṭa Rāśis

Karka = water insects such as crustaceans, crabs, shrimps etc.

Vṛścika = land insects such as scorpions, arachnids, spiders, centipedes etc.

Now, let us focus on the Catuṣpāda Rāśis

Meṣa = goats grazing on a mountaintop

Vṛṣabha = cow and bull grazing in a grassland

Siṅha = Lions and other wild animals from the jungle

Makar-1 = a deer on a crocodile body (Mṛga)

Dhanu-2 = a centaur with a horse's body

Sunidhi: Guruji, some people classify Karka as Jalacara. Shouldn't it be so?

Ācārya: They do so because Karka represents a flowing river; therefore, its creatures, such as freshwater fishes, are Jalacara. But fishes are generally represented by Mīna. So, we should classify it as Kīṭa only.

Maharṣi Parāśara also supports classifying Karka as Jalacara. In Bṛhatparāśara 27.26-29, while explaining the Rāśi Dikbala, he states, (a) Deduct 7H from a Bhāva containing Kanyā, Mithuna, Tulā, Kumbha or Dhanu-1. (b) If Meṣa, Vṛṣabha, Siṅha, or Makara-1, Dhanu-2 is in a Bhāva, deduct 4H from it. (c) If the Bhāva is in Karka or Vṛścika, deduct 1H from it. (d) Deduct 10H from the Bhāva falling in Makara-2 or Mīna.

What is explained above are the places where the strength is zero. The Dikbala, therefore, is in the opposite Bhāva, i.e., 1H - Kanyā, Mithuna, Tulā, Kumbha or Dhanu-1; 10H - Meṣa, Vṛṣabha, Siṅha, or Makara-1, Dhanu-2; 7H - Karka or Vṛścika; and, 4H - Makara-2 or Mīna.

Kailāśa: What is its impact on a Kuṇḍalī?

Ācārya: If someone has a Manuṣya Rāśi with Guru/Budha in Udaya, the person is exceedingly intelligent; if Jalacara Rāśi with Candra/Śukra is in 4H, the person is good with relaxation techniques, nurturing and healing; if Kīṭa Rāśi with Śani is in 7H, the person is good in trading (connecting) and secret services/research (getting into the depth of matter); and, if Catuṣpāda Rāśis with Sūrya/Maṅgala is in 10H, the person is highly action-oriented.

Kailāśa: That makes sense, Guruji. Dhanyavād!

Jayanta: Now, the author describes the number of feet of the Graha. This implies that in previous ślokas, the author didn't imply that Guru/Budha are Manuṣyas etc.

2.34. Guru, Budha and Śukra are Manuṣya (Dvipāda); Śani, Sūrya and Maṅgala are Catuṣpāda; Candra and Rāhu are Bahupāda (multiple feet) Grahas. Candra is a fast-moving (Śīghragati) Graha; Śani and Budha are birds. Śani and Rāhu walk on their knees (weak feet) and the rest of the Grahas walk on their feet.

द्विपादा जोववित्शुक्राः शन्यर्काराश्चतुष्पदाः। शशिसर्पौ बहुपादौ शनिसौम्यौ च पक्षिणौ ॥२५॥ शनिस जानुगतो पद्भ्यां यान्तीतरे ग्रहाः।

बृहस्पति बुध शुक्र इनकी द्विपद संज्ञा है तथा शनि सूर्य मंगल इन ग्रहों की चतुष्पद संज्ञा कही गई हैं, चन्द्रमा राहु ये बहुपद तथा शनि बुध ये पक्षिसंज्ञक कहे जाते हैं, शनि और राहु की जानु गति होती है और इन से भिन्न ग्रह पैर से चलते हैं।

Kailāśa: There are still differences in opinion. According to this author, Sūrya is a Catuṣpāda, whereas according to Ācārya Vaidyanātha, he is like a bird. Śani and Maṅgala are Catuṣpāda, Candra and Rāhu are Sarīsṛpa; Budha is a bird; and Guru and Śukra are Manuṣya. The issue is Budha being assigned as Manuṣya, Śani as Pakṣi and Sūrya as Catuṣpāda.

Jayanta: Yes, differences in opinion are likely in a complex subject such as this. Each author tries to portray their understanding with their writings.

2.35. There are three Vīthis (pathways) for the Rāśis, namely Meṣa-vīthi, Vṛṣabha-vīthi and Mithuna-vīthi. In Meṣa-vīthi the Rāśis Vṛṣabha, Mithuna, Karka and Siṅha rise; in the Mithuna-vīthi the Rāśis Vṛścika, Dhanu, Makara and Kumbha rise; in the Vṛṣabha-vīthi the remaining Rāśis - Meṣa, Mīna, Tulā and Kanyā rise.

उदीर्यतेऽजवीभ्यां तु चत्वारो वृषभादयः ॥२६॥ युग्मवीभ्यामुदीर्यन्ते चत्वाशे वृश्चिकादयः । उक्षवीभ्यामुदीर्यन्ते मीनमेषतुला स्त्रियः ॥२७॥

2.36. Draw the Rāśi Cakra as in the following figure. Starting from the East with Vṛṣabha and other Rāśis in the clockwise direction, the 12 Rāśis constitute the Āruṛha Cakra

राशिचक्र - समालिख्य प्रागादि वृपभादिकम् । प्रदक्षिणक्रमेणैव द्वादशारूढसंज्ञितम् ॥२८॥ वृषश्चैव वृश्चिकस्य मिथुनस्य शरासनम् । मकरश्च कुलीशस्य सिंहस्य घट उच्यते ॥२६॥ मोनस्तु कन्यकायाश्च तुलायो मेष उच्यते ।

2.37-38. The following pairs of Rāśis: Vṛṣabha and Vṛścika, Mithuna and Dhanu, Karka and Makara, Siṅha and Kumbha, Mīna and Kanyā, Meṣa and Tulā aspect each other mutually in the Pratisūtra manner.

मेषस्य वृषभं छत्रं मेषच्छत्रं वृषस्य च ॥३॥ युग्मं कर्कटसिंहानां मेषच्छ्त्रमुदाहृतम् । कन्यायाश्च परं छत्रं तुलाया वृषभस्तथा ॥४॥ वृषभस्य युगच्छत्रं धनुषो मिथुनं तथा । नकस्य मिथुनच्छन्नम् मेषः कुंभस्य कीर्तितम् ॥५॥ मीनस्य वृषभच्छत्रं छत्रमेवमुदाहृतम् ।

प्रतिसूत्रवशादेति परस्परनिरीक्षिताः ॥३०॥ गगनं भास्करः प्रोक्तो भूमिश्चन्द्र उदाहृतः।

ग्रह एक सूत्रस्थ एक दूसरे को देखते हैं। सूर्य को आकाश और भूमि को चंद्रमा समझना चाहिये।

Jayanta: The author describes now the Kārakatvas of the Grahas, including association of 8 animals and objects.

2.39. According to the Śāstras, it is stated that Sūrya is Ākāśa (sky.) and Candra the earth; Sūrya is male and Candra female; Sūrya is Prāṇa and Candra is the Deha.

2.40. According to the Śāstras, Budha is the flag (Dvajā), Rāhu the smoke (Dhūma), Candra the Lion, Guru the Dog, Śani the Bull, Maṅgala the Donkey, Śukra the Elephant, and Sūrya the Crow.

Ācārya: It is common to associate 6 animals and two objects (Dvajā and Dhūma) with the Grahas. The animals are Siṅha (lion), Svāna (dog), Vṛṣabha (bull), Khara (donkey), Gaja (elephant) and Crow.

However, a different association is given by Praśnamārga. According to Ācārya Harihara Sūrya, Maṅgala, Guru, Budha, Śukra, Śani, Candra, and Rāhu respectively denote Dhvaja (flag), Dhūma (smoke), Siṅha (lion), Svāna (dog), Vṛṣabha (bull), Khara (donkey), Gaja (elephant) and Vāyasa (Crow).

Praśnamārga:

7.3-6. In Aṣṭamaṅgala Praśna, Sūrya, Maṅgala, Guru, Budha, Śukra, Śani, Candra, and Rāhu, respectively denote Dhvaja (flag), Dhūma (smoke), Siṅha (lion), Svāna (dog), Vṛṣabha (bull), Khara (donkey), Gaja (elephant) and Crow. They denote Garuṛa, Cat, Siṅha, Vṛṣabha, Serpent, Mouse, Gaja and Rabbit, respectively. Dhvaja and Siṅha are related to Pṛthvībhūta; Gaja and Vṛṣabha are related to Jalabhūta; Dhūma relates to Agni; Khara relates to Vāyubhūta; Svāna and Crow relate to Ākāśabhūta.

Ācārya: The association of numbers 1 to 8 with Grahas, Yonis, Mṛga and Bhūta are as follows:

Table 10

#	Grahas	Yoni (Source)	Mṛga (Animal)	Bhūta (Element)
1	**Sūrya**	Banner	Eagle	Earth
2	**Maṅgala**	Smoke	Cat	Fire
3	**Bṛhaspati**	Lion	Lion	Earth
4	**Budha**	Dog	Dog	Ether
5	**Śukra**	Bull	Serpent	Water
6	**Śani**	Donkey	Rat	Air
7	**Candra**	Elephant	Elephant	Water
8	**Rāhu**	Crow	Rabbit	Ether

Jayanta: Now, the method of ascertaining Chatrarāśi is delineated.

2.41. In this Śāstra Āruṛha Chatra is defined as follows: one must learn the Rāśi of the Bhacakra where the Pṛcchaka stands, belongs to the Mithuna Vīthi. It is the 6th Rāśi from Makara. And if at Praśna, the Udayarāśi is Meṣa; the Chatrarāśi is the 6th Rāśi from Meṣa, that is Kanyā.

2.42. Some others define Chatrarāśi thus: the number of Rāśis separating the Rāśi where the Pṛcchaka stands (Āruṛha) and Sūrya's Vīthi must be counted from the Udayarāśi when the Praśna is made to determine the Chatrarāśi.

Sunidhi: What is Chatrarāśi, Guruji?

Ācārya: It is the Rāśi of the symbolic umbrella, which conceals things. It also protects one from the hot sun.

Kailāśa: Kindly explain its computation, Guruji!

Ācārya: For that, we need three things, Āruṛha, Sūrya's Rāśi and Udayarāśi. From Sūrya's Rāśi, we must determine the Sūrya's Vīthi.

Kailāśa: What is Sūrya's Vīthi?

Ācārya: Vīthi is a pathway, so it implies the pathway of Sūrya. Vīthi Rāśi can be Meṣa, Vṛṣabha and Mithuna. To find Vīthi Rāśi, Bhacakra is divided into 3 sectors, Vṛṣabha-Siṅha, Vṛścika-Kumbha and the remaining (Mīna-Meṣa/Kanyā-Tulā).

Vṛṣabha-Siṅha is related to Meṣa Vīthi, Vṛścika-Kumbha is related to Mithuna and the remaining ones (Mīna-Meṣa/Kanyā-Tulā) are related to Vṛṣabha Vīthi.

Sunidhi: What is next after we know Sūrya's Vīthi?

Ācārya: Count Udaya from Āruṛha (Āruṛha2Udaya), and count as many Rāśis from Sūrya's Vīthi (Vīthi2Chatra). Supposing Udaya is Siṅha, Āruṛha is Vṛṣabha and Sūrya is in Meṣa. Sūrya's Vīthi is Vṛṣabha.

(1) Arudha2Udaya: Counting Udaya (Siṅha) from Āruṛha (Vṛṣabha), we get 4 Rāśis. (2) Udaya2Chatra: Now, counting 4 Rāśis from Sūrya's Vīthi (Vṛṣabha), we arrive at Siṅha as the Chatrarāśi.

In this case, it is the same as Udaya, but it need not be the case always. Also, refer to Praśnamārga 9.34 for computation of Chatrarāśi.

Sunidhi: Kindly explain the method given by this author. It appears different.

Ācārya: It is different, but it yields the same result. It also involves 2 steps: (1) Āruṛha2Vīthi: Count Sūrya's Vīthi from Āruṛha. (2) Count as many Rāśis from Udaya (Udaya2Chatra).

Therefore, in the example, Udaya is Siṅha, Āruṛha is Vṛṣabha and Sūrya's Vīthi is Vṛṣabha. Āruṛha2Vīthi = 1. Udaya2Chatra = counting 1 Rāśi from Udaya (Siṅha), we arrive at Siṅha as the Chatrarāśi.

You can see that the results are the same.

Sunidhi: How to find the Āruṛha? Should we get it from the direction of the Pṛcchaka?

Ācārya: It is one of the methods if the Pṛcchaka has come to visit you. Else, you can know it from other methods such as a number from 1 to 108 or placing a gold coin or cowries. Any method will work, provided that the Pṛcchaka is sincere and you have performed your daily Sādhanā.

Jayanta: The Udaya Chatra for the Rāśis are given below:

2.43-45. For Meṣa, Vṛṣabha; and for Vṛṣabha, Meṣa; for Mithuna Karka and Siṅha, Meṣa. For Kanyā, Makara; for Tulā, Vṛṣabha; for Vṛścika, Mithuna; and for Dhanu, Mithuna. For Makara, Mithuna; for Kumbha, Meṣa; and for Mīna, Vṛṣabha.

Ācārya: Here is another method of determining Chatra from Udayarāśi, but this method is less common. The Chatra for different Udayarāśis are as follows:

Meṣa – Vṛṣabha
Vṛṣabha – Meṣa
Mithuna – Meṣa
Karka – Meṣa
Siṅha – Meṣa
Kanyā – Makara
Tulā – Vṛṣabha
Vṛścika – Mithuna
Dhanu – Mithuna
Makara – Mithuna
Kumbha – Meṣa
Mīna – Vṛṣabha

The śloka for this is मेषस्य वृषभं छत्रं मेषच्छत्रं वृपस्य च ॥३॥ युग्मं कर्कटसिंहानां मेषच्छत्रमुदाहृतम् । कन्यायाश्च परं छत्रं तुलाया वृषभस्तथा ॥४॥ वृषभस्य युगच्छत्रं धनुषो मिथुनं तथा । नक्रस्य मिथुनच्छत्रम् मेषः कुंभस्य कीर्तितम् ॥५॥ मीनस्य वृषभच्छत्रं छत्रमेवमुदाहृतम् ।

Jayanta: Now the dṛṣṭi of Rāśis are explained.

2.46. A Graha has four kinds of dṛṣṭies from its place, namely 7H full-aspect; 5H-9H half-aspect; 4H-8H, three-quarters; 10H, one-quarter. उदयात् सप्तमे पूर्ण अर्धं पश्येतिकोणभे ॥६॥ चतुरस्त्रे त्रिपादं च दशमे पादएव च ॥

Ācārya: This is the standard rule of all Grahas in Parāśarī Jyotiṣa. But it should be pādadṛṣṭi to 3H-10H. They are called Pūrṇadṛṣṭi, Dvipādadṛṣṭi, Tripādadṛṣṭi, and Padadṛṣṭi. 7H is Kāmadrsti and normally Pūrṇadṛṣṭi, 4H-8H is Caturasra (protection) dṛṣṭi, and they are normally Tripādadṛṣṭi, 5H-9H is Jñānadṛṣṭi, and they are normally Dvipāda, and 3H-10H is Upacayadṛṣṭi (growth) and it is Padadṛṣṭi.

Kailāśa: Guruji, according to Maharṣi Parāśara 26.4, the Dṛṣṭis increase gradually in slabs of quarters, i.e. ¼, ½, ¾ and full for 3H-10H, 5H-9H, 4H-8H and 7H. This is aligned with what the author said.

Jayanta: The author also says that a Grahas dṛṣṭies its 3H-11H by Padārdha dṛṣṭi i.e., half of a quarter 1/8 (12.5%) एकादशे तृतीये च पदार्धं वीक्षणं भवेत् ॥७॥.

Ācārya: This is a different opinion from Maharṣi Parāśara! According to the Maharṣi, Grahas do no aspect their 11H. But some scholars do believe in a mild aspect on 11H. Normally, 3H is considered Padadṛṣṭi.

Jayanta: The dṛṣṭis of the Grahas and Rāśis are stated now.

2.47. Sūrya, Candra, Śukra and Budha are strong in their full dṛṣṭies.

2.48. Guru in his half-aspect, Maṅgala in his three-fourth and one-eighth dṛṣṭies, and Śani in his quarter-aspect too are powerful. The "Paśvādi" Rāśis (Meṣa, Vṛṣabha, Siṅha and Vṛścika), aspect cross-wise and the "Manuṣya" Rāśis (Mithuna, Kanyā, Tulā, Dhanu and Kumbha) aspect on a level-basis.

Ācārya: What it means is that Sūrya, Candra, Śukra and Budha are powerful when they are aspecting a place with their Pūrṇadṛṣṭi. Guru is powerful when he dṛṣṭies with Dvipādadṛṣṭi (5H-9H), Maṅgala is powerful when he dṛṣṭies with Caturasradṛṣṭi (4H-8H), and Śani is powerful when he dṛṣṭies with Upacayadṛṣṭi (3H-10H).

Kailāśa: In a way, it indirectly states that Sūrya, Candra, Śukra and Budha have full influence on their 7H, Guru has it in his 5H/9H, Maṅgala in 4H/8H and Śani in 3H/10H. This is the same as the regular rule.

Ācārya: The śloka supporting this is रवीन्दुसितसौम्यास्तु बलिनः पूर्णवीक्षणे । अर्वेक्षणे सुराचार्य्यस्त्रिपादपादार्धयोः कुजः ॥८॥ पादेक्षणे बली सौरिः वीक्षणे बलमीरितम् ।

Jayanta: Kindly explain the Rāśi's dṛṣṭi also.

Ācārya: Manuṣya have Samadṛṣṭi i.e., forward; Catuṣpāda have Tiryagdṛṣṭi, i.e., sideways sight, the Pakṣi have Urdhvadṛṣṭi, i.e., upward sight, and Sarīsṛpa have Adhodṛṣṭi, i.e., downward sight. They apply to both Grahas and Rāśi.

तिर्यक पश्यन्ति तिर्यञ्चो मनुष्याः समदृष्टयः ॥६॥ ऊर्द्ध वेक्षणे पत्ररथाः अधोनेत्रं सरीसृपः।

Regarding the Manuṣyādi classification of Grahas and Rāśis, you must refer to 2.32-34. They are as follows:

Manuṣya: Mithuna, Kanyā, Tulā, Dhanu, Kumbha.

Catuṣpāda: Meṣa, Vṛṣabha, Siṅha.

Sarīsṛpa: Karka, Vṛścika.

Pakṣi: Makara, Mīna.

Kailāśa: Guruji, why is Dhanu classified as Manuṣya and Makara Pakṣi? Dṛṣṭi is based on the head, and therefore, Dhanu is considered Manuṣya. Makara and Mīna have weak knees, a characteristic of Pakṣi; therefore, they are considered Pakṣi.

Jayanta: The dṛṣṭis of the Grahas are stated below.

2.49-50. The Pakṣi Rāśis (i.e. Makara and Mīna) look upwards; the Sarīsṛpa Rāśis (Karka and Vṛścika) look downwards; Guru and Candra have Samadṛṣṭi (they aspect each other). Sūrya has Urdhvadṛṣṭi; Maṅgala has Tiryagdṛṣṭi; Śukra and Budha have Adhodṛṣṭi. Rāhu and Śani look alike.

अन्योऽन्यालोकितौ जीवचन्द्रौ उर्ध्व वेक्षणो रविः ॥१०॥ पश्यत्यरः कटाक्षेण पश्यतोऽथ कवीन्दुजो । एकदृष्ट यार्कमन्दौ च ग्रहाणामवलोकनम् ॥११॥

According to Pt Ramvyas Pandey, बृहस्पति और चंद्र एक दूसरे को देखते हैं। सूर्य ऊपर को देखता है। मंगल और बुध कटाक्ष से देखते हैं, सूर्य और शनि एक दृष्टि से देखते है इस प्रकार ग्रहों का अवलोकन है। It means Guru and Candra aspect each other. Sūrya looks upwards. Maṅgala and Budha aspect sideward through the corner of their eyes. Sūrya and Śani aspect each other with a single gaze. This is how the Grahas aspect.

Jayanta: Now, the direction of the lost things is specified.

2.51-52. If an article is lost, Meṣa signifies east; Siṅha and Dhanu south-east; Vṛṣabha south; Makara and Kanyā south-west; Mithuna west; Tulā and Kumbha north-west; Karka north; Vṛścika and Mīna north-east directions in which it is likely to be found.

मेषः प्राच्यां धनुः सिंहान्नाश्च दक्षिणे । मृगकन्ये च नैरृत्यां मिथुनः पश्चिमे तथा ॥१२॥
वायुभागे तुलाकुम्भौ उदीच्यां कर्क उच्यते । ईशभागेऽलिमीनौ च नष्टद्रव्यादिसुचकाः ॥१३॥

Kailāśa: Guruji, this does not follow the traditional assignment of direction to Rāśis. Could you explain this?

Ācārya: The direction associated with the Rāśis is shown in the diagram. This is indeed unique. Normally, the directions are either in the form of E-S-W-N repeating or E-E-S-S-S-SW-W-W-NW-N-N-NE.

NE	E	S	W
NW			N
SW			SE
SE	NE	NW	SW

But, this starts with E-S-W-N, and then for each assignment of E-S-W-N after that, it adds, S-S-N-N-S-S-N-N, covering all the corner directions.

Sunidhi: Guruji, what is the rationale behind the direction order E-S-W-N?

Ācārya: That is the natural order, which is clockwise. E is followed by S, which is followed by W and then N. This manifest in two ways in Rāśis. They are shown below. In the 1st manifestation, the corner Rāśis are not included, whereas, in the 2nd manifestation, they are included.

N	E	S	W
W			N
S			E
E	N	S	W

NE	E	E	SE
N			S
N			S
NW	W	W	SW

Jayanta: Now, the direction of the Grahas.

2.53. As Sūrya, Śukra, Maṅgala, Rāhu, Śani, Candra, Budha and Guru, respectively, the directions E, SE, S, SW, W, NW, N and NE, the lost object can be found according to the Graha indication.

Kailāśa: They are the regular direction of the Grahas. Isn't it?

Ācārya: Indeed, they are the eight directions governed by the Dikpālas. There are 10 directions, including the upward and downward, governed by Ketu (upward) and Lagna (downward).

The Dikpālas are E Indra (Sūrya), SE Agni (Śukra), S Yāma (Maṅgala), SW Nirṛti (Rāhu), W Varuṇa (Śani), NW Vāyu (Candra), N Kubera (Budha) and NE Īśāna (Guru).

There are four Kendra directions called cardinal direction, E, S, W, and N, and four Koṇa directions, SE, SW, NW, and NE. The four corner directions are called Āgneya Koṇa, Nairṛtya Koṇa, Vāyavya Koṇa and Aiśānya Koṇa.

The vibrations of the directions are according to their Dikpāla. For honour and influence, you should pray to Indra facing E; for wealth, pray to Kubera, facing north.

Kailāśa; That is so revealing, Guruji!

Ācārya: Yes, it is. Different Mandirs are also aligned to the directions depending on their purpose.

Kailāśa: Guruji, how would we know the direction of the Mandir?

Ācārya: Every Mandir has a Navagraha Vigraha, which is like a compass that tells you the direction of the main Vigraha or the Mūrti of the Devatā.

In a Navagraha Vigraha Surya is in the centre, Śukra E, Maṅgala S, Śani W, Bṛhaspati N, Candra SE, Rahu SW, Ketu NW and Budha NE. From Sūrya's face, you can identify the direction of the Mandir's face and which direction you will face while worshipping the main Devatā.

You can also use a compass. Face the main Vigraha and check which direction you are facing. You are activating the blessings of that Devatā.

While worshipping the main Vigraha, you are facing NE, Guru's direction; then the Mandir is for the blessing of Jñāna (knowledge) and Santāna (children). You can think about all of Guru's Kārakatvas.

For instance, when you face the main entrance of Śrī Kedāranātha Mandir, you will be facing north – Budha – Kubera. This can help remove your financial woes and help rejuvenate you (Budha = child = rejuvenation).

When you worship Sūrya facing E with Gāyatri Mantra, you slowly move towards self-realisation and remove your Tamas (darkness, ignorance). When you worship Sūrya facing W in the evening, the helps you get blessings of Śani, removing your past negative Karmas.

Worshipping Viṣṇu, when Sūrya is in the north, helps you remove financial difficulties and give success in the undertaking. Worshipping Śakti, when Sūrya is below the earth (Midnight), will give you success in battles and overcoming enemies as that activates Maṅgala's vibrations.

Sunidhi: Guruji, this is so enlightening.

Ācārya: This gives rise to four Sandhyās, Prātaḥ, Madhyānha, Sāyaṁ, and Turiya. You must worship Sūrya (Brahmā – creation), Viṣṇu, Maheśvara, and Devī in those Sandhyās with their Gayatris. You should either use Prasiddha Mantra or get initiation from a Guru into their tradition!

Jayanta: Now the gender of the Rāśi and Grahas are explained.

2.54-55. Meṣa, Mithuna, Dhanu, Kumbha, Tulā and Siṅha are Ojarāśis. The other six Vṛṣabha, Karka, Kanyā, Vṛścika, Makara and Mīna are Yugmarāśis. Sūrya, Maṅgala and Guru are Puruṣa Grahas; Śukra, Candra and Rāhu are Strī Grahas; and the rest Śani, Budha and Ketu are Eunuch Grahas.

Ācārya: Ojarāśis are masculine (Puruṣa), and Yugmarāśis are feminine (Strī). The Grahas are arranged in Vāra order based on Puruṣa and Strī. Sūrya, Maṅgala, Guru, Śani are masculine, with Śani as masculine eunuch. Candra, Budha, and Śukra are feminine, with Budha as a feminine eunuch. Rāhu is masculine and Ketu is feminine (feminine eunuch).

Jayanta: Now, whether the Rāśis like to stay in the company or alone is explained.

2.56. Tulā, Dhanu, Mithuna and Kumbha are Ojarāśis living in company, while Meṣa and Siṅha are Ojarāśis living separately. Vṛṣabha, Karka, Vṛścika, and Kanyā are Yugmarāśis living alone, while Makara and Mīna are Yugmarāśis living together.

तुलाकोदण्डमिथुना घटयुग्मं नराः स्मृताः । एकाकिनो मेपसिंह वृषकर्कालिकन्यकाः ॥१७॥ एकाकिनः स्त्रियो प्रोक्ताः त्रयुग्मौ प्रकरान्तिमौ । एकाकिनोऽर्केन्दुकुजाः शुक्रज्ञार्काहिमन्त्रिणः ॥१८॥ एते युग्मग्रहाः प्रोक्ताः शास्त्र ज्ञानप्रदीपके ।

Ācārya: Among the Ojarāśis, the Manuṣya Rāśis (Tulā, Dhanu, Mithuna and Kumbha) stay in a community. The Paśu Rāśis (Meṣa and Siṅha) stay in solitude. Among the Yugmarāśis, the Pakṣi Rāśis (Makara and Mīna) stay in a community, whereas Paśu/Kīṭa Rāśis (Vṛṣabha, Karka, Vṛścika) stay in solitude.

Sunidhi: What is the effect of that Guruji?

Ācārya: Community Grahas/Rāśis like teamwork, while the other Rāśis/Grahas like to work independently!

2.57. Sūrya, Candra and Maṅgala are separate Grahas, while Śukra, Budha, Śani, Rāhu and Guru are Grahas living together, i.e. Yugma 5 Grahas.

Ācārya: Among the Grahas Śukra, Budha, Śani, Rāhu and Guru like to stay in the community, whereas Sūrya, Candra and Maṅgala like to stay alone. Therefore Śukra, Budha, Śani, Rāhu and Guru are called Yugma Grahas. Here Yugma means two or company of at least two people.

Jayanta: Now, the Varṇas of the Rāśis are explained.

2.58. Karka, Vṛścika and Mīna are Brāhmaṇas; Meṣa, Siṅha and Dhanu are Kṣatriyas; Mithuna, Tulā and Kumbha are Vaisyas; and Vṛṣabha, Kanyā and Makara are Śudras. विप्राः कार्यालिमीनाश्च धनुः सिंहक्रिया नृपाः ॥१६॥ तुलायुग्मघटा वैश्याः शूद्रा नकोक्षकन्यकाः ।

Ācārya: This is straightforward: Jalarāśi = Brāhmaṇa, Agnirāśi = Kṣatriya, Pṛthvīrāśi = Vaiśya and Vāyurāśi = Śudra.

Sunidhi: Guruji, why must we classify a person in Jāti or caste? That is unfair. This causes all kinds of social problems.

Ācārya: These are not Jāti, but Varṇas. This is how society works. The work is classified into knowledge work (Brāhmaṇa), Governance/Security (Kṣatriya), Trading (Vaiśya), Agriculture and manual labour (Śudra). People are gravitated to different Varṇas depending on their capability and merit.

You may be born as a Śudra but can become a Brāhmaṇa if you practice knowledge like Vidura was born to a maidservant (Pariśrami) and Maharṣi Vyāsa.

Still, he becomes one of the foremost Brāhmaṇa. You become what you are regardless of your birth. Birth is only a starting point, but your ending can differ.

Do not get influenced by the modern-day propagandist, who confuse Varṇa with Jāti and spread misinformation about Sanātana Dharma!

Jayanta: Now, the Varṇas of the Grahas are stated.

2.59. Likewise among Grahas, Guru and Candra are Brāhmaṇa Grahas; Sūrya and Maṅgala, Kṣatriya Grahas; Budha is Vaisya; Śukra Śudra; and Śani and Rāhu Nīca (sinful or fallen). नृपौ अर्ककुजौ विप्रो बृहस्पतिनिशाकरौ ॥२०॥ बुधा वैश्यो भृगुः शूद्रो नीचा वर्कभुजङ्गमौ ।

Sunidhi: Guruji, there is a difference in opinion here from mainstream Jyotiṣa!

Ācārya: Yes, there is. Normally Guru/Śukra are considered Brāhmaṇa, Sūrya/Maṅgala Kṣatriya, Candra/Budha Vaiśya, Śani Śudra, Rāhu Mlecchā (Vidharmi – follower of non-Vedic Dharma), and Ketu Monks (outside of the Varṇas).

Kailāśa: Surprisingly, the author designates Śukra, the Guru of the Asuras, as Śudra and Śani/Rāhu as fallen. Candra is saumya but not as knowledgeable as Guru and Śukra, so classifying him as Brāhmaṇa does not make sense.

Ācārya: The author may have tried to add his perspective. So, you may try if this works.

Jayanta: Now the author gives the colour of the Rāśis and Grahas.

2.60. Meṣa, Dhanu and Siṅha are red; Karka, Vṛṣabha and Tulā are white; Kumbha, Vṛścika and Mīna are dark (Shyama); and Mithuna, Kanyā and Makara are black (Kṛṣṇa). रक्ताः मेषधनुः सिंहाः कुलीरोक्षतुलास्सिताः ॥२१॥ कुम्भालिमीनाः श्यामाः स्युः कृष्णयुग्मांगनामृगाः ।

Kailāśa: Again, there are deviations from the conventional rules.

Ācārya: Yes, there is! According to the conventional rules, the colours related to the Rāśis are (1) Meṣa = Blood red, (2) Vṛṣabha = White, (3) Mithuna = Green, (4) Karka = Pale red, (5) Siṅha = Off white, (6) Kanyā = Variegated, (7) Tulā = Black, (8) Vṛścika = Yellow, (9) Dhanu = Tawny, (10) Makara = Multicolour, (11) Kumbha = Deep brown, (12) Mīna = colourless like water.

2.61. Among Grahas, too, are colours to be noted; Śukra white; Maṅgala red; Guru golden-limbed; Budha green; Candra white; Sūrya red; Śani and Rāhu black.

Kailāśa: The colour related to the Grahas are the same as the conventional rules.

Ācārya: Indeed! The Grahas are normally adorned in robes of these colours. For instance, Sūrya is adorned in a red robe, Candra in a white, etc. Sometimes, Śani is shown in a blue robe and Rāhu in black.

Kailāśa: Guruji, according to Maharṣi Parāśara (3.42a), the robes worn by the Grahas are in the order of (1) Sūrya – Red silken, (2) Candra – While silken,

(3) Maṅgala – Red, (4) Budha – Black silken, (5) Bṛhaspati – Saffron, (6) Śukra – Silken, (7) Śani – Multi-coloured clothes, (8) Rāhu – Multi-coloured clothes and (9) Ketu – Rags.

Jayanta: Now, the shape denoted by the Grahas are described.

2.62. Sūrya has a squarish body; Candra is round; Maṅgala is octagonal; Budha is square; Guru has a long body; Śukra a large form; Śani too large in form; Rāhu is round. चतुरस्त्रं च वृत्तं च कुशमव्यं त्रिकोणतः । दीर्घवृत्तं तथाष्टात्र चतुरस्त्रायतं तथा ॥२४॥ दीर्घायिते क्रमादेते सूर्याद्याः क्रमशो मताः । सूर्य आदि नव ग्रहों का स्वरूप क्रमशः इस प्रकार है. चौकोना, वृत्ताकार, बीच में पतला त्रिभुज, दीर्घवृत्त (अंडाकार), अष्टभुज, चौकोना, आयत और लंबा ।

Sunidhi: Guruji, can you explain how to interpret them?

Ācārya: They indicate the shape of the face of people ruled by the Grahas, Sūrya – squarish, Candra – circular and so on.

2.63. Sūrya has 5 Raśmis; Candra 21; Maṅgala 2; Budha 9; Guru 10; Śukra 16; and Śani 4. पञ्चैकविंशयो दृष्टी नवदिक षोडशाब्धयः ॥२५॥ भास्करादिग्रहाणां च किरणाः परिकीर्तिताः ।

2.64. The Rāśis have the following number of Raśmis: Meṣa 8; Vṛṣabha 11; Mithuna 6; Karka 11; Siṅha 3; Kanyā 6; Tulā 14; Vṛścika 14; Dhanu 10; Makara 100; Kumbha 4; and Mīna 34. वसु रुद्राश्च रुद्राश्च वह्निषट्कं चतुर्दशम् ॥२६॥ विश्वशा शतवेदाश्च चतुस्त्रिंशदजादिना । कुलीराजतुलाकुम्भकिरणा वसुसंख्यया ॥२७॥ मिथुनोक्षमृगाणां च किरणा ऋतुसंख्यया । सिंहस्य किरणाः सप्त कन्याकार्मुकयोस्तथा ॥२८॥ चत्वारो वृश्चिकस्योक्ताः सप्तविंशत् झषस्य च ।

८, ११, ११, ३, ६, १४, १३, १०, १००, ४, ४ और ये संख्यायें क्रमशः मेषादि राशियों की किरणों की घोतक हैं। किसी के मत में कर्क, मेष, तुला और कुंभ इनकी किरणों की संख्या ८ है। मिथुन वृष और मकर की ६, सिंह, कन्या और मकर की ७, वृश्चिक की ४, और मीन की किरणसंख्या २७ है ।

2.65-67. But there are others giving different figures for the Rāśis: Karka, Meṣa, Tulā and Kumbha 8 each; Mithuna, Vṛṣabha and Makara 6; Siṅha 7; Kanyā and Dhanu 7; Vṛścika 4 and Mīna 27. Another version is that from Meṣa onwards to Mīna, the Raśmis are respectively, 7, 8, 5, 3, 7, 11, 2, 4, 6, 8, 7 and 20. सप्ताष्टशरवह्न्यद्रिरुद्रयुग्धाब्धिषड्वसु ॥२६॥ सप्तविंशतिसँख्याश्च मेषादीनां परे विदुः । कुछ आचार्य ऐसा भी मानते हैं कि मेषादि राशियों की संख्या कमशः ७, ८, ५, ३, ७, ११, २, ४, ४, ६, ८ और २७ ये हैं।

Kailāśa: According to Maharṣi Parāśara (73.1), the Raśmis of the Grahas are Sūrya 10, Candra 9, Maṅgala 5, Budha 5, Guru 7, Śukra 8 and Śani 5. This is used for determining the Raśmibala.

Sunidhi: The Raśmis, according to Jinendramāla, are:

1.53. (1) Meṣa 7; (2) Vṛṣabha 8; (3) Mithuna 5; (4) Karka 8; (5) Siṅha 7; (6) Kanyā 11; (7) Tulā 2; (8) Vṛścika 4; (9) Dhanu 6; (10) Makara 8; (11) Kumbha 8; (12) Mīna 27.

1.54. (1) Sūrya 5; (2) Candra 21; (3) Maṅgala 7; (4) Budha 9; (5) Bṛhaspati 10; (6) Śukra 16; (7) Śani 4; (8) Rāhu 4.

Jayanta: Now, the status of the Grahas are described.

2.68. Maṅgala, Candra and Śani are short-statured; Guru, Budha and Rāhu are tall; and Sūrya and Śukra are middling. कुजेन्दुशनयो ह्रस्वा दीर्घा जीवबुधोरगाः ॥३०॥ रविशुकौ समौ प्रोक्तौ शास्त्रे ज्ञानप्रदीपके । मंगल चन्द्रमा और शनि ये ह्रस्व, वृहस्पति बुध राहु ये लंबे कद तथा सूर्य शुक्र ये समान कदके इस ज्ञानप्रदीपक में कहे गये हैं ।

Sunidhi: This is straightforward. This denotes the heights of people ruled by the Grahas. Tall = Guru/Budha/Rāhu. Middling = Sūrya/Śukra and Short = Maṅgala/Candra/Śani.

Kailāśa: Isn't Śani described as tall and emaciated?

Ācārya: Yes, that is right. But, normally, if other factors are not supportive, Śani ruled people and objects are shorter. If Śani has Saumya influences, it can indicate someone tall and emaciated.

Jayanta: Now, the distance denoted by the Grahas are described.

2.69. Regarding the distance in yojana to which the individual Graha's influence extends, it is stated that Sūrya, Śani and Budha 8, Śukra 16; Guru 9; Maṅgala 7, and Candra 21. आदित्यशनि सौम्यानां योजनं चाष्टसंख्यया ॥३१॥ शुक्रस्य षोडशोक्तानि गुरोश्च नवयोजनम् । सूर्य, शनि और बुध इनके योजन की संख्या ८ होती हैं। शुक्र की योजन संख्या १६ और गुरु की नव है ।

Sunidhi: Why is the distance stated in Yojana?

Ācārya: That is the ancient measure of distances. The diameter of Grahas, distance from Sūrya etc., are measured in Yojanas. One's travels from one place to another were also measured in Yojanas.

Kailāśa: How much is a Yojana in modern measures?

Ācārya: It is about 8-9 miles or 12-14 km. There were different usage in different places. They are useful in locating a lost object, how far a thief has travelled etc.

Jayanta: Now, the age of the Grahas are described.

2.70-71. About their respective ages, Maṅgala is 16 years; Śukra 7; Budha 20; Guru 30; Candra 70; Sūrya 50; Śani and Rāhu 100 years. भूमिजः षोडशवयाः शुक्रः सप्तवयास्तथा ॥३२॥ विंशदवयाश्चन्द्रसुतः गुरुस्त्रिंशद्वयाः स्मृतः । शशांकः सप्ततिवयाः पञ्चाशद् भास्करस्य वै ॥३३॥ शनैश्चरस्य राहोश्च शतसंख्यं वयो भवेत् । मंगल की अवस्था १६ वर्ष की, शुक्र की सात की, बुध की बीस की, गुरु की तीस की, चन्द्रमा की सत्तर की, सूर्य की पचास की, शनि और राहु की अवस्था सौ वर्ष की है।

Sunidhi: What is the applicability of age, Guruji?

Ācārya: There are several applicability, i.e., finding the age of a thief, the age of your partner or spouse, you are planning to marry etc.

Kailāśa: There seem to be differences in opinions among the scholars about age.

Ācārya: Yes, there are some differences. The following is based on Praśnamārga 14.2

Depending on the Grahas owning (or occupying) the Praśna Lagna (or Āruṛha), the age of the Pṛcchaka is Bālacandra/Maṅgala under 5, Budha 8, Śukra 16, Guru 30, Sūrya/Vṛddhacandra 70, Śani/Rāhu 70+.

Sunidhi: What are infant and aged Candra?

Ācārya: Candra is Bāla from S1 till S5. He is Vṛddha from K8 till K15 (Amāvasyā). Between S5 and K8, the age can be calculated by proportion.

According to Daivajñavallabha 9.5:

The ages of the Grahas, Candra, Maṅgala, Budha, Śukra, Bṛhaspati, Sūrya and Śani are respectively those of (1) suckling child (2) boy (3) celibate (4) young man (5) middle-aged person (6) old man (7) and very old man. Roughly the ages are Candra- under 5, Maṅgala- 5 to 8, Budha- 8 to 16, Śukra- 16 to 30, Bṛhaspati- 30 to 50, Sūrya- 50 to 70 and Śani- 70 and above.]

Jayanta: Now, the taste of the Grahas is explained.

2.72. Śani and Rāhu love bitter taste; Guru sweet; Śukra sour; Maṅgala salty; Budha astringent and Sūrya hot. तिक्तौ शनैश्चरो राहुः मधुरस्तु बृहस्पतिः ॥३४॥ अम्लं भृगुर्विधुः क्षारं कुजस्य क्रूरजा रसाः । तवरः सोमपुत्रस्य भास्करस्य कटुर्भवेत् ॥३५॥ शनि और राहु तिक्त, बृहस्पति मधुर, शुक अम्ल, मंगल खारा, बुध कसैला और रवि कटु-ग्रह हैं।

Sunidhi: There are deviations even in taste matters.

Ācārya: Yes, there is! Seven tastes are recognized in Jyotiṣaśāstra, including six pure and one mixed. The governors of the tastes are (1) Sūrya – Pungent, (2) Candra – Salty, (3) Maṅgala – Bitter, (4) Budha – Mixed, (5) Bṛhaspati – Sweet, (6) Śukra – Acidulous (sour), (7) Śani – Astringent (like in pulses or raw guava or spinach). Phaladīpikā 2.31 also gives the same list.

Sunidhi: How to use this principle?

Ācārya: Depending on the Graha in Lagna or owning the Lagna, the native likes these tastes.

In Praśna, this is useful in determining the taste of the food served or eaten, i.e., in Bhojana Praśna. This can also indicate the preference for tastes among family members.

Jayanta: The distinguishing mark in the body described now.

2.73. One must ascertain distinguishing marks on the right side of one's body with the help of Sūrya, Budha, Maṅgala and Guru; the left side by Rāhu, Candra, Śukra and Śani.

2.74. There are distinct marks to be found for Śukra in the face; Maṅgala in the rear; Guru on the shoulder; Budha in the armpit; Candra on the head; Sūrya in the buttocks; Śani in the thighs, and Rāhu in the feet.

Ācārya: The distinguishing marks of the Grahas are as follows:

Right side: Sūrya, Budha, Maṅgala and Guru

Left side: Rāhu, Candra, Śukra and Śani

Sunidhi: This is based on which principle, Guruji?

Ācārya: Masculinity = Right side, and Femininity = Left side. Therefore, masculine Grahas, Sūrya, Maṅgala and Guru have marks on the right side, and the feminine Grahas Candra and Śukra on the left side.

Kailāśa: How about Budha and Śani?

Ācārya: They are normally considered eunuchs. Besides, Budha is feminine, and Śani is masculine. But the author seems to have interchanged that. Also, Rāhu is Masculine, and Ketu is feminine. So their mark should be on the right or left side accordingly.

Sunidhi: Where to use this, Guruji?

Ācārya: You can use them to verify someone's Lagna or identify a thief based on body marks.

Jayanta: The horns denoted by the Grahas are explained now.

2.75. Budha and Sūrya are broken-horned; Candra has no horn; Maṅgala is sharp-horned; Guru and Śukra are long-horned; Śani and Rāhu have crooked, bent horns.

Kailāśa: Guruji, not all Grahas denote Catuṣpāda or animals. So how come they have horns?

Ācārya: That is an excellent question. When you have ascertained the subject of a Praśna is a certain animal, i.e., one kept in a zoo, or domesticated or killed in hunting etc., the kind of animals are known by their horns.

Sunidhi: Can you give some examples?

Ācārya: Some animals do not have horns, like elephant, tiger, lion, horse, zebra, dog, cat etc. Some animals have horns, like cows, bulls, buffalo, dear and several other plant-eating mammals (Catuṣpāda).

Kailāśa: Carnivores do not have horns, whereas herbivores have horns.

Ācārya: Normally, carnivores do not have horns, but herbivores are divided into two classes, horned and non-horned. Cow, Bull, Deer etc., have horns, whereas Horse, Zebra, Donkeys etc., do not.

The Grahas are divided into 5 classes.

No horn: Candra

Long-horn: Guru and Śukra

Sharp-horn: Maṅgala

Crooked-horn: Śani and Rāhu

Broken-horn: Budha and Sūrya

Jayanta: The Rāśis are now classified into standing, walking etc.

2.76. Vṛṣabha, Siṅha, Vṛścika and Kumbha are Sthira and standing Rāśis. Karka, Makara, Tulā and Mīna are Cara and walking Rāśis. Mithuna Kanyā, Dhanu and Mīna are Dvisvabhāva sleeping Rāśis.

Ācārya: This is based on the Cara, Sthira, Dvisvabhāva Rāśis. Cararāśis have high energy, and therefore, they are designated as walking. Sthirarāśis have low energy, and therefore, they are designated as standing. The Dvisvabhāva Rāśis have middling energy; therefore, they are designated sleeping.

Jayanta: The Rāśis are now classified as forests etc.

2.77-78. Dhanu and Meṣa indicate the border of forests; Kanyā and Mithuna mean towns; Siṅha, Dhanu, Tulā, Mīna and Makara indicate water; Karka a river; Vṛṣabha a canal; Kumbha a milk pot; Vṛścika a well. धनुर्मेषवनं प्रोक्तं कन्यका मिथुनं पुरे ॥३७॥ हरिर्गिरौ तुलामीनमकराः सलिलेषु च । धनु और मेष इनका स्थान वन है, कन्या और मिथुन का ग्राम, सिंह का पर्वत और तुला मीन और मकर का स्थान जल में है । नद्यां कुलीरः कुल्यायां वृषः कुंभः पयोघटे ॥३८॥ वृश्चिकः कूपसलिले राशीनां स्थितिरीरिता । कर्क का स्थान नदी में, वृष का कुल्या (क्षुद्रजलाशय) में कुंभ का जल के घड़े में, वृश्चिक का स्थान कुए के पानी में है - यही राशियों की स्थिति है ।

Ācārya: They are some more indications of the Rāśis.

Meṣa and Siṅha are forests, Meṣa is a mountainous forest, and Dhanu is a forest abounding horses, zebra, deer etc.

Kanyā and Mithuna are villages because they are Manuṣya Rāśis and owned by Budha. Both indicate places of social interaction; Mithuna is a drawing room or playroom, whereas Kanyā is a garden.

Vṛścika denotes a waterfilled well. Karka's place is near a river, and Vṛṣabha is near a small water body. Vṛṣabha is Sthirarāśi, with a strong influence of Candra and Śukra, and therefore, indicates a waterbody but steady, like a small pond or lake. Kumbha denotes a place with a water pot.

Sunidhi: Is this related to finding the location of a lost object?

Ācārya: Yes, that is right!

Jayanta: Further indications of the Rāśis are explained.

2.79. The Rāśis from Meṣa onwards to Mīna respectively indicate; (1) a forest, (2) a paddy field, (3) a garden, (4) a canal, (5) a mountain, (6) forest-land (7) river-bank (8) big well (9) tank (10) river (11) water-pot, and (12) well. In these places, the lost property can be found.

Ācārya: The indications of a Rāśi are dependent on a combination of Manuṣyādi, Carādi attributes and its symbols.

Budha: Cara indicates movement like Meṣa – mountainous trail, Karka – flowing river, Tulā – a marketplace with transactions and movement of people, and Makara – a swampy land on which boats and river animals such as crocodiles are plying.

Sthira indicates steadiness like Vṛṣabha – a grassland or a granary where grains are stored, Siṅha – a jungle with a fort, Vṛścika – a well with stagnant water, and Kumbha – a pitcher holding water.

Dvisvabhāva indicates some movement like Mithuna – a drawing room where people are having conversations, Kanyā – a garden where children are playing, Dhanu – a jungle where horses and zebras are moving around, and hermits are moving around their cottages, Mīna – a boundless ocean with water tides.

Jayanta: Further indications of the Rāśi are explained.

2.80. Kumbha, Kanyā, Mithuna and Tulā indicate village; Meṣa, Vṛścika. Dhanu and Siṅha indicate forest; Karka, Vṛṣabha, Makara and Mīna indicate water.

Ācārya: They are based on the Manuṣyādi classification of the Rāśis. Mithuna, Kanyā, Tulā and Kumbha are Manuṣya Rāśi, therefore, indicating a place where people live, i.e., town, villages etc.

Meṣa, Vṛścika, Dhanu and Siṅha are Catuṣpāda and Kīṭa Rāśis, indicating a jungle filled with wild animals and poisonous creatures.

Karka, Makara and Mīna are Jalarāśis and indicate places abounding water such as rivers, swamps, and oceans. Vṛṣabha also denotes a small waterbody, as indicated before.

Jayanta: Now, the places denoted by the Grahas are stated.

2.81. Regarding Grahas, the places can be recognized thus: Maṅgala means earth; Śukra and Candra indicate water; Budha and Rāhu refer to the plain ground with no thorns but studded with pits; Guru and Sūrya to the sky; Śani, a battlefield. If the Grahas, however, are strong, the following indications must be noted; Sūrya, Śani and Maṅgala refer to earth; Guru and Śukra to the sky; Candra and Budha to the midway. This is the view of a few Jyotiṣīs.

वने चापि कुलिरेक्षनक्रमीनाः जलस्थिताः॥४१॥ विपिने शनिभौमार्कि भृगुचन्द्रौ जले स्थितौ। मेष, वृश्चिक, धनु और सिंह वन में तथा फर्क वृष, मकर और सोम ये जल में रहते हैं। इसी प्रकार शनि, भौम और सूर्य वन में, शुक्र और चंद्रमा जल में ...

बुधजीवौ च नगरे नष्टद्रव्यादि सूचकौ ॥४२॥ भौमे भूमिर्जलं काव्ये शशिनो बुधभागिनः। बुध और बृहस्पति नगर में नष्ट द्रव्य के सूचक होते हैं। इसी तरह मंगल के बलवान होने पर भूमि, शुक्र के बली होने पर जल चंद्रमा और बुध के बलवान होने पर ...

निष्कुटश्चैव रंधव गुरुभास्करयोर्नभः॥४३॥ मंदस्य युद्धभूमिश्च बलोत्तरखगे स्थिते। गृहोद्यान, बृहस्पति से छिद्र, सूर्य से आसमान, शनि के बलवान होने पर युद्ध की भूमि - ये नष्टद्रव्य के सूचक होते हैं।

सूर्याकरबले भूमौ गुरुशुकवले खगे ॥४४॥ चंद्रसौम्य मध्ये श्चिदेवमुदाहृतम्। सूर्य, मंगल और शनि के बलवान् होने पर भूमि में गुरु और शुक्र के बली होने पर आकाश में चन्द्रमा और बुध के बली होने पर बीच - ये किन्हीं किन्हीं का मत है।

Ācārya: Maṅgala is Bhumiputra, born from the earth, and therefore, is the Kāraka for Pṛthvī (even though Budha is Pṛthvī tattva). Śukra and Candra reside in water as they are Jalagrahas. Budha and Rāhu denote a plane ground. Guru and Sūrya denote the sky; Guru because he denotes Ākāśa tattva, and Sūrya because he shines on the sky. Śani denotes a battlefield, as that is where many people die!

Jayanta: Now, the association of Rāśis and different times of the day is explained.

2.82-83. Others express that the time of day, night or twilight must be determined by ascertaining the Rāśi where Sūrya is posited. Others say that Cararāśis means night, Sthirarāśis day, and the Dvisvabhāva Rāśi twilight.

निशादिवससन्ध्याश्च भानुयुग्राशिमादितः ॥४५॥ चरराशि वशादेवमिति केचित्प्रश्नचक्षते । कुछ लोग चर, स्थिर और द्विस्वभाव राशियों के वश से बात, दिन और सन्ध्या का क्रमशः निर्देश करते हैं।

Ācārya: Some people consider Cara as Rātri, Sthira as Dina and Dvisvabhāva as Sandhyā.

2.84. The time duration denotes by the Grahas are given below; Śani, one year; Sūrya 6 months; Budha 2 months; Guru 1 month; Śukra 15 days; Maṅgala 1 Vāra; and Candra 1 Muhūrta (48 min).

ग्रहेषु बलवान्यस्तु तद्वशाइलमोरयेत् ॥४६॥ शनेवर्षं तदर्धं स्याद्भानोर्मासद्वयं विदुः । ग्रहों का बल विचार करते समय जो बलवान हो उसी के अनुसार उसका बळ कहना चाहिये। शनि का डेढ़ वर्ष काल हैं, सूर्य का दो मास...

शुक्रस्य पक्षो जीवस्य मासो भौमस्य वासरः ॥४७॥ इंदोर्मुहूर्तमित्युक्तं ग्रहाणां वलतो वदेत् । शुक्र का एक पक्ष, बृहस्पति का एक मास, मंगल का एक दिन चंद्रमा का पक मुहूर्त काल है। प्रश्न विचारते समय ग्रहों का बलाबल विचार कर तदनुसार फल कहना चाहिये।

Ācārya: The time periods of Grahas are:

1 y – Śani

6m – Sūrya

1m – Guru

2m – Budha

15d – Śukra

1w/1d – Maṅgala

1 Muhūrta – Candra

2.85. The Grahas in Ucca have the following measurements in terms of minutes: Śani 24 min; Sūrya 12 min; Budha 10 sec; Śukra 2½ sec; Guru 5 sec; Maṅgala 1 ¼ sec and Candra ¼ sec.

2.86. If the Graha is in its Svarāśi, it means day; in a Mitrarāśi, 1 month; and in a Śatrurāśi or Nīcarāśi, a longer duration.

2.87. The 24 hours of the day are divided into 8 Yāmas of 3 hrs. They are owned by Grahas from Vāreśa Yāmakāla order, i.e., Sūrya, Maṅgala, Guru, Budha, Śukra, Śani, Candra and Rāhu.

They are also positioned from Sūrya onwards in Vāra order, in the 8 directions from E. In the first Yāma on Ravivāra, Sūrya is in E, Maṅgala is SE; Guru is S, Budha is SW, Śukra is W, Śani is NW, Candra is N, and Rāhu is NE.

In the 2nd Yāma, Sūrya moves to SE; therefore, Rāhu moves to E. Now count from Rāhu onwards from E. Similarly, in 3rd Yāma, from Candra in E, and so on.

In the second Yāma (i.e. 9 a.m. to 12 noon), Sūrya would have moved to the southeast, and likewise, all other Grahas would have moved regularly till we found Rāhu in direct east. The directions of the Grahas will likewise change in the 3rd,4th,5th, 6th,7th and 8th Yāmas. The movements of the Grahas in terms of the Rāśis, too, can be determined thus. Each Rāśi is divided into 4 Pādas, and the 12

Rāśis have 48 Pādas. In each Yāma, every Graha has 6 Pādas to move, i.e., in the first Yāma (6 to 9 a.m.) Sūrya will be in movement in 4 Pādas of Meṣa and 2 Pādas of Vṛṣabha, while Maṅgala will be in 2 Pādas of Vṛṣabha and 4 Pādas of Mithuna and so on for other Grahas.

सूर्यारजीवविच्छुक्रशनि चन्द्रभुजङ्गमाः । प्रागादिदिक्षु क्रमशश्चरेयुर्यामसङ्ख्यया ।
प्रागादीशानपर्यन्तान्वारेशाद्यन्तकान् ग्रहान् ॥८७॥

Ācārya: There are several classifications of an Ahorātra or Nychthemeron.

Horā: 24 segments of an Ahorātra – they imbibe the same quality as Vāras. Therefore, they are also called Kṣaṇavāra. They are also called Kālahorā.

Kāla: 16 segments of an Ahorātra – this is the basis of Rāhukālam.

Yāma: 8 segments of an Ahorātra – this is the basis of several computations in Praśna and Patāki Cakra.

Yāmārdha: half of a Yāma and similar to Kāla.

When a day is divided into 8 segments, each is known as a Yāma, which spans about 3 hours. When a Yāma is further divided into 2 parts, each is known as a Yāmārdha.

Sunidhi: How is Rāhukālam determined?

An Ahorātra is divided into 16 Kālas, 8 for the day and 8 for the night. The Dinakālas commence at Sūryodaya, and the Rātrikālas commence at Sūryāsta. The Rātrikālas commence from the 5th Graha in the Kāla order from the Vāreśa. For instance, on a Ravivāra, the Rātrikālas commence with Śukra, Somavāra – Bṛhaspati and so on.

The Grahas lord the Kalās in order Sūrya ☉ → Maṅgala ♂ → Bṛhaspati ♃ → Budha ☿ → Śukra ♀ → Śani ♄ → Candra ☽ → Rāhu ☊. This gives rise to Rāhukālam. Like Rāhukāla, the remaining seven Grahas also have their Kalās. During the day, the Rāhukālam for Ravivāra onwards is 8th, 2nd, 7th, 5th, 6th, 4th and 3rd Kālas. During the night, the Rāhukālam is counted from the 5th Graha of Vāreśa.

Sunidhi: What is the basis of the Kāla order, Guruji?

Ācārya: This is based on Kālacakra. In this Cakra, the 8 Grahas are the lords of eight directions, and the Cakra also has 28 Nakṣatras assigned to it. The following direction illustrates this.

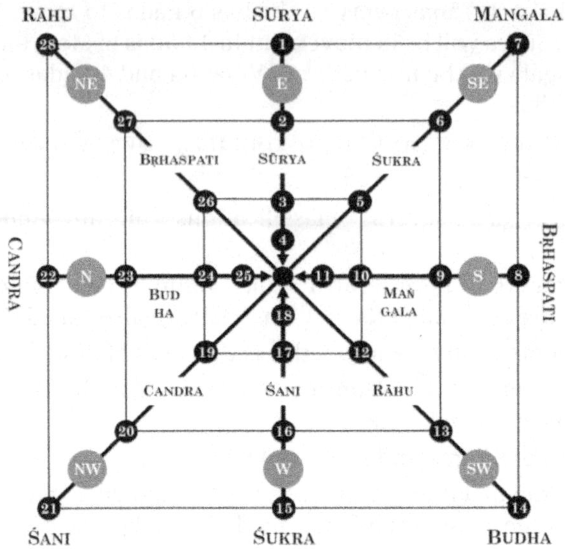

Sunidhi: What is this Cakra used for, Gurudeva?

Ācārya: This a several hidden esoteric usage. This is used for tracking the movement of Yogini.

Jayanta: Guruji, kindly tell us about the movement of Yogini in Kālacakra.

Ācārya: This knowledge is highly secretive and is known only to some Daivajñas. Understanding this is difficult, let alone applying it. But let me explain this.

The knowledge stems from Praśnamārga 16.81-116. The following ślokas are from Praśnamārga.

16.81. By examining Kālacakra, Nakṣatra, etc., we can work out Yogini and Mṛtyu. From these processes also, some effects can be predicted.

Kailāśa: What is Mṛtyu, Gurudeva?

Ācārya: We shall learn how to determine that. It is an indicator of destruction and death.

Let us start with reviewing the Nakṣatras. In this Cakra, like Sarvatobhadra and other Cakras, there are 28 Nakṣatras, including Abhijit. The Nakṣatras are assigned numbers 1 to 28 for ease of reference. Abhijit is an intercalary Nakṣatra that falls between Uttarāṣāṛhā and Śravaṇa.

1 Aśvinī, 2 Bharaṇī, 3 Kṛttikā 4 Rohiṇī, 5 Mṛgaśirā, 6 Ārdrā 7 Punarvasu

8 Puṣya, 9 Aśleṣā, 10 Maghā, 11 P.phālgunī, 12 U.phālgunī, 13 Hastā, 14 Citrā

15 Svāti, 16 Viśākhā, 17 Anurādhā, 18 Jyeṣṭhā, 19 Mūla, 20 P.āṣāṛhā, 21 U.āṣāṛhā

22 Abhijit, 23 Śravaṇa, 24 Dhaniṣṭhā, 25 Śatabhiṣā, 26 P.bhādra, 27 U.bhādra, 28 Revatī

Kailāśa: What is the span of Abhijit?

Ācārya: Abhijit starts from the last Caraṇa of Uttarāṣāṛhā and extends till the 1/15th part of Śravaṇa. It lies between 276°40' to 280°53'20" in the Bhācakra, which is Makara 6°40' to 10°53'20".

Kailāśa: Dhanyavād Guruji,

Ācārya: Let us now learn about assigning the Tārās to the Kālacakra. That is the first step.

Sunidhi: I am looking forward to it, Guruji!

Ācārya: The śloka is

16.82-84. Draw three squares, one inside the other and prepare a Cakra. Beginning from the centre of the top horizontal line (E), establish the 28 Tārās in the 28 parts in the order shown in the diagram. Starting from No. 1, the count should be done in the order in which the figures are shown in the Cakra.

You should remember the following schema.

TC → C → TR → RC → C → BR → BC → C → BL → LC → C → TL

Here T = Top, B = Bottom, R = Right, L = Left, C = Centre.

This can also be written as

E → C → SE → S → C → SW → W → C → NW → N → C → NE

There are four primary directions, E, S, W, and N and four secondary directions, SE, SW, NW, and NE. The direction of motion from the main directions is inward (towards the centre). It is outward for the corner directions.

Also, are four Nakṣatras in the primary directions and 3 Nakṣatras in the secondary.

It is like a fort with 3 concentric walls. Each wall has 8 Nakṣatras, which gives rise to 24 Nakṣatras. The remaining 4 Nakṣatras are in the inner sanctum or the centre of the fort.

Kailāśa: Guruji, I think I can construct the Kālacakra from the rules mentioned.

Ācārya: The next is to find three objects, Prāṇa, Deha and Mṛtyu. As the name suggests, Prāṇa is life, Deha is body, and Mṛtyu is death. The śloka is as follows:

16.85. (1) Prāṇa: Assign the Tārā held by Sūrya at Praśna to 1. Count from this to the Tārā held by Candra at Praśna, and the point arrived at is Prāṇa. **(2) Deha:** Assign Janmatārā to 1 and count from it to the Prāṇa Tārā. The point arrived at is Deha. **(3) Mṛtyu:** Assign Kṛttikā to 28 and count from here to Praśna Tārā in an anti-clockwise order. The point arrived at is Mṛtyu. If all these three points fall in the same line, it indicates death.

Jayanta: Guruji, kindly explain it. It isn't very clear.

Ācārya: Suppose at a Praśna, Sūrya is in Aśleṣā (9), and Candra in Citrā (14), Guḷika is in Śatabhiṣā (25), while the Janmatārā is Mṛgaśirā (5).

(1) Prāṇa: Count Praśna Candratārā from Praśna Sūryatārā, and the count so arrived is the Prāṇa. **Prāṇa** = Praśna Candratārā – Praśna Sūryatārā + 1 = 14 - 9 + 1 = 6. Therefore, Prāṇa falls in 6.

(2) Deha: Count Praśna Candratārā from Janmatārā, and the count so arrived is the Deha. **Deha** = Praśna Candratārā – Janmatārā + 1 = 14 - 5 + 1 = 10. Therefore, Deha falls in 10.

(3) Mṛtyu: Count Praśna Candratārā from Kṛttikā that is assigned to 28, in reverse order. **Mṛtyu** = Kṛttikā - Praśna Candratārā - 28 = 3 - 14 - 28 = -39. Since it is negative, we must add to it multiples of 28. Adding 56, we arrive at 17. Therefore, Mṛtyu falls in 17.

Kailāśa: So, we count where the Tārās of Sūrya, Candra etc., are from other Tārās and identify where the Prāṇa, Deha and Mṛtyu area?

Ācārya: That is right. When they are in the same line, death occurs.

Sunidhi: What if two are in the same line?

Ācārya: If Mṛtyu is in the same line as Deha, health suffers. If it is in the same line as Prāṇa, the person becomes low-spirited or dejected. He may have psychological suffering. If Deha and Prāṇa are in the same line, it is good – the person is high-spirited.

Sunidhi: So, in the example you mentioned above, 6, 10 and 17 do not fall in a straight line, and therefore, this is not life-threatening.

Ācārya: Yes, tha is right! This is explained in the next śloka.

16.86. (1) If **Deha and Mṛtyu** fall on the same line, the sickness is prolonged. **(2)** If **Prāṇa and Mṛtyu** fall on the same line, the person will be dull and have fits occasionally. **(3)** Assign Kṛttikā to 1. Count the Tārās held by Guḻika, Sūrya and Janmatārā from Kṛttikā. Death is likely if the three points fall in the same line (except the central vertical).

Sunidhi: Kindly explain this!

Ācārya: Even though no special designation is attached to the count arrived now, we should call them Prana2, Deha2, and Mrtyu2.

Prana2 = Praśna Sūryatārā – Kṛttikā + 1 = 9 – 3 + 1 = 7.

Deha2 = Praśna Guḻikatārā – Kṛttikā + 1 = 25 - 3 + 1 = 23.

Mrtyu2 = Janmatārā – Kṛttikā + 1 = 5 - 3 + 1 = 3.

There is no threat since points 7, 23, and 3 do not fall in the same line.

Kailāśa: After knowing the Prāṇa, Deha and Mṛtyu, what is next?

Ācārya: The next is to ascertain the position of Yogini.

Kailāśa: What are Yoginis, Guruji?

Ācārya: It is a vast topic, but let me give a brief background.

Yogini originated from Yoga, which means union. Yogini is the feminine form of Yogī or a female Yoga practitioner. A yogini is the sacred feminine force manifested as an aspect of Parvati and revered in the yogini Mandirs of India as the Sixty-four Yoginis.

In the 11th-century collection of legends, the Kathāsaritsāgara, a yogini, is one of a class of females with magical powers, sometimes enumerated as 8, 60, 64 or 65. The Hatha Yoga Pradīpikā mentions yoginis.

In Yogini Daśā, the 8 Yoginis contribute to 36 years. They are 1. Maṅgala, Sūrya, Dhānya, Bhrāmarī, Bhadrikā, Ulka, Siddha and Saṅkaṭā. They contribute 1y, 2y, 3y, 4y, 5y, 6y, 7y and 8y. They are associated with the Grahas, Candra, Sūrya, Guru, Maṅgala, Budha, Śani, Śukra and Rāhu.

Kailāśa: What do we do knowing the position of Yogini in Kālacakra?

Ācārya: Praśnamārga states the following:

16.87. Count from Kṛttikā to Praśna Sūryatārā. If this coincides with the point signified by Janmatārā and Yogini, the native may die. Some relatives may die if all three points fall in the same line. The movement of Yogini is given in the forthcoming ślokas.

Sunidhi: Kindly explain this, Guruji.

Ācārya: Suppose the Janmatārā is Mṛgaśirā and Praśna Sūryatārā is Dhaniṣṭhā, and Yogini is at 12. Counting from Kṛttikā to Janmatārā, we arrive at 3. Again, counting from Kṛttikā to Dhaniṣṭhā, we arrive at 21. Life is not threatened since the three factors do not fall at the same point or line.

Kailāśa: So, how to ascertain their position?

Ācārya: In this regard, Praśnamārga states the following:

16.88-89. Yogini rises on Ravivāra to Śanivāra in the following manner: Ravivāra East (1), Somavāra North (22), Maṅgalavāra Southeast (7), Budhavāra Southwest (14), Bṛhaspativāra South (8), Śukravāra West (15) and Śanivāra Northeast (21) respectively. After rising, it travels throughout the day through all 8 directions and returns to the starting point by Sūryāsta. At night it starts from the same point and moves again through various directions.

Kailāśa: How to interpret this, Guruji?

Ācārya: An Ahorātra is divided into two parts, Dina and Rātri or about 12 hrs or 30 Ghaṭis. Each of these parts is further divided into eight parts, called Yāmārdhas (or Kāla), about 1.5 hrs or 3.75 Ghaṭis.

The Yogini rises at Sūryodaya in the direction of Vāreśa and moves in the order of the 6th Kāla, which is Sūrya → Śani → Bṛhaspati → Rāhu → Śukra → Maṅgala → Candra → Budha.

This defines the rising and setting of various Kalās.

In each Yāmārdha, the Yogini covers 6 Tārās, and therefore, Yogini's stay in a Tārā is 0.25 hrs, or 15 min or 0.625 Ghaṭi or 37.5 Vighaṭika.

Therefore the Yogini covers each Tārā twice, excluding the 8 Tārās on the outermost square, i.e., 28, 1, 7, 8, 14, 15, 21 and 22.

There are 28 Tārās, and 2 cycles of it, make it 56. From 56, if we deduct 8, we get 48. Therefore, in a duration of a Dina or Rātri (30 Ghaṭis), the Yogini stays in 48 Nakṣatras, each about 15 min. The precise duration depends on the Dinamāna and Rātrimāna.

The following table shows the movement of Yogini on different Vāras and Kālas. For instance, on a Ravivāra, the Yogini rises in E (Sūrya's direction in Kālacakra), and in the first Kāla travels through Nakṣatras 1, 2, 3, 4, 19 and 20. In Somavāra, the Yogini rises in N (Candra's direction in Kālacakra) and moves through the Nakṣatras 22, 23, 24, 25, 12 and 13 in the first Kāla.

They rise in the Nakṣatra associated with the Nakṣatra in the Kālacakra.

Table 11

Kāla	**Ravi vāra**	**Soma vāra**	**Maṅgala vāra**	**Budha vāra**	**Bṛhaspat ivāra**	**Śukra vāra**	**Śani vāra**
1st	Sūrya E (1) 1,2,3,4,19, 20	Candra N (22) 22,23,24, 25,12,13	Maṅgala SE (7) 7,6,5,25,2 4,23	Budha SW (14) 14,13,12, 3,4,2	Bṛhaspati S (8) 8,9,10,11, 26,27	Śukra W (15) 15,16,17, 18,5,6	Śani NW (21) 21,20,19, 11,10,9
2nd	Śani NW (21) 21,20,19, 11,10,9	Budha SW (14) 14,13,12, 3,4,2	Candra N (22) 22,23,24, 25,12,13	Sūrya E (1) 1,2,3,4,19, 20	Rāhu NE (28) 28,27,28, 18,17,16	Maṅgala SE (7) 7,6,5,25,2 4,23	Bṛhaspati S (8) 8,9,10,11, 26,27
3rd	Bṛhaspati S (8) 8,9,10,11, 26,27	Sūrya E (1) 1,2,3,4,19, 20	Budha SW (14) 14,13,12, 3,4,2	Śani NW (21) 21,20,19, 11,10,9	Śukra W (15) 15,16,17, 18,5,6	Candra N (22) 22,23,24, 25,12,13	Rāhu NE (28) 28,27,28, 18,17,16
4th	Rāhu NE (28) 28,27,28, 18,17,16	Śani NW (21) 21,20,19, 11,10,9	Sūrya E (1) 1,2,3,4,19, 20	Bṛhaspati S (8) 8,9,10,11, 26,27	Maṅgala SE (7) 7,6,5,25,2 4,23	Budha SW (14) 14,13,12, 3,4,2	Śukra W (15) 15,16,17, 18,5,6
5th	Śukra W (15) 15,16,17, 18,5,6	Bṛhaspati S (8) 8,9,10,11, 26,27	Śani NW (21) 21,20,19, 11,10,9	Rāhu NE (28) 28,27,28, 18,17,16	Candra N (22) 22,23,24, 25,12,13	Sūrya E (1) 1,2,3,4,19, 20	Maṅgala SE (7) 7,6,5,25,2 4,23
6th	Maṅgala SE (7) 7,6,5,25,2 4,23	Rāhu NE (28) 28,27,28, 18,17,16	Bṛhaspati S (8) 8,9,10,11, 26,27	Śukra W (15) 15,16,17, 18,5,6	Budha SW (14) 14,13,12, 3,4,2	Śani NW (21) 21,20,19, 11,10,9	Candra N (22) 22,23,24, 25,12,13
7th	Candra N (22) 22,23,24, 25,12,13	Śukra W (15) 15,16,17, 18,5,6	Rāhu NE (28) 28,27,28, 18,17,16	Maṅgala SE (7) 7,6,5,25,2 4,23	Sūrya E (1) 1,2,3,4,19, 20	Bṛhaspati S (8) 8,9,10,11, 26,27	Budha SW (14) 14,13,12, 3,4,2
8th	Budha SW (14) 14,13,12, 3,4,2	Maṅgala SE (7) 7,6,5,25,2 4,23	Śukra W (15) 15,16,17, 18,5,6	Candra N (22) 22,23,24, 25,12,13	Śani NW (21) 21,20,19, 11,10,9	Rāhu NE (28) 28,27,28, 18,17,16	Sūrya E (1) 1,2,3,4,19, 20

Sunidhi: Guruji, this is quite complex.

Ācārya: I have simplified it in the above table. The table shows Yogini's movement through the different directions and the Tārās in different Kālas.

Kailāśa: I can understand this, Guruji!

For instance, on Ravivāra, the Yogini rises in the Eastern direction with Sūrya Kāla, which corresponds to 1st Tārā, and in the first Kāla travels through 1, 2, 3, 4, 19 and 20, staying in each of them, 15 min approx.

In the 2nd Kāla, she starts in the NW direction in Śani's Kāla, which corresponds to the 21st Tārā. In this Kāla, she moves through the Tārās, 21, 20, 19, 11, 10 and 9.

Ācārya: Let me explain this further.

In the following table, I have given the sequence of Yogini through the Kālagrahas (1st column), the directions, the Nakṣatras (from Kṛttikā), and the six Nakṣatras through which the Yogini moves during the span of the Kāla.

Table 12

#	Kāla Graha	Direction	First Nakṣatra	Six Nakṣatras
1	Sūrya	E	1	1, 2, 3, 4, 19, 20
2	Śani	NW	21	21, 20, 19, 11, 10, 9
3	Bṛhaspati	S	8	8, 9, 10, 11, 26, 27
4	Rāhu	NE	28	28, 27, 28, 18, 17, 16
5	Śukra	W	15	15, 16, 17, 18, 5, 6
6	Maṅgala	SE	7	7, 6, 5, 25, 24, 23
7	Candra	N	22	22, 23, 24, 25, 12, 13
8	Budha	SW	14	14, 13, 12, 3, 4, 2

Sunidhi: Kindly explain with an example.

Ācārya: Alright! Let us work out an example to understand this.

The time right now is 11:45 am in Singapore (GMT+8), on 15 March 2021, Somavāra. The JD is 2459288.65625.

Singapore coordinates are 1.3521° N, 103.8198° E.

Sūryodaya is at 7.176, and Sūryāsta is at 19.283.

Dinamāna is 12.106 and Rātrimāna is 11.893.

The Iṣṭaghaṭi is 11.75 -7.176 = 4.574 hrs or 11.435 Ghaṭis.

The day elapsed is 4.574/12.106 = 37.782%.

Kāla is 4.574/12.106 * 8 = 3.023 = 4.

This is the 4th Kāla of Somavāra, i.e., Śani NW (21), and the Nakṣatra movement is in the order 21, 20, 19, 11, 10, 9.

In the above computation, the decimal left is 0.023. Therefore, the Yogini Nakṣatra is 0.023 * 6 = 0.138 = 1. This is the 1st Nakṣatra, which is 21.

Therefore, we conclude that the Yogini is in the 21st Nakṣatra (from Kṛttikā).

Sunidhi: Guruji! Kindly also give the rise of Kalās for different Vāras.

Ācārya: Here you go! This is different from the normal reckoning of the Kālas.

The Yogini Kāla sequence is Sūrya → Śani → Guru → Rāhu → Śukra → Maṅgala → Candra → Rāhu.

However, the regular Kāla sequence is Sūrya → Maṅgala → Bṛhaspati → Budha → Śukra → Śani → Candra → Rāhu.

Table 13: Yogini Kāla Sequence

Kāla	Ravi vāra	Soma vāra	Maṅgala vāra	Budha vāra	Guru vāra	Śukra vāra	Śani vāra
1st	Sūrya	Candra	Maṅgala	Budha	Guru	Śukra	Śani
2nd	Śani	Budha	Candra	Sūrya	Rāhu	Maṅgala	Guru
3rd	Guru	Sūrya	Budha	Śani	Śukra	Candra	Rāhu
4th	Rāhu	Śani	Sūrya	Guru	Maṅgala	Budha	Śukra
5th	Śukra	Guru	Śani	Rāhu	Candra	Sūrya	Maṅgala
6th	Maṅgala	Rāhu	Guru	Śukra	Budha	Śani	Candra
7th	Candra	Śukra	Rāhu	Maṅgala	Sūrya	Guru	Budha
8th	Budha	Maṅgala	Śukra	Candra	Śani	Rāhu	Sūrya

Table 14: Regular Kāla Sequence

Kāla	Ravi vāra	Soma vāra	Maṅgala vāra	Budha vāra	Guru vāra	Śukra vāra	Śani vāra
1st	Sūrya	Candra	Maṅgala	Budha	Guru	Śukra	Śani
2nd	Maṅgala	Rāhu	Guru	Śukra	Budha	Śani	Candra
3rd	Guru	Sūrya	Budha	Śani	Śukra	Candra	Rāhu
4th	Budha	Maṅgala	Śukra	Candra	Śani	Rāhu	Sūrya
5th	Śukra	Guru	Śani	Rāhu	Candra	Sūrya	Maṅgala
6th	Śani	Budha	Candra	Sūrya	Rāhu	Maṅgala	Guru
7th	Candra	Śukra	Rāhu	Maṅgala	Sūrya	Guru	Budha
8th	Rāhu	Śani	Sūrya	Guru	Maṅgala	Budha	Śukra

Kailāśa: What is the reasoning behind the Yogini Kāla sequence?

Ācārya: I have explained this before. But let me still tell you. This is based on the 6th Graha in the Kāla sequence, i.e., Sūrya → Maṅgala → Bṛhaspati → Budha → Śukra → Śani → Candra → Rāhu.

For instance, the 6th Graha from Sūrya is Śani, which comes after Sūrya. The 6th Graha from Śani is Guru, who comes next.

Ācārya: The next śloka of Praśnamārga explains how to identify the Yogini's Nakṣatra. I have explained this before, but let us review what Ācārya Harihara states here.

16.90. Convert the time (of Praśna/Janma) into Vighaṭis from Sūryodaya. Divide this by 225. The quotient is the number of Yāmas expired from Sūryodaya. Divide the remainder by 37.5. The quotient represents the point of Yogini in the diagram. The path of Mṛtyu is similar to that of Yogini. But there is a difference about its rising (of Mṛtyu). Every day it rises in the Northwest and passes through the directions like Yogini.

Kailāśa: Why the Vighaṭis must be divided by 225?

Ācārya: In an Ahorātra, there are 60 Ghaṭis and 3600 Vighaṭis. If you divide the day into 16 segments, each measure 225 Vighaṭis. These Yāmas are further divided into 6 parts, each measuring 37.5 Vighaṭis. Each of them corresponds to a Nakṣatra.

Just follow the steps I explained before.

Kailāśa: Guruji, what happens at night?

Ācārya: It completes the day cycle of 8 Yāmārdhas and again starts with the Yāmārdha of the Vāreśa. For instance, on a Ravivāra, after traversing the Yāmārdha of Sūrya to Budha, the Yogini traverses again from Sūrya to Budha from Sūryāsta.

Kailāśa: Now that we know how to compute Yogini, what is next?

Ācārya: Next, we learn how to find the position of Mṛtyu in a day. Here is the śloka from Praśnamārga.

16.91. According to some, on any given day, Mṛtyu rises in NW in the first Yāma (21); S in the 2nd (8); NE in the 3rd (28); W in the 4th (15); SE in the 5th (7); N in the 6th (22); SW in the 7th (14) and E in the 8th (1). At the end of the 8th Yāma, it comes to the East, where it rises in the first Yāma of the Night, repeating the same cycle.

Sunidhi: Kindly explain this, Guruji!

Ācārya: Yogini rises at different points on different Vāras, but Mṛtyu rises at the same point, 21, corresponding to Northwest (Śani). The position of Mṛtyu can be located on the same basis as that of Yogini. The following table gives the position of Mṛtyu for different Vāras.

On Śanivāra, Yogini and Mṛtyu pass through the same Tārā at all times.

Table 15: Mṛtyu Rāśi

Kāla	Ravi vāra	Soma vāra	Maṅgala vāra	Budha vāra	Guru vāra	Śukra vāra	Śani vāra
1st	Śani	Śani	Śani	Śani	Śani	Śani	Śani
2nd	Guru	Guru	Guru	Guru	Guru	Guru	Guru
3rd	Rāhu	Rāhu	Rāhu	Rāhu	Rāhu	Rāhu	Rāhu
4th	Śukra	Śukra	Śukra	Śukra	Śukra	Śukra	Śukra
5th	Maṅgala	Maṅgala	Maṅgala	Maṅgala	Maṅgala	Maṅgala	Maṅgala
6th	Candra	Candra	Candra	Candra	Candra	Candra	Candra
7th	Budha	Budha	Budha	Budha	Budha	Budha	Budha
8th	Sūrya	Sūrya	Sūrya	Sūrya	Sūrya	Sūrya	Sūrya

Ācārya: Now, Praśnamārga talks about the Rāśi correspondence of Yogini and Mṛtyu.

16.92. If Yogini and Mṛtyu rise in the position of primary directions (E, S, W or N), take it as the end of the Cararāśi. When these rise in the secondary directions (SE, SW, NW or NE), take it as the middle of Dvisvarāśis.

Sunidhi: How to interpret this, Guruji?

Ācārya: According to this śloka, we can locate the positions of Yogini and Mṛtyu in Rāśis.

If Yogini or Mṛtyu occupies points denoting East, West, North or South, then the Rāśis are the Cararāśis, i.e., Meṣa, Karka, Tulā and Makara.

If Yogini or Mṛtyu rises in a corner, i.e., NE, NW, SW, or SE, then it is said to be in a Ubhayarāśi, viz., Mithuna, Kanyā, Dhanu or Mīna.

No Sthirarāśis are allotted to them.

We should consider the Rāśi directions Meṣa E, Karka S, Tulā W, and Makara N for Cararāśis. For Dvisvarāśis, we should consider Mithuna SE, Kanyā SW, Dhanu NW and Mīna NE, as shown in the table below.

Table 16

#	Kāla Graha	Direction	First Nakṣatra	Six Nakṣatras	Rāśi	Rāśi Quality
1	**Sūrya**	**E**	1	1, 2, 3, 4, 19, 20	**Meṣa**	Cara
2	**Śani**	**NW**	21	21, 20, 19, 11, 10, 9	**Dhanu**	Ubhaya
3	**Bṛhaspati**	**S**	8	8, 9, 10, 11, 26, 27	**Karka**	Cara
4	**Rāhu**	**NE**	28	28, 27, 28, 18, 17, 16	**Mīna**	Ubhaya
5	**Śukra**	**W**	15	15, 16, 17, 18, 5, 6	**Tulā**	Cara
6	**Maṅgala**	**SE**	7	7, 6, 5, 25, 24, 23	**Mithuna**	Ubhaya
7	**Candra**	**N**	22	22, 23, 24, 25, 12, 13	**Makara**	Cara
8	**Budha**	**SW**	14	14, 13, 12, 3, 4, 2	**Kanyā**	Ubhaya

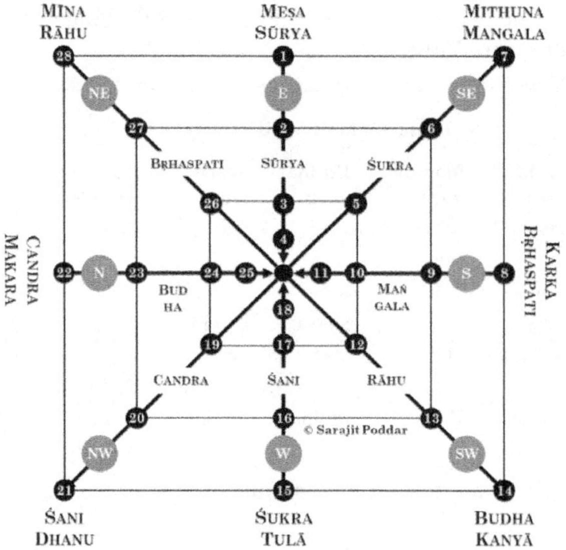

The Rāśis are also indicated in the diagram below, which shows that the primary directions are mapped to the four Cararāśis and the corners are mapped to the four Dvisvarāśis.

In śloka 16.94, the use of this allocation of Rāśi to the direction is given.

It is said that wherever the Yogini is, she tramples the 4th house from it and cuts the 7th with her sword. That means the 4th and 7th house from the Rāśi occupied by Yogini is severely damaged.

Ācārya: Now, the appearance of the Yogini is described.

16.93. Yogini has two frontal teeth, and she is fearful. She is yellow-complexioned. Her eyes are red. Her terrible voice can be heard in all quarters.

She has a special taste for killing. Her dress is of red hue as twilight. She adorns herself with the spoils of killing. Her bangles are serpents. She has a sword in hand which she uses to kill all. She is always deep drunk.

Sunidhi: Yogini is described as a fearful being, drunk and intends to kill others.

Ācārya: Yes, she is a dangerous creature, highly destructive. She is of the nature of the negative attributes of all Grahas. Each of her depictions has an association with a Graha. The frontal teeth are related to Rāhu, yellow colour, Guru, terrible voice, Maṅgala + Budha, a taste for killing, Maṅgala + Śani, dress in red, Maṅgala, bangles as a serpent, Rāhu/Ketu, sword in hand, Sūrya, and drinking, Śani.

Kailāśa: It appears that when a Graha becomes evil due to its placement and Yoga, it gives rise to a being like Yogini, who manifests death!

Ācārya: The fearful appearance of Yogini is described to impress the unfortunate effects flowing from its position in the chart.

Sunidhi: It makes sense, Guruji!

Ācārya: Now, the houses impacted by Yogini are explained.

16.94. Yogini tramples on 4H from the Rāśis she stands in; and cuts 7H with her sword.

Sunidhi: So, we know which Bhāvas are affected by Yogini,

Ācārya: Yes, Yogini affects 4H (Śani) and 7H (Maṅgala) from itself. If the Āruṛha Rāśi of the Pṛcchaka falls in 4H or 7H from Yogini, the Pṛcchaka dies. Of the two Rāśis, 7H is the worst.

Kailāśa: Guruji, trampling may signify health suffering and cutting death.

Ācārya: Yes, that sounds right!

Praśnamārga also states that there are differences in opinion about the Nakṣatras through which Yogini traverses. It states:

16.95. According to Vāras, there is no difference of opinion about the rise of Yogini in different directions. Still, regarding its path, some authors hold different views, which are explained below.

16.96-98. On Ravivāra, Yogini moves through 1, 7, 2, 4, 3, 5, 6 and 8 in the eight Yāmas. Somavāra 7, 5, 8, 2, 1, 3, 4 and 6; Maṅgalavāra 2, 8, 3, 5, 4, 6, 7 and 1; Budhavāra 4, 2, 5, 7, 6, 8, 1, 3; Bṛhaspativāra 3, 1, 4, 6, 5, 7, 8, 2; Friday 5, 3, 6, 8, 7, 1, 2 and 4; and Śanivāra 6, 4, 7, 1, 8, 2, 3 and 5. The numbers 1 to 8 respectively denote directions 1E, 2SE, 3S, 4SW, 5W, 6NW, 7N and 8NE, and also the eight Yāmas.

Ācārya: There are some issues with the translation of Dr Raman, which I have corrected in the above translation. The issues are in Ravivāra, Budhavāra and Śanivāra.

In this method, the Yoginis do not move through a designated path daily, in the order 1, 6, 4, 8, 5, 2, 7, 4 from the Vāreśa.

Table 17

Kāla	Ravi vāra	Soma vāra	Maṅgala vāra	Budha vāra	Guru vāra	Śukra vāra	Śani vāra
1st	1	7	2	4	3	5	6
2nd	7	5	8	2	1	3	4
3rd	2	8	3	5	4	6	7
4th	4	2	5	7	6	8	1
5th	3	1	4	6	5	7	8
6th	5	3	6	8	7	1	2
7th	6	4	7	1	8	2	3
8th	8	6	1	3	2	4	5

Sunidhi: Guruji, what is the basis of this movement?

Ācārya: It is based on the jumps. It moves with the following jump from the 1st Kāla, i.e., 7, 4, 3, 8, 3, 2, and 3 in the order 1, 2, 3, 4, 5, 6, 7 and 8 (the Kālagraha order, Sūrya, Maṅgala, Guru, Budha, Śukra, Śani, Candra, Rāhu).

In the normal reckoning (as explained before), the jump is uniform to every 6th in the Kālagraha order, but in this reckoning (irregular), it is different, i.e., 7th, 4th, 3rd, 8th, 3rd, 2nd, and 3rd.

For instance, on Ravivāra, 1st Yāma is 1 (Sūrya). It is followed by the 7th in the order 1, 2, 3, 4, 5, 6, 7 and 8, which is 7. It is followed by the 4th from 7, which is 2. The next is the 3rd from 2, which is 4. This goes on in this manner.

Let me state below the Grahas through whose Kāla the Yogini would traverse in different Yāmas of the Vāras. This would make the reckoning easier. In the header, I have also indicated the directions ruled by the Kālagrahas in Kālacakra.

Table 18

Kāla	Ravi vāra E	Soma vāra N	Maṅgala vāra SE	Budha vāra SW	Guru vāra S	Śukra vāra W	Śani vāra NW
1st	Sūrya	Candra	Maṅgala	Budha	Guru	Śukra	Śani
2nd	Candra	Śukra	Rāhu	Maṅgala	Sūrya	Guru	Budha
3rd	Maṅgala	Rāhu	Guru	Śukra	Budha	Śani	Candra
4th	Budha	Maṅgala	Śukra	Candra	Śani	Rāhu	Sūrya
5th	Guru	Sūrya	Budha	Śani	Śukra	Candra	Rāhu
6th	Śukra	Guru	Śani	Rāhu	Candra	Sūrya	Maṅgala
7th	Śani	Budha	Candra	Sūrya	Rāhu	Maṅgala	Guru
8th	Rāhu	Śani	Sūrya	Guru	Maṅgala	Budha	Śukra

Ācārya: Now, the movement of Yogini at night is explained.

16.99. Thus, after rising in a particular Dik, Yogini traverses through the various Diks in different Yāmas and reaches the 8th Dik after 8 Yāmas.

Ācārya: On a Ravivāra, Yogini traverses from Sūrya to Rāhu, which is to the 5th Dik in the Kālagraha order. On Somavāra, she traverses from Candra to Śani, again the 5th Dik in the Kālagraha order.

In the previous reckoning, the Yogini traverses to the 4th Graha in Kālagraha order by Sūryāsta. However, in this reckoning, she traverses to the 8th Graha.

Sunidhi: Guruji, this is still confusing. Kindly explain this further.

Ācārya: Suppose on a particular Vāra she rises at a particular Dik - say Ravivāra, 1st Yāma, Sūrya E. In the 2nd Yāma, she reaches the 7th Dik from it; in the 3rd Yāma, the 4th from it; in the 4th Yāma, the 3rd from it; in the 5th, the 8th from it; in the 6th, 3rd from it; in the 7th, the 2nd from it; and in the 8th Yāma the 3rd from it. This is the order in which the Yogini moves on all days in the second reckoning.

In other words, the Yogini returns to the 8th Dik from the starting Dik at the end of the 8th Yāma. As mentioned, the movement is 1, 7, 4, 3, 8, 3, 2, 3 from the previous one.

Reckoning from the 1st Yāma, the order is 1, 7, 2, 4, 3, 5, 6, 8. Thus, in a day, the place where the Yāma starts reaches the 8th from where it started. After that, it starts again from the same place at night and moves in the same order.

This means, on a Ravivāra, after traversing from Sūrya to Rāhu, She moves through Sūrya to Rāhu from Sūryāsta. The cycle repeats at night (Rātri) as it moves during the day (Divā/Dina).

Sunidhi: Dhanyavād, Guruji!

Ācārya: Now, let us focus on finding the sphuṭa of Yogini and Mṛtyu. In this regard, Praśnamārga states the following:

16.100. Multiply the Iṣṭaghaṭis by 96. Divide the product by 30. The quotient is the Rāśi. Reduce the remainder to degrees, minutes, etc. Expunge multiples of 12. (a) Note the Rāśi Yogini is in at the required time, (b) Then deduct (a) from (b). The exact sphuṭa of Yogini is obtained. By a similar process, the position of Mṛtyu can also be known.

Kailāśa: Kindly provide an example, Guruji!

Ācārya: Let us take our previous example.

Time: 11:45 am in Singapore (GMT+8), on 15 March 2021, Somavāra.

Sūryodaya is at 7.176, and Sūryāsta is at 19.283.

Dinamāna is 12.106 hrs and Rātrimāna is 11.893 hrs. In Ghaṭis, they are 30.265 and 29.733.

The Iṣṭaghaṭi is 11.75 -7.176 = 4.574 hrs or 11.435 Ghaṭis.

Iṣṭaghaṭi * 96/30 = 11.435 * 96/30 = 36.592r = 0.592r = 17.76° = Meṣa 17:45:36

Now, what is Yogini's Rāśi? It is ascertained as per Praśnamārga 16.92. We previously found that the Kāla is 4th, owned by Śani (NW). It is mapped to Dhanu. In the corner direction, Yogini rises in the "middle" of Dvisvabhāva Rāśi. So Yogini should be Dhanu 15°.

Deducting Meṣa 17:45:36 (17.76°) from Dhanu 15:0:0 (245°) we get 17.76° - 245° = 132.76 = Siṅha 12:45:36. This is the Rāśi and sphuṭa of Yogini.

Now, let us find Mṛtyusphuṭa.

The 4th Kāla for Mṛtyu is owned by Śukra (W) and mapped to Tulā 30° (end of Cararāśi).

Deducting Meṣa 17:45:36 (17.76°) from Tulā 30:0:0 (210) we get 17.76° - 210° = -192.24 = 167.76 = Kanyā 17:45:36. This is the Rāśi and sphuṭa of Mṛtyu.

Jayanta: Guruji, what is the reasoning behind multiplying the Iṣṭaghaṭi by 96 and dividing it by 30?

Ācārya: That is an excellent question. A day (or night) has 8 Kālas (or Yāmardhas). Each of them is mapped to 12 Rāśis. Therefore, there are 8 * 12 = 96 Rāśis in a Dina or Rātri of 30 Ghaṭis. Therefore, Iṣṭaghaṭi is divided by 30 and multiplied by 96 to determine the Rāśi rising at the moment.

Each Kāla has 12 Rāśis; therefore, the Rāśis elapsed can be known by noting the Kāla elapsed.

In our example, Iṣṭaghaṭi is 4.574 hrs or 11.435 Ghaṭis. Yāmas elapsed is 11.435/30 * 8 = 3.049. It is 0.049 of 4th Kāla. 0.049 equals 0.049 * 12 = 0.588 Rāśi = 17.64° = Mesha 17:38:24. This is close to what we arrived before, and the difference is due to rounding off error.

However, the formula is not precise as it does not account for the difference between Dinamāna and Rātrimāna. The Dinamāna is 30.265 ghaṭis. Therefore, the calculation should be 11.435/30.265 * 96 = 36.272 = 0.272r = 8.16° = Meṣa 8:9:36.

Kailāśa: Then why must we count it from Cara and Dvisvabhāva Rāśis?

Ācārya: That is because, in the Yāmas, the reckoning is not always from Meṣa. It is the end of a Cararāśi if the Yogini/Mṛtyu is in a Primary (E/S/W/N) direction and middle of a Dvisvabhāva Rāśi if the Yogini/Mṛtyu is in a Secondary (SE/SW/NW/NE) direction.

In our example, Kālasphuṭa "Meṣa 17.64°" reckoned from Kanyā 15° is 132.76°. Seen from Meṣādi (Meṣa 0°), it is Siṅha 12:45:36. Similarly, Mṛtyu's reckoning point is Tulā 30° from where Kālasphuṭa is 167.76°, which is Kanyā 17:45:36 (from Meṣādi).

Ācārya: The effects of Mṛtyu passing through different directions are given now.

16.101. If the Praśna is made when Mṛtyu is passing into the interior, predict that the Pṛcchaka dies. If Mṛtyu happens to go out, then the native will not die. A tree will fall if he goes out through E (Sūrya). A cow will die if he issues out through SE (Maṅgala). If he goes out through S (Guru), some of his near relatives will die. If he goes through SW (Budha), an animal, such as deer, will die near. A female buffalo will die if he goes out through W (Śukra). If he goes out through NW (Śani), the high amongst Caṇḍālas will die. If he goes out through N (Candra), the low amongst Caṇḍālas will die. If he goes out through NE (Rāhu), a Brāhmaṇa nearby will die. Carefully study the diagram and see when he goes in and out by noting points.

Jayanta: It seems that Mṛtyu moving through different directions indicates the death of something nearby, which can be a tree, animal or human.

16.102. According as at the time Praśna is put Mṛtyu issues out through SW/W (Budha/Śukra), then servants or quadrupeds of the Pṛcchaka will die. If these events happen, then it can be predicted that the issues will not die.

16.103-104. In the Pūrvārdha of a Yāma, if Mṛtyu enters through E (Sūrya) at Praśna, the death of a person belonging to the ruling class may happen in a near place. If Mṛtyu enters through SE (Maṅgala), fire hazards must be feared. If through S (Guru), some person falls unconscious due to excessive eating of nuts; if SW (Budha), the Pṛcchaka himself may get sick by eating nuts; if W (Śukra), he will have watery diseases as dysentery, vomiting, etc.; if NW (Śani), trouble from thieves and consequent uproar; *if N (Candra), not mentioned*; if through NE (Rāhu), sudden fits. If these ominous signs occur, you can predict the death of the questioner is certain.

Sunidhi: The entry of Mṛtyu through N is not mentioned here.

Ācārya: Now, the rising of Mṛtyu on different Vāras is stated.

16.105. According to Sārasaṅgraha, Mṛtyu rises thus at Sūryodaya. Ravivāra in E (Sūrya), Maṅgalavāra SE (Maṅgala), Guruvāra S (Guru), Budhavāra SW (Budha), Śukravāra W (Śukra), Śanivāra NW (Śani) and Somavāra N (Candra). It traverses through the 8 points of the compass thrice in the daytime and thrice in the night-time in a clockwise direction. 'Kala' also rises in the same Diks as Mṛtyu but traverses through the cardinal points in an anticlockwise direction thrice in the daytime and thrice in the nighttime.

Jayanta: According to Śara Saṅgraha, Mṛtyu does not rise with Śani and ends with Sūrya every day (as per 16.91). It instead rises in the Kāla of Vāreśa, coinciding with Sūryodaya.

Ācārya: Now, another method of rising of Yogini stated, which is different from what is explained before.

16.106-107. Yogini stays along with Kāla and Mṛtyu in the Dik (direction), where these rise daily during the first Yāma. In the 2nd Yāma Yogini stays in the rising direction of the next day; in the 3rd, in the rising direction of the 3rd day; in the 4th Yāma, the fourth day and so on. On the 8th, it will stay in NE on all days. East signifies Meṣa and Vṛṣabha. The first and the second parts of Yāma denote Meṣa and Vṛṣabha, respectively. Similarly, the south signifies Karka and Siṅha, the west Tulā and Vṛścika and the north Makara and Kumbha. SE, SW, NW and NE represent Kanyā, Dhanu, Mīna and Mithuna. Yogini dṛṣṭies the 7th Rāśi from the sign occupied by it. Death may occur if the Āruṛha of the Pṛcchaka happens to be the 4th or 7th from Yogini.

Kailāśa: Kindly explain the difference, Guruji!

Ācārya: Previously, we noted that Yogini traverses the 8 Yāmas from Sūryodaya in the order of Sūrya → Śani → Bṛhaspati → Rāhu → Śukra → Maṅgala

→ Candra → Budha. This is each successive 6th Graha in Kālagraha order, i.e., Sūrya, Maṅgala, Guru, Budha, Śukra, Śani, Candra, Rāhu.

However, according to Śara Saṅgraha, Yogini traverses in the Vāra order, i.e., Sūrya (E) → Candra (N) → Maṅgala (SE) → Budha (SW) → Guru (S) → Śukra (W) → Śani (NW). In the 8th Kāla on all Vāras, it moves to Rāhu (NE)

Sunidhi: Dhanyavād, for explaining this. If I understand this correctly, we should follow the first approach delineated by Ācārya Harihara, i.e., the 6th Graha of Kālagraha approach.

Ācārya: That is right! Now, let us review the movement of Yogini through the Tithis.

16.108. The movement of Yogini through the various tithis is described in the form in which Yogini's movement during the Vāras is stated now.

16.109-115. Yogini rises and moves during the eight Yāmas in the eight directions on different Tithis as follows:

1st/9th: E, N, SE, SW, S, W, NW and NE

2nd/10th: NW, NE, SE, E, SW and NW

3rd/11th: SE, NE, S, W, SW, NW, N and E

4th/12th: SW, SE, W, N, NW, NE, E and S

5th/13th: S, E, SE, NW, W, N, NE and SE

6th/14th: W, S, NW, NE, N, E, SE and SW

7th/15th: NW, SW, NE, SE, S and W

8th/_: NE, NW, E, S, SE, SW, W and N

The same arrangement holds good both for Śukla and Kṛṣṇa Pakṣa.

Kailāśa: What is the basis of this movement, Guruji? Mantreśa

Ācārya: If you examine the Tithis, 1, 3, 4, 6 and 8, you will find that starting from the 1st Kāleśa, the next Kāleśa is the 7th Graha in the Kālagraha order, i.e., Sūrya, Maṅgala, Guru, Budha, Śukra, Śani, Candra and Rāhu. The following are the 4th, 3rd, 8th, 3rd, 2nd and 3rd.

Applying the same principle to Tithis 2, 5 and 7, we find the Diks and the Kāla Lords in the tables below. The Diks given by Dr Raman are incomplete and inconsistent for the mentioned Tithis. Therefore, I made the corrections. Also, I made the first Kāleśa for the 2nd/10th Tithis, which should be N (Candra) instead of NW (Śani).

Kailāśa: Why 2nd/10th should be Candra-N instead of Śani-NW?

Ācārya: That is because, if you look carefully, the first Kāleśa is Sūrya to Rāhu in Vāra order (except 2nd). This tells us that the Tithis are owned by Sūrya to Rāhu from 1st Tithi onwards.

Table 19

	1	2	3	4	5	6	7	8
Kāla	9	10	11	12	13	14	15	-
1st	E	***N***	SE	SW	***S***	W	***NW***	NE

	1	2	3	4	5	6	7	8
2nd	N	***S***	NE	SE	***E***	S	***SW***	NW
3rd	SE	***W***	S	W	***SW***	NW	***S***	E
4th	SW	***SW***	W	N	***S***	NE	***SE***	S
5th	S	***N***	SW	NW	***SE***	N	***E***	SE
6th	W	***E***	NW	NE	***E***	E	***NE***	SW
7th	NW	***NE***	N	E	***NE***	SE	***N***	W
8th	NE	***N***	E	S	***N***	SW	***NW***	N

Table 20

	1	2	3	4	5	6	7	8
Kāla	**9**	**10**	**11**	**12**	**13**	**14**	**15**	**-**
1st	Sūrya	***Candra***	Maṅgala	Budha	***Guru***	Śukra	***Śani***	Rāhu
2nd	Candra	***Guru***	Rāhu	Maṅgala	***Sūrya***	Guru	***Budha***	Śani
3rd	Maṅgala	***Śukra***	Guru	Śukra	***Budha***	Śani	***Guru***	Sūrya
4th	Budha	***Budha***	Śukra	Candra	***Guru***	Rāhu	***Maṅgala***	Guru
5th	Guru	***Candra***	Budha	Śani	***Maṅgala***	Candra	***Sūrya***	Maṅgala
6th	Śukra	***Sūrya***	Śani	Rāhu	***Sūrya***	Sūrya	***Rāhu***	Budha
7th	Śani	***Rāhu***	Candra	Sūrya	***Rāhu***	Maṅgala	***Candra***	Śukra
8th	Rāhu	***Candra***	Sūrya	Guru	***Candra***	Budha	***Śani***	Candra

Kailāśa: Why are the Tithis in pairs besides Aṣṭamī?

Ācārya: That is because there are two cycles of Tithis. In the first cycle, there are 8 Tithis, 1st to 8th. The second cycle repeats from the 9th Tithi.

Kailāśa: Does that mean that 1st/9th Tithis are lorded by Sūrya, 2nd/10th by Candra and so on?

Ācārya: Yes, that is what we infer. To find the Tithi Graha Lord, we must divide a Tithi by 8 and take the remainder. The remainder from 1 to 8 represents the Tithi Lord as 1 Sūrya, 2 Candra, 3 Maṅgala, 4 Budha, 5 Guru, 6 Śukra, 7 Śani, and 8 Rāhu.

That is why the Tithi Kāla (Yamārdha) commences from those Grahas.

Jayanta: How to find these in a real-life scenario?

Ācārya: Like a Vāra (between two Sūryodayas) is divided into 16 segments, similarly, a Tithi is divided into 16 segments.

The duration of a Tithi is 12°. Suppose on a day, Sūrya is Mithuna 15:52:22 (75.872), and Candra is Vṛścika 29:14:11 (239.236). Sūrya2Candra = 239.236 - 75.872 = 163.364. Tithi = 163.364/12 = 13.614 = 14th Tithi. It is the same as the 6th Tithi, lorded by Śukra.

The decimals 0.614 represent the portion of the Tithi elapsed. Converting it to Yāma, we have 0.614 * 16 = 9.8 = 10th. The first half of 8 Tithi-Kāla is complete, and the second half is the 2nd Kāla. 2nd Kāla of Śukra's Tithis is Guru. Therefore, the Tithi Kāleśa is Guru (S). Tithis Yogini is in the South at this time.

Sunidhi: Guruji, how to use this knowledge?

Ācārya: This is stated by the next śloka of Praśnamārga.

16.116. If Yogini dṛṣṭies the Janma or Āruṛha Lagna, the Pṛcchaka will meet with his death.

Sunidhi: It means the Tithi-Yogini must not aspect the Janma or Āruṛha Lagna?

Ācārya: Yes, that is right. Also, look for any dṛṣṭi on Praśna Lagna, Āruṛha or Praśna Candra. Any dṛṣṭi in these places indicate danger to life.

Sunidhi: How to know the Rāśi of Tithi Yogini?

Ācārya: You can use the Rāśi identified before. I am giving the table here again. We found that the Tithi Yogini is in S in Guru's Kāla. This is mapped to the Karka end.

Table 21

#	Kāla Graha	Direction	Rāśi	Rāśi Quality
1	Sūrya	E	Meṣa	Cara
2	Śani	NW	Dhanu	Ubhaya
3	Bṛhaspati	S	Karka	Cara
4	Rāhu	NE	Mīna	Ubhaya
5	Śukra	W	Tulā	Cara
6	Maṅgala	SE	Mithuna	Ubhaya
7	Candra	N	Makara	Cara
8	Budha	SW	Kanyā	Ubhaya

Jayanta: Guruji. Should we not use the principle of Iṣṭaghaṭi/30 * 96?

Ācārya: The classical text mentions nothing of that sort, but you can experiment. But this should be modified to Tithi elapsed * 96. We already found the Tithi elapsed as 0.614. Multiplying it by 96, we arrive at 0.614 * 96 = 58.944r = 10.944r = Kumbha 28:19:12. You can reckon it from Karka 30° as before.

Again, this is open to experimentation.

Jayanta: Dhanyavād, Gurudeva!

Ācārya: Now, let us focus on Jñānapradīpikā. Here an Ahorātra is divided into 8 Yāmas of 3 hrs. Per 2.87, they are ruled by the Yāmagrahas from the Vāreśa at Sūryodaya, in the order, **Sūrya, Maṅgala, Guru, Budha, Śukra, Śani, Candra, and Rāhu**. This is also the Kālagraha order.

They correspond to directions Sūrya E, Maṅgala SE, Guru S, Budha SW, Śukra W, Śani NW, Candra N, and Rāhu NE in Kālacakra. Since the movements are clockwise, i.e., E, SE, S, SW, W, NW, N and NE, the Kālagraha order is crucial.

Kailāśa: How did the Grahas move in in the 8 Yāmas?

Ācārya: In the first Yāma, the Vāreśa is in the E, and the 7 following Grahas are in SE to NE. In the 2nd Yāma, the Vāreśa moves to SE, and the remaining Grahas also shift their places by one. The following table illustrates it for Ravivāra.

Table 22: Grahas in different Diks in differen Yāmas on Ravivāra

Yāma	E	SE	S	SW	W	NW	N	NE
1st	Sūrya	Maṅg	Guru	Budha	Śukra	Śani	Candra	Rāhu
2nd	Rāhu	Sūrya	Maṅg	Guru	Budha	Śukra	Śani	Candra
3rd	Candra	Rāhu	Sūrya	Maṅg	Guru	Budha	Śukra	Śani
4th	Śani	Candra	Rāhu	Sūrya	Maṅg	Guru	Budha	Śukra
5th	Śukra	Śani	Candra	Rāhu	Sūrya	Maṅg	Guru	Budha
6th	Budha	Śukra	Śani	Candra	Rāhu	Sūrya	Maṅg	Guru
7th	Guru	Budha	Śukra	Śani	Candra	Rāhu	Sūrya	Maṅg
8th	Maṅg	Guru	Budha	Śukra	Śani	Candra	Rāhu	Sūrya

In this manner, we must draw one table for each Vāra, giving rise to seven tables. This is provided in the book's main body and not provided again.

Kailāśa: Dhanyavād, Guruji!

Ācārya: Let us examine another opinion regarding assigning Grahas to different Diks on different Vāras and Yāmas. This is based on the Vāra order instead of the Kālagraha order.

2.88. From E to NE are the Grahas posited from the 1st Yāma to the 8th Yāma of the day. In the first Yāma is Vāreśa in E, and it passes on to SE in the second Yāma and so on. At Praśna, one must ascertain in what direction the Vāreśa is situated. In the next direction would be the Vāreśa the next day, and to the next is the Vāreśa of the succeeding day. That is, in the first Yāma on Ravivāra, Sūrya is in E, Candra in SE, Maṅgala in S, Budha in SW, Guru in W, Śukra in NW and Śani in N.

Jayanta: Should we not follow the Kālagraha order instead of the Vāra order?

Ācārya: This is just another opinion. We should follow the Kālagraha order per the author's first śloka, i.e., 2.87. This is someone else's opinion, which is considered secondary by the author. That is because this is mentioned after mentioning the Kālagraha order.

Table 23: Assigment of Grahas to Diks based on Vāra order

Yāma	E	SE	S	SW	W	NW	N	NE
1st	Sūrya	Candra	Maṅgala	Budha	Guru	Śukra	Śani	Rāhu
2nd	Rāhu	Sūrya	Candra	Maṅgala	Budha	Guru	Śukra	Śani
3rd	Śani	Rāhu	Sūrya	Candra	Maṅgala	Budha	Guru	Śukra
4th	Śukra	Śani	Rāhu	Sūrya	Candra	Maṅgala	Budha	Guru
5th	Guru	Śukra	Śani	Rāhu	Sūrya	Candra	Maṅgala	Budha
6th	Budha	Guru	Śukra	Śani	Rāhu	Sūrya	Candra	Maṅgala
7th	Maṅgala	Budha	Guru	Śukra	Śani	Rāhu	Sūrya	Candra
8th	Candra	Maṅgala	Budha	Guru	Śukra	Śani	Rāhu	Sūrya

Kailāśa: Noted, Guruji!

Ācārya: I have provided the above table based on the Vāreśa order. The author mentions it till Śani. However, I have added Rāhu; else, one of the parts will be lord-less.

Kailāśa: That makes sense, Guruji! Normally, we add Rāhu after Śani in the Vāreśa order.

Ācārya: The author clarifies the two opinions of the scholars, of which we should follow the predominant opinion, which is based on the Kālagraha order. We should also call them Yāmagraha order and the Grahas in different directions as Yāmagraha. They are also called Jāmakkol in Tamil.

2.89. Some state the Vāreśa (Yāma lords) to be respectively Sūrya, Candra, Maṅgala, Budha, Guru, Śukra and Śani. But others affirm (as per 2.87) they are successive: Sūrya, Maṅgala, Guru, Budha, Śukra, Śani, Candra and Rāhu. These Grahas serve as the base to determine past, current, and future events. At Praśna, one must count the Rāśis Candra is from the Udayarāśi, and some state that it will take that many days for the fruition of their desires. Others believe that the number of Rāśis the Navāñśa of Candra is from the Udayarāśi Añśeśa at Praśna denotes the number of days taken for the fulfilment of their desires.

Kailāśa; Noted, Guruji!

Ācārya: The author now tells us a method of timing events. There are two approaches.

1_Count from Udayarāśi to Candra.

2_Count Candrāñśa from Udayarāśi Añśeśa.

Sunidhi: Kindly clarify the second approach.

Ācārya: Suppose at a Praśna, Candra is in Dhanu Rāśi and Meṣa Añśa, and Lagna is in Dhanu Rāśi, Vṛścika Añśa. Maṅgala is in Siṅha Rāśi Meṣa Añśa. As per method 1, the work will be done in a day. As per the 2nd method, Candrāñśa (Meṣa) is 9 Rāśis away from Udayarāśi Añśeśa (Siṅha), indicating 9 days.

Sunidhi: it is clear, Guruji!

Ācārya: Now, the author gives an important aspect called Arka Lagna and Kāla Lagna. Every hour from Sūryodaya is in sequence mapped to Arka Lagna and Kāla Lagna.

Kailāśa: Guruji, isn't it how the Horā Lagna moves – 1 hour per Rāśi?

Ācārya: Yes, it is! Let us see more about these Lagnas. They move through the directions in order E, SE, S, SW, W, NW, N, NE.

2.90. From Sūryodaya to Sūryāsta, the first hour is called Arka Lagna; the second hour is Kāla Lagna, and so on; alternately, the day is divided into these two Lagnas. And these Lagnas must be posited in E, SE, S etc., in regular order. From this, one can determine at Praśna - which direction it implies, either as Arka or Kāla Lagna. This direction must be taken as the Āruṛha direction, and the lord of the Graha there at the time can also be determined (per 2.87-88).

Ācārya: The author gives an example of using these Lagnas and identifying the ruling Graha.

Sunidhi: Kindly explain, Guruji!

2.91. Take, for example, the Praśna made at 11:35 am, which means that it falls in the Kāla Lagna in the NW direction: Then we have to take this as Āruṛha in the NW direction. According to śloka 2.89, the lord of Āruṛha is Śukra. One must ascertain where Śukra is posited at Praśna, and the property loss must be decided in that direction.

Ācārya: Suppose someone puts a Praśna at 11:35. Suppose the Sūryodaya is at 6 am (assumed, when it is stated). The number of hours elapsed is 5:35 hrs, equivalent to the 6th Rāśi. It is a Kāla Rāśi and is mapped to the 6th direction from E, i.e., E, SE, S, SW, W, **"NW"**, N, NE.

Which Graha is it mapped to?

Jayanta: The Yāmagraha order is Sūrya, Maṅgala, Guru, Budha, Śukra, **"Śani"**, Candra, and Rāhu. The 6th Graha in the sequence is Śani. Therefore, it should be mapped to Śani.

Ācārya: That is right. But it appears that the author has considered the Vāreśa order, i.e., Sūrya, Candra, Maṅgala, Budha, Guru, Śukra, Śani, and Rāhu. The 6th Graha is Śukra in this sequence, as the author states.

Jayanta: Both Yāmagraha and Vāreśa orders appear relevant for different purposes.

Ācārya: Indeed, it appears so!

Now the author explains the computation of Kālahoreśa.

2.92. Here is given some calculation which the student must learn from his teacher. This employs the distance of Lagna from Sūrya. Since, it is unclear, I have not reproduced it here. अर्कोनलग्नस्य लवाः खयाणचन्द्रावशेषै रहितास्त्रिभक्ताः। वारान्वितास्सप्तहृताः कृतास्ते कालाख्यहोरापतयोर्कतस्स्यः ॥९२॥

Kailāśa: Kindly explain this, Guruji!

Ācārya: Kālahorā is same as Horā. In an Ahorātra, there are 24 Horās, also called hours. There are 3600 Vighaṭis in an Ahorātra; dividing it by 24 gives us 150 Vighaṭis.

In an Ahorātra, Lagna makes one full cycle of the zodiac to meet Sūrya. This is the duration of two Sūryodayas. Therefore, Horā can be computed from Lagna's distance from Sūrya. One Ahorātra is 360° motion of Lagna from Sūrya. Therefore, in a Horā, Lagna traverses 15° from Sūrya. Each 15° distance of Lagna from Sūrya is a Horā.

To find Horā, divide Lagna – Sūrya by 15°. The result should be rounded off and divided by 7. The remainder should be counted from the Vāreśa in Horeśa order, which is Śani, Guru, Maṅgala, Sūrya, Śukra, Budha, Candra. This order is based on the speed of Grahas. The Vāreśa order is based on the 4th Graha of the Horeśa order.

Kailāśa: Kindly explain with an example.

Ācārya: Suppose on a Ravivāra, Sūrya was in Siṅha 8:10:33 (128.176) and Lagna Dhanu 9:44:54 (249.748). Surya2Lagna = 249.748 - 128.176 = 121.572. Dividing by 15, we get 8.105. Rounding it "up", we get 9. Dividing 9 by 7 and considering the remainder gives us mod (9, 7) = 2. Counting 2 from Sūrya in the order of reducing speed, we get Sūrya → Śukra → Budha. So the Horeśa was Budha.

Kailāśa: We can get the Kālahorā from the time elapsed from Sūryodaya. Isn't it?

Ācārya: Yes, that is right. But if the sphuṭa of Sūrya and Lagna is available, we should follow the abovementioned method.

Kailāśa: That makes sense, Guruji!

Ācārya: Now, the Dhātvādi attribute of Rāśis and Grahas are explained.

2.93. Meṣa, Karka, Tulā and Makara are called Dhātu Rāśis; Vṛṣabha, Siṅha, Vṛścika and Kumbha are called Mūla Rāśis; Mithuna, Kanyā, Dhanu and Mīna are called Jīva Rāśis.

Kailāśa: What is Dhātvādi attribute?

Ācārya: Rāśis are classified into Dhātu-Mūla-Jīva, which is called the Dhātvādi attribute of the Rāśis.

The Rāśis are Dhātu-Mūla-Jīva in the order of Cara, Sthira, Dvisvabhāva. Therefore, the Cararāśis, Meṣa, Karka, Tulā and Makara are Dhātu; Sthirarāśis, Vṛṣabha, Siṅha, Vṛścika and Kumbha are Mūla and Dvisvabhāva Rāśis Mithuna, Kanyā, Dhanu and Mīna are Jīva.

Kailāśa: Guruji, what is the basis of this classification?

Ācārya: That is an outstanding question. Nowhere is it written why Cararāśis must be Dhātu, Sthira Mūla and Dvisvabhāva Jīva? But I can provide you with my understanding.

Jayanta: That will be helpful, Guruji!

Ācārya: The classification is based on the fixedness of the entities associated with the Rāśis. Plants and vegetation (Mūla) are fixed on the ground; therefore, they are Sthira. Jīva (humans and animals) are mobile but need the earth's hard surface to walk, so they cannot move in all directions. Therefore, they are Dvisvabhāva.

This is extended to other creatures, such as birds and insects, who can move in all directions. This is because all creatures originated from water and then on land, as they needed a medium for their movement (water or land). Even birds and insects need a medium (air) for their movement since flapping their wings in a vacuum will not have any effect.

Dhātu, on the other hand, is not bound by anything. Any object, metallic or non-metallic, can move in any direction and is not bound by any medium. They are completely free. Even a spaceship moves in a vacuum. Therefore, they are Cara.

Jayanta: This makes sense!

Ācārya: Let us examine the Dhātvādi attribute of the Grahas.

2.94. Maṅgala, Candra, Śani and Rāhu are called Dhātu Grahas; Śukra and Sūrya are Mūla, and Guru and Budha are Jīva.

Jayanta: We know that Guru is called Jīva in Nāḍī Jyotiṣa.

Ācārya: Guru is a Jīva Graha and governs the entire living world with higher intellect, i.e., humans, bipeds etc. Budha is another Jīva Graha that governs all creatures' thought-processing power (Bodhana Śakti).

Śukra and Sūrya govern the entire plant world. Sūrya denotes their ability to photosynthesize their food, and Śukra denotes their ability to propagate sexually and asexually. Śukra and Sūrya both represent the rejuvenation abilities of plants.

The remaining four Grahas denote Dhātu, which can be anything, not plant or animal. All objects, metallic or non-metallic, are considered Dhātu.

Sunidhi: Dhanyavād, Guruji, for explaining the nuances of this classification.

Ācārya: Now the author explains certain exceptions.

2.95. Candra in Svarāśi is like Sūrya and becomes Mūla; In other places, he is Dhātu; **Śani** in his Svarāśi becomes Mūla; **Budha** in his Svarāśi becomes Dhātu.

Table 24

#	Graha	Svarāśi	Other Rāśis
1	***Candra***	*Mūla*	*Dhātu*
2	**Maṅgala**	Dhātu	Dhātu
3	***Śani***	*Mūla*	*Dhātu*
4	**Rāhu**	Mūla	Mūla
5	**Sūrya**	Mūla	Mūla
6	**Śukra**	Mūla	Mūla
7	**Guru**	Jīva	Jīva
8	***Budha***	*Dhātu*	*Jīva*

Ācārya: now, the metals ruled by the Grahas are explained.

2.96. Maṅgala is copper; Budha brass; Guru gold; Śukra silver; Candra bronze; Śani and Rāhu are iron.

Table 25

#	Graha	Metal	Notes
1	**Sūrya**	Not mentioned	Normally it is copper.
2	**Candra**	Bronze	Bronze is a metal alloy of ***copper and tin***, known for its durability and strength. It has been used for tools, weapons, art, and various applications throughout history, playing a crucial role in human advancements.
3	**Maṅgala**	Copper	Copper is a reddish-brown metal known for its excellent electrical conductivity and corrosion resistance. It is widely used in electrical wiring, plumbing systems, and various industrial applications.
4	**Budha**	Brass	Brass is a metal alloy composed mainly of ***copper and zinc***, known for its yellowish appearance and favourable combination of strength and malleability. It is commonly used in musical instruments, decorative items, and plumbing fittings.

#	Graha	Metal	Notes
5	**Guru**	Gold	Gold is a precious metal prized for its rarity, beauty, and high value throughout history. It is used in jewellery, investment, and various industrial applications, including electronics and dentistry.
6	**Śukra**	Silver	Silver is a lustrous white metal known for its high electrical and thermal conductivity. It is used in jewellery, silverware, photography, and industrial applications such as electrical contacts and mirrors.
7	**Śani**	Iron	Iron is a strong and abundant metallic element that is essential for the production of steel and the construction of various infrastructures. It is widely used in manufacturing, transportation, and construction industries due to its durability and versatility.
8	**Rāhu**	Iron	- do -

Sunidhi: What is the difference between the different alloys of copper, brass, bronze, bell metal etc? Also, what are Tambra, Kansa and Pītal as used in Indian civilization?

Ācārya: Copper, Iron, Tin and Zinc were the important metals of ancient Indian civilization. Copper has been used in making alloys with Tin and Zinc for ages. Following are some more details.

Copper "Tambra" is a pure metal known for its excellent electrical conductivity and corrosion resistance. It has a characteristic reddish-brown colour and is widely used in electrical wiring, plumbing systems, and industrial applications.

Brass "Pītal" is an alloy made primarily of copper and zinc. It has a yellowish appearance and offers a favourable combination of strength and malleability. Brass is commonly used in musical instruments, decorative items, and plumbing fittings.

Bronze "Kansa" is another copper alloy, mainly composed of copper and tin. It has a reddish-brown colour similar to copper but is harder and more durable. Bronze has been historically significant, crucial in tools, weapons, and art during the Bronze Age.

Bell metal is a type of Bronze "Kansa" with a specific composition of copper and tin, typically with a higher proportion of tin. It is called bell metal due to its use in making bells for musical instruments. Bell metal provides a rich tone and is valued for its resonance and sonorous qualities.

While all these alloys contain copper, their additional elements and proportions are the main difference. Copper is the base metal, brass incorporates zinc, bronze combines copper and tin, and bell metal is a specific type of bronze with a higher tin content for making musical bells. Each alloy has distinct properties and applications in various industries and artistic endeavours.

Sunidhi: Thank you for clarifying this.

Ācārya: Now the effect of the Grahas in their Svarāśis or other Rāśis and the yuti with other Grahas are mentioned.

2.97. If Maṅgala Sūrya, Śani and Śukra are in their Svarāśis, they keep to their respective metals. If Candra, Budha and Guru are in their Svarāśis or Mitrarāśis, they keep to their respective metals. If two or three Grahas are in a Rāśi, either the respective metal of the Grahas or the dominant metal should be mentioned.

Kailāśa: Will the Grahas indicate a separate metal when outside their Svarāśis?

Ācārya: When the Grahas are in their Svarāśis, they indicate pure metals, but when they are in someone else's Rāśi, they indicate an alloy. If they are conjunct with other Grahas, they also indicate an alloy or the stronger metal among them.

Kailāśa: How about non-metals? The Grahas must also rule some non-metallic "Dhātu" objects. Isn't it?

Ācārya: Indeed! That is explained in the next śloka.

2.98. Sūrya is found of granite stones; Budha of mud pots; Candra sand; Śukra pearls; Maṅgala coral; Śani iron, and Guru copper sulphate. शिलां भानोर्बुधस्याहुर्मृत्पात्रं तूषरं विधोः । सितस्य मुक्तास्फटिके प्रकाळं भूसुतस्य च । आयसं भानुपुत्रस्य मन्त्रिणश्च मनश्शिलाम् ॥९८॥

Ācārya: The non-metallic "Dhātus" denoted by the Grahas are Sūrya – granite (produced by volcanic eruptions), Candra – sand (formed by oceans), Śukra – pearls and Sphaṭika (crystals), Maṅgala – coral (formed by the skeletons of dead coral insects), Śani – iron (high compressive strength), and Guru (a bluestone used in several mystical purposes).

Kailāśa: The rulership appears to be based on how these materials originated and where they are found.

Ācārya: Yes, these Kārakatvas are based on several factors, which are based on the Guṇas, Bhūtas etc., of the Grahas.

2.99. When Grahas are in their Uccarāśis, they are stated to be purified Dhātus by their Sphutas and "Ghaṭita" (i.e. associated with other Dhātus). If they are in Nīca, they are then stated to be impure Dhātus and "Aghaṭita" (not associated with other Dhātus). स्वोच्चादिके धाम्यधातुस्तथाधाम्यं तु नीचगे । घटिताघटितं ब्रूयाच्छास्त्रे ज्ञानप्रदीपके ॥९९॥

Ācārya: Let me also give the ślokas from the Hindi translation of Pt Ramvyas Pandey. Some of them are missing in the translation of Pt Kadalangudi Natesa Sastri.

स्वक्षेत्रभानुरुच्चंद्रो धातुरन्यश्च पूर्ववत् । स्वक्षेत्रभानुजो वल्ली स्वक्षेत्रधातुरिन्दुजः ॥५६॥ विशेषता यह है कि, सूर्य अपने का, और चन्द्रमा उच्च का धातु होते है । शनि स्वक्षेत्र में मूल और बुध क्षेत्र में धातु होता है, शेष ग्रह पूवत्रत् ही रहते हैं ।

ताम्रो भौमस्त्रपुर्ज्ञश्च कांचनं धिषणो भवेत्। रौप्यं शुक्रः शशी कांस्य: अयसं मंदभोगिनौ ॥६०॥ मंगल, तामा, बुध त्रपु (पीतल?), गुरु सोना, शुक्र चांदी, चंद्रमा कांसा, शनि और राहु लोहे होते हैं ।

भौमार्कमंद शुकास्तु स्वस्थ लोहस्वभावकाः । चन्द्रागुरवः स्वस्वलोहोः स्त्रक्षेत्र मित्रपाः ॥६१॥ मिश्र मिश्रफलं ज्ञात्वा ग्रहाणां च फलं कूमात् । मंगल सूर्य शनि शुक ये अपने २ भाव में लौहकार के होते हैं, चन्द्रमा बुध बृहस्पति अपने क्षेत्र तथा मित्र क्षेत्र में होने से लौहकारक कहे गए हैं। मिश्र में मिश्रित फल का आदेश क्रम से करना चाहिये ।

शिला भानोबुधस्याहुः मृत्पात्रं चोपरं विदुः ॥६२॥ सितस्य मुक्तास्फटिके प्रवालं भूसुतस्य च । अयसं भानुपुत्रस्य मंत्रिणः स्यान्मनः शिला ॥६३॥ नीलं शनेश्च वैडूर्य्यं भृगोर्मरकतं विदुः । सूर्यकान्तो दिनेशस्य चंद्रकान्तो निशापतेः ॥६४॥ तत्तदग्रहवशान्नित्यं तत्तद्राशिवशादपि । सूर्य को शिला, बुध का मृत्याच्च और उपर, शुक्र का मोती और स्फटिक मणि, मंगल का मूंगा, शनि का लोहा, गुरु का मनःशिला (धातु विशेष) शनि का नीलम और वैडूर्य, शुक का मरकत, सूर्य का सूर्यकान्त, चंद्र का चंद्रकांत, ये रत्न मन विचारते समय तदुराशि और ग्रह पर से बताने चाहिये ।

बलाबलविभागेन मिश्रे मिश्रफलं भवेत् ॥६५॥ नृराशौ नृखगैर्दृष्टे युक्ते वा मर्त्यभूषणम् । तत्तद्राशिवशादन्यत् तत्तद्रूपं विनिर्दिशेत् ॥६६॥ इति धातुचिंता। बली, निर्बल का विचार करके दृढ़ और अदृढ़ फल बताना चाहिये । यदि मिश्रफल हो तो फल भी मिश्र होता है। यदि नरराशि मनुष्यग्रह द्वारा दृष्ट किंवा युक्त हो तो धातुसंबंधी प्रश्न में मानवभूषण बताना चाहिये। शेष राशि और ग्रह के स्वरूपवश।

2.100. Śani's favourite stone is Sapphire. Śukra's cat's-eye; Budha's emerald; Sūrya's Sunstone (Sūryakānta) and Candra's Moonstone (Candrakānta).

Ācārya: Now, the precious gemstones denoted the Grahas are delineated.

Sūrya – Sūryakānta maṇi – Ruby

Candra – Candrakānta maṇi – Moonstone

Maṅgala – Coral – Pravāla

Budha – Emerald – Panna – Marakaṭa

Guru – Puṣparāga – Yellow sapphire

Śukra – Diamond – Vajra maṇi

Śani – Blue sapphire – Nīlama

Rāhu – Hessonite – Gomedika

Ketu – Vaidurya maṇi – Cats eye

The author states some differences in the Gemstones associated with Grahas. I have provided my views above.

Jayanta: We should also add pearl for Candra and Turquoise for Śukra.

Ācārya: Indeed, we should!

2.101-102. If an Ojarāśi is dṛṣṭied by or associated with a Puruṣa Graha, then one can predict the loss of ornaments worn by men. In other places appropriate prediction must be made in accordance with the nature of the Rāśis and Grahas. The colour of the article must be judged according to the strength of the Graha and Rāśi. If both are of equal strength, the result will be of a mixed nature. नृराशौ नृखगैर्दृष्टे युक्ते वा मर्त्यभूषणम् । तत्तद्राशिवशादन्यत्तत्तद्रूपं विचिन्तयेत् ॥१०१॥ तत्तदूग्रहवशाद्वर्णं तत्तद्राशिवशादपि । बलावलविभागेन मिश्र मिश्रफलं वदेत् ॥१०२॥

Ācārya: Ojarāśis are masculine. If an Ojarāśi has yutidṛṣṭi of Puruṣagrahas, the object in question may be an ornament worn by men.

Alternatively, if a Yugmarāśi has yutidṛṣṭi of Strīgrahas, then the ornaments must be worn by women. If the influences are mixed, the indications are also mixed.

3. MŪLACINTA

Ācārya: After covering Dhātu, next is to focus on Mūla, plants and vegetation. Mūla meets root, and the plant kingdom is known from the roots that bind them to the ground. Therefore, they are denoted by Sthirarāśis.

3.103. Based on earlier Śāstras, this account about plants and Grahas is being narrated.

3.104. Maṅgala is related to grains and pulses; Budha and Guru to crops like rice and wheat-Budha to bushes, Sūrya to trees; Candra to creepers and clinging vines. Guru to sugarcane. Śukra to tamarind tree. Śani, Maṅgala and Rāhu to bitter trees like Neem (Margosa, Azadirachta *indica*) and thorny plants.

Ācārya: Different Grahas are associated with different plants and vegetation.

Sūrya: Trees

Candra: Creepers

Maṅgala: Grains and pulses, dāl such as Moong, Masoor, Toor and Urad.

Budha: Rice and wheat

Guru: same as Budha

Śukra: Tamarind

Śani/Maṅgala: Bitter trees like neem

Rāhu: Thorny plants and trees such as honey locust

Sunidhi: Doesn't Guru represent fruit-bearing trees?

Ācārya: According to Maharṣi Parāśara, yes! Śloka 3.39-40 of Bṛhatparāśara states that Sūrya rules strong trees, Śani useless trees, Candra milky trees, Maṅgala bitter ones, Śukra floral plants, Bṛhaspati fruitful ones and Budha fruitless.

Kailāśa: I suppose Budha is the Kāraka for all vegetation.

Ācārya: Budha is the governor of leaves and is associated with plants and vegetation. He is the Kāraka for non-violence and shunning killing animals for food. But in Dhātvādi classification, Budha is considered Jīva, and Sūrya/Śukra are classified as Mūla.

Therefore, generally considered, Budha is the Kāraka for vegetation, further subdivided based on their kind and utility.

Sūrya is the Kāraka for strength, and he rules strong trees used for building materials - such as houses etc. We find a dictum that when Sūrya is in the 4H from Kārakāñśa, the native lives in a wooden house.

The governance of trees by the Grahas are - (1) Sūrya - strong trees, (2) Candra - milky trees, (3) Maṅgala - bitter trees, (4) Śukra - floral plants, (5) Bṛhaspati - fruit-bearing trees, (6) Budha - fruitless trees, those having leaves only, (7) Śani - useless trees.

Sunidhi: Thank you for clarifying this, Guruji!

Ācārya: Let us also check the governances as per Phaladīpikā.

According to Phaladīpikā 2.37., the tree governances are,

(1) Sūrya: Tall and inwardly strong trees

(2) Śukra: creepers

(3) Ketu and Rāhu signify bushes

(4) Maṅgala and Śani indicate thorny trees

(5) Guru signifies fruit-bearing trees

(6) Budha fruitless trees, i.e., with good foliage and grasses

(7) Śukra and Candra signify those that are full of sap and blossoming

(8) Candra represents all herbs

(9) Śani represents the sapless and weak trees

(10) Rāhu indicates the śāla (Shorea robusta), or Sakhua tree

Kailāśa: I suppose Ketu rules all kinds of trees whose leaves are used for intoxicants/narcotic drugs, such as cannabis, poppy etc.

Ācārya: Yes, that is right.

Kailāśa: Thank you for clarifying this, Guruji!

3.105. Meṣa and Vṛścika are related to grains and pulses; Vṛṣabha, Karka and Tulā to creepers; Kanyā and Mithuna to trees; Kumbha and Makara to thorny bushes; and Mīna to sugarcane.

Ācārya: Now, the focus is on the Rāśis. The Rāśi association is based on their owners.

(1) Maṅgala: Meṣa/Vṛścika: Grains and pulses

(2) Candra/Śukra: Karka/Vṛṣabha/Tulā: Creepers

(3) Budha: Mithuna/Kanyā: Trees with dense foliage

(4) Śani: Makara/Kumbha: Thorny bushes

(5) Guru: Dhanu/Mīna: Sugarcane

Kailāśa: Guruji, Guru governs sweet taste; therefore, Sugarcane is governed by him. Isn't it?

Ācārya: That is right. Besides, Maṅgala is bitter and, therefore, should govern trees such as Neem. Candra/Śukra are watery and, therefore, should govern is succulent like aloe vera and has a lot of sap, such as rubber tree. Śani should govern all kinds of useless bushes. In this manner, you can associate the Graha Kārakatvas with the plant kingdom.

Kailāśa: I suppose the Saumyas (Guru/Śukra/Candra/Budha) should govern the beautiful trees laden with flowers and fruits. Isn't it?

Ācārya: Yes, that is right. Guru rules all fruit trees such as mango, guava, jackfruit etc. Śukra governs all flowing plants such as Champa, Jasmine, Lily etc. Budha governs all trees and plants known for their dense foliage, such as bamboo.

Besides, the author also states other views on this matter. All Saumyas are stated to be related to thornless trees, and Krūras to thorny ones. Of these,

Sūrya is related to twin thorny plants and trees; Maṅgala to stunted thorny plants and Śani and Rāhu to bent and crooked thorny ones.

Let us see some more classification in the next śloka.

3.106-109. All Krūras are thorny trees; Budha is a thick bushy plant; and Śukra is a thornless tree. Plantain is ascribed to Candra; trees growing on mountains and hills to Sūrya; tall trees with long leaves like the coconut to Guru; Śani and Rāhu are related to date palms and trees with sap or without sap. Śani, Candra and Sūrya are related to weak trees; while Śukra and Guru are to strong plants and trees. Śani, Guru, Maṅgala and Rāhu, if posited in their own Rāśis, refer to trees which look seemingly strong outside. All Grahas in their own Rāśis refer to real strong trees, while in other Rāśis, related to apparently strong trees, say some Jyotiṣīs.

Sunidhi: Kindly elaborate on this.

Ācārya:

(1) The Krūras govern thorny trees
(2) Budha: Thick bushy plant
(3) Candra: Plantain or bananas
(4) Sūrya: Trees growing on mountains and hills
(5) Guru: Tall trees with long leaves like the coconut
(6) Śani/Rāhu: Date palms and trees with sap or without sap
(7) Śani/Candra/Sūrya: Weak trees
(8) Guru/Śukra: Strong trees
(9) Śani/Guru/Maṅgala/Rāhu in Svarāśi: Trees that look seemingly strong outside

Besides, according to some scholars, Grahas in their Svarāśis refer to "truly" strong trees, while other Rāśis related to "apparently" strong trees.

Sunidhi: Dhanyavād, Guruji!

Ācārya: Let us see the association of Grahas to different parts of a plant.

3.110. Sūrya is connected with the bark, Candra with the tubers, Maṅgala with flowers, Budha with leaves, Guru with fruits, Śukra with unripe fruit, Śani with roots, and Rāhu with creepers. Likewise, these parts can also be applied to the appropriate Rāśis of the Grahas.

Ācārya: The association are:

(1) Sūrya: Bark
(2) Candra: Tubers
(3) Maṅgala: Flowers
(4) Budha: Leaves
(5) Guru: Fruits
(6) Śukra: Unripe fruits
(7) Śani: Roots
(8) Rāhu: Creepers

Kailāśa: Why is Maṅgala the governor of flowers? Should it not be Śukra?

Ācārya: That is an excellent question. Normally Śukra is the Kāraka for beauty and governs flowering plants or a tree laden with flowers. But when it comes to the parts of a plant, things are a little different.

Maṅgala and Śukra govern the male and female parts of a flower.

The stamen is the male reproductive organ of a flower. It consists of two main parts: Anther and Filament. The anther is the top portion of the stamen. It produces and contains pollen and male gametes (sperm cells). The filament is the long, slender stalk that supports the anther.

The pistil or carpel is the female reproductive organ of a flower. It consists of Stigma, Style and Ovary. The stigma is the topmost part of the pistil. It is sticky or feathery to capture pollen. The style is a slender tube-like structure that connects the stigma to the ovary. The ovary is the enlarged basal portion of the pistil. It contains one or more ovules, which house the female gametes (egg cells).

Kailāśa: But why associate flower with Maṅgala?

Ācārya: It appears that the author associates the unfertilized stage of a flower with Maṅgala and fertilized stage of the flower with Śukra. The fertilized stage of a flower gives rise to fruit.

Kailāśa: Now, it appears to make sense.

Ācārya: Alright, let us focus on the other governances of the Grahas.

3.111. Budha is associated with green gram; Śukra with white dāl; Maṅgala with peanuts; Candra with sesamum; Sūrya with beans; Guru with red dāl; and Śani and Rāhu with black gram.

The association of Grahas with grains are as follows:

(1) Sūrya – beans

(2) Candra – sesame seeds

(3) Maṅgala – peanuts

(4) Budha – green gram or moong

(5) Guru – red gram or masoor

(6) Śukra – white gram, cowpea or lobia

(7) Śani/Rāhu – black gram or urad

Sunidhi: Which Graha governs the horse gram?

Ācārya: According to some classical texts, Ketu governs it.

Kailāśa: How about the grains such as rice, wheat etc.?

3.112. Regarding crops, Maṅgala is related to rye and Budha to paddy.

Ācārya: Normally, the governances are as follows:

(1) Sūrya: Wheat or crops that grow in arid land

(2) Candra: Rice or crops that grow in water-logged land

(3) Maṅgala: Rye, as per the author

(4) Budha: Paddy, as per the author

Normally Budha rules all kinds of grasses, such as Durba and Sabai grass (*Eulaliopsis binata*).

Jayanta: According to Jinendramāla 3.11. (1) Candra is white paddy; (2) Maṅgala is millet; (3) Śukra is white sesamum seed; (4) Budha, Bṛhaspati and Śani are beans of their respective colour. (5) Also, the four Śubhagrahas and Śani are hard grains, and (6) the three-remaining Krūragrahas are pod grains (pulses, such as peas, dāl etc., which grow inside pods).

Ācārya: Where these crops grow is also mentioned in terms of Grahas.

3.113. Maṅgala and Sūrya correspond to hilly tracts; Budha and Rāhu to anthills; Candra and Śukra to watery regions; Guru to mountain slopes; and Śani to black granite tracts.

Sunidhi: Kindly elaborate, Guruji!

Ācārya: The Grahas govern a certain kind of land. They are specified here.

(1) **Sūrya/Maṅgala:** Agni: hilly tracts (like Meṣa/Dhanu)
(2) **Candra/Śukra:** Jala: watery regions (like Karka/Mīna/Vṛṣabha)
(3) **Guru:** Mountain slopes (like Dhanu)
(4) **Śani:** black granite tracts (like Makara). Rāhu should also indicate the same.
(5) **Budha/Rāhu:** anthills. Normally, Ketu is related to an anthill.

Ācārya: The author now specifies how to use these Kārakatvas.

3.114. The prediction must be made properly and investigated by determining the appropriate colour, juice, caste, jewel, weapon, leaf, fruit, bark, root, etc., of the various Grahas, their rising position (Āruṛha) and the Chatra.

Kailāśa: Where and how to use them?

Ācārya: They are used in several places, including lost objects, food, crops, objects concealed in the mind or fist etc. In such a Praśna, Udaya, Āruṛha and Chatra must be examined to conclude something.

4. MANUṢYA KĀṆḌA

Ācārya: After reviewing the principles of Dhātu and Mūla, let us focus on Jīva. We start by reviewing humans' (Manuṣya) association with different Grahas.

4.115. Candra is the mother of the universe, as Sūrya is the father. Guru, Śukra, Maṅgala, Budha and Śani are the five elements of the universe.

Sunidhi: These Kārakatvas are well known.

Ācārya: Tell me what they are:

Sunidhi: They are as follows:

(1) Sūrya – Father
(2) Candra – Mother
(3) Maṅgala – younger siblings
(4) Budha – maternal uncles and aunts

(5) Guru - children, preceptor and elders, paternal grandparent

(6) Śukra - spouse

(7) Śani - servant, elder sibling

(8) Rāhu - foreigner

(9) Ketu - Maternal grandparent, monk

Ācārya: That is good. Let us focus on the Tattvas.

Sunidhi: They are

(1) Agni - Maṅgala

(2) Pṛthvī - Budha

(3) Vāyu - Śani

(4) Jala - Śukra

(5) Ākāśa - Guru

Kailāśa: Isn't Sūrya of Agnitattva and Candra of Jalatattva? Why haven't you included them?

Ācārya: Kailāśa, they are not the governor of the Tattvas. They are of the Tattvas. The Grahas are primarily classified into Prakāśagrahas (Sūrya/Candra), Bhūtagrahas (Maṅgala to Śani) and Chāyāgrahas (Rāhu/Ketu).

Next comes the association of the senses:

4.116. The five Grahas are related to the five senses; Guru to sound; Śukra to touch; Maṅgala to sight; Budha to taste; and Śani to smell.

Ācārya: The sense organs are called Indriya. There are two kinds of Indriyas, Jñānendriya and Karmendriya.

Jñānendriya is the organ of perception. The five Jñānendriya or "sense organs" - Ears, Skin, Eyes, Tongue and Nose. They perceive sound, touch, vision, taste and smell.

Karmendriya is the "organ of action". The five Karmendriyas Hasta, Pada, Vāk, Pāyu and Upastha. They are used for grasping, walking, speaking, excreting and procreating.

Kailāśa: What are the other attributes of the human body?

Ācārya: According to the Śāstras, there are several attributes human body. This includes 5 Jñānendriya, 5 Karmendriya, 5 Tanmātra, 4 Antahkaraṇa, 10 Nāḍī, 7 Cakra, 7 Dhātu, 10 Vāyu, 5 Koṣa, 9 Dvāra, 6 Ripus, 3 Maṇḍala, 3 Doṣa, 3 Guṇas and 5 Avasthā

5 Jñānendriya: Eye, Ear, Nose, Tongue, Skin.

5 Karmendriya: Mouth, feet, hand, anus, genital.

5 Tanmātra: Light, sound, taste, smell, consciousness

4 Antahkarana: Māna - to think; Buddhi - to understand; Aham - to self-identify; Citta - to reflect.

10 Nāḍī: Suṣumnā, Ida, Piṅgala, Gandhari, Hastajihvā, Yaśasvini, Pūṣā, Alambuṣā, Kuhu, and Śaṅkhinī.

7 Cakra: Mūlādhāra – Root; Svādhiṣṭhāna – Sacral; Maṇipura – Solar Plexus; Anahata – Heart; Viśuddha – Throat; Ajñā – Third Eye; Sahasrāra – Crown.

7 Dhātu: Rasa Serum; Rakta Blood; Māṁsa Flesh; Meda –fats; Asthi Bone; Majjā bone marrow; Śukra Semen

10 Vāyu: Prāṇa – situated in the heart; Apāna - situated in the top of the head and passing downwards; Samāna - situated in the pit of the throat; Vyāna – pervading the whole body; Udāna - situated in the navel; Nāga – which effects the motions and speech; Kūrma – causing horripilation; Karikarā - seated in the face; Devadatta – that which is exhaled in yawning; Dhananjaya – that which remains in the body after the death and escapes by splitting the head.

5 Koṣa: Annamaya; Prāṇamaya; Manomaya; Vijñānīya; Anandamaya.

9 Dvāra: Two eyes; Two ears; Two nostrils; The mouth; The anus; Urinary orifice.

6 Ripu: Kāma, Krodha, Lobha, Moha, Mada and Mātsarya.

3 Maṇḍala: Agni Maṇḍala – lower abdomen; Āditya Maṇḍala – stomach; Candra Maṇḍala – head and shoulders.

3 Doṣa: Vāta, Pitta; Kapha.

3 Guṇas: Sattva, Rajas, Tamas.

5 Avasthā: Jāgrata, Svapna, Suṣupta, Turīya, Turīyatīta.

Sunidhi: Guruji, this is enlightening.

Kailāśa: Are the Grahas have the same grasping power as the Indriyas?

4.117. These five Grahas have different powers of knowledge, namely Guru 5, Śukra 4, Maṅgala 3, Budha 2, and Śani 1, i.e. that Guru is capable of grasping the five senses of sound, touch, sight, taste, and smell; Śukra to the four senses of touch, sight, taste and smell; Maṅgala to three senses of sight, taste and smell; Budha to the two senses of taste and smell; and Śani only to the one sense of smell only.

Ācārya: According to Jñānapradīpikā, the Grahas have different grasping power that ranges from Guru, Śukra, Maṅgala, Budha, and Śani. These are the Tattvagrahas or Bhūtagrahas.

(1) Guru: smell, taste, sight, touch, sound

(2) Śukra: smell, taste, sight, touch, ~~sound~~

(3) Maṅgala: smell, taste, sight, ~~touch, sound~~

(4) Budha: smell, taste, ~~sight, touch, sound~~

(5) Śani: smell, ~~taste, sight, touch, sound~~

Jayanta: What does it signify?

Ācārya: The Jñānendriya represent how we acquire knowledge. Guru is the most capable of acquiring knowledge, followed by Śukra and others. You can acquire knowledge through such sense organs depending on the Graha influencing your Jñāna Bhāva.

Now, the author explains other Kārakatvas of the Grahas.

4.118-119. Conch, pearl, and shell belong to the Budha group, and Bug, louse, bee and ant belong to the Maṅgala group. All species of six-legged insects belong to the Śukra group. Devas, humans, cows, snakes, and Pakṣi belong to the Guru group. Plants which have only a single sensory awareness belong to the Śani group.

Ācārya: The following are the association of different creatures based on their ability to use their sensory organs. This excludes Sūrya and Candra. The creatures that have developed 5 sensory organs are governed by Guru, four by Śukra and so on.

(1) Guru: 5 senses: Devas, Manuṣya, cows (cattle), snake, and Pakṣi

(2) Śukra: 4 senses: six-legged insects

(3) Maṅgala: 3 senses: Bug, louse, bee and ant

(4) Budha: 2 senses: Conch, pearl, and shell

(5) Śani: 1 sense: Plants

Kailāśa: The Bhūtas are associated with so many things. It is enlightening to know that Grahas are associated with things based on the predominant usage of certain senses.

Ācārya: Indeed. Śani governs plants, who respond to only one sense: touch.

The following ślokas deal with the Bhūtas with the senses.

4.120-121. It is stated that of the five elements, Ākāśa has only one attribute, namely, sound; and Vāyu has two attributes, sound and touch; Agni has three attributes, namely, sound, touch and sight; Jala has the four attributes of sound, touch, sight, and taste. Finally, the 5th element Pṛthvī has the five qualities of sound, touch, sight, taste and smell. Referring then to the parts of the body, Guru corresponds to the body, Śukra tongue. Budha to nose, Maṅgala to eyes and Śani to ears. Further, Guru is analogous to Dvipāda, Śukra to Catuṣpāda, Budha to Bahupāda, Maṅgala to Pakṣi and Śani to Kīṭa and Sarīsṛpa (crawling insects crustaceans and frogs are stated to have no legs. Lice and bugs are stated to have many legs. Tortoise and Iguana are crawling animals).

Ācārya: The senses governed by the Bhūtas are as follows:

(1) **Ākāśa:** Sound

(2) **Vāyu:** Sound, and Touch

(3) **Agni:** Sound, Touch, and Sight

(4) **Jala:** Sound, Touch, Sight, and Taste

(5) **Pṛthvī:** Sound, Touch, Sight, Taste, and Smell

Further, the Graha Kārakatvas of creatures based on their number of feet (Pada) is as follows:

(1) **Śani:** Sarīsṛpa: No legs: snakes. *Amphibians:* crocodile, tortoise, frog, lizard, iguana, etc.

(2) **Guru:** Dvipāda: 2 legs: human, chimpanzee, monkey, orangutan etc.

(3) **Maṅgala:** Pakṣi: 2 legs: birds.

(4) **Śukra:** Catuṣpāda: 4 legs: cattle, horse, zebra, tiger, lion, wolf etc.

(5) **Śani:** Kīṭa: 6 legs: ant etc. *Crustaceans:* crab, shrimp etc.

(6) **Budha:** Bahupāda: many legs: bugs, lice, millipede, centipede etc.

Deciphering thoughts:

Ācārya: Now the author focuses on deciphering one's thoughts from the Praśna. This is a complex area of Jyotiṣa, and one requires years of experience to be good at it.

4.122. Predicting what one thinks: As Makara and Mīna are Vāyurāśis and if Śani and Maṅgala are posited there, one can predict that Pṛcchaka is thinking of the wildfowl or the crow.

Ācārya: The matters mentioned here, such as thinking about a wildfowl (a hen) or a crow, may not be relevant for many; therefore, the indications must be adapted to modern circumstances.

Sunidhi: How to apply them in modern circumstances, Guruji?

Ācārya: By taking note of the parameters used for making the judgement. Here the author considers the Bhūta of the Rāśis and the Grahas posited in them.

Sunidhi: But isn't Makara Pṛthvī Rāśi and Mīna, Jala?

Ācārya: That is right. However, it appears that the author has considered the Bhūta of the lord. Even in that case, Makara should be Vāyu, but Mīna should be Ākāśa.

Sunidhi: Why did he conclude on wildfowl and crow?

Ācārya: That is because, according to 2.48, Makara and Mīna are Pakṣi Rāśis. The selection of crows is due to Maṅgala, and wildfowl is also due to Maṅgala.

Sunidhi: That makes sense. I think wildfowl (cockerel or hen) are related to Maṅgala (Meṣa), as they are often used for rooster fights, and Meṣa is the Uccarāśi of Sūrya, the ruling bird.

Kailāśa: How can you say that Sūrya rules roosters?

Ācārya: That is because roosters are the first to wake up with the first Sūryaraśmi and act as alarm clocks.

Therefore, the key takeaway is that we must consider the Rāśi and Graha in Udaya. Even though the author does not specifically state that we must consider Udaya, we should. Normally the subject of a Praśna relates to Lagna or Candra in the Praśna Kuṇḍalī. Sometimes, it is associated with the Horeśa or the strongest Graha in the Kuṇḍalī.

4.123. If in those Rāśis Śukra is posited, the thinking is about a swan; if Budha, it is a parrot; if Candra, it is a peacock. The same must be predicted if the above Grahas aspect the two Rāśis Makara and Mīna.

4.124. If Sūrya has yutidṛṣṭi on those Rāśis, the eagle is being thought about. If it is Guru, it is the white heron; if it is Rāhu, it is a long-tailed cuckoo; if it is Budha, a cock; and If it is Śukra, it is an owl.

Ācārya: Now that we know that Makara and Mīna are Pakṣi Rāśis, the placement of different Grahas indicates different kinds of birds.

(1) Sūrya: Eagle

(2) Candra: Peacock

(3) Maṅgala: Rooster

(4) Budha: Cock, Parrot

(5) Guru: White heron

(6) Śukra: Owl, Swan

(7) Śani: Crow

(8) Rāhu: Long-tailed cuckoo

(9) Ketu: Not mentioned

Sunidhi: Guruji, Devī Lakṣmī is often depicted with an owl, and Devī Sarasvatī is often depicted with a Swan. Also, Devī Pārvati is depicted with a parrot.

Kailāśa: Why would Devī Sarasvatī be depicted with a Swan?

Ācārya: Swan is also governed by Guru, as that is the Uccarāśi of Śukra. Śukra also owns Naisargika 2H (Vṛṣabha), which stands for speech. She is Vākdevi, the goddess of speech.

Similarly, Śanideva is depicted riding a crow. Crow is also associated with Śrāddha, the rites of the dead!

Kailāśa: If the mentioned Grahas are not placed in the Rāśis, but aspect the Rāśis, then also the results prevail?

Ācārya: Yes! If the Rāśi is vacant, but dṛṣṭied by a Graha, then the results of that Graha would prevail. This is clarified in the next śloka.

4.125. If the Graha is in or aspecting Rāśis other than Makara and Mīna, the effects of those Rāśis must be predicted. If the Grahas are Saumya, the birds also would be auspicious; and if the Grahas are Krūra, the birds thought about would be cruel.

Sunidhi: What about other Rāśis?

Ācārya: Then, the matters of those Rāśis would prevail.

Kailāśa: Also, depending on the governing Graha, the birds are gentle or cruel.

Ācārya: Indeed. Candra – peacock; Budha – parrot; Guru – heron; Śukra – swan. They are gentle birds. On the other hand, Sūrya – eagle, Maṅgala – rooster, Śani – crow etc. These are fierce birds.

Kailāśa: Which Graha governs vulture?

Ācārya: Vultures live on dead animal carcases, and therefore, they are governed by Śani and Rāhu.

Kailāśa: How about hawks?

Ācārya: They are of the family of eagles. Therefore, kites, hawks etc., are governed by Sūrya.

Kailāśa: I heard that eagles could spot their prey from a long distance.

Ācārya: That is because Sūrya is the Kāraka for vision! They have very good vision.

4.126-128. If Ucca Sūrya is in the Udayarāśi or aspecting it, the person thought about will either be a ruler of the earth or one associated with him; if Sūrya is in Meṣa (his exalted Rāśi) and dṛṣṭies the Udayarāśi, the person thought about is a king or emperor; if Sūrya is in his Svarāśi and dṛṣṭies the Udayarāśi, the person is commander-in-chief; if Sūrya is in his Mitrarāśi and dṛṣṭies the Udayarāśi, the person is attached to the king; if Sūrya is in a Samarāśi and dṛṣṭies the Udayarāśi, the person is a warrior. But if the Udayarāśi is in any Rāśi other than Meṣa and is dṛṣṭied by Sūrya, the person thought about should be predicted appropriately according to what is stated above, i.e. as one doing work on bronze, or a potter; or one selling bronze ware; or a breaker of shells; or one seeking chemical powders; or a goldsmith etc.

Ācārya: Now the effect of Sūrya on the Praśnalagna on the subject of Praśna is delineated. The following are the effects of Sūrya occupying/aspecting Udaya from different Rāśis:

(1) Ucca: A king or his associate

(2) Sva: A commander-in-chief

(3) Mitra: A king's associate

(4) Sama: A warrior

If Lagna is in a Rāśi other than Meṣa and Sūrya dṛṣṭies it, then the person in thought could be associated with bronze, pottery, chemical, gold etc. Depending on the Rāśis held by Sūrya, different indications can be estimated.

4.129. If an Ojarāśi is rising and it is dṛṣṭied by Guru, the prediction must be made as stated in previous ślokas for Sūrya, with the provision that the man to be seen will be a Brāhmaṇa; and in the case of an Ojarāśi rising dṛṣṭied by or associated with Budha, the person to be seen will be an ascetic.

4.130. If the rising Ojarāśi is dṛṣṭied by Śukra, the person will be of the lower class; and in the rising Ojarāśi dṛṣṭied by Candra or Rāhu, the person will be of depressed class. But there are some special cases, as in the following.

Ācārya: Now, the Oja and Yugma attribute of the Udayarāśi and dṛṣṭi of Grahas are delineated.

(1) Guru: A Brāhmaṇa

(2) Budha: An ascetic

(3) Śukra: lower class

(4) Candra/Rāhu: depressed class

4.131. If Meṣa is rising and dṛṣṭied by Sūrya, the person will be a servant; if dṛṣṭied by Candra, the person will be a doctor; if dṛṣṭied by Budha, the person will be vaiśya and a gang of thieves; if dṛṣṭied by Rāhu (some will say, Candra) the person may be a poisoner a Caṇḍāla or a thief.

4.132. If dṛṣṭied by Śani, the person will be a woodcutter; if dṛṣṭied by Rāhu, the person will be a fisherman; a flower-seller, a breaker of shells, a dancer, a handicraftsman, a carpenter, a washerman, or a sculptor.

4.133. If dṛṣṭied by Śukra, the person may be a seller of snuff or pearl-diver. The caste of the person must be determined by judging the Rāśis and the occupants of the Rāśis. From the strength of the different Grahas, the finding of lost objects must be determined.

Ācārya: The following are the indications of various Grahas aspecting Meṣa Lagna and the person who may have committed the theft in a Corapraśna.

(1) Sūrya: A servant

(2) Candra: A doctor

(3) Budha: A vaiśya and a gang of thieves

(4) Śani: A woodcutter

(5) Rāhu: A fisherman, a flower-seller, a breaker of shells, a dancer, a handicraftsman, a carpenter, a washerman, or a sculptor.

(6) Rāhu (Candra): a Caṇḍāla or a thief, a fisherman

(7) Śukra: A seller of snuff or pearl-diver

Kailāśa: As per Praśnaśāstra, the age and Varṇa of the thief should be judged from the Rāśi (Agni, Pṛthvī etc.). Isn't it?

Ācārya: Yes, we should! The author states that the caste of the person must be determined by judging the Rāśis and the occupants of the Rāśis. This is explained in detail in Book 23A: The Praśna Fundamentals.

5. THE FINDING OF LOST OBJECTS

Ācārya: Now, we focus on finding the lost objects. It starts with identifying the lost object. Even though in a modern context, this may be diverse and different from what the author describes here, we should learn about the Kārakatvas of Grahas in different Rāśis.

5.134. If Maṅgala is in Meṣa, the thought is about the loss of a goat; if Sūrya is there, the thought is a Bengal tiger; if Budha, it is a monkey.

5.135. If Śukra is in Meṣa, the idea is a cow; if it is Candra, the idea is a bull; if it is Guru, it is a horse; if Śani, it is a buffalo; if Rāhu, it is a deer.

Kailāśa: That is interesting. So, does that mean the Grahas denote different things in different Rāśis?

Ācārya: Yes, they do! Depending on the Manuṣyādi, Dhātvādi, Carādi, Bhūta etc. classification of Rāśis, the Grahas denote different things. The following are the Graha indications in Meṣa Rāśi.

(1) Sūrya: Bengal tiger

(2) Candra: Bull (Nandi)

(3) Maṅgala: Goat, sheep

(4) Budha: Monkey

(5) Guru: Horse

(6) Śukra: Cow
(7) Śani: Buffalo
(8) Rāhu: Deer

Jayanta: Meṣa is a Catuṣpāda Rāśi, and therefore, the Grahas denote different animals (Catuṣpādas). Isn't it?

Ācārya: That is right!

5.136. If Śukra is in Vṛṣabha, the idea thought about is a cow just given birth to a calf; if Maṅgala, it is a deer; if Budha, it is a monkey; if Guru, it is a horse; if Candra, it is a cow that has given birth to a calf; if Sūrya it is 'Śarabha', a kind of lion and if Śani or Rāhu, it is a buffalo.

Ācārya: Now, let us focus on Vṛṣabha, another Catuṣpāda Rāśi. The indications of the Grahas are:

(1) Sūrya: A Śarabha (a kind of lion)
(2) Candra: A cow that has given birth to a calf (a mother cow)
(3) Maṅgala: Deer
(4) Budha: Monkey
(5) Guru: Horse
(6) Śukra: Cow
(7) Śani: Buffalo
(8) Rāhu: Buffalo

Sunidhi: The indications are almost the same as Meṣa.

Ācārya: Yes, with some differences. Vṛṣabha is the Rāśi of cow and bull, and therefore, Candra/Śukra govern a cow (female bovine). Candra is the mother and, therefore, denotes a cow that has given birth to a calf, i.e., a mother cow. Śukra rules a cow that has not given birth to a calf yet.

Sunidhi: Guruji, what is a Śarabha?

Ācārya: Śarabha (शरभ,) or Śarabha is an eight-legged part-lion and part-bird beast in Sanātana Dharma, who is described as more powerful than a lion or an elephant, possessing the ability to clear a valley in one jump.

According to the Paurāṇic legends, Śarabha an incarnation of Śrī Śiva and to subdue the fierce manifestation of Śrī Viṣṇu, Śrī Nṛsiṅha. The Śiva Purāṇa describes Śarabha as lion-faced, with matted hair, wings and eight feet, and a thousand arms.

After slaying Hiranyakashipu, Śrī Nṛsiṅha's wrath threatened the world. At the behest of the Devatās, Śrī Shiva sent Śrī Virabhadra to tackle Śrī Nṛsiṅha. When that failed, Śrī Shiva manifested as Śarabha. The Śiva Purāṇa mentions Sharabha attacking Śrī Nṛsiṅha and immobilising him. He thus quelled Śrī Nṛsiṅha's terrifying rage.

According to Liṅga Purāṇa and the Śarabha Upanishad, Śarabha then decapitated and de-skinned the man-lion form so Śrī Śiva could wear the hide and lion head as a garment. After Śrī Nṛsiṅha's form was destroyed, Śrī Viṣṇu assumed his normal form and retired to his abode after duly praising Śrī Śiva. From here on that Śrī Śiva came to be known as "Śarabheshamūrti" or "Siṅhaghnamūrti". This is, however, now acceptable to the Vaiṣṇavas.

According to Vaiṣṇava tradition, when Śarabha tried to hold Śrī Nṛsiṅha and carry him high into the sky, Śrī Nṛsiṅha took the form of a two-headed eagle - Gaṇḍabheruṇḍa - who was even stronger than Śarabha, and now with renewed rage. After a hot pursuit, when Gaṇḍabheruṇḍa met Śarabha, a fierce 18-day-long battle ensued between them. On the eighteenth day, Gaṇḍabheruṇḍa defeated Śarabha and tore him into shreds.

Gaṇḍabheruṇḍa then pleaded and appealed to Śrī Nṛsiṅha to forgive him for his actions, after which the Devatā regained his sense of calm. As a mark of respect, Śarabha removed the skin of his body and presented it to Gaṇḍabheruṇḍa. Peace having been restored to the universe, Śrī Vishnu and Śrī Shiva assumed their true forms and returned to their abodes of Vaikuṇṭha and Kailaśa, respectively.

Sunidhi: Dhanyavād Guruji, for the enlightening legend. I bow to the effulgent and fierce forms of Śrī Nṛsiṅha, Śrī Śarabha and Śrī Gaṇḍabheruṇḍa.

5.137. If Maṅgala is in Karka, it is a donkey; if Maṅgala in Makara, it is a buffalo; if Maṅgala in Vṛṣabha, it is a lion; if Maṅgala in Mithuna, it is a dog; and if Maṅgala in Kanyā, it is a fox.

Ācārya: The following are the indications of Maṅgala in different Rāśis

(1) Meṣa: Goat, Sheep

(2) Vṛṣabha: Deer, Lion

(3) Mithuna: Dog

(4) Karka: Donkey

(5) Siṅha: Tiger

(6) Kanyā: Fox

(7) Tulā: ____

(8) Vṛścika: ____

(9) Dhanu: ____

(10) Makara: Buffalo

(11) Kumbha: ____

(12) Mīna: ____

5.138. If Maṅgala is in Siṅha, the thought in the Pṛcchaka's mind is a tiger; and if Sūrya or Candra are in Siṅha, the idea is a lion; and if Śukra in Siṅha, it is a dog; if Budha in Siṅha, it is a monkey; and if other Grahas are in Siṅha, the prediction of an animal akin to dog can be made.

Ācārya: The effects of Grahas in Siṅha are as follows:

(1) Sūrya: Lion

(2) Candra: Lion

(3) Maṅgala: Tiger

(4) Budha: Monkey

(5) Guru: Dog-like creature

(6) Śukra: Dog

(7) Śani: Dog-like creature

(8) Rāhu: Dog-like creature

5.140. If Śukra is in Tulā, the idea in mind is about the loss of a calf; if it is Candra, the idea is a cow; if Guru, Candra and Maṅgala are in Dhanu, the idea is a horse; if along with Śani Sūrya is also in Kumbha; the thought is about a mad elephant if Rāhu is in Kumbha, it is a buffalo, and if Budha and Guru are in Kumbha, it is a monkey.

5.141. If in Kumbha are posited Śukra, Sūrya and Candra, the idea is a cow; if Guru and Sūrya aspect Kumbha, it is a pregnant cow; if dṛṣṭied by Śani, it is a barren cow'; and if dṛṣṭied by Maṅgala, it is an old cow with no more calving. A wise man can make such predictions.

Ācārya: Following are some more indications:

(1) Śukra in Tulā: calf

(2) Candra in Tulā: cow

(3) Candra/Guru/Maṅgala in Dhanu: horse

(4) Śani/Sūrya in Kumbha: a mad elephant

(5) Rāhu in Kumbha: buffalo

(6) Budha/Guru in Kumbha: monkey

(7) Śukra/Candra/Sūrya in Kumbha: cow

(8) Guru/Sūrya in Kumbha: a pregnant cow

(9) Guru/Sūrya in Kumbha dṛṣṭied by Śani: a barren cow

(10) Guru/Sūrya in Kumbha dṛṣṭied by Maṅgala: an old cow with no more calving

Jayanta: Guruji, what are the other Kārakatvas of Grahas and Rāśis regarding animals (Catuṣpāda)?

Ācārya: For that, we must refer to Praśnamārga, which deals with this subject in detail in the context of hunting (called Mṛgaya Praśna). The following ślokas are from Praśnamārga.

24.198. If 8H happens to be owned by Maṅgala or occupied by him, or if Maṅgala is posited in a Kendra, a pig with its young ones shall be shot dead. If Sūrya occupies a Kendra, a tiger shall be shot dead. If Śukra occupies 1H, 8H or 11H and Budha is in a Kendra, no animal is shot dead. If Śukra occupies 1H, 8H or 11H and Maṅgala is in a Kendra, a pig shall be shot, but it will escape.

24.199. If Udaya is a Cararāśi occupied by Maṅgala, Gu̲lika is posited in 8H, and Śani stands in 4H, a pig shall be captured in the hunt.

24.200. Sūrya, Śani, Maṅgala and Rāhu occupying 4H, 7H, 1H and 10H indicates the death of many animals in the hunt.

24.201. When Krūras occupy Cararāśis and Saumyas are in Sthirarāśis, and Gu̲lika is in 3H, many animals, such as tigers, etc., shall be killed.

24.202. If Krūras occupy Kendras, 5H or 9H, Māndi is in 3H, and Makara is Udaya, animals shall be captured in the hunt. When Candra and Maṅgala are in 8H, Gulika is in 3H, and Yamaghaṅṭaka occupies 9H, a pregnant animal shall be killed. The nature and kind of the animals must be ascertained from the Dreṣkāṇa Lagna.

24.203. That which helps the easy killing or capture of animals in a hunt is the elevation or depression of the ground. This can be known from the Rāśi or Graha. The number of animals to be captured should be ascertained from the number of Grahas in Asta, in Nīca, or Śatru Rāśis.

24.204. In Sārasaṅgraha, animals have been classified under various heads as bipeds, quadrupeds, etc., and Grahas also have been allotted relationships to animals. They are given below:

24.205. (1) Sūrya governs lion and other superior animals; **(2)** Candra, rabbit and other gentle animals; **(3)** Maṅgala, tiger, leopard and such cruel animals; **(4)** Budha, pig and hog; **(5)** Bṛhaspati, elephant and horse; **(6)** Śukra, deer and stag; **(7)** Śani, donkey and camel and **(8)** Rāhu, creeping animals as Godha (monitor lizard). **(1)** Sūrya/Śani govern bipeds, **(2)** Candra/Budha, six-legged creatures or the hexapods, **(3)** Maṅgala/Bṛhaspati four-legged creatures, or the quadrupeds and **(4)** Śukra/Rāhu, 8 legged creatures or the octopods.

24.206. According to some authors, **(1)** Sūrya governs lion; **(2)** Candra, rabbit; **(3)** Maṅgala, tiger; **(4)** Budha, pig; **(5)** Bṛhaspati, wild elephant; **(6)** Śukra, small animals; **(7)** Śani, animals that live on thorns, etc., as camel; and **(8)** Rāhu, creeping and crawling ones such as snakes.

24.207. Meṣa, Vṛṣabha, Siṅha, Dhanu govern Catuṣpada. We shall now describe the animals as given in Kṛṣṇīyam.

24.208-211. (1a) Sūrya in Dhanu indicates elephant; **(1b)** in Siṅha, lion; **(1c)** in Vṛṣabha, deer and stag.

(2a) When Candra is in Dhanu, it is horse; **(2b)** in Siṅha, lion; **(2c)** in Meṣa, goats; **(2d)** in Vṛṣabha, oxen and cows.

(3a) When Maṅgala occupies Dhanu, it is horse; **(3b)** Siṅha, tiger; **(3c)** Meṣa, goats; and **(3d)** Vṛṣabha, oxen.

(4) When Budha is in Dhanu, Siṅha, Meṣa or Vṛṣabha, it denotes hog and monkey.

(5a) Bṛhaspati in Dhanu denotes horse; **(5b)** in Siṅha, camel; **(5c)** in Meṣa/Vṛṣabha, camel and donkey.

(6a) When Śukra occupies Dhanu, it is a horse; **(6b)** Siṅha/Meṣa, elephant and donkey; and **(6c)** Vṛṣabha, wild ox.

(7a) When Śani occupies Dhanu, it denotes elephant; **(7b)** in Siṅha, baboon (monkey); **(7c)** in Meṣa, he-buffalo; **(7d)** in Vṛṣabha, she-buffalo.

Mano Muṣṭi Chinta

Ācārya: If a person has something in his mind and he asks the Daivajña to predict it, the method of detecting it is called 'Chintana', which is detailed below:

Kailāśa: Looking forward to learning more about this.

5.142. This is a subtle subject which is going to be described. If Guru is in Kumbha or its Trikoṇas, i.e. in Mithuna and Tulā, or if Guru dṛṣṭies these Rāśis, the person has an elephant in his mind; and the same answer can be given if Saumyas aspect Mīna and Dhanu.

Ācārya: Guru denotes an elephant (Airāvata, Indra's elephant). If Guru is in or dṛṣṭies Vāyu trikoṇa (Mithuna/Kumbha/Tulā), then the person has an elephant in mind. The same occurs when Lagna rises in Guru's Rāśi with Saumyadṛṣṭi.

The following relates to hunting Praśna (Mṛgaya Praśna).

24.212. Grahas that occupy Kendras and Trikoṇas indicate animals that could be seen while hunting, while Graha, joined with Guḻika, indicates the animal to have been shot dead.

Ācārya: The ślokas from Praśnamārga is covered above. Some information from Jñānapradīpikā is presented here.

(1) Grahas in Kendrakoṇa indicate the animals seen during hunting

(2) Grahas joining Guḻika, indicate the animals that were shot dead

Do note that Śukra in 1H/8H/11H ensures that the animal is not shot dead, as Śukra grants life to the animal being hunted. Budha in a Kendra also ensures that.

5.143. If Śani is in Meṣa, the idea thought about is a monkey or an elephant. If it is Maṅgala in Meṣa, the thought is a goat. If Budha is in Meṣa, it is a dancer or a singer.

5.144. If Guru, Śukra and Sūrya are in Meṣa, the idea is a textile merchant; and the same is the answer if Candra is in Meṣa; if Śani is in Siṅha, the person is thinking of his enemy.

Ācārya: The following gives the indications of Grahas in Meṣa

(1) Sūrya: a textile merchant

(2) Candra: a textile merchant

(3) Maṅgala: goat

(4) Budha: dancer, singer

(5) Guru: a textile merchant

(6) Śukra: a textile merchant

(7) Śani: monkey, elephant

5.145. If Śani is in Vṛṣabha, he is thinking about a buffalo; if Śani is in Tulā, the idea is about a man with a wheel; if Śani is in Vṛścika, he is thinking of illness; if Śani is in Meṣa, he is thinking of death and pain. The Daivajña must consider these five categories of a Graha's Mitra, Ucca, Sva, Sama and Śatru; he must give predictions per what is stated in ślokas 5.127-128.

Ācārya: The following are the indications of Śani in different Rāśis

(1) Meṣa: death, pain

(2) Vṛṣabha: buffalo

(3) Mithuna: ____

(4) Karka: ____

(5) Siṅha: ____

(6) Kanyā: ____

(7) Tulā: a man with a wheel

(8) Vṛścika: an illness

(9) Dhanu: ____

(10) Makara: ____

(11) Kumbha: ____

(12) Mīna: ____

Ācārya: Now, let us examine the effects of Dhātvādi Rāśi and Grahas on the person's thoughts.

5.146. If the Dhātu Rāśis (Meṣa, Karka, Tulā and Makara) are dṛṣṭied by Dhātu Grahas (Maṅgala, Candra and Śani) or become Chatrarāśis, the thought is stated to be about Dhātus. The same is the case with Mūla Rāśis and Jīva Rāśis, too, i.e. if they are dṛṣṭied by Mūla or Jīva Rāśis respectively or become Chatrarāśis. Some pandits affirm that even if Mūla Grahas (Sūrya and Śukra) are in Dhātu Rāśis, they are stated to be Jīvas.

Ācārya: Among Rāśis, Cara = Dhātu, Sthira = Mūla and Cara = Jīva. Among Grahas, Dhātu = Maṅgala, Candra, Śani and Rāhu; Mūla = Śukra and Sūrya and Jīva = Guru and Budha. Refer to 2.94 śloka of this text.

Kailāśa: So, if these Rāśis and Grahas rise in Praśna Lagna, the person must be thinking about the associated Dhātumūlajīva. Right?

Ācārya: Also examine the Rāśi and Graha in Chatrarāśi. That is equally important.

Sunidhi: How about Āruṛha?

Ācārya: Yes, you should examine that Rāśi also. Essentially, the three Rāśis, Udaya, Āruṛha and Chatra, must be examined. The Chatrarāśi indicate the hidden dṛṣṭies of the Praśna, but the Āruṛha represents the apparent dṛṣṭies. Use Udaya over Āruṛha only when it is much stronger than Āruṛha.

5.147. If Jīva Rāśis are dṛṣṭied by Mūla Grahas or associated with them, the thought is only about Mūlas; if the Mūla Rāśis are dṛṣṭied by the Jīva Grahas, or associated with them, the thought is about Dhātu products.

Ācārya: The following indicate the combination of Dhātu, Mūla and Jīva.

Dhātu Rāśi + Dhātu Graha = Dhātu

Mūla Rāśi + Mūla Graha = Mūla

Jīva Rāśi + Jīva Graha = Jīva

Dhātu Rāśi + Mūla Graha = Jīva

Dhātu Rāśi + Jīva Graha = ____

Mūla Rāśi + Dhātu Graha = ____

Mūla Rāśi + Jīva Graha = Dhātu

Jīva Rāśi + Dhātu Graha = ____

Jīva Rāśi + Mūla Graha = Mūla

5.148. As stated above, if the three kinds of Rāśis, Dhātu, Mūla and Jīva are dṛṣṭied by or associated with any of the three kinds of Grahas, Dhātu, Mūla or Jīva, prediction about the idea thought about should be made after considering the strength of the various Grahas. If other Grahas aspect Candra, the size of the Grahas (per 5.68-69) must be considered and their respective products predicted.

5.149. One must take into consideration the qualities and attributes of Udaya, Āruṛha, and Candra Rāśi and the nature of the Grahas associated with or aspecting these. After that, predictions must be made in respect of the idea thought about in terms of Dhātu, Mūla, Jīva, caste colour etc., described in ślokas 5.97-101.

Ācārya: While making predictions about a lost object or things concealed in the fist or mind, one must examine the attributes of the Rāśis and the Grahas aspecting or occupying them. This should be examined from three Rāśis, Udaya, Āruṛha and Candra. We must also examine the Chatrarāśi, which indicates hidden things, i.e., not visible or apparent.

5.150-152. The loss of an article, the hidden article in the fist or the idea thought about must be predicted thus: If the Grahas are in Kendras and if the Grahas are in their Sva/Ucca/Mitra Rāśi or if they aspect the Kendras, the desired result will come into effect. From Udayarāśi, all ideas about Dhātus; from Āruṛha thoughts about Mūla and Chatra, everything about Jīva can be predicted. By studying the Kendras, the idea thought about can be predicted by studying the Panapharas (2H/5H/8H/11H); the article hidden in the fist can be stated by studying the Apoklimas (3H/9H/6H/12H) the loss of an article can be traced from these, the success of the venture can be determined. From śloka 5.122-152, the methods of determining the loss of property or the idea thought about are detailed, and one must apply them appropriately as the occasion demands before prediction.

Ācārya: This śloka is crucial for understanding several dṛṣṭies of Praśna related to Dhātumūlajīva, a lost object, or one that is concealed in the mind or fist.

The three Rāśis, Udaya etc. are associated with Dhātumūlajīva classification:

(1) Udaya: Dhātu

(2) Āruṛha: Mūla

(3) Chatra: Jīva

Therefore, depending on the nature of Praśna, one must focus on one of the three Lagnas more than the other. Again different attributes of the Kendra, Panaphara and Apoklima should be examined.

(1) Kendra: Examination of mental thought

(2) Panaphara: Examination of object concealed in the fist

(3) Apoklima: Recovery of lost objects.

6. ON ĀRUṚHA RĀŚI

Ācārya: Now let us focus on Āruṛha.

Sunidhi: Guruji, how is Āruṛha determined?

Ācārya: It is determined based on Nimitta. There are several methods of determining this. You can follow any of them:

(1) Cowries: You can pick a bunch of cowries energised with Mantras and remove multiples of 12. What remains denotes the Āruṛha Rāśi.

(2) Number: You can ask for 1 to 108 and remove multiples of 12. What remains denotes the Āruṛha.

(3) Clock: In a clock, note the minutes. Divide it by 5; the quotient denotes the Āruṛha.

(4) Speech: Note the first Akṣara of the Praśna put by the Pṛcchaka. The corresponding Rāśi is the Āruṛha.

(5) Touch: Note the body part touched by the Pṛcchaka while asking the Praśna. That becomes the Āruṛha.

(6) Random number: You can carry a Jyotiṣa or Adhyātma book you regularly study. Open a random page number and remove multiples of 12. What remains is the Āruṛha.

(7) Direction: Note the direction of the Pṛcchaka and the corresponding Rāśi. That becomes the Āruṛha.

(8) Gold coin: You can carry a gold coin and ask the Pṛcchaka to place it in any Rāśis drawn on a table or ground. That becomes the Āruṛha. You can substitute a gold coin with another object of gold, such as a gold ring. It can be another object of Sūrya, such as a Ruby.

Sunidhi: Dhanyavād, Guruji. Any recommendation?

Ācārya: Depending on the situation, you can use any of them. Normally, I use the 1 to 108 number method.

Kailāśa: Thank you for elucidating these rules of identifying Āruṛha. If we have a doubt, should we verify through another method?

Ācārya: No, if you have already identified the Āruṛha using a method, you "cannot" use another method to verify it or validate it. It will "not" work. Good, bad or ambiguous – whatever situation may result after the determination of the Āruṛha, that should be it. You have to give out the prediction from that only!

Kailāśa: Thank you for clarifying this!

Ācārya: Let us now focus on identifying a lost object through Praśna. The focus right now is on Āruṛha.

6.153. If Candra is in Āruṛha, there is no Joss of property; it is only hidden from sight for the time being. It is indestructible and can be found. If Candra is in 10H from the Āruṛha, there will be an increase in profit; if it is in 4H, the prediction is as stated earlier, i.e. lost property can be recovered, but if it is in 7H, loss of property must be predicted.

Ācārya: The Kendras from Āruṛha are crucial here. If Candra is one of the Kendras, then we can easily estimate the recovery of the property. Else, other methods must be adopted.

The following are the results of Candra in different Kendras from Āruṛha:

(1) 1H: The object is not lost. It is misplaced somewhere and can be found. If the Praśna is whether someone destroyed the object, the answer is that – not it is not destroyed. It is intact and can be recovered.

(2) 4H: The lost object can be recovered.

(3) 10H: The lost object can be recovered. Besides, the native will gain from several other things.

(4) 7H: The lost object cannot be recovered. It is taken somewhere out of sight, from where recovery is not likely. 7H is the Dvāra from which the object is taken out of sight.

Jayanta: So when we cast a Praśna on a lost object, we should examine Candra from Āruṛha.

Ācārya: Yes, that is right. Such Praśna is called Naṣṭa Praśna. If we find that the object is stolen, it is called Cora Praśna. Only if it is a Cora Praśna we identify the thief etc.

Jayanta: Dhanyavād!

6.154. If Lagna is in a Trika from Āruṛha, the lost property cannot be recovered. In addition to financial loss, the enemy will be strengthened.

Ācārya: Let us examine other indications in this regard.

If Lagna is in a Trika from Āruṛha, then the lost object cannot be recovered. Besides, there will be financial losses etc. If it is a Praśna about conflict, then the enemy becomes stronger if this Yoga exists.

Jayanta: So, in a Praśna, we should examine the disposition of Lagna and Āruṛha before anything else. Isn't it?

Ācārya: Indeed! My Praśna Guru, Śrī Krishnan ji, taught me that when Āruṛha and Lagna are in 2H-12H or 6H-8H from each other, the Praśna leads to failure or immense difficulties. If there are other favourable yogas in the Kuṇḍalī, they will be successful after obstacles and difficulties. This is an important Yoga in Praśna.

Besides, check the position of Lagna from Āruṛha. The Bhāva indicated by this placement is activated and plays some role in a Praśna.

6.155. The respective effects of the position of Lagna about the Āruṛha are as follows: in 1H, it is related to the body; in 2H, family; in 3H, brothers; in 4H, mother; in 5H, children; in 6H, enemy; in 7H, spouse; in 8H, death; in 9H, preceptor; in 10H, work; in 11H, gain; and 12H, expenses.

Kailāśa: So, if Āruṛha is in 10H from Lagna, there are indications of 10H in the Praśna. Is that right?

Ācārya: Let me correct you. You should not check the placement of Āruṛha from Lagna. It should be Lagna from Āruṛha. In your example, Lagna will be in 4H from Āruṛha; therefore, 4H matters are crucial in a Praśna.

Kailāśa: Can we use this principle to zoom into the matter of Praśna?

Ācārya: Yes, this is one of the methods. There are other methods such as Horeśa, strongest Graha in the Kuṇḍalī, disposition of Candra from Lagna/ Āruṛha, Chatra etc. But if you choose to use this method, you can do so. Follow whatever catches your attention and appeals to your heart.

Kailāśa: Dhanyavād, Guruji!

Ācārya: Now, the focus is to decipher one's thoughts.

6.156. If Sūrya, Candra, Śukra, Guru and Budha are in Ojarāśis, the idea thought about is men; if Lagna is dṛṣṭied by Śani and has relations with Maṅgala, the idea is about lost property; if Lagna is only having relation with Maṅgala, the idea is about strife or conflict; if it is only dṛṣṭied by Śani, the idea is about thieves or poisoning.

Ācārya: This is known from the Graha having yutidṛṣṭi with Lagna. If Lagna is in an Ojarāśi and is occupied by any of Sūrya, Candra, Śukra, Guru and Budha, it is about a man. But if it is Yugmarāśi which those Grahas occupy, it is about a woman.

Regardless of Lagna being Oja or Yugma, if Śani is Lagna with Maṅgala's yutidṛṣṭi, it is about some lost object. Instead of Śani, if Maṅgala is with yutidṛṣṭi on Lagna, then it is about some strife or conflict.

Instead, if Śani has yutidṛṣṭi on Lagna without the involvement of Maṅgala, then it is about some thief or poisoning.

Kailāśa: These are very specific conditions. What is the principle behind deciphering someone's thoughts?

Ācārya: You can read someone's thoughts from Lagna rising at Praśna.

What you need to do is as follows:

(1) Rāśi: Check the attributes of Rāśi, including Carādi, Dhātvādi, and Manuṣyādi classifications. Also, check the Bhūta classification of the Rāśi.

(2) Graha: Check the Graha in the Lagna. If Lagna is vacant, check the Graha aspecting the Lagna. Examine the Kārakatvas of the Graha, both Naisargika and Bhāveśaika (based on Bhāva ownership).

(3) Lagneśa: If Lagna has no Graha occupying/aspecting it, then Lagneśa prevails. Examine the Bhāva occupied by the Graha.

(4) Lagna from Āruṛha: Examine the Bhāva held by Lagna from Āruṛha.

(5) Blending: Blend the above indications to get a fair idea of Praśna's subject.

(6) Horeśa and Highest Ṣaḍbala Graha: If you wish to fine-tune the analysis, you also consider these Grahas. For all practical purposes, the examination of Horeśa is adequate.

Kailāśa: Thank you for clarifying this, Guruji!

Ācārya: Let us check the other indications stated by the author.

6.157. If Lagna is either associated with or dṛṣṭied by Sūrya, the idea in the Pṛcchaka's mind is about a king or god; if dṛṣṭied by or associated with Guru, the idea is about noble and good things; and if associated with or dṛṣṭied by Budha or Śukra, the person is thinking about marriage matters.

Ācārya: If Sūrya influences Lagna, the Praśna is about King or God (Sūrya's Kārakatvas). If it is Guru, it is about Śubha activities (like marriage and childbirth, promotion etc.). If it is Budha/Śukra, then it is about marriage.

Kailāśa: Why is Budha related to marriage?

Ācārya: There are two sides of marriage. One is about getting into the domain of a married person – Śukra rules this. The other is about leaving your childhood and entering the next stage – Budha rules this. If Budha influences the Lagna, the Praśna could be about whether I will complete my education and step into the next stage – i.e., start earning. It can also be, will I have to complete my education and get married?

The Praśna can manifest in different manners, and therefore, one should assess the Praśna after quickly examining the Lagna, Graha influencing the Lagna etc., as mentioned above.

7. ON CHATRARĀŚI

Ācārya: Let us focus on Chatrarāśi. Refer to 2.42 for the computation. We can compute Chatrarāśi from Udaya, Āruṛha and Sūrya's Vīthi.

Sunidhi: Kindly explain again, Guruji.

Ācārya: Follow the two steps (1) Āruṛha2Vīthi: Count Sūrya's Vīthi from Āruṛha. (2) Count as many Rāśis from Udaya (Udaya2Chatra).

Sunidhi: Dhanyavād!

7.158. If the Chatrarāśi is in 2H/12H to Udaya/Āruṛha, all undertakings will fail. But if Guru is in Chatrarāśi or dṛṣṭies it, all work will be successful.

7.159. If the Chatrarāśi is in 3H/11H to Udaya/Āruṛha, all undertakings will be successful. But if a Krūra is in or dṛṣṭies the Chatrarāśi, there will be a certain failure of any work undertaken.

Ācārya: Now, let us examine the position of Chatra from Udaya/Āruṛha.

(1) **2H-12H placement:** Failure in the undertaking.

(2) **3H-11H placement:** Success in the undertaking.

(3) **5H-9H placement:** Success in undertaking and overall happiness.

(4) **Krūrayutidṛṣṭi:** Some obstacles and failures.

(5) **Saumyayutidṛṣṭi:** Smooth realization of results.

(6) **Mixed yutidṛṣṭi:** Mixed results.

7.160. If a Saumya is in or dṛṣṭies the Chatrarāśi, all enterprises will meet with success. If both Saumyas and Krūras have a connection with the Chatrarāśi, the Śāstra of Jñānapradīpikā teaches that the results will be of mixed nature.

Jayanta: What if the results from Udaya and Āruṛha contradict? Which one to consider?

Ācārya: In that case, you have to assess the relative strength of Āruṛha and Udaya before pronouncing the results. Also note the matters that must be examined from Udaya, Āruṛha and Candra. In different Praśnas, different emphasis is given to the three Rāśis.

7.161. If the Chatrarāśi happens to be 5H/9H, all undertakings will be successful. If it is associated with a Saumya, success will come; and if with a Krūra, failure would be the result. But the result will be mixed if both Krūras and Saumyas are there.

Ācārya: Let us see below the generic effect of Chatrarāśi falling in 2H-12H or 6H-8H from Udaya/Āruṛha.

7.162. If the Chatrarāśi is in 2H, 8H, 6H or 12H, the lost property cannot be recovered; diseases will not be cured; the wished-for fruit cannot be attained; and enmity will not cease.

Sunidhi: Kindly elaborate, Guruji!

Ācārya: I have explained this before in the context of Āruṛha. The mutual disposition of Rāśis in the 2H-12H or 6H-8H form is not conducive. They indicate difficulties and failures. The same goes with the disposition of Chatra in 2H-12H or 6H-8H from Udaya/Chatra.

According to 5.150-152, from Udayarāśi, all ideas about Dhātus, Āruṛha, thoughts about Mūla and Chatra, and everything about Jīva can be predicted. Therefore, different emphasis should be given to the different Rāśis depending on the nature of the Praśna.

8. ON UDAYARĀŚI

Ācārya: Let us study the principles of Udayarāśi.

Kailāśa: Isn't Udayarāśi the Praśna Lagna?

Ācārya: Indeed! The Rāśi rising on the eastern horizon at Praśna, Muhūrta or Janma is called Lagna. Since it is rising, it is also called Udaya or Udaya Lagna.

Kailāśa: What are the other Lagnas then?

Ācārya: There are four Lagnas at the moment. Udaya, Daśama, Asta and Pātāla. They represent the four cardinal points in a Kuṇḍalī, 1H, 10H, 7H and 4H. The sphuṭas of 1H and 7H are 180° apart, and that of 4H and 10H are also 180° apart.

Besides these Lagna, which are related to the position of Rāśis on the celestial sphere, there are several other Lagnas, such as Bhāva, Horā, Ghaṭī,

Vighaṭi, Āruṛha, Chatra etc. Therefore, if there is a chance of misinterpretation, it is better to call Lagna Udaya as that is unambiguous, meaning the Rāśi is rising.

8.163. If Guru is in the Udayarāśi, good will result; more property and victory will come; ill-will and enmity die; and all enterprises will certainly succeed.

8.164. If Budha is in the Udayarāśi, the warrior will defeat his enemy and return with the (victor's) spoils. If Candra dṛṣṭies the Udayarāśi, the man who goes out to accomplish a work will come back with achievement; he will succeed in litigation. The same good result will be if Guru, Budha and Candra are in Chatrarāśi.

8.165. If Candra is in Udayarāśi, the person will gain property in many ways and get his desired ends. The same prediction can be given if Candra is in Chatrarāśi or Āruṛha Rāśi.

8.166. If Śukra is in Udayarāśi, there will be gain in property, acquisition of women, curing of illness, victory and friendliness with erst-while enemies. The same will happen if Śukra is in Chatrarāśi.

Ācārya: Following are the effects of Grahas in Udayarāśi at a Praśna. If the Udayarāśi is vacant, dṛṣṭi of Grahas should be considered. Generally, Saumyas in the Lagna or aspecting the Lagna indicate good things, and Krūras troublesome things.

(1) Sūrya: loss of property, ill-will and unfriendliness, illness and death

(2) Candra: accomplishment at work, success in litigations, acquiring property through many ways, getting desired ends

(3) Maṅgala: same as Sūrya

(4) Budha: the warrior defeats his enemy and gains from the enemy.

(5) Guru: good results; more property and victory; ill-will and enmity disappear; enterprises certainly succeed

(6) Śukra: gain in property, acquisition of woman, curing of illness, victory and friendliness with erst-while enemies

(7) Śani: same as Sūrya

(8) Rāhu: bondage, fear of thieves, poisoning and even death

(9) Ketu: same as Rāhu

8.167. If Śani, Sūrya or Maṅgala is in Udaya, Chatra or Āruṛha Rāśi, there will be loss of property, ill- will and unfriendliness, illness and death.

8.168. If Rāhu is associated with the Uḍaya, Chatra or Āruṛha Rāśi, there will be bondage, fear of thieves, poisoning and even death.

Ācārya: The following śloka gives the generic effects of Saumyas and Krūras in certain houses.

8.169. Misery must be predicted if Krūras are in 2H, 9H or 8H. But prosperity must be predicted if Saumyas are in those places or Kendras.

Sunidhi: Kindy explain this!

Ācārya: You can follow the following guidelines:

(1) Kendrakoṇa and Dhana are considered Śubha Bhāvas. Saumyas are welcome in these Bhāvas.

(2) Trikas (6/8/12) are Aśubha Bhāvas. Grahas in these Bhāvas are considered troublesome.

(3) Triṣaḍāyas (3/6/11) are good places for Krūras. They confer good things.

(4) Krūras in 3H-6H make one courageous and aggressive and fight for victory, but Saumyas here make one timid and docile. Saumyas in these Bhāvas are good for saintly people.

(5) 11H is good for both Saumyas and Krūras. They all confer financial gains.

(6) 2H/5H/9H/11H are specifically known for finances. Saumyas in 2H/5H/9H and all Grahas in 11H promote one's financial well-being.

(7) 4H/8H/12H are sensitive Bhāvas (Mokṣatrikoṇa) and must be free from Krūras. Saumyas are welcome, but Krūras cause serious harm in these places.

(8) Vakrī Grahas should not be in a Trika; else, they make one's life hell. Saumya Vakrī is lesser troublesome than Krūra Vakrī. If a Krūra Vakrī afflicts a Saumya in a Dusthāna through yutidṛṣṭi, or a Saumya Vakrī is afflicted in a Trika by Krūrayutidṛṣṭi, then also life becomes hell. The person is constantly troubled by this Graha's indications (Naisargika or Bhāveśaika).

(9) Bādhaka and Bādhakeśa should be carefully examined as they source obstacles and hidden troubles. Their affliction makes things worse. Rāhu is most diabolical when he associates with Bādhaka.

Sunidhi: Dhanyavād, Guruji!

Ācārya: These are only the key ones. You should study the other books on Bhāva analysis for more details.

Sunidhi: Noted, Guruji!

8.170. If Krūras are in or aspecting the Lagnas, namely Udaya, Chatra or Āruṛha, destruction will result. But if Saumyas are in or aspecting these Lagnas, good will accrue.

Ācārya: Following is another general rule but is extremely crucial. If all three Lagnas, Udaya, Chatra or Āruṛha are afflicted by Krūras, untold suffering and destruction of the object of the Praśna occur. If dignified Saumyas fortify them, good things about the Praśna occur.

9. ON RECOVERY OF LOST OBJECT

Ācārya: Let us focus on the recovery of the lost object.

9.171. If Udaya is in Tulā and Āruṛha is in Meṣa, the loss of property will certainly be recovered. If it is the reverse, i.e. Udaya is in Meṣa and Āruṛha is in Tulā, the property cannot be recovered. If Udaya is in Vṛścika and Āruṛha is in Vṛṣabha, not only will the lost property be recovered, but additional gains will accrue. If it is otherwise, i.e., Āruṛha-Vṛścika, Udaya-Vṛṣabha, the lost property cannot be regained.

Sunidhi: Kindly explain, Guruji!

Ācārya: The principles given here are based on the Āruṛha and Udaya in the 1-7 axis. When I say Āruṛha in a Rāśi, you must consider the Udaya in 7H. The 7H denotes where the object is taken out and where it will be recovered – since it is the Dvāra (door).

9.172. One can regain the lost property if Udaya is in Mithuna and Āruṛha is in Dhanu. In the reverse case, the lost property cannot be traced. If Āruṛha is in Makara and Udaya is in Karka, there will be a success in the venture. In the reverse case, i.e. Āruṛha-Karka and Udaya-Makara, failure will be the result.

9.173. If Udaya is in Siṅha and Āruṛha is in Kumbha, there will be certainty of regaining lost property. In the reverse case of Āruṛha-Siṅha and Udaya-Kumbha, one cannot regain the property. If Udaya is in Kanyā and Āruṛha-Mīna, there will be success in regaining the property. In the reverse case of Āruṛha-Kanyā and Udaya-Mīna, failure will be the result.

Ācārya: Let us see the Rāśi pairs indicating recovery or no recovery.

(1) Meṣa Āruṛha – recovery

(2) Vṛṣabha Āruṛha – recovery

(3) Mithuna Āruṛha – no recovery

(4) Karka Āruṛha –no recovery

(5) Siṅha Āruṛha – no recovery

(6) Kanyā Āruṛha – no recovery

(7) Tulā Āruṛha – no recovery

(8) Vṛścika Āruṛha – no recovery

(9) Dhanu Āruṛha – recovery

(10) Makara Āruṛha – recovery

(11) Kumbha Āruṛha – recovery

(12) Mīna Āruṛha – recovery

Kailāśa: Guruji, there is a pattern in this.

Ācārya: Indeed! There is a pattern. The Bhacakra is divided into two zones, (1) Dhanu-Vṛṣabha and (2) Mithuna-Vṛścika. When Āruṛha falls in Rāśis Dhanu to Vṛṣabha, they indicate recovery, provided Udaya is in 7H of Āruṛha. Instead, if Āruṛha falls in Mithuna to Vṛścika, and Udaya is in 7H, there is no recovery.

Effects of Carādi attributes of Rāśis

Ācārya: Now, let us focus on the effects of Shira and Dvisvarāśi.

Jayanta: Cararāśi indicates changes in the status quo, Sthirarāśi indicates no change, and Dvisvarāśi indicates the accomplishment of the task with difficulties and obstacles. Is that right?

9.174. If Udaya, Āruṛha and Chatra are in Sthirarāśis, and the Pṛcchaka asks about death, there will be no death; if he asks about lost property, he will get back that property; and if he asks about illness, he will not be cured of it.

Ācārya: That is right, Jayanta!

There are three important Lagnas in a Praśna, Udaya, Āruṛha and Chatra. When all three are in Sthirarāśi, there is no change in status quo, such as:

(1) If the Praśna is about an illness, the patient does not recover.

(2) If the Praśna is about death, it does not occur, as if someone has put a blocker to it.

(3) If someone asks about a lost object, it means that the object has not gone anywhere, and the Pṛcchaka will be able to recover it.

9.175. If Udaya, Āruṛha and Chatra are in Dvisvarāśis, and the Pṛcchaka asks about lost property, he will not get back that property; if about illness, it will not be cured; and if about enmity, the truce arrived at between the parties cannot last long.

Ācārya: If the three Lagnas fall in Dvisvarāśis, there are obstacles. The following can be said about different Praśnas:

(1) In a lost object Praśna, the object cannot be recovered

(2) In an illness related to Praśna, it will not be cured. Instead, it can be aggravated.

(3) In a hostility-related Praśna, there can be peace talks which will falter later.

9.176. If Udaya, Āruṛha and Chatra are in Cararāśis, there will certainly be success in all fields; gain of a woman, recovery of lost property, curing of diseases, and accomplishment of all enterprises undertaken.

Sunidhi: So, we should expect changes or improvement in Cararāśi?

Ācārya: Yes, we should! Cararāśis are like flowing rivers (Karka) and indicate improvement. So, in different Praśnas, the indications are as follows:

(1) In a success related Praśna, there is a success.

(2) There is a marriage (gain of partner), recovery of lost property, recovery from sickness and success in undertakings.

(3) There is a well-known dictum, which is when Udaya or Lagneśa is in a Cara/Śīrṣodayi Rāśi and dṛṣṭied by a Saumya, success is guaranteed.

Sunidhi: Thank you for clarifying this.

9.177. Good or bad results must be predicted by properly assessing the strength of the various Grahas in the Rāśis. If Udaya is in a Cararāśi and Saumyas are posited therein, all kinds of work undertaken will succeed.

Ācārya: We should predict the results from the Rāśis held by Āruṛha, Udaya and Chatra, and Grahas posited there. From the attributes of the Rāśis and Grahas, we can estimate the result of the Praśna.

9.178. If Krūras or Asta Grahas are in Āruṛha, Udaya or Chatra, someone must have taken away the lost property, and no hope is there of recovery. But if Saumyas are there, hope of recovery can be predicted.

Ācārya: In a lost object Praśna, if Krūras or Asta Grahas occupy the 3 Lagnas, there is no chance of recovery. On the other hand, if Saumyas are in the 3 Lagnas, there is a high chance of recovery.

Kailāśa: Should we also consider the dṛṣṭi and ownerships?

Ācārya: Yes! We should also consider if the Rāśi is owned by a Saumya or Krūra, the dignity of the Rāśyeśa, and dṛṣṭi of Saumya or Krūra. All must be considered before pronouncing the judgement.

Sunidhi: Guruji, how to identify whether a Graha is Asta?

Ācārya: You need to check the distance of the Graha from Sūrya. The following are the orbs of combustion of Grahas: Maṅgala 17°, Budha 12° (vakrī) 14° (mārgī), Bṛhaspati 11°, Śukra 8° (vakrī) and 10° (mārgī), Śani 15°.

When the distance of a Graha is lesser than the mentioned orb, the Graha is Asta or Astāṅgata. Suppose in a Kuṇḍalī, Sūrya is 2°, and Vakrī Śukra is 9°; it means Śukra is not Asta. If Mārgī Śukra is 9°, he is Asta!

Sunidhi: This makes sense now!

Ācārya: So far, we have seen the effects of Grahas in 1H of Āruṛha/ Udaya/Chatra. Now the author gives the rules for examining the other Bhāvas from these 3 Rāśis.

9.179. If Saumyas are in 5H, 7H or 9H from Āruṛha, Udaya or Chatra, the lost property can be recovered. By determining the condition of the Grahas, Saumya or Krūra, weak or strong, in Udaya, Āruṛha or Chatra, the possibility of recovery or otherwise of lost property can be predicted.

Ācārya: Besides 1H, Saumyas in 5H/9H or 7H also promote the well-being of a Bhāva. Generally, Saumyas in Kendrakoṇa/Dhana from a Bhāva promotes the Bhāvas and Krūras in these places diminish it.

Among the said Bhāvas, 5H/7H/9H are the most crucial. 5H/9H are Trikoṇas, denoting the outcome/reward (fruit) of a Bhāva. 7H shows opposition and must not have Krūras; else, it indicates conflicts.

Kailāśa: How about Krūras. Where must the Krūras be placed?

9.180. If even a Krūra is in 3H or a Saumya in 5H from Udaya, Āruṛha or Chatra, the man who has taken the property will return it of his own accord.

Ācārya: The ideal places for Krūras are the Triṣaḍāyas, i.e., 3H, 6H and 11H. They indicate victory and overcoming obstacles.

Therefore, the author states that Krūras in 3H and Saumyas in 5H help in recovery.

Kailāśa: How about Saumyas in other Śubhabhāvas and Krūras in other Triṣaḍāyas?

Ācārya: They also help with the recovery. But the Yoga of Saumyas in 5H (good future) and Krūras in 3H (action and enterprise) help with certain recovery.

Kailāśa: This makes sense, Guruji!

9.181. If a Saumya or a Krūra is associated with Dhūma, the alleged lost property is not lost but is intact in the direction indicated by the Graha.

Ācārya: There are other Yogas that involve Upagrahas etc.

For instance, according to the author, if a Graha is with Dhūma, be it Saumya or Krūra indicates that the lost object is misplaced and can be recovered. It can be recovered in the direction indicated by the Graha conjunct with Dhūma.

Sunidhi: How to find Dhūma?

Ācārya: Dhūma = Sūrya + 133°20′ = Sūrya + 4r + 13°20′.

Sunidhi: Can you provide an example?

Ācārya: Suppose Sūrya is in Siṅha 8°10′33″. His sphuṭa is 4r8°10′33″. Adding 4r13°20′ makes it 8r21°30′33″. This is Dhanu 21°30′33″.

Sunidhi: Shouldn't 8r = Vṛścika?

Ācārya: No, when we reckon Grahasphuṭa, Meṣa is 0r, Vṛṣabha is 1r, Mīna is 11r and so on. It is the number of complete Rāśis. Therefore Siṅha is 4r, not 5r, and Dhanu is 8r, not 9r.

Kailāśa: Guruji, what is Dhūma?

Ācārya: Dhūma is an Aprakāśa Graha, and in that group, we have 5 Grahas, Dhūma, Vyatipāta, Pariveṣa, Indracāpa and Upaketu.

They are hidden, dark and invisible. Therefore, they are called Aprakāśa or not resplendent. All Grahas have brightness, so we can see them in the night sky. However, the Aprakāśa Grahas are some sensitive points around Sūrya, which affect us, and we can determine them through computations.

Dhūma is Sūrya + 4r13°20′. Vyatipāta is 12r – Dhūma, Pariveṣa is diagonally opposite to Vyatipāta; Indracāpa is 12r – Vyatipāta and Upaketu is Sūrya – 1r.

Kailāśa: Why must we know them?

Ācārya: They play a crucial role in a Kuṇḍalī, be it Jātaka, Praśna, Muhūrta or Medini. We must compute them. They afflict anything that joins them.

Kailāśa: what is the significance of their names? Why are they so named?

Ācārya: In Jyotiṣa, the names embody the attributes of the body. Dhūma is like a thick smoke through which you cannot see anything – like the smoke that appears when a house is on fire. Some say Dhūma is in the shape of fume clouds, while others opine it is a comet with a tail.

Vyatipāta means disruption, and its behaviour is like the fall of a meteor or a meteor shower. Pariveṣa means the halo around Sūrya or Candra. Indracāpa is a rainbow, and Upaketu is a comet. When these bodies are seen in the sky, i.e., smoky cloud, meteor shower, a halo around Sūrya or Candra, rainbow or a comet, they forbode evil.

Even though the Aprakāśa Grahas are Krūras, they are not the same. Their ways of working must be equated with their parents. **Dhūma** is like Maṅgala, violent; **Vyatipāta** is like Rāhu causing pain, suffering and troubles from unknown quarters; **Paridhi** is like Candra, indicating mental anxiety; **Indracāpa** is like Śukra, indicating relationship issues; **Upaketu** is like Ketu, indicating uncertainties and chaos.

Kailāśa: Dhanyavād for clarifying this, Guruji!

Ācārya: Let us examine other Yogas regarding lost objects.

9.182. If Candra is in a Pṛṣṭodaya Rāśi, the alleged lost property is not lost but is somewhere in the house itself. If that Rāśi is dṛṣṭied by Śani, the article is in a high place, and if that Rāśi is related to Maṅgala, it is not in the high place.

Ācārya: Examine Candra in a Praśnakuṇḍalī and decipher results based on his disposition. If Candra is in a Pṛṣṭodaya Rāśi (rising backwards), the alleged lost property is not lost but is somewhere in the house.

Sunidhi: Guruji, why must it be so?

Ācārya: That is because the Pṛṣṭodayi Rāśis are focused backwards, i.e., the thing is directed towards its origin. They denote a backward motion. Therefore, when Pṛṣṭodayi Rāśi/Añśa rises at Janma, the foetus tries to remain within the womb and not come out. That makes it difficult to deliver and is called Breech birth. In this case, the head is positioned upward and legs downward. In a normal birth, the head is downward and the head upwards, indicating that the foetus wishes to take birth.

Sunidhi: What are these Rāśis?

Jayanta: That is straightforward. Let me explain.

Rāśis are firstly divided into Sūrya's half and Candra's half. Sūrya's half is Siṅha to Makara, and Candra's half is Karka to Kumbha (in reverse).

Sunidhi: Why must Candra's Rāśi be seen in reverse?

Ācārya: Because masculinity is forward (right-handed) and femininity is reverse (left-handed). This is the principle of Prakṛti Cakra, which I have explained in my Jaiminīsūtra book.

Jayanta: Once we have established Sūrya's and Candra's half, the next is the Dinabalī and Rātribalī Rāśis. The Dinabalī Rāśis are strong during the day (Sūrya), and Rātribalī Rāśis are powerful at night (Candra).

In the Dinabalī and Rātribalī classification, Candra's Rāśis are Rātribalī and Sūrya's Rāśis are Dinabalī but with an exception. The exception is that it is reversed in the last four Rāśis. Mīna-Kumbha is Dinabalī even though they are from Candra's half. Whereas, Dhanu-Makara are Rātribalī even though they're from Sūrya's half.

Sunidhi: How are they related to Śīrṣodayādi Rāśis?

Jayanta: That is coming next.

The Dinabalī Rāśis are Śīrṣodayi, and Rātribalī Rāśis are Pṛṣṭodayi, but with an exception.

Mīna is Dinabalī but Ubhayodayi and Mithuna is Rātribalī but Śīrṣodayi. Therefore, the exceptions are in two Dvisvarāśis, Mīna and Mithuna.

Sunidhi: So how many Śīrṣodayi, Pṛṣṭodayi and Ubhayodayi Rāśis are there?

Ācārya: Why not you tell us now, Sunidhi?

Sunidhi: Let me try!

Meṣa – P, Vṛṣabha – P, *Mithuna* – **S**, Karka – P, *Siṅha – S, Kanyā – S, Tulā – S, Vṛścika – S*, Dhanu – P, Makara – P, *Kumbha – S*, Mīna – **U**.

So, there are 6 Śīrṣodayi, 5 Pṛṣṭodayi and 1 Ubhayodayi Rāśis.

Kailāśa: Guruji, what is the explanation behind Mīna and Mithuna reversal?

Ācārya: That is unclear. But we know another fact from this reversal. Normally, Ojarāśi indicates male and Yugmarāśi female. Right?

Kailāśa: Yes, Guruji!

Ācārya: However, when we reckon male and female births from the Rāśis, Mithuna indicates female and Mīna male, which is reversed.

Kailāśa: But why must that be?

Ācārya: One reason is that Guru is "predominantly" male, and Budha is "predominantly" female.

Kailāśa: How do we know which Graha is male and female?

Ācārya: That is simple. Oja (odd) is masculine, and Yugma (even) is feminine. In a Graha sequence in Vāra order, Oja places are occupied by Puruṣa Grahas and Yugma places are occupied by Strī Grahas.

Sūrya – *Candra* – Maṅgala – *Budha* – Guru – *Śukra* – Śani – *Ketu* – Rāhu.

In the sequence, the Grahas in even places, i.e., Candra, Budha, Śukra, and Ketu, are Strī Grahas. The Grahas in odd places, i.e., Sūrya, Maṅgala, Guru, Śani and Rāhu, are Puruṣa Grahas.

Kailāśa: But why did you reverse the sequence of Rāhu-Ketu?

Ācārya: That is because, in this sequence of reckoning, Rāhu-Ketu are Vakrī and, therefore, reversed.

Kailāśa: Isn't Budha and Śani Napuṅśaka (eunuch) Grahas?

Ācārya: That is right, but in the determination of sex, Budha is Strī Napuṅśaka (young girl before puberty), and Śani is Puruṣa Napuṅśaka (old men after sexuality has declined). Therefore, if they indicate a masculine or feminine birth, Budha indicates a girl, and Śani indicates a boy.

If there are Yogas of the birth of Eunuch, then Budha and Śani indicate the birth of Eunuchs. Even among them, if more traits of femininity are seen, they are denoted by Budha; if they are more masculine, they are denoted by Śani.

Kailāśa: Dhanyavād for clarifying this, Guruji!

Jayanta: The śloka states, "If that Rāśi is dṛṣṭied by Śani, the article is in a high place, and if that Rāśi is related to Maṅgala, it is not in the high place." Why is that so?

Ācārya: That is because of the attributes of the Grahas. Śani is of Vāyubhūta and therefore denotes things above the ground. Maṅgala is Bhūmisuta, i.e., the child of Bhū Devī, and therefore, denotes land or ground. Therefore, the object could be above the ground or on the ground depending on the dṛṣṭi of Śani or Maṅgala on Candra.

Ācārya: Now, the effects of Grahas on the Kendras are delineated for the lost object Praśna. It says what metal the object is made of, and it is lost in none of the cases. This means that it can be recovered. The Bhāva positions of Guru/ Budha/Śukra/Śani are their Dikbala positions.

9.183. If Guru is in Udaya, the lost property is made of gold, but it is not lost; if Śukra is in 4H from Udaya, the alleged lost object is made of silver and not lost.

9.184. If Śani/Maṅgala is in 7H, the lost object is made of iron, and it is not lost; if Budha is in Udaya/4H, the lost object is made of tin/zinc and is not lost.

9.185. If Candra is in 7H, the lost object is made of bronze and not lost; If Sūrya is in 5H, the lost object is made of brass and is not lost.

Ācārya: The following are the effects of the Grahas and their association with the metals and alloys:

(1) Sūrya: 5H: Brass

(2) Candra: 7H: Bronze

(3) Maṅgala: Same as Śani

(4) Budha: 1H*/4H: Tin/Zinc

(5) Guru: 1H*: Gold

(6) Śukra: 4H*: Silver

(7) Śani: 7H*: Iron

9.186. If Krūras are associated with 10H, the lost object is an animal (Catuṣpāda), and it is not lost; and if Udaya is in a catuṣpāda Rāśi with Rāhu, the animal must be considered as lost.

9.187. If Udaya is in a Dvipāda Rāśi with Rāhu, a Manuṣya (person) is in jail or bondage. If Udaya is in a Bahupāda Rāśi with Rāhu, an animal is lost. If Udaya is in a Pakṣi Rāśi with Rāhu, the above predictions must be stated, namely, that the man or the animal is in bondage.

Ācārya: There are a few other rules.

(1) If Krūras are in 10H or aspecting it, it could be an animal (cattle etc.) that is lost. It could also be a house pet, i.e., a dog or a cat. It may not be lost unless Rāhu is in Lagna in a catuṣpāda Rāśi. Meṣa, Vṛṣabha, Siṅha are Catuṣpāda Rāśis.

(2) If Rāhu is in Lagna in a Dvipāda Rāśi, then a person who is not found could be in Jail or kept in captivity. Kumbha, Mithuna, Tulā and Kanyā are Manuṣya (Dvipāda) Rāśis.

(3) If Rāhu is in Lagna in a Bahupāda Rāśi, then an animal is lost. Karka and Vṛścika are Bahupāda Rāśis.

(4) If Rāhu is in Lagna in a Pakṣi Rāśi, then it is possible that a person or an animal that is lost is in bondage. Makara and Mīna are Pakṣi Rāśis.

Kailāśa: When Rāhu is in the Lagna, it appears that the lost object, a person or an animal is in bondage.

Ācārya: Indeed! The person or the animal is forcefully kept against its will.

Now, where the lost object kept in the house can be known from the Rāśis/Grahas in Udaya.

9.188. If Udaya is in Karka or Vṛścika, the lost object is in a loft (height) or the middle of the house.

9.189-190. If Udaya is with Maṅgala, the lost object will be in a pot; if with Budha, it is certainly in a pot; if with Guru, the article is in a red clay pot; and if with Śukra, it is in the water jug; and if with Śani the article is in rice-cleansed water, and if with Candra the article will be in the salt jug.

(1) Udaya in Karka: The object is in a loft

(2) Udaya in Vṛścika: The object is in the middle of the house.

(3) Udaya with Maṅgala: The object is in a pot.

(4) Udaya with Budha: Same as Maṅgala.

(5) Udaya with Guru: The object is in a red clay pot.

(6) Udaya with Śukra: The object is in a water jug.

(7) Udaya with Śani: The object is in rice-cleansed water. This is the water that is thrown or kept aside after cleaning rice.

(8) Candra: The object is in a salt jug.

Kailāśa: How to know whether the thief is a man or a woman?

9.191. If Ojarāśis (in Udaya) are dṛṣṭied by Puruṣa Grahas, the thief is a man. Likewise, if Yugmarāśis (in Udaya) are dṛṣṭied by Strī Grahas, the thief is a woman.

Ācārya: If Udaya is in an Ojarāśi and dṛṣṭied by Puruṣagrahas, the thief is a man. Instead, if it is in a Yugmarāśi and dṛṣṭied by Strīgrahas, the thief is a woman.

The principle here is to check the predominance of masculine and feminine vibrations on Udaya. Therefore, one must check the Udaya in Rāśi/Navāñśa and the Grahas with yutidṛṣṭi on Udaya.

9.192. If from Udaya (in an Ojarāśi) a Puruṣa Graha is in an Oja Bhāva, the thief is a man. If Udayarāśi is Yugma, and if from that a Strī Graha is in a Yugma Bhāva, the thief is a woman. What is stated must be considered in light of the strength of Udaya and Āruṛha.

Ācārya: Yet another unique principle utilizes Oja and Yugma Bhāva.

Kailāśa: What is different? We already know Oja and Yugma Rāśi. Ojarāśis are masculine (Meṣa, Mithuna, Siṅha…) and Yugmarāśis are feminine (Vṛṣabha, Karka, Kanyā…).

Ācārya: The difference is that the Ojabhāvas are reckoned from Udaya and not from Meṣa. Therefore, the Ojabhāvas are 1H, 3H, 5H and so on. Similarly, Yugmabhāvas are 2H, 4H, 6H and so on.

Sunidhi: What is the significance of Oja and Yugma Bhāvas, Guruji?

Ācārya: It is similar to Oja and Yugma Rāśis. Just that Bhāvas replace the Rāśis. The Oja Bhāvas are masculine and Yugma Bhāvas are feminine.

Sunidhi: What are the key attributes of masculinity and femininity?

Ācārya: The following are the key attributes.

Masculinity:

(1) Physical strength: physical power, vigour, and athleticism.

(2) Assertiveness: assertive, confident, taking charge of situations.

(3) Independence: self-reliance and the ability to be self-sufficient

(4) Competitiveness: a drive to compete and achieve success.

(5) Courage: courage, bravery, and facing challenges head-on.

(6) Leadership: take on leadership roles and display leadership qualities.

(7) Rationality: logical thinking and problem-solving.

Femininity:

(1) Nurturing: compassion, empathy, and caring for others.

(2) Sensitivity: an ability to express and understand emotions.

(3) Collaboration: cooperative, collaborative, build strong relationships.

(4) Intuition: intuition, empathy, understanding non-verbal cues.

(5) Communication: skilled communicators, verbal and non-verbal.

(6) Adaptability: an ability to adapt to different situations and be flexible.

(7) Emotional expressiveness: expressing a wide range of emotions and being open about feelings.

Sunidhi: Dhanyavād, Guruji!

Ācārya: Let us focus on the principle of recovery of the lost object.

Kailāśa: Kindly elaborate, Guruji!

9.193. If Udaya is in Karka, Makara and Kanyā, the lost property cannot be recovered. If Udaya is in Tulā, Vṛṣabha and Kumbha, the lost property can be recovered. Except for Guru, the lost object cannot be obtained if any other Graha is in a hostile Rāśi.

Ācārya: This is based on the Udayarāśi. If Udaya is in Karka/Makara/Kanyā, the lost object cannot be recovered. If Udaya is in Vṛṣabha/Tulā/Kumbha, the lost object can be recovered.

Kailāśa: Why So?

Ācārya: The rationale is unclear!

9.194. Whatever Graha dṛṣṭies Candra, the thief will have the features of that Graha. The stolen article, too, will have some characteristics of that Graha.

Ācārya: This śloka is about assessing the feature of the thief and the lost object. Earlier, we have seen that the thief's features and the attributes of the lost object can be assessed from Udaya. According to this śloka, we must also assess it from Candra.

Kailāśa: Guruji, when to use Udaya and when Candra?

Ācārya: For that, identify the relative strength of the Rāśis.

Kailāśa: Guide us on how to identify the relative strength of the Rāśis.

Ācārya: You can use some thumb rules.

(1) A Rāśi with more Grahas is stronger.

(2) A Rāśi with a Uccagraha is stronger.

(3) If the Rāśis are vacant, the Rāśi whose lord is with higher dignity (Sva/Ucca/Mūlatrikoṇa/Mitra/Sama/Śatru/Nīca) is stronger.

(4) If both Rāśis have equal strength, then tha Naisargika Rāśibala is used, which is Dvisva > Sthira > Cara.

(5) If both Rāśis still have equal strength, then an Ojarāśi with its Lord in a Yugmarāśi and a Yugmarāśi with its Lord in an Ojarāśi is considered stronger.

Kailāśa: Dhanyavād, Guruji!

9.195. The lost object will be in the direction in which Āruṛha is situated. The time taken to recover the lost property can be reckoned in terms of days according to the Raśmis of the Grahas concerned or the months and years of the Grahas according to the circumstances of the case. Accordingly, the prediction must be made considering the nature of the Grahas and those aspecting Āruṛha, Udaya and Chatra.

Ācārya: Now, let us focus on the direction of the lost object. It is known from the direction of Āruṛha.

Sunidhi: Kindly elaborate, Guruji!

Ācārya: First, you understand that the directions are E – S – W – N. This is the clockwise direction of reckoning.

Then, you assign the primary (cardinal) directions to the direction in sets of two. So E = Meṣa/Vṛṣabha, S = Karka/Siṅha, W = Tulā/Vṛścika and N = Makara/Kumbha.

After that, you assign the secondary (corner) direction to the Dvisvarāśis, i.e., SE = Mithuna, SW = Kanyā, NW = Dhanu and NE = Mīna.

Sunidhi: Dhanyavād, Guruji. How about the days of recovery?

Ācārya: This can be known from the Raśmis of the Grahas aspecting Āruṛha or being positioned there. You need to estimate days, months and years based on other factors such as Cara/Sthira/Dvisvabhāva Rāśi occupied by the Grahas. Cara = Day. Sthira = Years, and Dvisvabhāva = Months.

Kailāśa: What is Udaya or Chatra is stronger than Āruṛha?

Ācārya: You must assess the relative strength between the three and consider the strongest among them.

9.196. The number of Rāśis separating Udayarāśi from Candrarāśi (Candra2Udaya) is situated gives the number of days by which success will be attained. If the Rāśis of Candra and Udaya are Cara, the above number gives the days for the fruition of the prediction. If they are Sthira, the number must be trebled.

Ācārya: Now, another method of timing success is given. This generic method can be applied to any Praśna dealing with success or failure. Count from Candra to Udaya i.e. Candra2Udaya = Udaya – Candra + 1. Here you should consider the indices of the Rāśis, i.e., Meṣa = 1, Vṛṣabha = 2 etc.

Suppose Udaya is Kanyā and Candra is in Mithuna. Then, Candra2Udaya = Udaya – Candra + 1 = 6 – 3 + 1 = 3 + 1 = 4. It can be 4 days or multiple of it. If Candra and Udaya are in Cara, the result manifests in days; if they are in Sthira, the period is trebled; if in Dvisvabhāva, then the period is doubled.

10. ON GAINS AND LOSSES

Jayanta: Guruji! What are we going to study next?

Ācārya: Now we shall examine the Yogas of gains and losses in a Praśna Kuṇḍalī. Praśna, such as whether I will gain this or that, should be answered through the principles laid down here.

10.197-199. If Grahas in Ucca (or Mitra) Rāśis aspect Udaya, Āruṛha or Chatra, gain of valuable goods, even of, kingdoms must be predicted. For females, gain of a husband, rewards, achievement of tasks undertaken and obtaining of desired things can be predicted. For males, gaining a wife and obtaining a job will be predicted by wise men. If however Grahas in Nīca/Śatru Rāśis aspect Udaya, Āruṛha or Chatra the reverse of the above predictions is indicated. That is, there will be loss all around. Likewise, prediction must be made regarding marriage.
सुवस्तुलाभं राज्यञ्च राष्ट्रलाभं स्त्रियः पतिम् । उपायनं स्वकार्याणां लाभालाभौ वदेत्सुधीः ॥ १९७॥
उदयादित्रिकान्खेटाः पश्यन्त्युश्चेश्वरा यदि । चिन्तितार्थागमाश्चैव स्त्रीलाभो राज्यसिद्धयः ॥१९८ ॥
तान्नीचद्वेषिणो खेटाः पश्यन्ति यदि नाशयेत् । एवं विवाहकार्येच शुभाशुभनिरूपणम् ॥१९९॥

Sunidhi: Guruji, what are the core principles?

Ācārya: Good things happen or come into your life when there is good dṛṣṭi of Grahas on Lagna (Udaya, Āruṛha or Chatra). When Grahas in Ucca/Mitra Rāśis (comfortably situated) aspect Lagna, good things are blessed to the person. Instead, if Grahas in their Nīca/Śatru Rāśi aspect Lagna, then the incoming of the good things are not ascertained.

Now, we must know the differences between the states of the Grahas.

A Graha in Uccarāśi indicates the gain of honour, recognition and power.

A Graha in Mitrarāśi indicates friendship.

A Graha in Śatrurāśi indicates hostility.

A Graha in Nīcarāśi indicates depravity.

Sunidhi: Noted Guruji!

10.200. If the lords of Udaya, Āruṛha and Chatra are dṛṣṭied by Saumyas, even an enemy will become a friend. If, however, Krūras aspect them, even a friend will become an enemy.

Ācārya: Saumyas indicate benevolent (or amicable) people, and Krūras denote the fierce (or malevolent) ones. Different Grahas denote different kinds of people.

When Saumyas aspect Lagna (Udaya, Āruṛha or Chatra), they help remove differences and bridge gaps. They help with reaching an amicable resolution of an issue. On the other hand, Krūras cause dissension and differences and ruin relationships.

Sunidhi: This means that the dṛṣṭi of Saumya is favourable, whereas Krūra dṛṣṭi is unfavourable.

Ācārya: You got it!

10.201. If a Krūra occupies or dṛṣṭies Udaya or Candra, there will be decline in longevity; if they occupy a Śatrurāśi, there will be bondage. If Candra does not reach a Śatrurāśi, the lost property has been taken out. उदयश्चन्द्रलग्नश्च रिपुः पश्यति वा युतः । आयुर्हानी रिपुस्थानं गतश्चेद्बन्धनं भवेत् । गतो न यदि नष्टश्चेब्दहिरेव गतं वदेत् ॥२०१॥

Ācārya: If the Praśna relates to a gain of longevity, then Krūrayutidṛṣṭi on Udaya/Candra declines this. If Krūras are in their Śatrurāśis in Udaya/Candra, that may indicate bondage.

Sunidhi: Why bondage?

Ācārya: that is because Śatrurāśi indicate hostility, and it means that the native is attacked by an enemy or is held against his will.

10.202. If a strong Candra or Guru is in Kendra in a Praśnakuṇḍalī, there is no loss in a Naṣṭa Praśna. If it is about death, it can safely be said there will be no death. If Krūras are in or aspecting the Kendras, the reverse prediction must be made, i.e., the property cannot be recovered, and death may occur.

Ācārya: Let us now examine the protection Yogas in Kuṇḍalī. The greatest protection among all is Saumya-Kendra Yoga.

Sunidhi: Kindly elaborate, Guruji!

Ācārya: This Yoga is formed when a Saumya is in a Kendra in dignity. Dignity means that the Graha must not be in its Nīca/Śatru Rāśi.

Sunidhi: What about Krūras?

Ācārya: Krūra-Kendra Yoga is just the reverse. While Krūras owning a Kendra is good, their presence in a Kendra is detrimental to good Yogas. Nīca Krūra in a Kendra is disastrous – it is as if someone has attacked your house's foundation pillar, making it destined to crumble in due course.

Sunidhi: Guruji, is this endorsed by a Śāstra? I heard just the reverse that Krūras in Kendras are favourable.

Ācārya: I never say anything that is non-Śāstraic.

To understand the effects of Saumyas vs Krūras on Kendras, we must examine two Yogas, Mālā and Sarpa. Mālā is garland, and Sarpa is serpent. Both can be worn on the neck, but one is favourable, and the other is dangerous (unless worn by Devādhideva Mahādeva).

Sunidhi: Kindly elaborate on these Yogas.

Ācārya: Sārāvalī 21.18b states that Mālā Yoga is formed when Saumyas exclusively occupy the Kendras. In contrast, Sarpa Yoga is formed when Krūras exclusively occupy the Kendras. Mālā and Sarpa are called Dala Yogas.

The Mālā Yoga is formed when Saumyas exclusively occupy Kendras. Among the 7 Grahas, there are 4 Saumyas and 3 Krūras. Candra, Budha, Bṛhaspati and Śukra are considered Saumya, while Sūrya, Maṅgala and Śani are considered Krūra. The nodes are not included in the Nābhasa Yogas, so keep them aside.

The classics state that Saumyas occupy 3 Kendras to produce the Mālā Yoga. Here, (1) the fourth Kendra should be unoccupied, and (2) 3 Saumyas referred to here are Budha, Bṛhaspati and Śukra. Candra is usually not included, as his Saumya quality depends on his Pakṣabala.

Similarly, when Krūras occupy 3 Kendras, the Sarpa Yoga is produced, provided the remaining Kendras should be unoccupied. Maharṣi Parāśara is noticeably clear about the 3 Kendras (instead of 4), while Sārāvalī is silent on this matter.

Sunidhi: What are the effects of these Yogas, Guruji?

Ācārya: As per Sārāvalī 21.41-42, one born with Mālā Yoga is always happy, endowed with conveyances, robes, wealth, and pleasures, splendorous and has many wives. On the other hand, the native under the Sarpa Yoga is crooked, lacks kindness, is always subject to grief and poverty and is forced to live in others' houses and eat their food.

Sunidhi: Dhanyavād Guruji!

Ācārya: Now you decide whether Krūras in Kendras are good or not.

Sunidhi: Guruji, from your explanation. Now, I do not doubt that Krūras in Kendras are troublesome.

Kailāśa: Guruji, are there other protection Yogas?

Ācārya: Indeed! There are a few others. Let me provide them from Bṛhatparāśara. They are called Ariṣṭabhaṅga Yogas. There are seven such Yogas!

(1) Budha, Guru and Śukra is in a Udaya Kendra.

(2) A strong (Sva/Ucca/Mitra) Guru in Lagna wards off all the evils.

(3) Lagneśa strongly placed in a Kendra.

(4) Saumyadṛṣṭi on Lagna for birth in Śuklapakṣa night. Krūradṛṣṭi on Lagna for birth in Kṛṣṇapakṣa daytime.

(5) Sūrya in 12H in Kanyā.

(6) Maṅgala subject to Guru yutidṛṣṭi.

(7) Krūras subject to Śubhakartari, and Kendrakoṇas are with Saumyas.

Kailāśa: Does that mean that when a dangerous Krūra is afflicting a Bhāva, Saumyas in Kendrakoṇa, 2H/12H from the Bhāva would protect it?

Ācārya: That is right.

Kailāśa: Thank you for clarifying this, Guruji!

Ācārya: Let us examine other Yogas for gains and losses.

10.203. If Krūras are in 4H, the enemy dare not come. If Saumyas are in 10H and 11H, all enterprises undertaken will be successful.

Ācārya: Krūras in 4H indicate that an expected invasion would not happen. On the other hand, Saumyas in 4H guarantees that. But, Sajala and Catuṣpāda Rāśis in 4H protect one's kingdom from invasion. We shall examine more such Yogas later in Yuddha Praśna.

Regarding Lābhālābha Praśna (i.e., about gains and losses), Saumyas in 10H and 11H promise success. In a fight or competition, Saumyas in 10H/11H from 7H indicate success to the opponent.

10.204. If Rāhu is in Udaya, Āruṛha or Chatra or in their Trikoṇas, the person who has gone far away from home will not return. He may be in bondage there.

Ācārya: Regarding Yātrā Praśna, Rāhu in Lagna (Udaya, Āruṛha or Chatra) indicate danger to the traveller (Lagna = traveller). He may be in bondage (held against his will) or in serious trouble.

10.205. If a Praśna relating to poison is asked in the above case, the person will die. The Pṛcchaka would go to the place where the person is confined, but his presence would be of no avail; there would be a loss of property, and all undertakings would fail.

Ācārya: In a Praśna regarding the whereabouts of a missing person, Rāhu in Lagna is truly a disaster. The person could be subject to harassment and bondage. If the Praśna is about if someone is poisoned – then the answer to the Praśna is yes, and the person may die.

Sunidhi: Why poison?

Ācārya: Poison is normally denoted by Śani, Māndi and Guḻika (Maharṣi Jaimini), and Rāhu is like Śani. So Śani-Rāhu Yoga in any manner indicates affliction by poison. Same goes with Yogas of other Grahas like Rāhu-Māndi, Rāhu-Guḻika, Śani-Māndi, Śani-Guḻika etc.

Sunidhi: Dhanyavād, Guruji!

10.206. If Śukra is in 10H from Candra and if Sūrya is in 10H from Guru at Praśna, all kinds of work undertaken by the Pṛcchaka would succeed.

Ācārya: There is a peculiar Yoga about Kendras from Śukra and Guru. Śukra and Guru are preceptors, and their strengths are paramount. Besides, Śukra and Candra are the Kārakas for 4H, and Guru and Sūrya for 10H.

If Candra and Sūrya are in Dikbala from Śukra and Guru, they guarantee success. Therefore, Candra in 4H from Śukra and Sūrya in 10H from Guru are crucial Yoga for success.

Kailāśa: This Yoga is so beautiful! I didn't realize we could check Dikbala from other Grahas.

10.207. Marital bliss, wealth, and prosperity will exist if Śukra is in 7H/10H from Udaya. The same good results will accrue if Candra is in 7H/10H from Udaya.

Ācārya: Now, let us examine the Yogas for happiness, specifically in married life. Candra/Śukra are the Kāraka for 4H (Sukha/happiness); therefore, when either is in 7H/10H from Udaya, happiness daws in the form of wealth, prosperity and marital happiness.

Kailāśa: Why 10H/7H?

Ācārya: 4H is the house of Sukha/Happiness. 7H being Bhāvātbhāvam of 4H, is the secondary Bhāva of happiness. 10H is the house of wealth and success. And Bhāvātbhāvam of 10H is also 7H.

Generally, the Kāraka for Sukha (4H, Candra/Śukra) in a Kendra from Udaya promises happiness, wealth and prosperity.

Kailāśa: This makes sense now, Guruji!

10.208. When the Grahas reach their Sva/Ucca/Mitra Rāśi, they confer all good benefits; and when they are in Nīca/Śatru Rāśi, all kinds of work will meet with failure.

Ācārya: Let us examine the Yoga for timing. In a Praśna, identify the Graha who is considering happiness and success. When the Graha transits its Sva/Ucca/Mitra Rāśi, what it promises in the Praśna Kuṇḍalī manifests.

Similarly, identify the most troublesome Graha among the Trikeśas, those in Trikas etc. When this Graha transits its Nīca/Śatru Rāśi, all hell breaks loose.

11. ON DISEASES

Jayanta: Guruji, should we focus on analysing diseases with Praśna now?

Ācārya: Let us do that.

11.209. Predictions about diseases and death are made in terms of the Śāstraic rules. 6H from Udaya indicates disease, and 8H, death.

Ācārya: What are the houses of diseases?

Jayanta: Diseases of several kinds and denoted by several Bhāvas.

6H: Attacks, injuries, wounds, and pathological sicknesses such as viral, bacterial, fungal, and protozoal infections.

8H: weaknesses, congenital disabilities.

Bādhaka: All kinds of hidden matters, such as the evil eye (dṛṣṭi), black magic and abhicāra.

Ācārya: Well done Jayanta!

Kailāśa: Should we also examine the Kārakas?

Ācārya: Yes, we should. Jayanta, what do you think about that?

Jayanta: Gurudeva, the Kārakas are:

Maṅgala: 6H: Injuries and pathological sicknesses. This Graha governs viral infections and itches.

Śani: 8H: weaknesses and disabilities caused by past life evil Karmas. Śani signifies this as he is limping.

Rāhu: Bādhaka: Rāhu is a Chāyāgraha and governs all forms of hidden things. Rāhu + Budha, Ketu + Budha, Maṅgala + Budha etc., indicate black magic and afflictions by Bhūtas, Pretas and Piśācas.

Ācārya: Good, Jayanta!

Kailāśa: Guruji, how to judge diseases from Praśna?

11.210. Whatever Grahas are in or aspecting 6H/8H, predictions regarding diseases and death must be made. If Krūras or Nīca/Śatru Grahas are in or aspecting 6H/8H, diseases would not be cured, nor death prevented.

Ācārya: Let us examine this sūtra from the author.

The diseases one suffers from should be known from the Grahas in 6H/8H. If there is no Graha in them, then the Grahas aspecting them must be examined.

If the Grahas in 6H/8H or aspecting them are Krūras or are in their Nīca/Śatru Rāśi, then the sickness is severe and would not subside soon. Affliction to 8H can eventually lead to demise.

Kailāśa: That makes sense, Guruji!

11.211. If Candra/Rāhu is in Udaya/6H/8H, diseases occur due to poisoning or abhicāra that are not cured. If Candra in Udaya is in Pṛṣṭodaya Rāśi, the illness will not be cured.

Ācārya: Now let us examine the sūtras of Candra and Rāhu.

Candra in Udaya/6H/8H indicates that the disease is serious and a dangerous sickness may afflict the person.

Kailāśa: I can understand Candra in 6H/8H as he manifests the indications of the Bhāva. But why must Candra in Udaya be considered unfavourable? Isn't Candra a Saumya?

Ācārya: That is a good question. According to the Śāstras, Candra in Udaya is not considered good unless he is in Meṣa, Vṛṣabha or Karka. In other Rāśis in Udaya, Candra manifests several troubles in life. The trouble is intense if Candra is with low Pakṣabala. Else, it is moderate.

Sunidhi: Candra is afflicted in a Trika, causing serious health troubles and even death. Is that true?

Ācārya: Yes, that is true; you must examine the Bālāriṣṭa Adhyāya of Bṛhatparāśara.

Sunidhi: Guruji, kindly give us the gist of the Yogas.

Ācārya: Alright, here you go!

9.3. Candra in a Trika with Krūradṛṣṭi. Life is somewhat extended if Candra is also with Saumyadṛṣṭi.

9.4. A Vakrī Saumya in a Trikoṇa with Krūradṛṣṭi. A Saumya in Lagna offers some respite.

9.5. Śani, Maṅgala and Sūrya in 5H cause the mother's and brother's death.

9.6. Maṅgala in 1H/8H with or dṛṣṭied by Śani/Sūrya and without Saumyadṛṣṭi.

9.7. Śani and Maṅgala Dṛṣṭi on Lagna, and Rahu with Sūrya + Candra.

9.8. Śani is in 10H, Candra in 6H and Maṅgala in 7H threaten the native and his mother.

9.9. Śani in Lagna, Candra in 8H and Guru in 3H. These are the Maraṇa Kāraka Sthānas of the three Grahas.

9.10. Sūrya in 9H, Maṅgala in 7H, Guru-Śukra in 11H.

9.11. Any of Sūrya, Candra, Śukra and Rāhu in 12H threaten life. But their dṛṣṭi on 12H counter evil.

9.12. Candra in 1H, 7H, 8H with a Krūra and without Saumyayutidṛṣṭi.

9.13-14. Birth in the morning or evening Sandhyā, in Candra's Horā or Candra Gaṇḍānta when Candra and Krūras occupy Udaya Kendra. Morning Sandhyā is 3 Ghaṭī before Sūryodaya, and evening Sandhyā is 3 Ghaṭī after Sūryāsta.

9.15. Vṛścika Udaya with all Krūras in the Eastern half (10H-3H) and all Saumyas in the Western half (4H-9H).

9.16. Udaya with Pāpakartari and Krūras in Trika.

9.17. Candra with Krūrayuti without Saumyayutidṛṣṭi and Krūras in 1H/7H.

9.18. Kṛṣṇa-Candra in Udaya and Krūras afflict 8H and Kendra.

9.19. Candra in 1H/7H/8H/12H with Pāpakartari.

9.20. Canda in 1H with Pāpakartari and Krūras afflicting 7H and 8H threaten the native and his mother.

9.21. Śani, Sūrya and Maṅgala in 12H, 9H and 8H without Saumyadṛṣṭi.

9.22. Krūras in 7H or in Udaya Dreṣkāṇa, and Kṛṣṇa-Candra is Udaya.

9.23. Weak Grahas in Apoklimas (12H, 3H, 6H, 9H).

Sunidhi: Dhanyavād Guruji, for narrating them here!

Ācārya: Let us examine the other principles laid down in Jñānapradīpikā.

Sunidhi: Kindly elaborate, Guruji!

11.212. In terms of the bodily organs, Meṣa is regarded as the head, Vṛṣabha the face, Mithuna the arms, Karka the hands, Siṅha the chest, Kanyā the breasts, Tulā the stomach, Vṛścika the armpits, Dhanu the arms, Makara the genitals, Kumbha the thighs, and Mīna the legs. Regarding the Rāśis, the affected parts of the body can be predicted.

Ācārya: First, let us examine the Rāśi assignments to the body parts. Jayanta, could you share your understanding here?

Jayanta: Absolutely! The Rāśis from Meṣa onwards governs the human body from head to toe. The mapping is as follows:

Meṣa: Head, skull, cranium, forehead

Vṛṣabha: Face, eyes, mouth

Mithuna: Arms, ears, throat, windpipe, lungs

Karka: Heart, chest, breast

Siṅha: Stomach

Kanyā: Lower abdomen, kidney, womb, uterus

Tulā: male genital

Vṛścika: rectum, female genital

Dhanu: Thigh

Makara: Knee

Kumbha: Shanks, calves

Mīna: Feet

Kailāśa: But there are some differences, according to the author. The differences start from Siṅha. The author explains the mapping of the body part to the Rāśis. I have marked the ones with differences with "*."

Meṣa: head

Vṛṣabha: face

Mithuna: arms

Karka: hands

Siṅha*: chest

Kanyā*: breasts

Tulā*: stomach

Vṛścika*: armpits

Dhanu*: arms

Makara*: genitals

Kumbha*: thighs

Mīna*: legs

Sunidhi: Guruji, which mapping should we follow?

Ācārya: Let us use the standard mapping, as the author mapping is generally not followed by the scholars.

According to Maharṣi Parāśara, the 12 Rāśis are mapped to 12 limbs of the Kālapuruṣa, which are here under (1) Head (śīrṣa), (2) face (ānane), (3) arms (bāhū), (4) heart (hṛt), (5) stomach (kroḍa), (6) hip (kaṭi), (7) lower abdomen (basti), (8) hidden parts (guhyo), (9) two thighs (uyugale), (10) two calves (jānuyugme), (11) ankles (jaṅghake) and, (12) feet (caranau dvau).

Kailāśa: Guruji, I have a doubt. Why is male genital mapped to Tulā and female genital to Vṛścika?

Ācārya: That is because, Tulā is a masculine Rāśi, and Vṛścika is a feminine Rāśi. There are several other reasons that I have explained in my previous books. Check the one on health and longevity.

Kailāśa: Noted, Guruji!

Ācārya: Now, let us examine the governorship of Grahas on body parts. Jayanta, what do you know about them?

11.213. In terms of the Grahas, the bodily organs are distributed; thus, Maṅgala is the head, Śukra the face, Rāhu the neck, Budha the arms, Candra the chest, Sūrya the stomach, Guru the lower portion below the navel, Śani the thighs, and Ketu the feet.

Jayanta: Guruji, you explained this in the health and longevity book of the series. You said Sūrya and other Grahas govern specific body parts/bodily constituents, and their afflictions cause diseases in those body parts.

You said, in How to Judge a Horoscope, Dr BV Raman opines that Sūrya governs the stomach, Candra, Heart, Maṅgala, head, Budha, chest, Bṛhaspati, thighs, Śani, legs, and the bones tibia and fibula, and Rāhu, the feet. The body parts mapping to the Grahas are as follows:

(1) Sūrya: bile, heart, brain, bead, eye, bone.

(2) Candra: breast, saliva, womb, bodily water, blood, lymphatic and glandular systems.

(3) Maṅgala: bile, ears, nose, forehead, ligaments, bone marrow, male genital.

(4) Budha: abdomen, tongue, lungs, bowels, nerve centres, bile, and muscular tissues.

(5) Bṛhaspati: phlegm, blood, thighs, kidneys, bodily fat, brain, arteries that carry oxygen.

(6) Śukra: ovaries, eyes, reproductive system, female genital, semen, phlegm.

(7) Śani: wind, legs, feet, digestive acids, knees, and muscular tissues.

Ācārya: Well done, Jayanta.

Kailāśa: Guruji, according to this author, the mapping is as follows:

Maṅgala: head

Śukra: face

Rāhu: neck

Budha: arms

Candra: chest

Sūrya: stomach

Guru: below the navel

Śani: thighs

Ketu: feet

Sunidhi: Which one to follow, Guruji?

Ācārya: Follow the one that is commonly followed. But also keep your mind open and check the classification given by the author's works.

Sunidhi: Noted, Guruji.

Kailāśa: Guruji, kindly tell us more about the diseased caused by the affliction of Grahas in the Kuṇḍalī and their association with the Trikas.

Ācārya: In that case, let us examine the ślokas from Phaladīpikā. You need to follow the following process to determine the Rogakāraka.

Identify the Grahas in 6H. They indicate pathological sicknesses such as cholera, typhoid, pneumonia, and food poisoning.

Identify the Grahas in 8H. They indicate physiological illnesses such as AIDs, Cancer, Hypertension, disabilities etc.

Identify the Grahas in 12H. They indicate bodily weaknesses.

Identify the Lords of 6H/8H/12H and the Grahas joining them.

One's illnesses in life can be traced to a combination of Grahas. When at least two of them join or have yutidṛṣṭi, then they become the prime Kāraka for diseases (Roga).

The following are the diseases signified by the Grahas:

Sūrya: high fever, pitta disorder, burns, epilepsy, heart disease, eye trouble, skin diseases, leukorrhea, brittle bones, danger from wood, fire weapon, poison and enemies. *Trouble to one's wife, children and danger from quadruped, thief, the sovereign, serpent, Yama Devatā, Śiva Devatā.*

Candra: excessive sleep, laziness, phlegm disorder, coughing, diarrhoea, carbuncle, typhoid fever, danger from horned and water animals, indigestion, lack of taste, trouble from women, jaundice, mental aberration, impurity of blood, *danger from water; danger from Bālagrahas, Devī Durgā, kinnaras, yama devatā, Sarpas and Yakṣinī.*

Maṅgala: excessive thirst, irritation of blood, bilious fever, leprosy, eye diseases, appendicitis, epilepsy, marrow-related ailments, roughness of the body, psoriasis, danger from fire, poison, weapons, bodily deformities, *trouble from the government, enemies and thieves, fighting with brothers, sons, enemies, and friends, fear from evil spirits, Gandharvas, and frightful demons and diseases affecting the upper limbs of the body (such as lungs, throat; teeth, tongue, ear, nose, etc.)*

Budha: mental disease, ailments of vocal organs, eye-disease, throat and nose ailments, fever, Tridoṣa ailments, skin diseases, anaemia, bad dreams, itches, scab, psoriasis, accidents due to the fire and poison; *troubles arising out of violence and imprisonment and harm from evil demons moving in the abodes of Gandharvas; and in fiery pits (where these evil spirits usually dwell), or Gandharvas, the Earth, mansions and horses, etc., as well as evil spirits.*

Guru: appendicitis (intestinal disorders), fever arising out of disorder in the entrails, diseases arising from sorrow, fainting or swooning, phlegmatic disorder, ear trouble, giddiness, *trouble in connection with Mandir matters, torture for knocking off hoarded wealth, harm resulting from the curses of brāhmaṇas and devatās, diseases engendered by kinnaras, yakshas, devatās,* *serpents, and Vidyādharas, etc., and troubles arising from serious offences done to wise men and elders.*

Śukra: anaemia, diseases caused by the irritation of phlegmatic and windy humours, trouble to the eyes, urinary diseases, diseases in the generative organ, strangury, trouble in cohabitation, *exudation of semen, loss (fading away) of bodily splendour as a result of intercourse with prostitutes, rickets, fear from witches; female ghosts and female deities and break of friendship with a dear friend.*

Śani: diseases caused by wind and phlegm, paralysis of the leg, misfortune, weariness, mental aberration, stomach ache, excess of internal heat, *desertion of servants, injury to the ribs, danger to wife and children, injury to some limb, mental anguish. He is responsible for causing a blow from a piece of wood or stone and trouble from (foul) ignominious goblins and the like.*

Rāhu: causes palpitation of the heart; leprosy, aberration of mind, danger from artificial poisoning, pain in the legs, trouble from goblins and serpents and ills to wife and children. **Ketu** indicates trouble through disputes with Brāhmaṇas and Kṣatriyas or from enemies. **Māndi (Guḻika)** causes fear from (seeing) corpses, poison, bodily pain and pollution (arising from the demise of one's near relations).

Kailāśa: Guruji, what are Vidyadhara, Kinnara, Yakṣa etc?

Ācārya: They are supernatural beings, and one may get afflicted by them when a certain Graha is weak/afflicted in a Kuṇḍalī. Therefore, the affliction is of two kinds, (1) this worldly illness and (2) otherworldly illness.

Normally, people are aware of this worldly illness. But one may get afflicted by supernatural beings and even the wrath of the Devatās such as Śiva Devatā, Yama Devatā etc.

Knowing the root cause of the issue can help in recovery. Medicine can cure these worldly illnesses, but it would not work for the otherworldly illnesses – for that, other remedies such as performing mantra japa, visiting Mandirs, performing Yajñas etc., should be undertaken.

Kailāśa: Thank you for explaining this. Are there other Yogas that we should be aware of?

Ācārya: There are several, but here are some more from Phaladīpikā (ślokas 10 and 11 from the sickness-related Adhyāya).

12H and 2H with Candra and Sūrya with or dṛṣṭied by Śani and Maṅgala indicate eye disease.

3H, 11H and Bṛhaspati with or dṛṣṭied by Śani and Maṅgala indicate ear disease.

Maṅgala in 5H with 6L/8L indicates stomach-ache.

8L and 6L in 7H and 8H with a Krūra indicate rectal disease.

Śukra with 6L/8L in 6H/8H, afflicted by Krūras, indicate genital diseases (STD).

The following are the effects of Grahas in 6H/8H:

Sūrya – fever; Maṅgala/Ketu – ulcer; Śukra – genital diseases; Bṛhaspati – consumption or tuberculosis; Śani – nervous diseases; Rāhu with Maṅgala yutidṛṣṭi – carbuncle; Śani-Candra – enlargement of spleen; afflicted Kṛṣṇa-Candra in a Jalatattva rāśi – watery disease (typhoid, cholera etc.) or consumption.

Kailāśa: Dhanyavād from guidance.

Jayanta: Guruji, kindly guide us about the approach of identifying diseases from the Kuṇḍalī.

Ācārya: The diseases caused by the afflictions to the Grahas are classified into two groups, (1) affliction to body parts, constituents, and functions and (2) non-localised ailments. When a Graha is afflicted, diseases occur in the (a) body parts, (b) bodily systems or (c) constituents governed by them.

Body parts: Ear, nose and eye ailments are localised ailments caused by the afflictions to the body parts

Bodily constituents: The watery constituent of the body is governed by Candra/Śukra, and Candra/Maṅgala governs blood. When the Grahas are afflicted, their constituents are affected.

Bodily functions: Grahas are also responsible for certain functions, such as reproductive function, governed primarily by Śukra and secondarily by Candra. Similarly, the body's shield against diseases, i.e., the immunity system, is governed by Śukra. When Śukra is afflicted, the immunity system is affected as well.

Non-localized ailments: Besides the diseases linked to body parts/ constituents/functions, others are not so specific, such as fever, inflammation, bodily pain, vomiting, etc. They are non-localised ailments.

Below, several ailments of the Grahas are listed. They are grouped under localized and non-localized. The localized ailments are related to affliction to body parts, constituents, and functions, whereas the non-localised ailments affect the whole body.

Let us take Sūrya. The grouping under localized ailments is "bone, right eye, heart, skin, belly, stomach, head, the general constitution of the body, cerebellum, brain, blood, lungs, heart, breasts, ovaries, seminal vesicle". The grouping under non-localized ailments is "fever of several kinds, inflammation, skin diseases, leprosy, dysentery etc."

This means that when Sūrya the Rogakāraka, there shall be pains in the bones, fractures of bones, etc. Similarly, there could be a disease of the right eye, heart, skin etc. The person may also suffer from non-localized ailments such as fever of several kinds, inflammation, skin diseases, leprosy, dysentery etc.

Kailāśa: This is very clear, Guruji!

Sunidhi: So, we should find the most weak/afflicted Graha in a Kuṇḍalī to decipher disease. Isn't it?

Ācārya: Look for the weakest/afflicted Graha present in 6H/8H or own that Bhāva. That Graha is the Rogakāraka.

You must also note that more than one Graha may cause disease. For instance, skin diseases can be caused by Sūrya, Maṅgala and Budha, even though Budha is the governor of the skin. However, the skin diseases' specific nature can differ depending on the Grahas involved.

Kailāśa: Noted, Guruji!

Ācārya: Following are the effects of Rogakārakas.

Sūrya: *(1) localised:* bone, right eye, Heart, skin, belly, stomach, head, the general constitution of the body, cerebellum, brain, blood, lungs, Heart, breasts, ovaries, seminal vesicle. *(2) non-localised:* fevers, inflammation, skin diseases, leprosy, dysentery.

Candra: *(1) localised:* bodily water, blood, blood plasma, lymphatic system, membranes, pericardium, veins, left eye, intestine, alimentary canal, kidneys, mind, heart, lungs, uterus, breast, mammary glands, appendix. *(2) non-localised:* sleeplessness, inertia, asthma, diarrhoea, a blood disorder, anaemia, jaundice, vomiting, diabetes, menstrual disorder, cough and cold, hydrocele.

Maṅgala: *(1) localised:* blood, marrow, head, neck, veins, genitals (penis), blood haemoglobin, rectum, urinary system, eyes, nose, veins, upper limbs (arms). *(2) non-localised:* poisoning, cuts, injuries, wounds, carbuncle, leprosy, itches, skin disease, blood pressure, amputation, loss of genital, bone fracture, ulcer, boils, tumours, cancer, piles, menstrual disorder, dysentery, vitality, smallpox, chickenpox, mumps, fistula, hernia.

Budha: *(2) localised:* belly, feet, chest, nerves, skin, nose, navel, gall bladder, lungs, tongue, mouth, hair, and skin. *(1) non-localised:* chickenpox, colic, navel, spinal epilepsy, system, affliction by poison, bone fracture, typhoid, madness, paralysis, fits, ulcers, indigestion, cholera, arms, neuroma, vertigo.

Bṛhaspati: *(1) localised:* thighs, fat, brain, memory, liver, pancreas, kidneys, lungs, ears, tongue, spleen, semen. *(2) non-localised:* diabetes, poor memory, memory loss, oedema, jaundice, tumours, the passage of albumin or semen in urine, blood poisoning, dyspepsia, and abscesses.

Śukra: *(1) localised:* bodily waters, face, eyes, genital (vagina), semen, urinary system, immune system, white blood cells, lustre of body, throat, pancreas, throat, glandular and endocrine system, chin. *(2) non-localised:* general debility, venereal diseases, gonorrhoea, syphilis, fading away of bodily lustre, epileptic fits, indigestion, trouble, diabetes, sexual incompetence, impotence, oedema, fever, goitre, gout, cysts, anaemia, urethral diseases, hernia.

Śani: *(1) localised:* limbs (lower limbs, legs), joints, bones, teeth, stomach, muscular system, skin, hair, ears, spleen. *(2) non-localised:* weakness, damage and loss of muscles, bone fracture, rheumatic pains, blindness, mental anxiety, wounds, bodily pains, muscular pains, joint pains, paralysis, hysteria, deafness, tumours, baldness.

Rāhu: *(1) localised:* feet, lungs, breathing, neck, throat. *(2) non-localised:* ulcers, boils, leprosy, breathing disorder, chocking, spleen enlargement, cataracts, hydrocele, varicose veins, bodily pains, epileptic fits, hiccups, stammering, afflicted by poison, smallpox, undiagnosable diseases

Ketu: *(1) localised:* belly, stomach, feet, eye, ear. *(2) non-localised:* boils, fever, lungs trouble, eye pain, stomach pain, bodily pains, intestinal worms, low blood pressure, speech defect, stammering, stuttering, brain diseases, phobias, undiagnosable diseases

Ācārya: After we know which Graha cause what diseases, let us see how to apply the knowledge. We need to blend the afflictions of both Grahas and Rāśis. Jayanta, kindly narrate what I have taught you.

Jayanta: Absolutely, Guruji!

Like Grahas, Rāśis are also associated with body parts. Affliction to a Rāśi by a Krūra or a Trikeśa can indicate disease in that body part.

The Rāśis are further mapped to the Bhāvas. For instance, whatever is said about Meṣa, also applies to 1H because Meṣa is 1H of Kālapuruṣa.

Also, a distinction is made between 6H and 8H. Normally, the diseases indicated by 8L pertain to the Rāśi, whereas the 6L pertain to the Bhāva.

12L indicates weaknesses in the body part and not diseases. The Agnitattva Rāśis, Meṣa, Siṅha, and Dhanu govern the vitality of a person. The Pṛthvītattva Rāśis, Vṛṣabha, Kanyā and Makara govern the bones and flesh. The Vāyurāśis Rāśis, Mithuna, Tulā and Kumbha govern the breathing, and the Jalatattva Rāśis, Karka, Vṛścika, Mīna govern the blood.

Ācārya: Good Jayanta. We need to blend the indications of both Grahas and Rāśis.

Regarding the 8H and 6H differences, let me explain further.

Suppose for a Mithuna Lagna person, 8L Śani is in Karka, in 2H. The disease can be related to Karka (chest/heart) or 2H (face/eyes/mouth). Since the affliction is caused by 8L, the Rāśi-based diseases take precedence. Therefore, the person may suffer from weakness in the chest/lungs.

Suppose in the same Kuṇḍalī, 6L Maṅgala is in Tulā, in 5H. The disease can be related to Tulā (male genital, kidney function, urine system etc.) or 5H (stomach, ulcer etc.). Since the affliction is caused by 6L, the Bhāva based diseases take precedence. Therefore, the person may suffer from a stomach injury, ulcer, etc.

The following is the mapping of Rāśis with body parts, systems and constituents.

(1) Meṣa: head, brain, mind

(2) Vṛṣabha: face, eyes, mouth, tongue, teeth, nose, ears, fingers, nails, bone, flesh

(3) Mithuna: neck, throat, collarbones, hands, breathing, respiration, growth of the body

(4) Karka: Heart, lungs, chest, breast, diaphragm, blood,

(5) Siṅha: upper abdomen, mind, Heart, liver, gall bladder, spleen, intestines, mesentery

(6) Kanyā: lower abdomen, navel, womb (kokh, kukṣi), kidneys, small intestine, bones, flesh, mental faculties

(7) Tulā: groins, genital, bladder, uterus, ovaries, prostate glands, pineal gland, seminal vesicle, large intestine, semen, breathing

(8) Vṛścika: rectum, genital, seminal vesicle, urine, blood

(9) Dhanu: thighs, femur, femoral arteries, the support system to the upper body

(10) Makara: knees, kneecap, kneepit (popliteal fossa), bones and flesh

(11) Kumbha: calves, legs in general, buttocks, left ear, breathing

(12) Mīna: feet, left eye, blood

11.214. In a Naṣṭa Praśna, the lost object will be in the place assigned to the Rāśi. Likewise, if Krūras are in or aspecting a Rāśi or if Kṣīṇa/Śatru Grahas are in a Rāśi, the corresponding body parts in terms of the Rāśi and Graha will be affected by disease. एतेष्वेव स्थलेषु स्यान्नष्टमेतेषु राशिषु । पावयुक्तेषु दृष्टेषु नीचारिस्थेषु रुग्भवेद् ॥२१४॥

Ācārya: The effects of the Rāśi are explained here. The location of the lost object can be denoted by the Rāśi in Udaya (or in 4H). One may refer to the details of Naṣṭa Praśna for further details. The Rāśi that a Kṣīṇa/Śatru Graha most afflicts. Kṣīṇa is weak and is often equated to Nīca. A Krūra in a Nīca/Śatru Rāśi is more dangerous than in their Sva/Ucca/Mitra Rāśi.

In Praśnaśāstra, the Grahas in 7H also denotes the nature of sickness, besides the Grahas in or aspecting 6H/8H/12H or their Lords. If a Trikeśa is with a Krūra in 7H, the disease is serious and requires immediate attention.

11.215. The time taken for cure of the illness will be in terms of the days, months, and years of the Grahas (per 2.84-85) aspecting Candra which aspects 6H. पश्यन्ति ये ग्रहाश्चन्द्रं व्याधिस्थानावलोकिनम् । पूर्वोक्तमासवर्षाणि दिनानि च वदेद्बुधः ॥२१५॥

Ācārya: If Candra aspects (or in) 6H, then the Graha that aspects Candra determines the period. Per śloka 2.84, the time duration denoted by the Grahas is given below; Śani, one year; Sūrya 6 months; Budha 2 months; Guru 1 month; Śukra 15 days; Maṅgala 1 Vāra; and Candra 1 Muhūrta (48 min).

11.216. If Krūras are in 6H/8H from Udaya, the disease will not be cured. But if, however, Saumyas are there, the disease will be cured.

Ācārya: Krūras in 6H/8H prolong the ailment, whereas Saumyas in these places help with recovery. However, Candra should be out of 8H and should be with high Pakṣabala. Guru/Śukra in 8h and Budha in 8H are specifically helpful with recovery.

11.217. But there is one special feature to be noted. The time to cure the illness will be the number of days the Saumyas takes to transit 6H/8H.

Ācārya: Now that we know that Saumyas in 6H/8H help with recovery, the same principle can be used for timing the recovery. When Saumyas pass through the same Bhāva and are fortified, not afflicted, they bring about recovery.

11.218. If Krūras are in 7H/11H from 6H (sickness), or if Candra is in 6H/8H, death is certain.

Ācārya: Some Yogas for danger to life are given here: Krūras in 4H/12H and Candra in 6H/8H. It is clear that Candra in 6H/8H does not aid with recovery but aggravates it. He does so even more when he is with low Pakṣabala and also afflicted by Krūrayutidṛṣṭi or Pāpakartari.

It is a well-known principle that Krūras in Mokṣatrikoṇa (4H/8H/12H) damage health and cause danger to life.

Ācārya: Now the author narrates the effects of Grahas in or aspecting 6H. Jayanta, can you summarise them?

11.219. If Maṅgala dṛṣṭies 6H (sickness), the person will have headache and fever. If Śukra dṛṣṭies it, he will get cholera; if Budha dṛṣṭies it, he will get boils in his armpits.

11.220. If Sūrya dṛṣṭies 6H, the person will suffer from stomach ache; If Śani dṛṣṭies it, he will have wind diseases or become lame; If Rāhu dṛṣṭies it, he will suffer from poisoning; and if Candra dṛṣṭies it, he will have eye-affliction. If Guru dṛṣṭies it, he will have piles; and the effects of Śukra will be like that of Candra, say some.

Jayanta: Here you go!

Sūrya – stomach-ache

Candra – eye ailments

Maṅgala – headache and fever

Budha – boils in the armpit

Guru – piles

Śukra – cholera and also like Candra

Śani – wind disease or lameness

Rāhu – poisoning

Ācārya: Well done, Jayanta! We have already examined the principles before. So, one should examine them. There are some additional indications – of ailments that commonly occur in people.

Let us examine the effects of Upagrahas on diseases.

11.221. If at Praśna, the Indracāpa is with or dṛṣṭies Pariveṣa, the person will be afflicted by leprosy. If Indracāpa is with or dṛṣṭies the Dhūma, the person will be tormented by ghosts and devils (Bhūta and Piśāca). मूलव्याधिः गुरुः पश्येज्वन्द्रवत्स्याद् भृगुः परे । परिघाविन्द्रकोदण्डदृष्टे प्रश्न युते सति । कुष्ठव्याधिमिति ब्रूयाद्धूमे भूताहतं वदेत् ॥२२१॥

Ācārya: Here are the effects of yutidṛṣṭi between two Upagrahas

Indracāpa + Pariveṣa = leprosy

Indracāpa + Dhūma = tormented by ghosts

11.222. If Indracāpa is with or dṛṣṭies a Graha, the person will have epilepsy; and if Indracāpa is with or dṛṣṭies Sūrya is dṛṣṭied, affliction by ghosts must be predicted. If Śani is similarly affected, the person will suffer from consumption; and if Maṅgala is similarly affected, the person will suffer from malaria. सर्वेऽपस्मारमादित्ये पिशाचपरिपीडनम् । काशं श्वासं च शूलं च शनौ शीतज्वरः कुजे ॥२२२॥

Ācārya: Here are the remaining ones:

Indracāpa + another Graha = epilepsy

Indracāpa + Sūrya = tormented by ghosts

Indracāpa + Śani = consumption or TB

Indracāpa + Maṅgala = malaria

11.223. If at Praśna, if Indracāpa/Pariveṣa aspects Śukra without Saumyayutidṛṣṭi, there will be no cure of the disease. But if a Saumya is in a Sva/ Ucca/Mitra Rāśi, the disease will be cured very soon. शुक्रे कोदण्डपरिधिदृष्टे प्रश्ने तु रोगिणाम् । न व्याधिशमनं किञ्चिद्यदि नेक्षन्ति चेच्छुभाः । रोगशान्तिर्भवेच्छीघ्रं मित्रस्वात्युच्च-संस्थिताः ॥२२३॥

Ācārya: Śukra is the Kāraka for immunity. Therefore, if Śukra is subject to Saumyayutidṛṣṭi, there is recovery. But if Śukra is afflicted by Indracāpa/ Pariveṣa yutidṛṣṭi, then the recovery is not seen.

Jayanta: Guruji, now the author explains the effects of Tārās on diseases.

11.224. If at Praśna, Udaya is in any of the nine Tārās, namely, Kṛttikā, Rohini, Mṛgaśirā, Ārdra, Punarvasu, Puṣya, Aśleṣā, Maghā and Pūrvāphālgunī, the parts of the body afflicted will be respectively head, forehead, brow, eye, nose, ear, lower lip, chin, and finger.

11.225. If Udaya is in the next nine Tārās, namely, Uttarāphālgunī, Hastā, Citrā, Svāti, Viśākhā, Anurādhā, Jyeṣtha, Mūla and Pūrvāṣāṛhā, the afflicted parts are respectively neck, chest, breast, stomach, waist, buttocks, genital, scrotum, and upper lip.

11.226. If Udaya is in the next nine Tārās, namely, Uttarāṣāṛhā, Śravaṇa, Dhaniṣṭhā, Śatabhiṣā, Pūrvābhādra, Uttarābhādra, Revatī, Aśvinī and Bharaṇī, the affected parts of the body are knee, calf, ankle, groin, back of the thighs, heel, and toes.

Ācārya: Yes, the Tārās are also associated with the body parts. However, there are two schemes. One commences with Aśvinī, and the other commences with Kṛttikā. The author uses the one that commences from Kṛttikā.

Kailāśa: Guruji, kindly elaborate on the mapping.

Ācārya: In the Textbook of Scientific Hindu Astrology, Prof PS Śāstrī gives the following mapping, which is based on the Kṛttikā = head concept. This is called the Nara Cakra.

I made some adjustments because he states that Bharaṇī is Heart, which is not correct since Kṛttikā is head. Bharaṇī should be the lower part of the feet. He also missed out on Puṣya and Aśleṣā, which I have added below. Punarvasu is also changed from the ears to the nose, as ears are allotted to Aśleṣā.

(3) Kṛttikā- skull, (4) Rohiṇī- forehead, (5) Mṛgaśirā- eyebrows, (6) Ārdrā- eyes, (7) Punarvasu- nose, (8) Puṣya- face, (9) Aśleṣā- ears, (10) Maghā- lips, chin, (11) Pūrvāphālgunī- right hand, (12) Uttarāphālgunī- left hand, (13) Hastā- fingers, (14) Citrā- neck, (15) Svāti- chest, (16) Viśākhā- breast, (17) Anurādhā- stomach, (18) Jyeṣṭha- right side, (19) Mūla- left side, (20) Pūrvāṣāṛhā- back, (21) Uttarāṣāṛhā- waist, (22) Śravaṇa- genitals, (23) Dhaniṣṭhā- anus, (24) Śatabhiṣā- right thigh, (25) Pūrvābhādra- left thigh, (26) Uttarābhādra- shanks, (27) Revatī- Ankles, (1) Aśvinī- upper part of the feet, (2) Bharaṇī- the lower part of the feet. Some scholars make use of this Cakra for pinpointing diseases.

Prof Śāstrī states that the Nakṣatras refer to certain ailments depending on the Caraṇa at birth or disease. Aśvinī1- sorrows; Aśvinī3- degenerating health; Bharaṇī2- inferiority complex, Kṛttikā1/4- biliousness, indigestion; Rohini1- colds; Mṛgaśirā3/4- high blood pressure, cardiac trouble; Ārdra3- skin; Ārdra4- bad sexual habits; Punarvasu2/3- indifferent health; Puṣya1- hypersensitivity; Puṣya2- cold and cough; Aśleṣā 2/4- weak health; Maghā 1- troubles from excessive sex; ...

... Maghā4- over eating; Pūrvāphālgunī4- boils, ulcers; Uttarāphālgunī2- bad health; Hastā3- worries, sensitivity; Citrā1- wrong thinking, pride; Svāti1/4- bad health; Viśākhā2- sedentary habits; Anurādhā1- digestive troubles; Anurādhā 4-constipation; Jyeṣṭha 2/3- frail health; Mūla1/2- frail health; Pūrvāṣāṛhā 3- sedentary habits; Uttarāṣāṛhā3- frail health; Śravaṇa2- sensuousness; Dhaniṣṭhā1- bad health; Śatabhiṣā2- irritability; Śatabhiṣā3- biliousness; Pūrvābhādra3- biliousness, liver troubles, constipation. Pūrvābhādra4- kidney and bladder troubles; Uttarābhādra1/2- epilepsy, irritability; Uttarābhādra4- mentally weak. Revatī2- excessive sex; Revatī3- personal uncleanliness.

Kailāśa: How about the one commencing with Aśvinī?

Ācārya: The below classification is based upon the mapping of Nakṣatras to the Rāśis. Since Meṣa governs the head, Aśvinī, Bharaṇī, and Kṛttikā must be mapped to various parts of the head.

Table 26

#	Nakṣatra	Body parts	Localised ailments	Non-localised ailments
1	Aśvinī ♈♈♈♈	♈: Head, brain, cranium, skull, the knees	Head injury, migraine, brain fever, headache, neuralgia, cerebral haemorrhage, coma, brain stroke, epilepsy, fainting	Malaria, chickenpox, viral infection

#	Nakṣatra	Body parts	Localised ailments	Non-localised ailments
2	**Bharaṇī** ♈♈♈♈	♈: Parts of the head and brain, cerebral hemisphere, organs within the head, forehead, eyes	Night blindness, cataract, forehead injury	Cold fever, debilitating sexual abilities, sexual diseases such as syphilis
3	**Kṛttikā** ♈♉♉♉	♈: Back portion of the skull and brain, vision ♉: Face, lower jaw, neck, throat, larynx, tonsils	Pimples, blood in the eyes, tonsillitis, swelling in the neck, boils, cerebral meningitis, brain fever	Hallucination, delusion, malaria, plague, smallpox, cuts, wounds, injury, accidents, explosions, fire, carbuncle, inability to excrete body wastes
4	**Rohiṇī** ♉♉♉♉	♉: Face, mouth, lips, tongue, palate, gums, teeth, neck, throat, tonsils, cerebellum Cervical vertebrae, both legs	Swelling in the neck, sore throat, cold, coughing, goitre, chest pain, breast pain, apoplexy[5]	Cold fever, irregular menses, swellings in the body, pains in the left feet
5	**Mṛgaśirā** ♉♉♊♊	♉: Face, chin, cheek, throat, larynx, palate, arteries, jugular veins, tonsils. ♊: Throat, vocal cord, arms, shoulders, ears, thymus gland, upper rib cage.	Face injuries, tonsillitis, pimples, throat pain, goitre, adenoids	Catching a cold, coughing, urinary infection, reduction of sexual desires, diphtheria, constipation
6	**Ārdrā** ♊♊♊♊	♊: Throat, arms, shoulders, ears	Throat infection, asthma, bronchitis, mumps, dry cough, ear infection, eosinophilia	Diphtheria
7	**Punarvasu** ♊♊♊♋	♊: Ear, throat, shoulder blades, fingers. ♋: Lungs, chest, respiratory system, diaphragm, stomach, liver, pancreas, thorax.	Pneumonia, pleurisy, ear swelling, lungs infection, tuberculosis, pneumonia, bronchitis, beriberi, stomach upset, dyspepsia, liver trouble	Blood disorder, blood impurity

5 Unconsciousness or incapacity resulting from a cerebral haemorrhage or stroke.

#	Nakṣatra	Body parts	Localised ailments	Non-localised ailments
8	**Puṣya** ♋♋♋♋	♋: Lower portion of lungs and rib cage, junction of food pipe and stomach, mouth	Pyorrhoea, periodontitis, tuberculosis, coughing, nausea, belching, hiccups, dyspepsia, inflammation in the respiratory system, gallstones	Cancer, eczema, Jaundice
9	**Aśleṣā** ♋♋♋♋	♋: Portion of lungs, oesophagus, diaphragm, stomach, liver, pancreas, body tissues and muscles, nails	Gastric troubles, flatulence, respiratory troubles due to wind problem, indigestion, coughing, phlegm	Hyperexcited, hysteria, nervousness, kidney inflammation, weak digestive juices, oedema, knees and leg pains, oedema
10	**Maghā** ♌♌♌♌	♌: Heart, back, spine, spinal cord, spleen, dorsal region of the spine, aorta, nose	Heart attack, irregular heartbeat, palpitation, sudden shock or grief, back pain, spinal-meningitis	Fainting, mental disease, poisoning, cholera, kidney stone
11	**Pūrvāphālgunī** ♌♌♌♌	♌: Heart, spinal cord, genital	Spine-curvature issues, heart problems, issues with the heart valves, blood pressure, hypertension, hypotension	Anaemia, leg pain, swelling of ankles, hydremia[6], aneurysm[7]
12	**Uttarāphālgunī** ♌♍♍♍	♌: Spinal cord, genital ♍: Small intestine, bowel, the lower and back portion of the liver, genital	Blockage in the intestine, stomach disorders, sore throat, bowel disorder	Swelling in neck and throat, spotted fever (tickborne illness), body pains, hypertension, hypotension, fainting, madness, blood, clotting, palpitation, tumours
13	**Hastā** ♍♍♍♍	♍: Bowel, small intestine, digestive glands, digestive enzymes, the two arms.	Gastric problems, stomach wind, stomach-ache, colic, irregular bowel syndrome, stomach worms, diarrhoea, dysentery, cholera blockage in the intestine	Short of breath, hysteria, typhoid, phobias, weakness of arms and shoulders

6 An increase in blood volume because of excessive plasma or water with or without a reduction in the concentration of blood proteins.
7 An excessive localized swelling of the wall of an artery

#	Nakṣatra	Body parts	Localised ailments	Non-localised ailments
14	**Citrā** ♍♍♎♎	♍: Belly, lower abdomen ♎: Kidney, appendix, womb, groins, loins, lumber vertebrae, vasomotor system, forehead.	Urinary infection, frequent urination (bahumutra doṣa), diabetes, kidney stone, kidney infection, renal haemorrhage, Bright's disease, appendicitis, hernia	White spots, skin disease, brain fever, lumbago[8], injuries, ulcers, acute pains, itching, inflammation, worms, leg pain, headache, sunstroke
15	**Svāti** ♎♎♎♎	♎: Skin, kidney, urethra[9], bladder, genital, teeth	Diabetes, deficiency of insulin, fainting, kidney infection, urinary infection, hernia, ulcer in the urethra or bladder	Giddiness, leprosy, skin trouble, eczema, polyuria
16	**Viśākhā** ♎♎♎♏	♎: Lower abdomen, parts near the bladder, kidneys, womb/uterus, pancreatic glands, both arms. ♏: Bladder, urethra, genitals, rectum, prostate gland.	Irregular menses, womb disease, fibroid, constipation, piles, hip bone injuries or fracture, kidney stone, prostate swellings or cancer, urinary disorder	Bodily pains, throat pain, nose-bleeding, coughing, nausea, oedema
17	**Anurādhā** ♏♏♏♏	♏: Hip bone, parts of the genital, parts of the rectum, nasal bone, bones in the crotch area, Heart.	Leukorrhea, bleeding piles, Menstrual suppression, menopause, sterility, constipation, thigh-bone injury, or fracture	Nasal catarrh, phlegm, sore throat, throat congestion, shoulder pain, tumour
18	**Jyeṣṭha** ♏♏♏♏	♏: Ovary, parts of womb, colon, hips, thighs, buttocks, parts of rectum, parts of the genital, sciatic nerve, bone marrow	Bleeding piles, bowel infection, fistula10, discomforts in the genital area, leucorrhoea	Pain in arm and shoulders, tumour

8 Pain in the muscles and joints of the lower back

9 The urethra is a part of the renal system. The kidneys, ureters, and bladder are also part of this system. The renal system is responsible for producing, storing, and eliminating liquid waste in the form of urine. The urethra transports urine that is stored in the bladder out of the body.

10 A fistula is a small tunnel that connects the infected gland inside the anus to an opening on the skin around the anus. Symptoms include pain and swelling around the anus, as well as pain with bowel movements.

#	Nakṣatra	Body parts	Localised ailments	Non-localised ailments
19	**Mūla** ♐♐♐♐	♐: Lower portion of the hip bone, thigh, femur, ilium, sciatic nerve, bone marrow, and both feet	Arthritis, rheumatism, hip disease, pulmonary troubles	Hypotension, mental derangement
20	**Pūrvāṣāṛhā** ♐♐♐♐	♐: Hip, thigh, sacral vertebrae, coccygeal vertebrae, filial arteries, and veins	Arthritis, rheumatism, sciatica, swelling in the knees, gout11, hip gout	Diabetes, respiratory disease, lung cancer, surfeit[12] cold, diabetes, lungs disorder, lungs cancer, bronchus problems, blood infection
21	**Uttarāṣāṛhā** ♐♑♑♑	♐: Thigh, femur, arteries ♑: Kneecap, patella, the skin of the entire body	Arthritis, rheumatism, sciatica, eczema, skin disease, leprosy, boils, pimples, carbuncles, skin rashes, eruptions	Dull pain, digestive trouble, heart palpitation, coronary thrombosis[13], gastric problems, irregular heartbeat, heart problems, eye infections, breathing troubles
22	**Śravaṇa** ♑♑♑♑	♑: Knees, the skin of the entire body, the lymphatic system, the two ears	Rheumatism, Eczema, skin diseases, pus formation, leprosy, boils, pimples, carbuncles, skin rashes, eruptions, pleurisy[14], filariasis	Tuberculosis, poor apatite, and digestion
23	**Dhaniṣṭhā** ♑♑♒	♑: Kneecap, bony system, back ♒: Ankles, limbs (arms/legs), calf muscles, back, skin	Rheumatism, skin diseases, pleurisy, boils, pimples, carbuncles, skin rashes, eruptions, pleurisy[15], filariasis, elephantiasis	Malaria, high fever, tuberculosis, dry cough, hiccups

11 A disease in which defective metabolism of uric acid causes arthritis, especially in the smaller bones of the feet, deposition of chalkstones, and episodes of acute pain.

12 A peculiar eruption, termed surfeit, which resembles mange, is sometimes the consequence of exposure to cold after a hot sultry day. This disease is perhaps generally left after a slight inflammation of the stomach, called a surfeit, occasioned by drinking cold liquors, or eating cold vegetables, when heated with exercise.

13 Coronary thrombosis is the formation of a blood clot inside a blood vessel of the heart. This blood clot restricts blood flow within the heart. It is associated with narrowing of blood vessels after clotting.

14 Pleurisy involves inflammation of the tissue layers (pleura) lining the lungs and inner chest wall. Pleurisy is often associated with the accumulation of fluid between the two layers of pleura, known as pleural effusion.

15 Pleurisy involves inflammation of the tissue layers (pleura) lining the lungs and inner chest wall. Pleurisy is often associated with the accumulation of fluid between the two layers of pleura, known as pleural effusion.

#	Nakṣatra	Body parts	Localised ailments	Non-localised ailments
24	**Śatabhiṣā** ♒♒♒♒♒	♒: Calf muscles, both sides of the chin	Leg pain, injury or fracture, limping, amputation, gout, rheumatism	Rheumatic Heart[16], heart attack, hypertension, palpitation, insomnia, leprosy, eczema, constipation, dracunculiasis[17]
25	**Pūrvābhādra** ♒♒♒♒♓	♒: Ankle ♓: Feet, toes	Swollen feet, ankle or leg swelling, corns in feet, and sweating feet.	Irregular circulatory system, gum ulcer, hernia, Jaundice, abdominal tumour, sprue[18], intestine defect, hypotension, increase of the heart size or the liver size
26	**Uttarābhādra** ♓♓♓♓♓	♓: Upper portion of the feet, two sides of the body	Gout, foot drop19, cold feet20, foot-fracture	Hernia, oedema, lack of appetite, indigestion, constipation, flatulence, tuberculosis, rheumatic pains
27	**Revatī** ♓♓♓♓♓	♓: Feet, soles, toes, armpits	Gout in feet, foot deformities, fracture of the foot or toes	Deafness, ear infection, muscular cramps, lassitude[21], nephritis[22], abdominal disorders, swelling in intestines, intestinal ulcer

Kailāśa: Guruji, can we identify the ailment by locating the Rogakāraka in the specific Tārā?

Ācārya: Yes, you should be able to. However, due to the differences in opinion, I would suggest you experiment with both the scheme, i.e., one commencing with Aśvinī and the other with Kṛttikā.

11.227. From the Tārās, the respective affected parts can be predicted as above. Finding the Tārā near Sūrya, the lost object can also be predicted.

---

16 Rheumatic heart disease is a complication of rheumatic fever in which the heart valves are damaged. Rheumatic fever is an inflammatory disease that begins with strep throat. It can affect connective tissue throughout the body, especially in the heart, joints, brain, and skin.

17 Dracunculiasis, also called Guinea-worm disease (GWD), is an infection by the Guinea worm. A person becomes infected when they drink water that contains water fleas infected with guinea worm larvae.

18 Celiac disease, also known as celiac sprue or gluten-sensitive enteropathy, is a chronic disorder of the digestive tract that results in an inability to tolerate gliadin, the alcohol-soluble fraction of gluten. Gluten is a protein commonly found in wheat, rye, and barley.

19 Foot drop is a gait abnormality in which the dropping of the forefoot happens due to weakness, irritation or damage to the common fibular nerve including the sciatic nerve, or paralysis of the muscles in the anterior portion of the lower leg. It is usually a symptom of a greater problem and is not a disease.

20 Since metabolism controls both heartbeat and the body's temperature, an underactive thyroid could contribute to reduced circulation and colder feet. Other less common causes of cold feet include peripheral vascular disease or narrowing of the arteries due to plaques. Raynaud's phenomenon, where blood vessels spasm.

21 A state of physical or mental weariness; lack of energy.

22 Inflammation of the kidneys.

Kailāśa: What is the rule about the lost object and nearness of Sūrya's Tārā?

Ācārya: You can check this rule in the section dedicated to locating lost objects.

11.228. If a Saumya occupies Trikoṇa, Lagna or 10H, diseases will not afflict the person. On the other hand, if the Graha (Saumya) is Nīca/Śatru, the disease will afflict.

Sunidhi: Kindly elaborate on this rule of Saumyas.

Ācārya: Normally, Saumyas help with recovery, as explained in a previous śloka – that Saumyas in 6H/8H help with recovery. Normally, Saumyas give good health in Udaya, 10H or Trikoṇa. However, if a Saumya is afflicted in a Nīca/Śatru Rāśi, then they also cause disease depending on their Kārakatvas (body part, system, constituent ruled). Weak/afflicted Saumya in a Trika is equally troublesome.

12. ON DEATH

Ācārya: Let us discuss the principles of death.

Sunidhi: Sure, Guruji! Looking forward to your elaborations.

12.229. Wise men can predict the time of death as in the following.

Ācārya: Let us first examine the two states of Chatra, Ucca and Nīca.

12.230. If Āruṛha or Udaya becomes Chatra and hence declared to be in Ucca, the person concerned about when the Praśna is made will not certainly die.

Sunidhi: Does Chatra has Ucca/Nīca Rāśi?

Ācārya: Yes, it does! When Chatra is in Udaya/Āruṛha Rāśi, it is considered Ucca. Given below are the conditions of Nīca Chatra.

12.231. Tulā Chatra for Dhanu Udaya/Āruṛha is considered Nīca, and hence life is endangered. One cannot be certain of death here, but death is certain if Dhanu is the Chatra for Tulā (Udaya/Āruṛha). Likewise, if Mithuna is the Chatra for Meṣa (Udaya/Āruṛha), it is considered Nīca, and hence life is endangered. Death is certain in the reverse case Meṣa Chatra for Mithuna (Udaya/Āruṛha).

12.232. Kanyā Chatra for Karka (Udaya/Āruṛha) is considered Nīca; hence life is endangered. Instead, death is certain in Karka Chatra for Kanyā Āruṛha/Udaya. Mīna Chatra for Makara (Udaya/Āruṛha) is considered Nīca, and hence life is endangered. Instead, death is certain for Makara Chatra for Mīna (Udaya/Āruṛha). The Nīca Chatra indicates danger to life and no cure for the disease. But the Mṛtyu Chatra foretells certain death.

Table 27

#	Udaya/Āruṛha	Chatra	Result
1	**Dhanu**	Tulā	Danger
2	***Tulā***	*Dhanu*	*Death*
3	**Meṣa**	Mithuna	Danger
4	***Mithuna***	*Meṣa*	*Death*

#	Udaya/Āruṛha	Chatra	Result
5	**Karka**	Kanyā	Danger
6	***Kanyā***	*Karka*	*Death*
7	**Makara**	Mīna	Danger
8	***Mīna***	*Makara*	*Death*

Sunidhi: What is the principle behind it, Guruji?

Ācārya: This applies to Cara and Dvisvabhāva Rāśis, and the 4 Sthirarāśis are excepted.

When Udaya/Āruṛha is in a Cararāśi, and Chatra is in their 3rd Rāśi (a Ubhayarāśi), the person's life is endangered. The is a life threat, but death is doubtful. This is Chatra's Nīcarāśi.

On the other hand, if Udaya/Āruṛha is in a Dvisvarāśi and Chatra is in their 11th Rāśi (a Cararāśi), death is certain.

Sunidhi: Guruji, now it makes sense.

Ācārya: Now, the author delineates the cause of death.

12.233. If at Praśna, Sūrya is strong, death by fire is likely; if Śani is strong, death by hunger; if Candra is strong, death by water; and if Śukra is strong, death by freezing.

Sunidhi: How to know the source of death?

Ācārya: Normally, we should examine the source from the Grahas in 8H or those aspecting it. If there is no Graha in or aspecting 8H, we must consider 8L. If more than one Grahas are involved, consider the strongest among them as the Mṛtyukāraka. The Mṛtyukāraka indicates the cause of death in a Kuṇḍalī.

Sunidhi: Got it Guruji.

12.234. If Budha is strong at Praśna, death may occur by snow and storm; if Maṅgala is strong, death may be by weapons; if Rāhu is strong, death may be by poisoning; and if Guru is strong, death may be by some disease in the stomach.

Ācārya: Now, the Grahas indicating the nature of death are as follows:

(1) Sūrya: fire

(2) Candra: water

(3) Maṅgala: weapons

(4) Budha: snow or storm

(5) Guru: stomach ailments

(6) Śukra: freezing

(7) Śani: hunger

(8) Rāhu: poisoning

Sunidhi: Why does Budha indicate snow or storm?

Ācārya: Budha is Pṛthvītattva, and therefore, can indicate a tornado, which is caused by soil picked up by whirling wind. But there must be some airy element (Śani) also involved. Else, Budha also indicates landslide.

These are only some indications; the topic of death is vast.

Sunidhi: Kindly share more about it, Guruji!

Ācārya: Let us examine the principles laid down by the author first. We can examine the other principles later.

12.235-236. By finding Krūras in 6H, 8H or 7H from Candra, the nature of the death of the diseased person must be predicted. If, as stated above, Āruṛha happens to be the house of death (8H) and from there in 8H is Candra dṛṣṭied by Krūras, death to the diseased one must be told by the wise.

Ācārya: Normally, the nature of death is seen from 8H and 3H (8th from 8H), but the author states that e must examine the Krūras in 6H, 8H or 7H from Candra. This must be another principle besides the commonly used one.

Sunidhi: Does that mean that the indications of death from the Grahas mentioned above must be seen from 6H, 7H, and 8H?

Ācārya: We should check it from 8H and 3H first and then from 6H and 7H. If we were to examine only Krūras in 6H, 7H and 8H, then the author would not have spelt out Budha, Śukra and Guru. That means even the Saumyas can cause death if mandated to (by their placement, aspect or ownership of 8H). I will share more principles later.

Now the author gives some indications for timing death.

Sunidhi: What are they, Guruji?

12.237. If Sūrya is in 3H from Udaya, or a Krūra is in 10H, death in 10 days is likely. If Śukra/Guru is in 3H from Udaya, the death of the diseased person in 7 days must be predicted.

Ācārya: These are only a few indications. There are more!

12.238. If a Krūra is in Udaya/4H/8H, death in 8 days is likely. If a Krūra is in 2H from Udaya, death in 14 days is likely.

12.239. If a Krūra is in 10H, death in 3 days must be predicted. If a Krūra is in 7H from Udaya, death in 10 days is likely. Along with this, one must reckon the days and months given for various Grahas and give the prediction accordingly.

Ācārya: These are some indications of days in the next few days.

3 days: a Krūra in 10H

7 days: Śukra/Guru in 3H

8 days: a Krūra in 1H/4H/8H

10 days: a Krūra in 7H

10 days: Sūrya in 3H

14 days: a Krūra in 2H

Sunidhi: Dhanyavād, Guruji! Kindly tell us more about the cause of death!

Ācārya: Alright! Let me narrate the principles from Bṛhatparāśara!

44.25: Sūrya in 3H: legal punishments.

44.26: Candra in 3H: tuberculosis

44.27: Maṅgala in 3H: wounds, weapons, fire and thirst

44.28: Śani/Rāhu in 3H: poison, water, fire, fall from heights, or confinement.

44.29: Candra + Gulika in 3H: insects, or leprosy

44.30: Budha in 3H: fever

44.30: Guru in 3H: swelling, or tumours.

44.31: Śukra in 3H: Urinary diseases.

44.31: Many Grahas in or aspecting 3H: death through many diseases.

44.32: Saumyas in 3H: death in an auspicious place (like a shrine)

44.32: Krūras in 3H: death in a sinful place.

44.32: Both Saumyas and Krūras in 3H: mixed results about the place of death.

44.33: Guru/Śukra in 3H: Consciousness prevail at death. Other Grahas in 3H - unconsciousness before death.

44.34: 3H in Cara, Sthira or Dvisva Rāśi: death in a foreign place, one's house, or on the way.

44.35: Sūrya in 8H: death through fire.

44.35: Candra in 8H: death through water.

44.35: Maṅgala in 8H: death through weapons.

44.35: Budha in 8H: death through fever.

44.36: Guru in 8H: death through sickness.

44.36: Śukra in 8H: death through hunger.

44.36: Śani in 8H: death through thirst.

44.37. Saumyayutidṛṣṭi on 8H and 9L with a Saumya: death in a shrine. Krūrayutidṛṣṭi on 8H and 9L with a Krūra: death in a place other than a shrine.

Kailāśa: What happens to the body after life leaves it?

Ācārya: The body disintegrates into the Pañca Mahābhūta. There are several methods of disposing of the body according to the Śāstras. Let us examine them.

44.38. 8H in Agni Dreṣkāṇa: the body is burnt in fire (Agnidāha).

44.38. 8H in Jala Dreṣkāṇa: the body will be offered to water (a river)

44.39: 8H in a Miśra Dreṣkāṇa: the body is dried up (mummification or buried inside the earth).

44.39: 8H in Sarpa Dreṣkāṇa: animals, crows, eat the body away.

Kailāśa: Dhanyavād Guruji, I didn't know there were so many ways to dispose of dead bodies.

Ācārya: Five kinds are due to 5 Mahābhūtas. Agni (Sūrya/Maṅgala) represent Agnidāha; Pṛthvī (Budha) denotes mummification or burial; Vāyu (Śani/Rāhu) denotes leaving the body in the air to be eaten by animals and birds, and Jala (Śukra/Candra) denotes offering the body to water.

Kailāśa: What is the 5th kind, Guruji?

Ācārya: The 5th kind is of Ākāśabhūta, which is exceedingly rare.

Kailāśa: What is it, Guruji?

Ācārya: Some highly exalted devotees merge into the divine consciousness spontaneously, and their physical bodies disappear (disintegrate into Pañca Mahābhūta spontaneously). They do not leave a trace of their body to be cremated or buried.

Kailāśa: How is it possible, Guruji?

Ācārya: Miracles do happen! But they are rare!

Now, what happened to Yudhiṣṭhira? Where did he leave his body?

Did you hear the legend of Mīrābāi?

Sunidhi: Guruji, this is so interesting. Kindly share!

Ācārya: On the auspicious occasion of Kṛṣṇa Janmashtami (in 1547), Mīrābāi was immersed in an ecstatic state as she sang and danced with unparalleled devotion. In her rapture, she moved gracefully towards the sacred Mūrti of Bhagavan Śrī Kṛṣṇa, but amidst her devotion, she stumbled and fell gently at the feet of the adorned Mūrti, surrounded by a bed of fragrant flowers. In a whisper, she expressed her conviction that Kṛṣṇa was calling her, and she joyously responded, "I am coming."

In a breathtaking turn of events, a sudden bolt of lightning illuminated the surroundings, and the colossal doors of the sanctum sanctorum majestically closed, enveloping the divine presence within. The ambience was charged with an aura of mysticism and reverence.

Minutes later, as the doors opened again, the devotees were astonished to find Mīrābāi absent from the mortal realm. Her saree had mysteriously merged with the divine Mūrti of Śrī Kṛṣṇa. Amidst the divine silence, the ethereal sound of Mīrābāi's soulful singing harmonized with the celestial melody of Kṛṣṇa's divine flute.

Mīrābāi had attained Mokṣa, liberation from the cycle of birth and death – through her unwavering love and devotion to Śrī Kṛṣṇa. Her divine union with the Devatā is a testament to the transcendental power of true Bhaktiyoga.

Devotees believe that Mīrābāi's earthly journey concluded within the renowned Dwarka Mandir, where she merged her being with the sacred Mūrti of Śrī Kṛṣṇa. However, some alternate accounts suggest that she attained oneness with the divine Devatā at a Mūrti in the sacred town of Vṛndāvana.

Sunidhi: Guruji, this is so spiritually enlightening.

Ācārya: Indeed, it is.

Kailāśa: Guruji, are there other accounts of such miracles?

Ācārya: Another such account is the merging of Śrī Caitanya Mahāprabhu into the Mūrti of Śrī Jagannatha.

This is mentioned in Śrī Caitanya Maṅgala, the authorised biography of Caitanya Mahāprabhu. In Śeṣa Khanda, Chapter four, Sri Locana Daśā Thākura states

On the auspicious day of Āṣāṛhā Saptami, a Ravivāra afternoon during the third Prahara (12:00-3:00), a profound event unfolded at the revered Gundicha Mandir, where Lord Caitanya Mahāprabhu graced the scene.

Surrounded by his close associates like Srivasa Paṇḍita, Mukunda Dutta, Śrī Govinda, Kāśi Miśra, and others, Lord Caitanya Mahāprabhu entered the sanctum of Śrī Jagannātha with an overwhelming sense of love and devotion. He embraced the divine Mūrti tightly and, in an instant, vanished from their sight, leaving the witnesses astounded.

As Mahāprabhu entered the Mandir, the doors gracefully closed behind him. The passing time without his return filled his devoted companions with anxiety and concern. Seeking a way to ascertain the events inside the sanctum, they approached the Brāhmaṇa Paṇḍā of Gundicha Mandir and earnestly requested him to open the Mandir doors.

After a moment of anticipation, the Paṇḍā disclosed a revelation that stirred their hearts. He conveyed, "The Lord is not physically present within the confines of Mandir, but I had the profound privilege of witnessing an extraordinary union. I beheld Gaura, Lord Caitanya, in a divine embrace with Prabhu, Śrī Jagannātha. This revelation I share with certainty."

Meanwhile, in the sacred land of Nilācala, Puri, the King of Orissa, Śrī Prataprudra, became aware of the heart-rending cries of the Śrī Śrī's devotees. The news deeply affected him and his entire family, causing them to lose consciousness in sorrowful empathy for the revered Mahāprabhu and his mysterious communion with Śrī Jagannātha.

This extraordinary incident left an indelible mark on the hearts of all who witnessed or heard of it, and it served as a testament to the profound love and divine connection between Śrī Caitanya Mahāprabhu and Śrī Jagannātha. The divine play of the Supreme brought solace to the devoted souls and continued to inspire countless seekers on their spiritual journey through time.

Kailāśa: What an extraordinary legend, Guruji!

Ācārya: Indeed, that is the power of Bhakti!

Another legend is of Sant Kabir, who received his spiritual initiation from Sant Ramanand.

One of the cherished legends that resonates deeply with Kabir's legacy revolves around his funeral. After Kabir's passing, his devoted disciples found themselves in a gentle dispute. The Muslim disciples sought to claim his body for burial, adhering to their religious customs. In contrast, the Hindu disciples wished to perform the sacred act of cremation per their beliefs.

In this moment of uncertainty, a miraculous event unfolded. Though no longer in the mortal realm, Kabir graced his disciples with his divine presence. He appeared to them and offered a solution to their dilemma. "Lift the burial shroud," he softly instructed.

As the disciples gently lifted the burial shroud that enveloped Kabir's form, a surprise awaited them. Instead of the mortal remains they had expected, they discovered a bed of fragrant flowers emanating an ethereal aura that filled the air.

The disciples shared the blessed flowers in a spirit of unity and reverence. The Muslim disciples chose to bury the flowers, honouring the essence of Kabir's teachings within their sacred burial grounds. At the same time, the Hindu disciples reverently embraced the sacred flowers and committed them to the holy flames of cremation, symbolizing their profound connection to Kabir and his teachings.

This divine event left a lasting impression on Kabir's disciples, reminding them of the universality and transcendence of his spiritual teachings. It showcased the harmony and love that underlined Kabir's life and work, transcending the boundaries of religion and embracing the essence of humanity. The legend of Kabir's funeral continues to inspire and unite people from diverse backgrounds, fostering a sense of unity and respect for all spiritual paths.

Kailāśa: Guruji, why are we discussing Sant Kabir? Is he not of Muslim descent?

Ācārya: So, what? Can't a Muslim become an enlightened being?

Kailāśa: Guruji, I am unsure about it. Our Śāstras are so different from theirs!

Ācārya: One's path is determined by the path adhered to by the person. Think about the Janma, Mṛtyu and reincarnation. Depending on the previous birth Karmas, a person can be born into different religions.

Sometimes, a Hindu saint can be born into a Muslim family and vice-versa. Everything that manifests is based on the past life of Karmas and the quality of the time (Kāla and Yuga). Therefore, saints are above their birth religion. What matters is the universality of their messages.

Look at some of his Doha. You decide what you want to believe. I do not wish to influence someone's understanding.

Here are a few of his Dohas dedicated to Śrī Rāma. These Dohās by Sant Kabir beautifully reflect his devotion to Lord Rāma.

राम नाम जपो जीवन की चाँदनी। पारस पत्थर मोक्ष की सिंदुरि लेप जानी॥

Chant the name of Śrī Rāma, it's the moonlight of life. It turns the philosopher's stone into the sacred vermilion of liberation.

राम नाम बिना जग बैरी। राम नाम बिना कोई न सहारी॥

Without the name of Śrī Rāma, the world becomes an enemy. Without the name of Rāma, there is no true companion.

बिनु राम नाम बिना रहे नूर। तेतीस करोड़ पंडित कौर॥

Without the name of Śrī Rāma, there is no light. Even thirty-three million scholars remain ignorant.

राम नाम जप की दूरी। काम विकार मिटे नूरी॥

Chant the name of Śrī Rāma as your constant companion. It dispels the allure of desire and brings divine illumination.

Sunidhi: Guruji, these are so enlightening. Dhanyavād for sharing!

Kailāśa: Guruji! This all makes sense now. I fell into the trap of judging someone based on their birth. We must form our opinion about someone from one's actions and teachings.

Ācārya: Sanātana Dharma is a path. One can be born to a parent on this path, or someone can acquire this path through action. It is not to judge someone merely based on their birth. We must assess their contribution to Dharma.

Jayanta: Guruji, the discussion has been enlightening.

Kailāśa: Guruji, you mentioned 8H in different Dreṣkāṇas, viz., Saumya, Krūra, Miśra and Sarpa. Kindly enlighten me about them.

Ācārya: There are 36 Dreṣkāṇas, and each of them has specific forms. That is called Dreṣkāṇa Svarūpa.

Sunidhi: Guruji, what are they?

Ācārya: Here are the forms (Svarūpa) of the 36 Dreṣkāṇas. I have also provided their special designations, such as Saumya, Krūra, Jala, Āyudha, Catuṣpada etc. Also given are the diseases and death caused by them when they become the 22nd Dreṣkāṇa.

Meṣa1: A *man* with a white cloth around his waist, dark-complexioned, intent on protecting one who is seeking his refuse, dreadful look, red eyes, *axe uplifted* in his hand. ***Krūra, Āyudha, Catuṣpāda, death through spleen or gallbladder ailments, poisoning, snakes.***

Meṣa2: A *woman* wearing red coloured cloth, intent on feating and adorning herself with ornaments, potbellied, horse-faced, thirsty and one-legged. ***Saumya, Catuṣpāda, death through watery ailments, insects, forest.***

Meṣa3: A *man* with wicked nature, skilled in fine arts, tawny hue complexion, intent on working, his resolve is broken in the end, a staff uplifted in his hand, wearing a red coloured cloth, furious. ***Miśra, Āyudha, death through drowning.***

Vṛṣabha1: A *woman* with torn ringlets, potbelly, burnt cloth, thirsty, fond of food and ornaments. ***Miśra, Saumya, Jala, death through animals like horse, camel, ass.***

Vṛṣabha2: A man possessing knowledge of lands, grains, houses, cows, arts, ploughing and carts, hungry, sheep-faced, dirty clothes and shoulders like the hump of an ox. ***Saumya, Catuṣpada, death through fire, murder, bile ailments, rheumatism***

Vṛṣabha3: A *man* with a body like that of an elephant, white teeth, legs like that of a Śarabha, yellowish colour, and clever in capturing sheep and deer. ***Jala, Catuṣpada, death through fall from vehicles, battle, weapons, in the sea.***

Mithuna1: A *woman*, fond of needlework, beautiful, fond of adorning ornaments, issueless, lifted hands and in menses. ***Saumya, Catuṣpada, death through lung infections, cough.***

Mithuna2: A man living in a garden, adorned in armour, with a bow, warlike, armed with weapons, face like that of Garuṛa, fond of play, children, ornamentation and wealth. ***Miśra, Āyudha/Pakṣi, death through poison, typhoid, animals.***

Mithuna3: A *man* adorned, decked with gems, armoured with a quiver and bow, skilled in dancing, drumming and arts, and poet. ***Jala, Āyudha, death through vehicles, rheumatism, animals.***

Karka1: A *man*, holding fruit, roots and leaves, elephant-bodied, residing on sandal trees in the forest, legs like that of Śarabha and horse-necked. ***Jala, Catuṣpada, Kolamukha, death through water animals, enemies, bad dreams, drinks.***

Karka2: A *woman* worshipped on the head by lotus flowers, with serpents, full-blown youthfulness, living in forests on the branch of palāśa and crying. ***Krūra, Sarpa, death through lightning, poison, fire, assault.***

Karka3: A *man* covered with serpents, flat-faced, and crossing the ocean in a boat in search of his wife's jewels. ***Miśra, Sarpa, death through venereal disease, tumour, overheat.***

Siṅha1: A man resembling a vulture and a jackal on the salmali (cotton) tree with a dog, dressed in dirty garments, leaving father and mother and crying (shouting). ***Krūra, Āyudha, Catuṣpada, Pakṣi, death through water, drowning, poison, disease in feet.***

Siṅha2: A man resembling a horse's body with white garlands on the head, wearing krishnajina and kambalam, fierce as a lion with a bow in hand and bent nose. ***Miśra, Āyudha, death through lungs trouble, Pleurisy, oedema, forest.***

Siṅha3: A man with a bear's face acts like a monkey, with long-bearded and curved ringlets, holding a stick, fruit and flesh. ***Krūra, Āyudha, Catuṣpada, Gridhramukha (?), death through surgery, weapons, fall, assault.***

Kanyā1: A woman with a pot full of flowers, covering her body with dirty garments, fond of money and clothes, and going to the home of the preceptor. ***Saumya, Pakṣi, death through head diseases, windy complaints, rheumatism.***

Kanyā2: A man with a pen in hand, dark-complexioned, the head tied around a cloth, counting gains and expenditure, body covered with dense hair and holding a big bow. ***Jala, Pakṣi, death through fall from elevated places, poisonous creatures, forest.***

Kanyā3: A woman, yellowish, covered by a great white silk cloth, tall, holding a pot and spoon, and going to a Mandir with great sanctity. ***Saumya, Pakṣi death through drowning, explosions, animals or by a man or a woman.***

Tulā1: A man seated in a shop in the middle of the road, holding balances, clever in weighing and measuring with a small scale for weighing gold, and diamonds, thinking of his money and the prices of the articles in his shop. ***Saumya, Pakṣi, death through animals, women, fall from elevated places.***

Tulā2: A man with a *vulture's face*, hungry and thirsty, holding a pot ready to fall and thinking of his wife and children. ***Miśra, Pakṣi, Gridhramukha, death through stomach troubles, Foods.***

Tulā3: A *man* decked with gems, wearing a golden quiver and armour and frightening animals in the wilderness, *resembling a monkey* and holding in his hand fruit and flesh. ***Krūra, Catuṣpada, death through snakes, cruel or water animals.***

Vṛścika1: A beautiful *woman* without her clothes and ornaments, coming from the middle of a great ocean to the shore, dislocated from her original place, snakes coiled around her legs. ***Krūra, Sarpa, death through weapons, poison, or drinks given by a woman or man.***

Vṛścika2: A *woman* fond of home and happiness for her husband's sake and *covered with serpents* with a body resembling a tortoise and a pot, i.e. potbellied. ***Krūra, Sarpa, Pakṣi, death through fat, obesity, prostrate ailments, hip fracture.***

Vṛścika3: A man like a lion with a broad flat face, resembling a *tortoise*, frightening dogs, deer, *boars* and jackals, protecting localities covered with sandalwood trees. ***Miśra, Catuṣpada, Kolāmukha (?), death through bones ailments, stones, and mines.***

Dhanu1: A *man* with a human face and a horse's body with a bow in hand residing in a hermitage, protecting sacrificial articles and Maharṣis. ***Miśra, Pakṣi, death through venereal diseases, rectal, colon ailments.***

Dhanu2: A beautiful *woman*, golden-coloured, picking up gems from the ocean and sitting in a bhadrāsana fashion. ***Saumya, Ratna Bhandār, death through weapons, knife, rheumatism, poison.***

Dhanu3: A man with a long beard, gold-complexioned, holding a stick, sitting in a splendid posture and keeping silks and deer skins. ***Saumya, Āyudha, death through water animals, water, abdominal troubles.***

Makara1: A *man* covered with much hair, teeth like those of a crocodile, *a body like that of a pig*, keeping yokes, nets and bandages, and with a cruel face. ***Krūra, Catuṣpada, Pakṣi, Nigaḍa, Kolāmukha, death through wild animals, scorpion bites, and water creatures.***

Makara2: A *woman* skilled in arts, broad eyes like lotus petals, greenish-dark, searching all kinds of articles and wearing iron ear ornaments. ***Saumya, Catuṣpada, death through fire, Weapon, fever, evil spirits.***

Makara3: A *man* with a body like kinaras, with a quiver, arrows and bow, and bearing a pot on the shoulder decked with gems. ***Miśra, Catuṣpada, death through shot by revolver etc., fever, thieves, diseases caused by women***

Kumbha1: A *man* with a mind disturbed by oils, wines, water and food being brought to him, with a Kambala, silk cloth and deerskin and a face resembling a vulture. ***Krūra, Āyudha, death through stomach disorder, venereal diseases, water, forest.***

Kumbha2: A *woman*, covered with a dirty cloth in a forest, bearing pots on her head and dragging metals in a burnt cart loaded with cotton trees. ***Saumya, Āyudha, death through generative organs, diseases caused by women, mental disease.***

Kumbha3: A dark *man* with ears covered with long hair, wearing a crown and wandering with pots filled with iron, skin, leaves, gum and fruit. ***Saumya, Āyudha, Gridhramukha (?), death through animals, infection, Head diseases.***

Mīna1: A *man* decked with ornaments, holding in his hand sacrificial vessels, pearls, conch shells and gems, and crossing the ocean in a boat in search of jewels for his wife. ***Jala, Āyudha, death through acidity, stomach disorder, venereal disease.***

Mīna2: A *woman* with a colour more beautiful than that of Campaka flower, surrounded by her attendants, and sailing in a boat decked with long flags searching for the ocean's coast. ***Jala, Āyudha, death through oedema, water, travelling, vehicles.***

Mīna3: A *man* crying in a pit in a forest, naked, his body covered with serpents, and his mind distracted by thieves and fire. ***Krūra, Sarpa, death through poison, stomach worms, amoebiasis, stomach disorders.***

Kailāśa: Guruji, what is the use of knowing the Dreṣkāṇa Svarūpa?

Ācārya: They are of several uses. The features describe the person who has stolen something in a Naṣṭa Praśna. But they also resemble people appearing in our lives from different Dreṣkāṇas. They also indicate a person who may become the cause of someone's death.

Kailāśa: How are the Dreṣkāṇa classified into Krūra, Saumya, Miśra and Jala?

Ācārya: The Dreṣkāṇa of the Krūra is called Agni or Krūra Dreṣkāṇa. The Dreṣkāṇa of the Saumyas is called Jala Dreṣkāṇa. The Dreṣkāṇas of both Saumya and Krūra or those aspected by both Saumya and Krūra, are called Mixed Dreṣkāṇas. And the Dreṣkāṇa falling in 8H is called the Mṛtyu Dreṣkāṇa. Mṛtyu Dreṣkāṇa is also called Khara Dreṣkāṇa. Khara is the Sanskrit word for donkey and means heavy toil.

Kailāśa: How are the Dreṣkāṇa classified as Sarpa etc.?

Ācārya: They are classified based on the Svarūpa. For instance, the Dreṣkāṇa with serpents appearing in them, coiling the leg etc., are called Sarpa Dreṣkāṇa. They are poisonous. The following table gives several such classifications.

Table 28

#	Designations	Dreṣkāṇa
1	**Sarpa[23] (5)**	Karka 2, Karka 3, Vṛścika 1, Vṛścika 2, Mīna 3
2	**Nigaḻa (1)**	Makara 1. According to Jātakapārijāta it is Vṛścika 2. Dr. BV Raman also supports Makara 1.
3	**Āyudha[24] (4)**	Mithuna 3, Dhanu 1, Dhanu 3, Makara 3
4	**Pakṣi[25] (4)**	Mithuna 2, Siṅha 1, Tulā 2, Kumbha 1
5	**Dahana/ Krūra (11)**	Meṣa 1, Karka 2, Siṅha 1, Siṅha 3, Tulā 3, Vṛścika 1, Vṛścika 2, Vṛścika 3, Makara 1, Kumbha 1, Mīna 3
6	**Jala (6)**	Vṛṣabha 3, Mithuna 3, Karka 1, Kanyā 2, Mīna 1, Mīna 2
7	**Saumya (11)**	Mithuna 1, Kanyā 1, Tulā 1, Meṣa 2, Vṛṣabha 2, Dhanu 2, Makara 2, Kumbha 2, Kanyā 3, Dhanu 3, Kumbha 3
8	**Miśra (8)**	Vṛṣabha 1, Dhanu 1, Mithuna 2, Siṅha 2, Tulā 2, Meṣa 3, Karka 3, Makara 3

According to Maharṣi Parāśara (44.40), the 2nd and 3rd Dreṣkāṇa in Karka, the 1st in Vṛścika and the 3rd in Mīna are designated as serpent Dreṣkāṇas.

Jayanta: Guruji, since you touched upon the Dreṣkāṇas, kindly also explain how to see from where one has descended.

Ācārya: Let us see the śloka from Bṛhatparāśara.

44.41-42. O excellent of Brāhmaṇas, the stronger of the two Prakāśa Grahas, Sūrya and Candra, occupying a Dreṣkāṇa of Guru, denotes the descent from Devaloka. If the stronger one occupies the Dreṣkāṇa of Śukra/Candra, the descent is from the Pitṛloka. If the stronger one is in the Dreṣkāṇa of Sūrya/ Maṅgala, the descent is from the Yamaloka (world of the mortals), and if in Dreṣkāṇa of Budha/Śani, the descent is the Narkaloka.

Kailāśa: Guruji, kindly explain further.

Ācārya: This is a highly secretive śloka, and less is known about its usage. However, it classifies the spiritual planes (lokas) into four, (1) Devaloka, (2) Pitṛloka, (3) Manuṣyaloka or Martyaloka, and (4) Narkaloka.

The lokas are associated with Bhūtas. Devaloka = Ākāśa, Pitṛloka = Jala, Martyaloka = Agni and Narkaloka = Pṛthvī/Vāyu.

Kailāśa: So, how can a person find the Lokas of descent?

Ācārya: The first step is to find the stronger of Sūrya and Candra. Then find the Rāśi held by the stronger one in Dreṣkāṇa. You read the Loka from the Dreṣkāṇa Lord of the stronger Prakāśagraha.

Kailāśa: How to find the stronger of Sūrya and Candra?

Ācārya: You can use some thumb rules

(1) The Rāśi with more Grahas is stronger

(2) The Rāśi with a Uccagraha is stronger

[23] According to Balabhadra Karka 1-2, Vṛścika 1-2, and Mīna 3. According to Jātakapārijāta, all the 3 Dreṣkāṇa of Karka, Vṛścika and Mīna. According to Dr. BV Raman's How to Judge a Horoscope vol. 2, Vṛścika 1, Karka 3 and Mīna 3.

[24] According to Dr. BV Raman, Dhanu 1, Meṣa 1, Kanyā 2, Mithuna 2, Meṣa 3, Mithuna 3, Siṅha 3, Tulā 3, Dhanu 3.

[25] According to Dr. Raman, they are Siṅha 1, Kumbha 1, Tulā 2 and Vṛṣabha 3.

(3) The Rāśi, whose lord is with higher Ṣaḍbala, is stronger

(4) The Rāśi, whose lord is in a different oddity, is stronger

However, there are some differences in opinion among the scholars. Some scholars believe that instead of considering the stronger between Sūrya and Candra, we must consider the Rāśyeśa of the stronger Prakāśagraha.

Also, the Dreṣkāṇa we must be used here may not be the regular Parāśarī but another one, such as Jagannātha Dreṣkāṇa. The Parāśarī Dreṣkāṇa is mainly used for siblings, whereas Jagannātha Dreṣkāṇa is used for Karmaphala. There is another Dreṣkāṇa called Somanātha Dreṣkāṇa, that is used for sexuality.

In determining the past life abode, we should also examine the Dreṣkāṇa held by the Dreṣkāṇeśa of stronger Prakāśagraha. Suppose in a Kuṇḍalī, Sūrya is stronger and is in Meṣa Dreṣkāṇa (D3J); then the Loka can correspond to the Dreṣkāṇa (D3J) held by Maṅgala. If Maṅgala is in Guru's Dreṣkāṇa, the person may have descended from Devaloka.

There is much speculation in this area, and one must not use this until clear guidance is available on using this principle.

Kailāśa: What do you advise Guruji here?

Ācārya: I have already mentioned that. But besides that, you should also examine the dignity, such as the Ucca/Nīca status of the strongest Prakāśagraha in this Kuṇḍalī. Therefore, if Sūrya is the strongest and is in Meṣa Dreṣkāṇa (D3J), the person may have descended from Devaloka. If Sūrya is Nīca, he may have descended from Narkaloka. I also believe that Vargottama Graha in this Varga can indicate descent from higher Lokas.

Nevertheless, experiment with these principles.

Kailāśa: Sure, Guruji!

Jayanta: Guruji, also explain where the soul goes after death.

Ācārya: The principles are laid down by Maharṣi Parāśara, but one should use them in Puṇyacakra, i.e., the Kuṇḍalī created at the death moment. The principle is as follows:

44.43-45. According to the following Grahas in 12H, 7H, 6H, or 8H, the native will attain one of the different worlds after death: Guru Svargaloka, Candra/Śukra Pitṛloka, Maṅgala/Sūrya: Martyaloka, Budha/Śani: Narkaloka. If the said Bhavas are not occupied, the native will go to the world, indicated by the stronger of the Dreṣkāṇa Lords, related to 6H and 8H. The relative Graha's Ucca etc., will denote the high, medium and low status the native will obtain in the said world.

Jayanta: The Loka classification is the same as the previous śloka in which four Lokas exist. Instead of Devaloka, here Guru is assigned Svargaloka. They are essentially the same.

Kailāśa: Guruji, aren't there 7 Lokas and 7 Talas? Can't we see which among them the soul went?

Ācārya: We can. But let us review them in the book I have covered, the Puṇyacakra. But, since we have already examined the Yogas, please also check the following Yogas from Bṛhajjātaka.

25.14: Bṛhaspati, Candra/Śukra, Sūrya/Maṅgala, and Śani/Budha bring people from Devaloka, Pitṛloka, Tiryāgaloka (Martyaloka) and Narkaloka, respectively. According to the position of the Lord of the Dreṣkāṇa occupied by the more powerful between Sūrya and Candra, we should predict the high, middle or low state of the man in his previous birth.

25.15: The Dreṣkāṇeśa of 6H or 8H or the Graha in 7H indicates the state of man's future existence after death (in which Loka). If Bṛhaspati is Ucca and occupies 6H, 8H or a Kendra, the person attains Mokṣa. The same occurs when Lagna is in Mīna Rāśi, and a Śubha Navāñśa and Guru is the most powerful among the Grahas (others are powerless).

Ācārya: The śloka 25.15 is mostly applicable to Puṇyacakra. In Praśna also, this is applicable.

Kailāśa: Noted Guruji. Dhanyavād, for the clear explanations on the topic of death!

13. ON HEAVENLY ABODE

Kailāśa: Guruji, the author, next talks about the heavenly abode. How is this Praśna to be used?

Ācārya: It can help answer the Praśna, where is the departed soul of "this" person who has recently died. Or, where is the departed soul of this person (could be my father, my mother etc.)

13.240. If at Praśna, a Graha is in Uccarāśi, the dead man will attain the heavenly abode. If it is in a Śatrurāśi, the dead man will be reborn as an animal. If it is in a Nīcarāśi, he will go to hell. If it is in a Mitrarāśi, he will be reborn in a friend's house. If it is in a Svarāśi, he will be reborn among his family or relatives.

ग्रहोच्च स्वर्गमायाति रिपौ मृगकुले भवः । नीचे नरकमायाति मित्रे मित्रकुलोद्भव ॥१॥ स्वक्षेत्रे स्वजने जन्म मित्रं ज्ञात्वा वदेत् सुधीः। मृत्यु के समय ग्रहों के उच्च के रहने मृत प्राणी को पर स्वर्ग होता है शत्रु स्थान में रहने पर पशुयोनि में जन्म मित्र गृह में रहने पर मित्र कुल में जन्म और स्वक्षेत्र में रहने पर स्वजनों में जन्म बताना चाहिये ।

Sunidhi: Guruji, what happens when we die? Where does the soul go?

Ācārya: The soul never dies. It can either merge into Parabrahma from which it arose or stay independent till eternity. Based on one's Karma, one attains different states of existence after leaving one's mortal frame.

In Praśnaśāstra 1, I explained the different kinds of Mokṣa, which are Sarsti, Sarupya, Samipya, Salokya, and Sayuja. In Mokṣa, either one merge with Parabrahma (Sayuja) or remain close to one's Iṣṭadevatā (Samipya) or reside in the Loka of the Iṣṭadevatā, such as Brahmaloka, Vaikuntha, Śivaloka etc. (Salokya).

If one does not attain Mokṣa, one is born into Martyaloka (Pṛthvī), in which one must die to get released into one's true form (as Ātmā). When Ātmā takes on one mortal frame, one appears as a plant, animal, human etc. In the mortal frame, one experiences the effects of past Karma. One must shed their mortal frame to attain the Ātmā form.

Sunidhi: Does the Ātmā in a plant, animal and human are the same?

Ācārya: They are all Ātmā, and there is no difference between them. They are called Yonis. Depending on one's Karma, one is born into different Yonis.

Kailāśa: Guruji, isn't the female private part called Yoni?

Ācārya: Yes, that is because she gives birth to a child, and one's Yoni (species) depends on its mother. The generic meaning of Yoni is species.

Kailāśa: Guruji, tell us more about the Yonis.

Ācārya: According to the Sanātana Śāstras, the plant and animal kingdom are classified into 84 lakhs Yonis, and Manuṣya is merely one among them.

Śrīmad Bhagavadgītā states that a Jīvātmā (living soul) incarnates into one of these 84 lakh Yonis depending on the Karma performed in the past life and the Saṅskāras (mental impressions) one acquired.

If one's mental attribute is like a dog, perhaps a dog's body is suitable for the Jīvātmā to take birth. According to the Śāstras, there is no distinction between the Jīvātmā born in different Yonis. One who has taken birth to a human Yoni in one life can take birth as a dog, horse, cow, or any other Yoni that fits the mental, emotional, and spiritual attributes.

Kailāśa: That is enlightening. It means that the Jīvātmā within us and an ant is the same. The body is different due to its past Karma.

Ācārya: Indeed, that is true! The Śāstras emphasize that birth in a Manuṣya Yoni is exceedingly rare. Therefore, we must make the best use of it. This instrument (Manuṣya Janma) effectively realises the subtlest of subtle truth and God.

Kulārṇava Tantra 1.14 states, "चतुरशीतिलक्षेषु शरीरेषु शरीरिणाम् । न मानुष्यं विनान्यत्र तत्त्वज्ञानन्तु लभ्यते caturaśītilakṣeṣu śarīreṣu śarīriṇām । na mānuṣyaṃ vinānyatra tattvajñānantu labhyate", which means among the 84 lakhs Yonis Tattvajñāna is achieved only in the Manuṣya Yoni. Śloka 1.16 states सोपान भूतं मोक्षस्य मानुष्यं प्राप्य दुर्लभम् । यस्तारयति नात्मानं तस्मात् पापतरोऽत्र कः sopāna bhūtaṃ mokṣasya mānuṣyaṃ prāpya durlabham । yastārayati nātmānaṃ tasmāt pāpataro'tra kaḥ, meaning, who is more sinner than the one who does not make full use of the Manuṣya Yoni, which is exceedingly rare and which is like a staircase to Mokṣa.

In Uddhava Gita of 11th Canto (11.20.17) of Śrīmad Bhagavatam, Lord Kṛṣṇa states, नृदेहमाद्यं सुलभं सुदुर्लभं प्लवं सुकल्पं गुरुकर्णधारम् । मयानुकूलेन नभस्वतेरितं पुमान् भवाब्धिं न तरेत् स आत्महा nṛ-deham ādyaṁ su-labhaṁ su-durlabhaṁ plavaṁ su-kalpaṁ guru-karṇadhāram mayānukūlena nabhasvateritaṁ pumān bhavābdhiṁ na taret sa ātma-hā", which means, the human body, which can award all benefit in life, is automatically obtained by the laws of nature, although it is an incredibly rare achievement.

This human body can be compared to a perfectly constructed boat having the spiritual master as the captain and the instructions of Lord Kṛṣṇa as favourable winds impelling it on its course. Considering all these advantages, a human being who does not utilize his human life to cross the ocean of material existence must be considered the killer of his own Ātmā (this is figurative as Ātmā never dies).

Janma in Manuṣya Yoni is so precious that even the Devatās aspire to take birth in this Yoni. In this regard, of Śrīmad Bhagavatam 5.19.21 states, एतदेव हि देवा गायन्ति - अहो अमीषां किमकारि शोभनं प्रसन्न एषां स्विदुत स्वयं हरि: । यैर्जन्म लब्धं नृषु भारताजिरे मुकुन्दसेवौपयिकं स्पृहा हि न: etad eva hi devā gāyanti - aho amīṣāṁ kim akāri śobhanaṁ prasanna eṣāṁ svid uta svayaṁ hariḥ yair janma labdhaṁ nṛṣu bhāratājire mukunda-sevaupayikaṁ spṛhā hi naḥ, meaning, all the Devatās in heaven speak in this way: How wonderful it is for these human beings to have been born in the land of Bhāratavarṣa. They must have executed pious acts of austerity in the past, or Lord Mukunda Himself must have been pleased with them. Otherwise, how could they engage in devotional service in so many ways? We demigods can only aspire to achieve human births in Bhāratavarṣa to execute devotional service, but these humans are already engaged there.

According to Śrī Viṣṇu Purāṇa, waterborne creatures are 9 lakhs, immobile beings such as plants and trees are 20 lakhs, microbes, insects, and reptiles are 11 lakhs, birds 10 lakhs, humans 4 lakhs, which gives rise to 84 lakhs Yonis. Whereas according to Śrī Garuṛa Purāṇa, Aṇḍajā (egg born), Udbhijjā (seed born), Svedajā (sweat born) and Jarāyujā (womb born) are 21 lakhs each.

Similar ślokas about the different kinds of Yonis are found in other Purāṇas such as Padma Purāṇa etc., but all of them talk about 84 lakhs Yonis. In Jyotiṣaśastra, a Yoni other than Manuṣya Yoni is called a Viyoni. There are chapters dedicated to this subject in several classical texts - called Viyoni Janma. Therefore, the scope of Jyotiṣa is not limited merely to human births but to every other kind.

The Rāśis are divided based on the number of legs of creatures. Creatures without legs are called Sarīsṛpa (serpents) or Jalacara (aquatic animals such as fishes). Creatures with two legs are called Dvipāda, Manuṣya, Nara, human, or Dvipāda. Creatures with 4 Legs are Catuṣpāda, Paśu and all four-legged creatures; mainly, mammals are grouped into this. Creatures with more than four legs are Kīṭa which stands for insects, spiders, centipedes, millipedes, octopuses, and other creatures with six or more legs. The symbols of the Rāśis are related to this classification.

The Manuṣya Rāśis are Mithuna, Kanyā, Tulā, Dhanu Pūrvārdha and Kumbha. The Catuṣpāda Rāśis are Meṣa, Vṛṣabha, Siṅha, Dhanu Uttarārdha and Makara Pūrvārdha. The Jalacara Rāśis are, Karka, Mīna and Makara Uttarārdha. The only Kīṭa Rāśi is Vṛścika. Karka is sometimes classified as Kīṭa because it signifies aquatic insects such as shrimps, crabs, and crustaceans.

Similarly, the Grahas are classified as Dvipāda, Catuṣpāda etc. According to Jātakapārijāta 2.12. Sūrya and Budha are in the form (Svarūpa, Ākṛti) of Birds

(Vihaga), Candra Reptile (Sarīsṛpa), Bṛhaspati and Śukra Biped (Dvipāda) and Śani and Maṅgala Quadrupeds (Catuṣpāda). Therefore, the influence of these Grahas on Śukra should also be seen. Śukra is Dvipāda; therefore, Manuṣya Yoni is also denoted when he is strong.

Kailāśa: Guruji, how do we know in which Yoni one was in the past life?

Ācārya: Normally, in a Janmakuṇḍalī, the Yoni of the creature is known from the Rāśi occupied by Candra in the Dvādaśāñśa Kuṇḍalī. This is a complex area of analysis, and one should not jump to a conclusion straightaway merely by looking at the disposition of Candra in a Viyoni Rāśi.

Ācārya Varāhamihira states in Bṛhajjātaka 3.1 that Saumyas must be powerless, Krūras powerful, and Budha/Śani is in Kendras, or dṛṣṭi the Lagna. Therefore, without a thorough assessment, jumping to a conclusion is foolhardy. It is only after balancing the indications the conclusion must be reached.

Kailāśa: Dhanyavād, Guruji! So, the Ātmā is reborn in a Yoni according to their Karma. Right?

Ācārya: That is right. The author of Jñānapradīpikā states that if at Praśna, a Graha is in Uccarāśi, the dead man will attain the heavenly abode (स्वर्गमायाति). If it is in a Śatrurāśi, the dead man will be reborn as an animal (मृगकुले). If it is in a Nīcarāśi, he will go to hell (नरकमायाति). If it is in a Mitrarāśi, he will be reborn in a friend's house (मित्रकुलोद्भव). If it is in a Svarāśi, he will be reborn among his family or relatives (स्वजने जन्म मित्रं ज्ञात्वा).

However, the author does not explain these states of the Grahas must be checked where. From the study of other classical texts, we know that the Ātmā's state after death must be seen from 12H.

Kailāśa: Guruji, should we examine the Grahas in 12H from Praśnalagna?

Ācārya: Yes, that is right!

Ucca means going upward – therefore higher Lokas (Bhūḥ, Bhuvaḥ, Svaḥ, Mahaḥ, Janaḥ, Tapaḥ, Satyaḥ). Nīca means going downward – therefore lower Lokas (Atala, Vitala, Sutala, Talātala, Mahātala, Rasātala, Pātāla). Śatrurāśi means reincarnating in the animal world, whereas Sva/Mitra Rāśi indicate being born in the human world among relatives (Svajana) and friends (Mitrajana).

Kailāśa: How to know which Loka one moves to after death.

Ācārya: Good question, but we shall review this in the book on Puṇya Cakra.

14. ON FOOD

Ācārya: Now, the author covers the Praśna on food. This covers several things about a meal, such as the vessel in which the food is eaten, the vegetables etc.

14.241. I will now tell you about the kind of food eaten – about the vessels in which the meal was prepared, the articles of food like vegetables, pulses, etc., their tastes, the guests with whom the meal was taken, the plates on which food was served, the friends of the host and his enemies too all in detail.

Kailāśa: What are the key principles, Guruji?

Ācārya: To identify the nature of the food eaten or going to be eaten, we must examine the Udaya.

14.242. If at Praśna, Meṣa is rising, the food taken is mutton; if Vṛṣabha, it is beef; is Mithuna, Siṅha or Dhanu is rising it is fish. मेषराशौ भवेच्छागं वृषभे गव्यमुच्यते । धनुर्मिथुनसिह्नेषु मत्स्यमांसादिभोजनम् ॥

14.243. If it is Karka, Makara, Vṛścika or Mīna, the food eaten is ripe fruit; and if it is Kanyā, Tulā or Kumbha, the meal is pure (good quality) rice. नक्रालिकर्कमीनेषु परिपक्वफलादिकम् । तुलाकन्याघटेष्वेव शुद्धान्नमिति कीर्तयेत् ॥

Ācārya: The nature of food is known from the Udayarāśi. There are different ślokas and translations for this. The given translation is from Śrī Kadalangudi Natesha Śāstrī, which states Meṣa is mutton (goat, sheep), Vṛṣabha is beef (cow, bull) etc. However, a different version of this is available.

The following is from the translation of Śrī Ramvyas Pandey.

सहभोक्ता भोजनानि तत्तथानुभवो रिपून् । (१) मेपराशौ भवेच्छाकं वृषभे गव्यमुच्यते ॥२॥ धनुमिथुन सिंहेषु मत्स्यमांसादिभोजनम् । नक्रालिकर्किमीनेषु फलभक्ष्यफलादिकम् ॥३॥ तुलायां कन्यका-याश्च शुद्धान्नमिति कीर्तयेत् । **मेष** लग्न यदि बली हो तो **शाक भोजन** बताना चाहिये। वृष हो तो दही दूध घी आदि धनु मिथुन और सिंह हों तो मछली मांस, मकर, वृश्चिक, कर्क और मीन हो तो फलाहार और तुला कन्या हो तो शुद्ध अन्न बताना चाहिये ।

Sunidhi: What does it say, Guruji?

Ācārya: It states that, for Meṣa, the food is green leafy vegetables (i.e., food of goat and sheep); for Vṛṣabha, it is milk, yoghurt, ghī (made from the milk of cattle) etc. Dhanu, Mithuna and Siṅha indicate mutton and fish. Makara, Vṛścika, Karka and Mīna indicate fruits, and Kanyā and Tulā indicate pure grains (rice, wheat, millet etc.).

Sunidhi: Why do Dhanu, Mithuna and Siṅha indicate mutton and fish?

Ācārya: Siṅha is commonly known as the meat-eating Rāśi. Dhanu and Mithuna are included in it because they are the Ucca/Nīca Rāśi of Rāhu and Ketu. Rāhu and Ketu are the Chāyāgrahas and are interested in non-vegetarian food.

Sunidhi: Why so, Guruji?

Ācārya: In Sanātana Śāstra, food is divided into Sattva, Rajas and Tamas.

Sunidhi: Is this different from Vegetarian and Non Vegetarian food?

Ācārya: Vegetarian and Non-vegetarian classification is a Western concept based on food's origin. However, Sattva, Rajas and Tamas indicate the effects of food on our bodies and mind.

Sunidhi: Kindly elaborate more, Guruji!

Ācārya: The food imbibes in us the quality of Sattva, Rajas and Tamas.

Sattva (Sūrya, Candra and Guru) is balance, peace, harmony, purity and clarity. It represents the following:

(1) Illumination: purity, clarity, and goodness. It brings about a sense of calmness, tranquillity, and inner harmony.

(2) Wisdom: clear understanding of truth and wisdom, making decisions based on higher knowledge.

(3) Compassion: empathy, unconditional love for beings.

(4) Spiritual Inclination: drawn to spiritual practices and desire self-realization.

(5) Balanced: balanced and moderate approach to life, encouraging healthy habits and a disciplined lifestyle.

Rajas (Budha and Śukra) is the fulfilment of desires, achievements and turbulence: It represents the following:

(1) Dynamism: restlessness, ambition, and constant activity, the driving force behind pursuing desires and achievements.

(2) Passion: energy, passion, the drive to attain goals and fulfil desires.

(3) Attachment: possessiveness, frustration, mental agitation.

(4) Competitive: competitive, seeking success and recognition in various endeavours.

(5) Striving: in pursuit of material and worldly aspirations.

Tamas (Śani, Maṅgala, Rāhu, Ketu) is dullness, darkness, heaviness, stagnancy and inertia. It represents the following:

(1) Inertia: inertia, laziness, a lack of enthusiasm, ignorance, an absence of light or knowledge.

(2) Dullness: mental lethargy, confusion, and lack of clarity.

(3) Ignorance: delusion, an apathetic attitude towards self-improvement or spiritual growth.

(4) Resistance: resistance to change, a lack of motivation to take positive actions, and procrastination.

(5) Destructive: self-destructive behaviours and a negative impact on one's physical and mental well-being.

Kailāśa: So, one normally belongs to one of the above three Guṇas?

Ācārya: One has a mix of all three Guṇas, but one among them is predominant. One's choice of food is dependent on the Guṇas. Humans are complex animals; therefore, the predominance of a Guṇa is unclear. But the choice of food and Guṇas is more clearly seen in the animal kingdom.

For instance, cows, deers, horses, elephants etc., are of Sattva Guṇa, and they are predominantly herbivores. They are gentle and non-combative.

Lions and Tigers are of Rajas Guṇa, and they are carnivores. They are fierce, brave and combative.

Animals such as Hyena are of Tamas Guṇa, lacking the courage to fight, but like to steal others' food.

Sunidhi: What are the Sattva, Rajas and Tamas foods?

Ācārya: Here is a representative list. Even among vegetables, pulses and grains, some are Rājasika and Tāmasika. You can study them from a book dedicated to this subject.

Sāttvika: the Sāttvika diet incorporates grains such as rice, wheat, and oats, along with legumes and moong dal (whole green gram). It focuses on consuming fresh green vegetables like spinach and green beans, cooked with mild spices. The diet also includes fresh fruits such as pomegranates, apples, bananas, oranges, grapes, and freshly prepared fruit and vegetable juices. It also includes lightly roasted seeds and nuts, fresh buttermilk, curd (yoghurt), butter, and ghī (clarified butter). Healthy oils like coconut, sesame, and olive oil are encouraged. The use of beneficial spices such as ginger, cardamom, cinnamon, fennel, coriander, and turmeric is emphasized. Natural sweeteners like honey, jaggery, and raw sugar are preferred over refined sugars.

Rājasika: The Rājasika diet involves the consumption of meat and fish, as well as foods that are excessively spicy, salty, or sour. It includes spicy vegetables and an excessive potato, cabbage, broccoli, and cauliflower intake. The diet also comprises jams, jellies, flavoured and preserved foods. Alcoholic drinks like wines, soda, cola, and coffee are part of the Rājasika diet. Fried, roasted, salted foods and mustard are commonly included. Sour milk and cream are also part of this diet. Additionally, the Rājasika diet includes chillies, garlic, onions, pickles, vinegar, and brown or black chocolate.

Tāmasika: The Tāmasika diet comprises meat, fish, and foods made from white flour and those with preservatives or left overnight. It includes foods high in starch, canned and tinned items, jams, jellies, and preserved foods. Hard liquors like whisky and rum are part of this diet. Foods preserved with salt, such as french fries and chips, are also included. Consuming overly cold or pasteurized milk, curds, and cheese is discouraged. Moreover, the Tāmasika diet involves excessive fats, oils, sugars, and pastries consumption. Foods made from white sugar and white flour are best avoided in the Tāmasika diet.

Kailāśa: Dhanyavād Guruji.

Sunidhi: Guruji, what is the effect of a Graha in Praśna Udaya?

Ācārya: Like Rāśis, Grahas also indicate the food being partaken. If a Graha is in the Udaya, it prevails; else, the Rāśi prevails.

Sunidhi: What kind of food does the Grahas rule?

Ācārya: The tastes of Grahas are as follows:

Sūrya: Pungency, spicy. Food cooked with spicy ingredients like chilli peppers, hot sauces, or spices like cayenne pepper, black pepper, or red pepper flakes. These vegetables add a kick of heat and flavour to dishes.

Candra: Salty. Some naturally salty vegetables include seaweed, olives, and capers. Vegetables like celery and spinach also have a subtle salty flavour. Additionally, vegetables like pickles or preserved vegetables may have been soaked in brine or salt solutions, making them salty.

Maṅgala: Bitter. Bitter vegetables have a distinct bitter taste due to certain compounds. Vegetables like bitter melon, Brussels sprouts, dandelion greens, kale, and radicchio are bitter. They are valued for their health benefits and unique Flavors. They are nutritious additions to a balanced diet.

Budha: Mixed, like pickles etc. Vegetables with mixed tastes blend sweet, savoury, and slightly bitter or tangy flavours. Examples include bell peppers, tomatoes, zucchini, carrots, cabbage, asparagus, and sweet potatoes. They add complexity and interest to dishes and are versatile in various culinary applications.

Guru: Sweetish. Sweetish vegetables have a mild sweetness in their taste profile. Examples include carrots, sweet potatoes, corn, and beets. These vegetables offer a gentle and pleasant sweetness, making them appealing. They can be used in both savoury and sweet dishes, providing versatility in cooking.

Śukra: Sourish, acidic. Sourish vegetables have a subtle tangy or sour taste. Vegetables like tomatoes, green apples, lemons, limes, and tamarind are sourish. These vegetables add a refreshing and zesty flavour to dishes. They are often used in salads, marinades, and sauces to enhance taste.

Śani: Astringent, like raw banana, pulses, amla etc. Astringent vegetables make a nutritious and delicious combination. Lentils and spinach are commonly cooked together in various Indian dishes. They offer a rich source of protein, iron, and other essential nutrients. This flavourful pairing provides a wholesome and balanced meal option.

14.244. If at Praśna Sūrya is rising, the food has salty, hot and bitter taste; if it is Maṅgala rising, the food is mixed with honey and black in colour. भाना, तिक्तकदुक्षारमिश्रं भोजनमुच्यते । कृष्णानं क्षौद्रसंयुक्तं भूमिपुत्रस्य भोजनम् ॥

14.245. If it is Budha rising, the food is well-spiced and served with pickles. भर्जितान्युपदंशानि सौम्यस्याहुर्मनीषिणः । पायसान्नं घृतयुतं गुरोर्भोजनमीरितम् ॥

14.246. If it is Guru the food is served with ghī and sweets; if it is Śani, the food is rye mixed oil; and if it is either Rāhu or Ketu, the food is made of some grams. सतैलकोद्रवान्न च भवेन्मन्दस्य भोजनम् | चणकं राहुकेत्वोश्च रसवर्ग उहाहृतः ॥

14.247. From Guru rising one can predict cutlets (or vada) and dāl-mixed rice; from Candra to be predicted tubers, flowers and fish; from Śukra rising must be understood that the food consists of sweet, milk-products etc. जीवस्य मषवटकं सूपमिश्रं तु भोजनम् । चन्द्रस्य कन्द प्रसव मत्स्याद्यैर्भोजनं भवेत् । क्षौद्रापूपपयोयुग्भि व्यंजनैर्भोजनं भृगोः ॥

Ācārya: Besides, the Grahas rule certain kinds of food

Sūrya: salty, hot and bitter taste

Candra: tubers, flowers and fish

Maṅgala: food is mixed with honey and black coloured

Budha: food is well-spiced and served with pickles

Guru: served with ghī and sweets, cutlets (or vada) and dāl-mixed rice

Śukra: food consists of sweets, milk products

Śani: rye mixed oil

Rāhu/Ketu: made of some grams

Sunidhi: Dhanyavād Guruji.

Ācārya: How to know whether the food was tasty or repulsive?

14.248. If Udaya in an Ojarāśi is dṛṣṭied by Saumyas, the food is tasty and refreshing; and if it is a Dvisvarāśi dṛṣṭied by Krūras, the food will be moderate and little. But some predict that if a Dvisvarāśi is dṛṣṭied by a Krūra, the food will be old and rotten and taken on a hungry stomach.

Ācārya: Regardless of the Udaya Rāśi or Graha, if it is with Saumyadṛṣṭi, the food is tasty and refreshing. If it is with Krūradṛṣṭi, then the food may not be as tasty. The food is repulsive if there is an affliction to Udaya or a Nīca Graha in Udaya.

If Udaya is in a Dvisvarāśi, and that is with Krūradṛṣṭi, the food is old and rotten. One cannot eat them unless someone is very hungry. This can also lead to health troubles.

Sunidhi: How to predict if the food was vegetarian or non-vegetarian?

14.249. Non-vegetarian food is predicted by Sūrya and Maṅgala in Udaya; food with butter, milk, curd and ghī if it is Śukra, Candra or Rāhu in Udaya.

Ācārya: For this, we must understand the Kārakatvas of Grahas. Maṅgala is the Kāraka for violence and killing, and therefore, is the Kāraka for animal flesh and meat. Whereas Budha is the Kāraka for non-violence, and therefore, is the Kāraka for all leafy vegetables such as spinach and vegetables.

Guru is the Kāraka for fruits, such as mango, jackfruit, guava etc. Guru is also the Kāraka for fats, and rules butter, ghī etc. Candra is the nourisher and therefore rules milk and milk products. Śukra is the rejuvenator and, therefore, rules Yogurt, Amla etc. Śani rules alcohol, and Rāhu/Ketu rules other intoxicants.

Sunidhi: Thanks for clarifying, Guruji!

14.250-252. If a Krūra is in a Sajala Rāśi and (even if) associated with a Saumya or dṛṣṭied by it, articles of food fried in oil must be predicted. A wise man, by reckoning the nature of Rāśis and Grahas about food articles (per 12.243-247), should predict appropriately by noting the Udayarāśi and Graha at Praśna. All considerations must be considered before giving a prediction.

Ācārya: This is an interesting subject and helps us uncover the hidden aspects of a Graha's Kārakatvas.

15. ON DREAMS

Jayanta: Guruji, let us discuss dreams. This topic is interesting, and I am glad the author covers it here.

Ācārya: Analysing dreams is a standard component of a Praśna. However, it is a vast subject, and only a few principles are laid down here. To understand the intricacies of dream analysis, you must wait for my book on Praśnaśāstra 2 (Book 23B), where I have covered this topic in detail.

Jayanta: We shall wait for that, Guruji. However, kindly explain the basic principles now.

Ācārya: Let us examine the principles laid down by the author in this classical text.

The content of dreams is known from Udaya. The Rāśi and Grahas in Udaya determine the content of the dream. Here you must employ all attributes of the Rāśis and Grahas.

Cararāśi and Śīghragati Grahas indicate things which are mobile, i.e., involving some motion.

Sthirarāśi and Mandagati Grahas indicate stable things, i.e., fixed and not moving.

Dvisvarāśi indicates movement through obstacles or hurdles like a steeplechase.

Saumyarāśi and Grahas indicate gentler dreams. Krūrarāśi and Grahas indicate fiercer dreams.

Grahas in Nīcarāśi indicate poverty; in Uccarāśi, indicate wealth and honour; in Mitrarāśi, friendship; in Śatrurāśi, enmity, conflicts and fights; in Svarāśi, resting at home; in Mūlatrikoṇa, working in an office.

The Varṇas of people involved can be known from the Varṇas of Grahas and Rāśis. Agnirāśi = Kṣatriya, fighters, king; Pṛthvīrāśi = Vaiśya, trader, industrialist, financial experts; Vāyurāśi = Śudra, menial worker, farmer, factory worker, office staff; Jalarāśi = Brāhmaṇas, teachers, professors, priests etc.

Among the Grahas, Guru/Śukra = Brāhmaṇa, Sūrya/Maṅgala = Kṣatriya, Budha/Candra = Vaiśya, Śani = Śudra, Rāhu = Mleccha, foreigner, and Ketu = outcast, monks, Caṇḍāla, Aghoris.

The Dhātumūlajīva attributes of Rāśis and Grahas must be used. Cara = Dhātu, Sthira = Mūla and Dvisva = Jīva. Among Grahas, Dhātu = Maṅgala/Candra/ Śani/Rāhu; Mūla = Śukra/Sūrya and Jīva = Guru/Budha.

The Rāśi symbols also matter, such as Meṣa = goat, sheep mountain; Vṛṣabha = granary, grassland, cattle; Mithuna = a couple, private moments, conversation between people; Karka = a river or lake, with fishes, crabs and crustacean; Siṅha = dense jungle, wild animal, lion, tiger, a fort; Kanyā = a garden, orchard, young girls...

... Tulā = a marketplace, corporate office, financial transactions, trade deals, negotiations, people; Vṛścika = a deep well, crevice, a cave, a mine, poisonous creatures, snakes, scorpions, bees, insects; Dhanu = outskirt of a jungle, horses, zebra, battlefield; Makara = waterbody, swamp, crocodile, dolphins, deer; Kumbha: university, occult place, Smasāna, Cremation or burial ground, last rites, initiation into a spiritual order; Mīna = ocean, trade, cruise, seafood and pearl, Ṛṣis absorbed in their Tapasyā, out of body experiences.

Jayanta: Dhanyavād, Guruji!

15.253. Whatever things and events are seen in dreams shall now be narrated. In Meṣa Udaya, one dreams of Mandirs and storeyed houses. In Vṛṣabha Udaya with Sūryadṛṣṭi, the same kind of dream can be predicted.

15.254. In Vṛścika Udaya with Sūrya and Maṅgala, the dream is full of sadness and may be of a dead man. In Mithuna Udaya, the dream is of Brāhmaṇas and ascetics teaching scriptures.

15.255. In Karka Udaya, the dream is of going to the fields and returning home with grass in the hands.

15.256. In Siṅha Udaya is in, the dream is of hunters of mountains and buffaloes. In Kanyā Āruṛha/Udaya, the dream is of drinking water given by a woman.

15.257. In Tulā Udaya, the dream is of kings, gold and merchants. In Vṛścika Udaya, the dream is of bees and beasts. He sees bulls but is not frightened; he will drive them away.

15.258. In Dhanu Udaya, the dream is of flowers. He gets ripe fruits in his dream. In Makara Udaya, the dream is of rivers and girls. In Kumbha, the dream is of mirrors; In Mīna Udaya, the dream is of gold, lakes and tanks.

Sunidhi: Guruji! Kindly narrate the dreams according to this author.

Ācārya: They are as follows:

Meṣa: Mandirs and storeyed houses

Vṛṣabha: Mandirs and storeyed houses with Saumyayutidṛṣṭi

Mithuna: Brāhmaṇas and ascetics teaching scriptures

Karka: going to the fields and returning home with grass in the hands

Siṅha: hunters of mountains and buffaloes

Kanyā: drinking water is given by a woman

Tulā: kings, gold and merchants

Vṛścika: bees and beasts; sees bulls but is not frightened; he will drive them away; full of sadness and may be of a dead man with Sūrya/Maṅgala,

Dhanu: flowers, ripe fruits

Makara: rivers and girls

Kumbha: mirrors

Mīna: gold, lakes and tanks

Jayanta: Guruji, how is 4H related to dreams?

15.259. The dream is of silver vessels if Śukra is in 4H from Udaya. If Sūrya is in 4H, the dream is of dead men and of falling from barren trees. If Candra is in 4H, the dream is of swimming in the sea; and if it is Rāhu, the dream is of wine and poison.

Ācārya: 4H indicates the middle of the night (complete darkness). It is also the house of sleeping and relaxing (Sukhabhāva). It is the Bhāva of the conscious mind (Candra). Therefore, it is related to dreams.

Also, the author clarifies in 5.261 that dreams must be interpreted in terms of the Grahas in or aspecting 4H from Udaya.

However, from the examples given by the author, it appears that in 4H, the effects of Grahas must be seen instead of Rāśis.

Śukra = silverware

Sūrya = of dead men and of falling from barren trees

Candra = swimming in the sea

Rāhu = wine and poison

Sunidhi: Why is Sūrya in 4H related to a dead man falling from barren trees?

Ācārya: 10H relates to up (above the head), and 4H relates to down (below the feet). Sūrya in 4H has zero Dikbala, and therefore it means fallen Sūrya. Sūrya is a Mūlagraha and is the Kāraka for wood. Therefore, Sūrya in 4H indicates that.

Sunidhi: Thank you for explaining this.

15.260. But there is a special point to be noticed; if Śukra is in Chatra, Āruṛha or Udaya, the dream is of white mansions; and if Budha, the dream is of Devatās.

Ācārya: The author makes another point based on Grahas in Udaya, Āruṛha or Chatra.

Śukra in those places = dream is of white mansions

Budha in those places = Devatās

Sunidhi: Shouldn't Guru be involved in the dreams of Devatās?

Ācārya: Yes, that should be. Guru is involved in such dreams and Agni Trikoṇa (Meṣa/Siṅha/Dhanu). Agni is the communicator between this and the divine realms. Budha specifically denotes Vedapātha and invocation of Devatās through Mantras.

15.261. Dreams must be interpreted from the Grahas in 4H from Udaya and Grahas aspecting 4H.

16. OMENS

Jayanta: Now the author talks about omen.

Ācārya: Omens are normally seen from Udaya. The Rāśis and Grahas manifest different events in the surrounding. From such omens, good and bad quality of time can be assessed, and events predicted.

The author's principles are narrated before, which you should examine yourselves. The details of Omens are covered in the Praśnaśāstra Book 2 (Book 23B); therefore, I do not intend to discuss them here.

16.262. When giving predictions about travel, one must note that if a Dvisvarāśi rises at Praśna, the pilgrim will return home because of bad omens. If a Cararāśi is rising, he will not travel due to bad omens.

अथोभयर्क्षे पथिको दुर्निमित्तानि पश्यति । स्थिरोदये निमित्तानां निरोधेन न गच्छति ॥१॥ चरोदये निमित्तानां समायातीति ईरयेत् । यात्री द्विस्वभाव लग्न में जाने से दुःशकुन देखता है। स्थिर लग्न में शकुनों के प्रभाव से यात्रा को स्थगित कर देता है और चर में शुभ शकुनों के प्रभाव से सफलतापूर्वक लौट आता है।

16.263. If Candra rises in Udaya, bad omens by owls, partridges and pigeons are predicted.

16.264. If Guru is rising, the pilgrim will see crows and long-tailed sparrows. If Śani is rising, he will see a Pakṣi called "Kuliṅga" (sparrow), and if Budha, he will see a Pakṣi called "Piṅgala" (small kind of owl - *Bubo bubo*). If Sūrya is on the right side of Udayarāśi, he will see the eagle flying on his right side; and if Sūrya is on the left side, the eagle (Garuṛa) also will be seen on the left side. गुरूदये तथाकाक भारद्वाजादि पक्षिणः । मन्दोदये कुळिङ्गस्स्याज्ज्ञोदये पिङ्गळो भवेत् । सूर्यो दये च गरुडः सव्यासव्यवशा- द्भवेत् ॥

16.265. If a Sthirarāśi is rising at Praśna, he will see definite good omens while starting; if a Cararāśi, he will see birds flying cross-wise; and if a Dvisvarāśi is rising, he will see omens on the way.

16.266. What omens will be seen when Grahas are in Udaya? If it is Rāhu in Udaya, he will see the Iguana; if Candra, he will see partridges; if it is Budha, he will see a land rat; if it is Śukra, he will see a milkmaid bringing curd; and if it is Guru, he will see milk and ghī.

16.267. If it is Sūrya, he will see a white eagle; if Maṅgala, a fox; if Śani, fire and thief; these are the omens to be predicted.

16.268. If it is Maṅgala in Udaya, he will see a dog, bear or rabbit; if it is Śukra, he will see flying birds and a chameleon.

14. ON MARRIAGES

Jayanta: Kindly discuss Marriage. It is one of the common sources of Praśna.

Ācārya: Sure, let us examine the principles.

17.269-270. At Praśna regarding marriage, if Sūrya*, **Maṅgala** or Budha* is in Udaya, marriage will be celebrated soon, but the girl will be widowed shortly. प्रश्नं वैवाहिके लग्ने कुजसूर्यबुघा यदि । वैधव्यं शीघ्रमायाति सा नारी नात्र संशयः ॥

Pt Ramvyas Pandey: प्रश्ने वैवाहिके लग्न कुजः स्यादुदये यदि । वैधव्यं शीघ्रमायाति सा वधू नेति संशयः ॥१॥ प्रश्न लग्न में, यदि विवाह सवधी प्रश्न हो तो, यदि मंगल हो तो शीघ्र विना संदेह के वधू विधवा हो जायगी ।

Ācārya: The interpretation of the first śloka is erroneous in the translation of Pt Kadalangudi Śāstrī. It states that if at a marriage Praśna, Sūrya, Maṅgala or Budha in Udaya, the marriage is celebrated soon, but the girl is widowed.

However, since Sūrya or Budha in Lagna does not cause early widowhood, I looked up the śloka in Pt Ramvyas Pandey's translation, and it states that if Maṅgala is in Udaya, then the girl becomes a widow early.

Sunidhi: Why is that so?

Ācārya: That is because Maṅgala gives rise to Kujadoṣa (Maṅgala Doṣa), which is fatal for a marital partner.

Sunidhi: Guruji, kindly elaborate on this Doṣa.

Ācārya: Maṅgala Doṣa causes widowhood in both men and women. In śloka 80.47, Maharṣi Parāśara states that a woman becomes a widow if Maṅgala is in 1H, 12H, 4H, 7H, or 8H from Lagna, devoid of a Saumyayutidṛṣṭi.

The Maharṣi further states in śloka 80.48-49 that if a man and a woman possessing this yoga join in wedlock, the yoga ceases to have any effect.

Modern-day scholars extend this yoga to Candra and Śukra, increasing the probability of the yoga. However, as Maharṣi Parāśara states, if Maṅgala is subject to Saumyadṛṣṭi, the yoga is nullified.

Dr Raman states that the position of Śukra and Maṅgala are very important in judging marital relations. Maṅgala, whose element is fire, rules marriage, and when he is weak/afflicted in the Kuṇḍalī of a male/female, the marriage does not last long.

He considers several elements more important in determining marriage adaptability between two parties than this Doṣa. The evil influences due to the Maṅgala Doṣa are only one of the several elements.

Dr Raman quotes it from Kerala Śāstra *"dhana vyayecha pathale jamitre chashtame kuja; strinam bharthru vinasamcha bharthunam strivinasanam"*. This means, "If Maṅgala is in 2H, 12H, 4H, 7H or 8H in a Kuṇḍalī of the female, the husband dies. Similar situation in Kuṇḍalī of a male causes the death of the wife."

Kerala Śāstra replaces 1H with 2H, whereas Maharṣi Parāśara states, *"lagne vyaye sukhe vāpi saptame cā'ṣṭame kuje । śubhadṛgyogahīne ca patiṃ hanti na saṃśayaḥ ॥47॥"* This houses involved here are the Mokṣa Trikoṇa and the 1H-7H axis. This makes more sense!

2H is also endorsed by Jātakapārijāta, which states in śloka 14.34, "Maṅgala in 2H, 12H, 7H, 4H, or 8H in Kuṇḍalī may cause the death of his wife. If Maṅgala is in the same position as a female Kuṇḍalī, she proves detrimental to the husband."

Based on Dr Raman's recommendations, Kerala Śāstra and Jātakapārijāta, we understand that Maṅgala in the Mokṣatrikoṇa (4/8/12) or 2/7 from Lagna/Candra/Śukra cause Maṅgala Doṣa.

Dr Raman clarifies further, "The *Lagna* represents the body, the *Candra*, mind and *Śukra*, sexual relations. Therefore, the houses must be reckoned with from all three, viz., Lagna, Candra and Śukra. The Doṣa is considered weak when it exists from Lagna, a little stronger from Candra, and more powerful from Śukra.

If this Doṣa is found in the Kuṇḍalī of both the husband and wife, the Doṣa is cancelled. Of course, many good combinations assure marital felicity and much importance need not be given to this Doṣa.

Sunidhi: Dhanyavād, Guruji!

Ācārya: In this context, we should also examine the cancellation of this Doṣa!

Sunidhi: Kindly elaborate, Guruji!

Ācārya: Dr Raman states that the Yogas for cancellations are: (1) Maṅgala in Budha's Rāśi in 2H. (2) Maṅgala in Śukra's Rāśi in 12H. (3) Maṅgala in Svarāśi in 4H. (4) Maṅgala in Ucca/Nīca Rāśi in 7H. (5) Maṅgala in Bṛhaspati's Rāśi in 8H.

Sunidhi: Dhanyavād for elaborating on this, Guruji!

Ācārya: There are also three more Yogas for cancellation of this Doṣa. (1) Maṅgala in Siṅha/Kumbha; (2) Maṅgala in yuti with Guru/Candra, and (3) Guru/Śukra in Lagna.

Jayanta: Dhanyavād, Guruji. Let us examine the other Yogas stated by the author.

Ācārya: Let us do that. In the following Yogas, it is assumed that a girl or her parents put the Praśna. In such a Praśna, Udaya = bride and 7H = groom. The bride's family is seen from Udaya Rāśi and the Grahas in or aspecting it.

17.271. If Śani is in Udaya, the girl to be married will be poor, and she will have children who will soon die. If Candra is in Udaya, the couple will shortly meet with death. But the couple will live happily if Śukra, Guru or Budha are in Udaya.

Jayanta: Why is Śani in Udaya indicate that the girl is from a poor family?

Ācārya: Śani is the Kāraka for poverty, and Guru is the Kāraka for wealth.

Jayanta: Why is Candra in Lagna indicate danger to the couple?

Ācārya: Candra in Lagna is not favourable unless he is in Meṣa, Vṛṣabha or Karka.

Jayanta: Śukra, Guru or Budha are in Udaya, and the couple will live happily.

Ācārya: Indeed. Saumyas in Udaya indicate a happy married life, except for Candra.

Jayanta: How about other Grahas?

Ācārya: We have already seen Maṅgala, and the remaining ones are Sūrya, Rāhu and Ketu.

Sūrya in Udaya indicates an influential or royal family.

Rāhu and Ketu indicate that the family is an outcast or not well accepted by the community.

Jayanta: Guruji, now the Grahas in the remaining Bhāvas are explained.

17.272. If Candra is in 2H from Udaya, the girl to be married will give birth to many children. If Sūrya, Śani or Maṅgala is in 2H, the couple will be sorrowful and suffer from poverty. द्वितीयस्थे निशानाथे बहुपुत्रवती भवेत् । । ३ । । स्थितिमध्यर्कमन्दाराः मनःशोको दरिद्रता । यदि द्वितीय में चंद्र हो तो बहु पुत्रता और दशम में सूर्य मंगल और शनि हों तो मानसिक कष्ट और दारिद्र्य प्राप्त होता है ।

17.273. If Rāhu is in 2H, the wife will be unchaste. If Saumyas are in 2H she will live long with her husband, blessed with children. द्वितीये राहुसंयुक्ता सा भवेत् व्यभिचारिणी ॥४॥ शुभग्रहा द्वितीयस्था मांगल्यायुष्यवर्द्धना । द्वितीय स्थान में राहु हो तो कन्या व्यभिचारिणी और शुभ ग्रह हो तो मंगल और आयु से पूर्ण होती है ।

Ācārya: Let us examine the effects of Grahas in 2H.

Sūrya: the couple will be sorrowful and suffer from poverty

Candra: the girl will give birth to many children

Maṅgala: Same as Sūrya

Budha: the girl lives along with her husband, blessed with children

Guru: same as Budha

Śukra: same as Budha

Śani: Same as Sūrya

Rāhu: the girl will be unchaste

Ketu: Not mentioned

17.274. If Guru or Rāhu is in 3H from Udaya the wife will remain barren. But if other Grahas are in 3H she will be happy, prosperous and blessed. तृतीये राहुजीवौ चेत्सा वन्ध्या भवति ध्रुवम् ॥५॥ अन्ये तृतीयराशिस्था धनसौभाग्यवर्द्धना । राहु और वृहस्पति यदि तृतीय में हों तो स्त्री वन्ध्या होगी। उसी स्थान में अन्य ग्रह हों तो धन और सोहाग से भरपूर होगी ।

Ācārya: Grahas in 3H

Guru/Rāhu: the girl will remain barren

Sūrya/Candra/Maṅgala/Budha/Śukra/Śani: the girl will be happy, prosperous and blessed.

Ketu: Should be like Maṅgala.

17.275. If Krūras like Sūrya and Candra are in 4H, or even if Śani occupies it, the wife will have no breast milk to feed the babies. If Rāhu is in 4H, her husband will have a concubine. If Budha, Śukra, Maṅgala or Guru is in 4H she will be short-lived. नाथा दिनेशस्तिग्मो यदि तुर्ये ततोऽशुभः ॥६॥ शनिश्च स्तन्यहीना स्यादहिः सापत्न्यवत्यसौ । बुधजीवारशुक्राश्चत् अल्पजीवन त्यसौ ॥७॥ चतुर्थ में सूर्य हो तो (अशुभ फल), शनि हो तो सन्तानहीना, राहु हो सौत वाली होगी। वहीं बुध बृहस्पति, मंगल या शुक्र हो तो अल्पायु होगा ।

Ācārya: Grahas in 4H

Sūrya/Candra/Śani: the girl will have no breast milk

Maṅgala/Budha/Guru/Śukra: the girl will be shortlived.

Rāhu: the girl's husband will have a concubine

17.276. If Śani is in 5H from Udaya, the girl to be married will suffer from illness; if Śukra, Guru or Budha is in 5H, she will have many children.

17.277. If Sūrya or Candra is in 5H, the woman will be barren. If Rāhu is in 5H, her son will die. If Maṅgala is in 5H the woman will be barren. If Maṅgala is in 5H, destruction of her son can be predicted. पंचमे यदि सौरिः स्याद व्याधिभिः पीडिता भवेत् । शुक्रजीवबुधाश्चापि पशुश्चेत बहुपुत्रवत् ॥८॥ चन्द्रादित्यौ तु बन्दी स्यात् अहिश्चेत् मरणं भवेत् । आरश्चेत् पुत्रनाशः स्यात् प्रश्ने पाणिमहोचिने ॥६॥ पंचम में यदि शनि हो तो रोगिणी, शुक्र, बृहस्पति और बुध हों तो बहुत पशु पुत्र से युक्त, चन्द्रमा और सूर्य हो तो बन्दी, राहु हो तो मरण और मंगल हो तो पुत्रनाश यह वैवाहिक प्रश्न में बताना ।

Ācārya: Grahas in 5H.

Sūrya/Candra/Maṅgala: the girl will be barren

Rāhu: one of the sons would die

Śani: the girl will be diseased

Moving forward, the principles of Grahas in different Bhāvas are clear. I have also included the translation of Pt Ramvyas Pandey for cross-examination of the principles.

17.278. If Candra is in 6H from Udaya, the girl to be a married will soon be a widow. If Budha is in 6H, the married girl creates conflict in the house. If Śukra is in 6H, she will live long happily with her husband. Any Graha other than Candra, Budha and Śukra in 6H will confer increased happiness and prosperity to the girl to be married. षष्ठे शशो चेद्विधवा बुधः कलहकारिणी । षष्ठे तिष्ठति शुक्रचेदीर्घमांगल्य धारिणी ॥१०॥ अन्ये तिष्ठन्ति चेन्नारी सुखिनी वृद्धिमिच्छति । षष्ठस्थान में चन्द्रमा हो तो विधवा हो सो कहो, शुक्र हो तो सर्व मांगल्य घारिणी और अन्य ग्रह हों तो सुखी और वृद्धिमती कन्या होती है ।

17.279. The girl will soon be widowed if Śani is in 7H from Udaya. Sūrya in 7H will make the girl suffer from illness.

17.280. Candra in 7H will also afflict the married girl with fever. If Maṅgala is in 7H, another man will take her away.

17.281. Prosperity will come to the girl to be married, if Guru or Budha is in 7H. If Rāhu is in 7H, she will be widowed. She will die soon after marriage if Śukra is in 7H from Udaya. सप्तमस्थे शनो नारी तरसा विधवा भवेत् ॥११॥ परेणापहृता याति कुजे तिष्ठति सप्तमे । बुधजीवौ सन्मतिः स्याद्राहुश्चेद् विधवा भवेत् ॥१२॥ व्याधिग्रस्ता भवेन्नारी सप्तमस्थो रविर्यदि । सप्तमस्ये निशाधीशे ज्वरपीडावती भवेत् ॥ १३ ॥ शुक्रश्चेत्सप्तमे स्थाने सा वधूर्मरणं व्रजेत् । सप्तम में यदि शनि हों तो शीघ्र विधवा मंगल हों तो दूसरे से हरी जाकर अन्य गामिनी, बुध और बृहस्पति हों तो सद्बुद्धि वाली, राहु हो तो विधवा, सूर्य हो तो व्याधि ग्रस्त, चन्द्रमा हो तो बुखार की पीडा से आकुल और शुक्र हो तो मृत्यु को प्राप्त होती है ।

17.282. If Śukra, Guru and Rāhu occupy 8H from Udaya, they will cause destruction. But Śani and Budha in 8H will confer increased benefit to the girl to be married. Candra too in 8H will cause destruction. Sūrya or Maṅgala in 8H will make the girl get married twice. अष्टमस्थाः शुक्रगुरुभुजगा नाशयंति च ॥१४॥ शनिज्ञो वृद्धिदौ भौमचंद्रो नाशयतः स्त्रियम् । आदित्यारौ पुनर्भूः स्यात्प्रश्ने वैवाहिके वधू ॥१५॥ अष्टम में शुक्र गुरु और राहु नाश करने वाले शनि और बुध वृद्धि करने वाले, मंगल और चंद्र मारक, सूर्य और मंगल पुनर्विवाह कारक होते है

[Notes: Being betrothed to one, the wedding may not come through, and she will marry another.]

17.283. Budha in 9H from Udaya will rid the girl of all illness. Guru or Candra is in 9H indicate many children. If other Grahas are there in 9H (i.e. Sūrya, Maṅgala, Śukra, Śani, Rāhu or Ketu) the girl to be married will remain barren. नवमे यदि सोमः स्यात् व्याधिहीना भवेद वधूः । जीवचंद्रौ यदि स्यातां बहुपुत्रवती वधू ॥१६॥ अन्ये तिष्ठन्ति नवमे यदि वन्ध्या न संशयः । यदि बुध हो तो वधू नीरोग, बृहस्पति और चन्द्रमा हो तो पुत्रवती और अन्य ग्रह हो तो वन्ध्या होती है - इसमें सन्देह नहीं ।

17.284. If Candra is in 10H from Udaya, the girl will also remain barren. If Śukra is in 10H she will be unchaste. If Maṅgala or Śani is in 10H, she will become a widow. If Guru is in 10H, she will be poor, but if Budha, or Sūrya is in 10H she will be happy and prosperous. दशमे स्थानके चंद्रो वन्ध्या भवति भामिनी ॥१७॥ भार्गवो यदि वेश्या स्यात् विधवाकिकुजादयः । रिक्ता गुरुश्चेज्ज्ञादित्यौ यदि तस्या शुभं वदेत् ॥१८॥ दशम में चन्द्र हों तो वन्ध्या शुक्र हो तो वेश्या, शनि मंगल आदि हो तो विधवा, गुरु हो तो रिक्ता और बुध सूर्य हो तो अशुभ फल वाली होती है ।

17.285. All Grahas in 11H from Udaya confer wealth, children and happiness to the girl to be married. But if Candra is in 12H, unhappiness and destruction must be predicted. Śani and Maṅgala in the 12H or aspecting it make her a drunkard. लाभस्थानगताः सर्वे पुत्र सौभाग्यवर्द्धकाः । लग्नद्वादशचंद्रो यदि स्यान्नाशमादिशेत् ॥१९॥ एकादश स्थान में सभी ग्रह पुत्र और सौभाग्य के वर्द्धक तथा लग्न और द्वादश में यदि चंद्रमा हो तो नाशकारक होता है ।

17.286. If Budha is in 12H, the girl will have male issues; and if Guru is in the 12th, she will have wealth and grains in plenty; Rāhu or Sūrya in 12H will make her barren; but Śukra in 12H will make her happy and prosperous. शनिभौमौ यदि स्यातां सुरापानवती भवेत् । सर्पादित्यौ स्थितौ वन्ध्या शुक्रे सुखवती भवेत् ॥२०॥ द्वादश में यदि शनि और भौम हों तो मदिरा पान करने वाली, राहु और सूर्य हों तो वन्ध्या और शुक्र हो तो सुखी होगी।

18. ON LOVE AND CONJUGAL FELICITY

Ācārya: After Praśna of getting married, the next step is to cover Praśna after the marriage has occurred. This Praśna is put by a married man or a woman about their marital life and their partner. Praśna, such as "Is my partner having an extramarital affair", falls in this domain.

Jayanta: I suppose depending on who is asking the Praśna, the indications of the Bhāvas will be different.

Ācārya: That is right. Always Udaya = Pṛcchaka and 7H = partner. In the following principles, it is assumed that the husband puts the Praśna about his wife. Similar principles are applied with modifications if the wife puts the Praśna about her husband.

18.287. This Śāstra also teaches about the relationship between husband and wife, marital happiness, chastity, and impurity.

18.288. If Rāhu is in Trikoṇas of Āruṛha or Udaya, the wife of the Pṛcchaka would be undoubtedly quarrelsome.

Ācārya: For instance, if a man puts the Praśna for his wife, the above principle is used. It states that Rāhu in Trikoṇa to Āruṛha/Udaya indicate that the wife is quarrelsome. However, if a woman puts this Praśna, her husband would be quarrelsome.

Jayanta: How about the Praśna about the chastity of his wife?

18.289. The wife would be chaste if Candra is in 11H, 7H, 3H, or 10H from Udaya and dṛṣṭied by Guru.

Ācārya: 7H = wife. If Candra is in a Trikoṇa to 7H and dṛṣṭied by Guru, the wife is chaste.

Jayanta: I suppose Guru's dṛṣṭi on 7H or his presence in its Trikoṇa also indicate that the spouse is chaste. Isn't it?

Ācārya: That is right. Guru ensures chastity as he abides by the social boundary (set by the King and the Queen, Sūrya and Candra).

Kailāśa: When is the wife unchaste?

18.290. If Puruṣa Grahas are with or aspecting Candra, the person's wife will be unchaste.

Ācārya: In a Praśna involving husband and wife, the wife is seen from Śukra/Candra and the husband is seen from Maṅgala/Sūrya. Therefore, the wife could be unchaste if Candra is with a Puruṣagraha. However, if a woman puts the Praśna, if Maṅgala is with a Strī Graha (mainly Śukra), the husband is unchaste.

Kailāśa: When is the wife bad-natured?

18.291. If Candra in Nīca/Śatru Rāśi is dṛṣṭied by Krūras in 7H, it indicates that the person's wife would be abusing his relations and would stray away from social conventions. But if Candra is with or dṛṣṭied by Saumyas, she would be of good character.

Ācārya: Candra denotes the wife, and therefore, if Candra is in a Nīca/Śatru Rāśi, she could have a repulsive character. But, in addition, Krūras must also afflict 7H (wife).

If a woman puts the Praśna, her husband is seen from Maṅgala. If Maṅgala is in a Nīca/Śatru Rāśi, and 7H is afflicted, then the husband could be abusive.

Jayanta: The next principle states that the wife is chaste if Sūrya or Guru influences Candra.

18.292. If Sūrya or Guru is with or aspecting Candra, the wife would be beautiful and chaste.

Ācārya: That is true because Guru and Sūrya are of Sattvaguṇa. But ideally, Sūrya should be away from Candra, which indicates higher Pakṣabala, imbibing Candra with high Sattva.

Jayanta: Now comes the influence of Maṅgala and Śukra.

18.293. If Maṅgala is with or dṛṣṭied by Śukra, the wife would have liaison with other persons. If Maṅgala is with Guru and Budha, there would be a union with a virgin (chaste woman).

Ācārya: Maṅgala and Śukra yoga is explosive and is known to cause multiple extramarital affairs.

Kailāśa: Why so?

Ācārya: Maṅgala is the Kāraka for masculinity and Śukra, femininity. Maṅgala also denotes Brahmacārya or abstinence from sex, whereas Śukra indicates indulgence. Therefore, when they join or have dṛṣṭi Sambandha, it is as if a Brahmachari has left his strict discipline and is eager to indulge in sexual intrigues.

In a Praśna about chastity, be it by a man or wife about the partner, the involvement of Maṅgala and Śukra Yoga indicate a lack of chastity and multiple extramarital affairs.

Kailāśa: Śukra is the Kāraka for marriage, and Maṅgala is the Kāraka for celibacy. Isn't it?

Ācārya: That is right.

Kailāśa: Is that the reason why Maṅgala causes Kujadoṣa?

Ācārya: That is indeed the reason. Maṅgala causes the spouse's death so that the person becomes a forced bachelor and follows Brahmacārya.

18.294. If Maṅgala is in Śukra's Varga or Śukra is in Maṅgala Varga at Praśna, the person's wife will become a widow. She will also be corrupt.

Ācārya: Here is a Yoga from the author. If Maṅgala is in a Śukra's Varga, or vice-versa, it causes another kind of Kujadoṣa where the Pṛcchaka dies, and the spouse becomes a widow/widower. If this does not happen, then likely the spouse has extramarital affairs.

Kailāśa: It appears that the Vargas have some use in Praśna.

Ācārya: Yes, they do. Focus on Navāñśa Varga as that is the most important Varga. You may also check Dreṣkāṇa, in some cases (mostly in theft and death Praśna).

Kailāśa: Makes sense, Guruji!

18.295. If Śukra is in Sūrya Varga, the wife will have the happiness and prosperity of a royal princess. If Candra is in Guru Varga, she will happily have conjugal bliss.

Ācārya: Here is another Yoga. Instead of Maṅgala, if Śukra is in Sūrya Varga, the wife will have the happiness of a princess (instead of becoming interested in many men). Candra also indicates the wife. Now, if Candra is in Guru's Varga, she will have happiness in marriage.

Generally, in a man's Kuṇḍalī (or Praśna), Śukra/Candra in Guru's Varga and a woman's Kuṇḍalī (or Praśna), Maṅgala/Sūrya in Guru's Varga indicate a good-natured spouse, committed to the marriage.

18.296. At Praśna if Śukra is in a Varga (strength) of a Strīgraha, the wife is independent (स्वतन्त्रवती). And if Candra is associated with Śani, she will be unchaste (व्यभिचारिणी). चन्द्रः स्त्रीवर्गयुक्तश्चेत् स्त्री स्वतन्त्रवती भवेत् । शनैश्चरेण युक्तश्चेदतीव व्यभिचारिणी ॥२९६॥

18.297. If Śukra is in a Varga (strength) of a Krūra or is dṛṣṭied by it, the woman will be unchaste. If Candra is in a Varga of a Krūra or dṛṣṭied by it, there may be union with an enemy's wife (or woman of the enemy's camp). पापवर्गयुते दृष्टे शुक्रे चेद्व्यभिचारिणी । अरिवर्गयुतश्चन्द्रो यद्यमित्रवधूरतिः ॥२९७॥

18.298. If at Praśna, Candra is in 'Nīcavarga', the person will desire union with a low woman. If Candra is associated with a friendly Graha, he will have a union with a friendly kind of woman. नीचवर्गयुतश्चन्द्रो नीचस्त्रीभोगकामुकः । मित्रवर्गयुतश्चन्द्रो मित्रवर्गवधूरतिः ॥२९८॥

18.299. If at Praśna Candra is in Svarāśi, the person will have conjugal enjoyment with his wife. If Candra gets its Sva Varga the person will have union with a woman higher than his own class. स्वक्षेत्रे यदि शीतांशुस्स्वभार्यायां रतिर्भवेत् । स्ववर्गयुक्तश्चन्द्रश्चेत्स्वोच्चवंशस्त्रिया रतिः ॥२९९॥

18.300. If Candra is associated with an Udāsina Graha or dṛṣṭied by it, the person will have union with a Udāsina woman. उदासीनग्रहयुतो दृष्टो वा यदि चन्द्रमाः । उदासीनवधूभोग इतिचाहुर्मनीषिणः ॥३००॥

18.301. If Candra is associated with Śani in 1H, 10H, 7H or 5H, the person will in the night have union with a sleeping woman who has a thief's appearance. लग्ने च दशमेऽस्ते च पञ्चमे शनियुक् शशी । चोररूपेण कथयेद्रात्रौ स्वप्नवधूरतिम् ॥३०१॥

18.302. At Praśna, if Udaya is in an Ojarāśi and its lord too is in an Ojarāśi, the person will have a sexual relationship once. But if Udaya is in a Yugmarāśi and its lord too is in a Yugmarāśi, the enjoyment will be on two occasions. ओजोदये तदधिपे त्वेकमैथुनमुच्यते । समोदये तदधिपे समस्थे द्वे रती तथा ॥३०२॥

18.303. By determining the strength of the rising Graha and counting its Raśmis or the Raśmis of the Grahas aspecting it, the number of times of sex relationship must be predicted. लग्नेश्वरबलं ज्ञात्वा तेषां किरणसङ्ख्यया । अथवा कथयेद्विद्वांत्सन्द्रष्टृग्रहसङ्ख्यया ॥ ३०३ ॥

18.304. If Candra, is associated with Maṅgala or dṛṣṭied by it, the couple quarrel and sleep separately. If Śukra is associated with Śani or dṛṣṭied by it, there will be quarrel between the couple. चन्द्रे भौमयुते दृष्टे कलहेन पृथक्शयः भृगौ सौरियुते दृष्टे स्वस्त्रीकलह उच्यते ॥३०४॥

18.305. The couple's misunderstanding and strife is predicted also when Candra is associated with or dṛṣṭied by Śukra, in any one of the places: 4H, 3H, 5H or 7H from Udaya. चतुर्थे च तृतीये च पञ्चमे सप्तमेपि वा । चन्द्रे शुक्रयुते दृष्टे स्वस्त्रिया कलहो भवेत् ॥३०५॥

18.306. If there is a relationship with a Krūra in 7H and 10H, the woman's sari would be torn (due to the scuffle between the couple). तदीयवसनच्छेदं रचितं परिकीर्तयेत् । सप्तमे पापसंयुक्ते दशमे पापसंयुते ॥ ३०६ ॥

18.307. If Budha is in 3H the person (Pṛcchaka) will lie down on the floor due to quarrel with his wife. If at Praśna Candra is in Udaya and Maṅgala in 2H, the same condition will prevail in the night as stated above. तृतीये बुधसंयुक्ते स्त्रीविवादात्स्थले शयः। लग्ने चन्द्रयुते भौमे द्वितीयस्थे तदा निशि ॥३०७॥

18.308. If the Praśna is made at the time of Rāśi or Tārā Sandhi, the couple could be lying awake without sleep due to fear of thieves. If the above is dṛṣṭied by other Grahas, union with widow is possible. जागरं चोरभीत्यर्थे राशिनक्षत्रसंधिषु । दृष्टश्चेद्विधवाभोगमकरो-दिति कीर्तयेत् ॥३०८॥

18.309. If at Praśna, Candra in Rāśi or Tārā Sandhi is with Śukra or Budha, there is a union with a prostitute. If at Praśna, Krūras aspect Candra, regardless of his position, the wife could be loving another person. However, if Candra with Saumyadṛṣṭi, the wife will be friendly and loving to the husband. तस्संघौ शुक्रसौम्यौ चेत्तदा दास्याः पति वदेत् । यत्र कुत्रापि शशिनं पापाः पश्यन्ति चेत्तदा । पुंसि चासज्जयति वधूः शुभाश्चेत्पुरुषप्रिया ॥३०९॥

18.310. Candra, Sūrya and Guru are Sāttvika; Śukra and Budha are Rājasika and Śani and Maṅgala are Tāmasika. From the nature of the Grahas must be determined the character and habits of men and women. सात्विकाश्चन्द्रजीवार्का राजसौ शुक्रसोमजौ । तामसौ शनिभूपुत्रौ चैव स्त्रीपुंगुणास्मृताः ॥ ३१० ॥

19. OF CHILDREN

Ācārya: Now, let us focus on the birth of children. The first is the Praśna, which is about whether the woman is pregnant.

Kailāśa: What are the rules of such Praśna, Guruji?

Ācārya: Guru and Rāhu indicate pregnancy. Guru is the Santānakāraka, and Rāhu indicates the birth in the mortal realm.

Sunidhi: Isn't Rāhu the Kāraka for bondage and Ketu, liberation?

Ācārya: That is right. We get entangled in worldly affairs due to Rāhu.

19.311. As women ask about their children's birth, I shall narrate the Graha conditions precedent for them. The conception will occur if Rāhu is with Udaya, Āruṛha, or Candra.

Ācārya: Therefore, in a Praśna, if Rāhu is with Udaya, Āruṛha or Candra, the woman must be pregnant.

Guru is the Kāraka for children, and therefore, Guru promises pregnancy.

19.312. At Praśna, if Guru is in 5H, 9H or 7H from Udaya or Candra, or if Guru dṛṣṭies those Bhāvas, conception can be predicted.

Ācārya: The key Bhāvas of pregnancy are 5H and 9H (Bhāvātbhāvaṁ of 5H). Besides, the 7H is also important, indicating coming together or copulation. Guru in the three Bhāvas or aspecting them can indicate pregnancy. The Bhāvas can be seen from Udaya or Candra.

Sunidhi: How to know if the delivery will be a painful one or will be with ease?

19.313. If Guru gets the influence of Saumyas, birthing (confinement) of the child will be easy; if Guru is in Nīca/Śatru Rāśi, misfortune (death) to the child must be predicted.

Ācārya: That is known from the state of Guru and influences on him. If he is weak/afflicted, the birthing will be painful, complicated and dangerous. But instead, he is fortified, and with Saumyayutidṛṣṭi, the delivery is smooth.

Sex Determination:

Jayanta: Guruji, why is the author talking about Pariveṣa?

Ācārya: Pariveṣa is like an Aprakāśa Graha. The Aprakāśa Grahas are children of Grahas. For instance, Dhūma is the child of Maṅgala, Vyatipāta Rāhu, Pariveṣa Candra, Indracāpa Guru and Upaketu Ketu. They have similar characteristics to their parent Graha.

Candra is the mother – related to Pregnancy. Pariveṣa is the halo around Sūrya and Candra, responsible for the rainy cloud. Therefore, Pariveṣa is associated with pregnancy and childbirth.

19.314. If at Praśna, Pariveṣa is in Vṛṣabha, the woman will be pregnant. From the Grahas associated with Pariveṣa, the sex of the child in the womb can be determined. If at Praśna, Candra, in whatever Rāśi, is associated with a Saumya, conception will occur.

Sunidhi: How to use Pariveṣa?

Ācārya: The author explains that. Candra's Uccarāśi is Vṛṣabha. Therefore, Pariveṣa in Vṛṣabha indicates that the woman is pregnant. In such a case, the Graha associated with Pariveṣa indicates the sex of the embryo.

Sunidhi: Kindly elaborate more.

Ācārya: Before that, let us examine the principles where the woman is not pregnant.

Sunidhi: Sure, Guruji.

19.315. If 3H, 9H and 5H are with Śukra, Sūrya, and Candra, or if the three Grahas are together in any of the three places, conception will not occur.

Ācārya: If Śukra is with Sūrya and Candra, the lady is not pregnant. The same occurs when Śukra (sex), Sūrya (father) and Candra (mother) are in 3H, 5H and 9H. 3H is the house of sex (Mithuna), whereas 5H and 9H stand for children. While Guru/Rāhu in these places (5H/9H) indicates pregnancy, Śukra/Candra/Sūrya indicates the opposite.

Sunidhi: Thank you for clarifying this.

Ācārya: Now, let us examine the principles of determining the sex of the embryo.

19.316. I will now describe how the sex of the child in the womb can be determined. If at Praśna, Pariveṣa dṛṣṭies Udaya; there will be an abortion.

Ācārya: if Parivеṣa dṛṣṭies Udaya, abortion results. Pariveṣa must ideally be in Vṛṣabha for pregnancy.

Kailāśa: Guruji, for male and female birth, should we not examine the Puruṣa and Strī Grahas and Rāśis?

Ācārya: Yes, we should. All Ojarāśis are Puruṣa, and Yugmarāśis are Strī. But Guru's both Rāśis indicate a male, and Budha's Rāśis indicate a female regardless of their Oja/Yugma attribute.

Kailāśa: If I remember correctly, Sūrya onwards Grahas are in the order of Puruṣa and Strī. Right?

Ācārya: Yes, that is why Sūrya, Maṅgala, Guru and Śani are males, whereas Candra, Budha and Śukra are females. Among the Chāyāgrahas, Rāhu is a male, and Ketu is a female.

19.317. If Candra is in an Ojabhāva from Udaya, the child will be male. But Candra is in a Yugmabhāva from Udaya; the child will be female. From the Tārā and Rāśi at Praśna, the sex of the child also can be predicted.

Ācārya: Besides Oja and Yugma Rāśis, we must also consider the Oja and Yugma Bhāvas. From Udaya, 1, 3, 5, 7, 9 and 11 are Ojabhāvas, and 2, 4, 6, 8, 10 and 12 are Yugmabhāvas.

According to the author, Candra in an Ojabhāva indicates a male birth, and a Yugmabhāva indicates a female birth.

19.318. A male child will be born if Sūrya or Śani is in 3H, 9H, 10H or 11H from Udaya.

Ācārya: Also, if Sūrya/Śani (males) in 3H, 9H, 11H (Ojabhāva) indicate a male birth. Their disposition in 10H indicates a male child, despite it being a Yugmabhāva. That is because it is Sūrya's and Maṅgala's (males) Dikbala Bhāva.

19.319. If all the Grahas are in Ojarāśis, a male will be born. If all Grahas are in Yugmarāśis, a female child will be born.

Ācārya: A simple principle is that if at Praśna, all Grahas are in Ojarāśis, then a male is born due to the predominance of masculine vibrations. Instead, when all are in Yugmarāśis, a female is born due to the predominance of feminine vibrations.

Timing Delivery:

Sunidhi: How to time the delivery?

19.320. The time taken for Candra to transit from Āruṛha to its 7H or the number of Tārās in the Rāśis from Āruṛha to 7H will give the number of days by which the woman will deliver the child.

Ācārya: There are several methods. But one of the methods is to check Candra's Gocara. This method works if the pregnancy is due in days. If it is due in months, there are other methods.

In this method, find how far 7H is (from Candra) from Āruṛha. Candra transits a Rāśi in about 2.25 days. You can estimate the birth date by checking how long Candra will take to move from Āruṛha to his (Candra's) 7H. You can also count the Nakṣatra of Āruṛha and 7H of Candra. Candra takes about a day to cover a Nakṣatra. Therefore, this count of Nakṣatras can indicate the approximate birth day.

20. ON MISFORTUNES

Ācārya: Now, the misfortune overcoming the child is described below. I will leave it to you for self-study.

20.321-322. Now I will describe the misfortunes that are likely to overtake a child. If Candra is in 6H from Udaya, and a Krūra is in 7H from Candra (i.e., 12H of Udaya), the mother and the child will die. But if a Krūra is in 5H or 6H from Candra, only the mother will die.

20.323. If at Praśna, Candra is in 12H, the newborn's left eye, and if Sūrya is in 12H, the newborn's right eye will be blind.

20.324. If Krūras aspect Sūrya, the father's death, and if Sūrya and Candra are together or aspecting each other, the mother's death must be predicted.

20.325-326. If at Praśna Guru dṛṣṭies Sūrya and Candra, both the parents will suffer from illness. If Rāhu is in Udaya and is dṛṣṭied by Guru, the death of the newborn must be predicted. If Sūrya and Candra are in 12H from Udaya, both the eyes of the child will be blind. चन्द्रादित्यौ गुरुः पश्येन्मातापित्रोर्गदो भवेत् । यदि लग्नगतो राहुर्जीवदृष्टिविवर्जितः ॥३२५॥ जातस्य मरणं शीघ्रं वदेदत्र न संशयः । द्वादशस्थावर्कचन्द्रौ नेत्रयुग्मं विनश्यति ॥३२६॥

20.327. If Sūrya and Candra are in 6H/5H and are dṛṣṭied by Krūras, the death of the parents is certain. If Śani is in those Bhāvas, the brother's death, and if Maṅgala is there, the uncle's death must be predicted.

20.328. If Saumyas are in the Kendras of Udaya, Āruṛha or Chatra or if Saumyas are in Sva/Ucca/Mitra Vargas, all kinds of disasters or accidents will be prevented.

Illegitimate Birth

Ācārya: Guru's dṛṣṭi on Udaya or Candra promise that the child is legitimate. However, if neither are dṛṣṭied by Guru by they are dṛṣṭied by Krūras, the child is born illegitimate.

20.329. If Guru does not aspect Udaya or Candra, but only Krūras are aspecting the two Lagnas, the child is born to a different father (illegitimate birth).

Danger to the Parents

Kailāśa: Guruji, kindly provide the principles for danger to the mother and father.

Ācārya: Alright, let me provide them from Bṛhatparāśara.

Sunidhi: Sure, Guruji!

Ācārya: Firstly, let us examine the main factors of danger to them.

Sūrya is the Kāraka for the father and Candra for the mother

Sūrya with Krūrayutidṛṣṭi, or in Pāpakartari, indicate danger to the father. This is even more so if Krūras also afflict 7H from Sūrya.

Candra with Krūrayutidṛṣṭi, or in Pāpakartari, indicates danger to the mother. This is even more so if Krūras also afflict 6H/7H from Candra.

Krūras in 6H, 8H, or 4H from Sūrya causes danger to the father.

Krūras in 6H, 8H, or 4H from Candra causes danger to the mother.

Sunidhi: Dhanyavād Guruji! Kindly elaborate on the other Yogas for danger to the mother and the father.

Ācārya: The Yogas are listed below.

Danger to the Mother

9.24. The mother is in danger if Candra receives a dṛṣṭi from three Krūras. Saumyas, giving a dṛṣṭi to Candra, bring good to the mother.

9.25. 2H occupied by Rāhu, Budha, Śukra, Sūrya and Śani, the child's birth is after the father's death, and even the mother is in danger.

9.26. Candra is with a Krūra in 7H/8H from a Krūra with dṛṣṭi from a strong Krūra, mother's life is in immense danger.

9.27. Sūrya in Ucca/Nīca in 7H indicates that the mother dies immediately after the child's birth, and he is raised on goat milk.

9.28. Krūra in 4H in a Śatrurāśi from Candra and Kendras are without Saumyas, indicating the death of the mother.

9.29. Krūras in 6H and 12H indicate danger to the mother. Krūras in 4H and 10H indicate danger to the father.

9.30. Budha in 2H, Krūras in 1H and 12H destroy the entire family (both the mother and the father).

9.31. Guru in 1H, Śani in 2H and Rāhu in 3H indicate immense danger to the mother.

9.32. The mother gives up the child if Krūras afflict Koṇas from Kṛṣṇa-Candra without Saumyayutidṛṣṭi.

9.33. Maṅgala-Śani yuti in a Candra-Kendra in the same Navāñśa indicates that the child has two mothers, and yet it is short-lived.

Danger to the father

9.34. Śani in 1H, Maṅgala in 7H and Candra in 6H indicate danger to the father.

9.35. Guru is 1H, and Śani-Sūrya-Maṅgala-Budha in 2H indicate that the person loses his father near his marriage.

9.36. Sūrya with a Krūra or in Pāpakartari, and his 7H is with Krūra, indicating an early death of the father.

9.37. Sūrya in 7H, Maṅgala in 10H and Rahu in 12H indicate an early death of the father.

9.38. Maṅgala in 10H in a Śatrurāśi causes an early and troubled death of the father.

9.39. Śani in 1H, Candra in 6H, and Maṅgala in 7H indicate danger to the father.

9.40. Sūrya in Meṣa, dṛṣṭied by Śani, indicate that the father leaves the family before the child's birth or he is not alive. The same occurs when Sūrya is Meṣa is in Vṛścika Navāñśa.

9.41. 4H, 10H and 12H afflicted by Krūras indicate that both the parents will leave the child to its fate and wander from place to place.

9.42. Rāhu-Guru yuti in 1H/4H in a Śatrurāśi indicates that the father does not see the native till the native is 23.

21. ON SWORDS

Ācārya: The following principles are for predicting the fate of a sword. In ancient times, the war used to be fought using swords. The quality of the sword was important to ensure that it did not break and become the cause of defeat in a war. Therefore, such Praśna used to be important.

You can study them yourself to witness the beauty of Jyotiṣa. We may skip the discussion since they have no practical use today.

Jayanta: Noted Guruji!

21.330. I will now tell you all about the ownership and fate of swords. If Candra is associated with Rāhu, the sword will break. If Grahas in Nīca/Śatru Rāśis aspect Candra, the sword will also break.

21.331. But if Candra is with or dṛṣṭied by Saumyas and is in 7H, all good will come to the sword.

21.332-333. If Āruṛha, Udaya and Chatra are associated with Krūras, the person will be killed by the same sword; or an enemy will take the sword away during a fight. But if in the above places, Saumyas are posited, all good will come from the sword.

21.334-335. If a Krūra is in 7H from Khadga Lagna when the sword is shown to a Daivajña, it will be broken at its lower portion. If Krūras are in 5H/9H, the whole sword will be broken at its lower portion. If Krūras are in 10H/4H, the middle portion of the sword will be broken. If in 11H/3H, the pointed edge of the sword will be broken.

21.336. If Grahas in a Mitrarāśi aspect Udaya, Āruṛha or Chatra, the sword belongs to a friend; if Grahas in their own houses aspect the above Rāśis the sword belongs to the Pṛcchaka himself making the Praśna; if Grahas in Ucca aspect the above Rāśis, the sword belongs to one higher than himself; if Grahas in Nīca aspect the Rāśis, the sword belongs to one higher than himself; and if Grahas posited in Śatrurāśis aspect the above Rāśis (Udaya, Āruṛha and Chatra), the sword belongs to his enemy.

21.337-338. If Samadṛṣṭi Grahas (Candra and Guru) aspect Udaya, Āruṛha or Chatra, the sword belongs to the owner (Pṛcchaka). If Tiryagdṛṣṭi

Graha (Maṅgala) dṛṣṭies the Rāśis, the sword belongs to another; and if Adhodṛṣṭi Grahas (Śukra and Budha) aspect the Rāśis, the sword has been obtained after defeating the enemy, and the sword has fallen and been picked up by the present owner. Considering the various characteristics of the Grahas, the ownership or misplacement of the sword must be determined.

[**Notes:** Per 2.49-50, Guru and Candra have **Samadṛṣṭi** (they aspect each other). Sūrya has **Urdhvadṛṣṭi**; Maṅgala has **Tiryagdṛṣṭi**; Śukra and Budha have **Adhodṛṣṭi**. Rāhu and Śani look alike. Sama is forward, Tiryag is sideways, Urdhva is upward, and Adho is downward.]

22. ON SHADOWS AND SHAFTS

Ācārya: The following principles deal with finding underground treasure. They can be used for identifying hidden wealth buried underground. Again, you can study on your own.

22.339. To answer some Praśnas, the shadow of the person making the Praśna is measured, and based on its length, certain calculations are made, and predictions are given. Measure the shadow, leaving the foot, by your pace, add 28, multiply by 12. and divide the sum by 16. The prediction is given based on the remainder arrived at. This is called the Salya Śāstra.

22.340. Salya is of 16 kinds. They are: (1) skull (2) bone (3) brick (4) tile (5) firewood (6) Devamūrti (7) ash (8) corpse (9) charcoal (10) grain (11) wealth (gold) (12) rock (13) frog (14) cow's bone (15) dog's bone, and (16) Piśāca. कपालास्थीष्टकालोष्टकाष्ठदेवविभूतयः । शावाङ्गारकधान्यानि धनपाषाणदर्दुराः । गोस्थिश्वास्थि पिशाचाश्च क्रमाच्छल्यानि षोडश ॥३४०॥

22.341. Of these, if (10), (11), (13) and (14) come together (i.e. grain, gold, frog and cow's bone), it is reckoned as Śubha (Uttama). But other 'Salyas' are considered Aśubha. एषु शल्येषु मण्डूकस्वर्णगोस्थि च धान्यकम् । दृष्ट चेदुत्तमं चान्ये सर्वे स्युरशुभावहाः ॥३४१॥

[**Notes:** Let us take an example. Suppose the length of the shadow is 9 paces. By adding 28, the sum is 37. Multiplied by 12, the product is 444. Divided by 16, the remainder is 12. The 12th Salya is "Rock"- which is Aśubha.

22.342. What the wise men have stated as "Ahi Cakra" I shall describe now. This means the student can learn about wealth, 'Salya' and 'Sunya' (i.e. Zero).

22.343. The "Ahi Cakra" is drawn thus by 8 lines vertically and 5 lines horizontally, making 28 houses.

22.344. These 28 houses must be filled with the Tārās starting from Kṛttikā. Wherever Candra is found in these houses, it must be noted there is a Salya.

22.345. Taking the Tārā rising in the horizon at Praśna as the first, fill up the 28 houses with Tārās and count the number up to the Tārā where Candra is, and note the 'Salya' indicated by that number.

22.346. He, who is anxious to find treasure and is searching, should make the 'Ahi Cakra' at that place of his search.

22.347. Fill the Eastern 7 houses with the following Tārās: (1) Revatī (2) Aśvinī (3) Bharaṇī (4) Kṛttikā (5) Maghā (6) Pūrvāphālgunī (7) Uttarāphālgunī.

22.348. In the next seven houses, fill the Tārās: (1) Uttarābhādra (2) Pūrvābhādra (3) Śatabhiṣā (4) Rohiṇī (5) Aśleṣā (6) Pūrvāṣāṛhā and (7) Hastā.

22.349. In the next seven houses, fill the following Tārās: (1) Abhijit (2) Śravana (3) Dhaniṣṭhā (4) Mṛgaśirā (5) Ārdra (6) Punarvasu and (7) Chitta.

22.350. In the next seven houses, fill the following Tārās: (1) Uttarāṣāṛhā (2) Pūrvāṣāṛhā (3) Mūla (4) Jyeṣṭha (5) Anurādhā (6) Viśākhā and (7) Svāti.

22.351. Thus is formed the Ahi Cakra. Opposite Bharaṇī and Maghā rise two branches, and in between is the hole opposite Kṛttikā. In the Ahi Cakra, 14 houses belong to Candra, and the rest to Sūrya.

22.352. As indicated in the figure, three Tārās from Aśvinī, 5 Tārās from Ārdra, 4 Tārās from Pūrvābhādra and Revatī belong to Candra. Therefore, the Tārās belonging to Candra are: Aśvinī, Bharaṇī, Kṛttikā, Ārdra, Punarvasu, Puṣya, Aśleṣā, Maghā, Pūrvāṣāṛhā, Uttarāṣāṛhā, Śravana, Dhaniṣṭhā, Pūrvābhādra and Revatī. Tārās belonging to Sūrya are the remaining 14; Rohiṇī, Mṛgaśirā Pūrvāphālgunī, Uttarāphālgunī, Hastā, Citra, Svāti, Viśākhā, Anurādhā, Jyeṣṭha, Mūla, Abhijit, Śatabhiṣā and Uttarābhādra.

The following is the **Ahi Cakra**

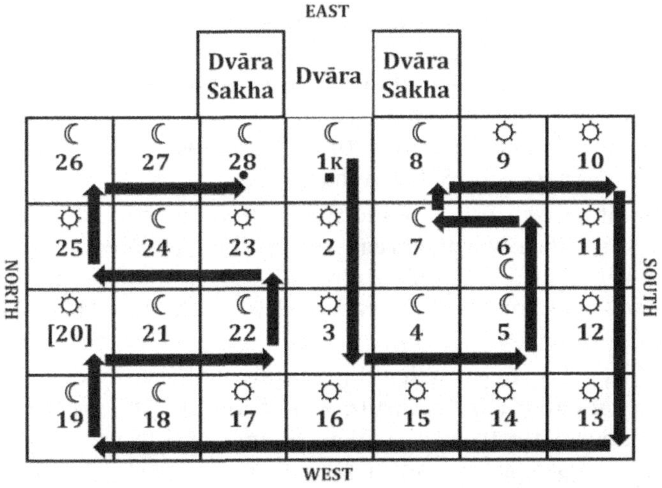

The Nakṣatras marked in the Cakra are 1-Kṛttikā; 2-Rohiṇī; 3-Mṛgaśirā; 4-Ārdrā; 5-Punarvasu; 6-Puṣya; 7-Aśleṣā; 8-Maghā; 9-Pūrvāphālgunī; 10-Uttarāphālgunī; 11-Hastā; 12-Citrā; 13-Svāti; 14-Viśākhā; 15-Anurādhā; 16-Jyeṣṭhā; 17-Mūla; 18-Pūrvāṣāṛhā; 19-Uttarāṣāṛhā; ***20-Abhijit***; 21-Śravaṇa; 22-Dhaniṣṭhā; 23-Śatabhiṣā; 24-Pūrvābhādra; 25-Uttarābhādra; 26-Revatī; 27-Aśvinī; 28-Bharaṇī.

The Nakṣatras marked with ☾ are ruled by Candra, and those marked with ☼ are ruled by Sūrya.

22.353. Ascertain Candra's Tārā at Praśna and the Nāḍīkā expired in that Tārā, multiply it by 25, and divide the product by 60. Leaving the quotient, the remainder must be counted from Candra's Tārā, and the resulting Tārā is called 'Dinendu'. उदयादिगता नाड्यो भग्नाः षष्ट्याप्तशेषके । दिनेन्दुभुक्तयुक्तोसौ भवेत्तत्कालचन्द्रमाः ॥३५३॥

22.354. Again taking the 'Nāḍīkā' expired in that Tārā by Candra, multiply by 60 and divide by 45. The quotient is again to be divided by 4. The remainder indicates the direction in which Candra will be at Praśna, considering 1 as East, 2 as South, 3 as West and 4 as North.

Jayanta: Kindly give an example.

Ācārya: Suppose at a Praśna, Candra is in Karka 29:18:51, i.e., 119.314. Multiplying it by 0.075, the Nakṣatra is 8.94855, i.e., 9th Nakṣatra Aśleṣā. The Nāḍīkā elapsed is 0.94855 * 60 = 56.913 = 56.

Therefore, Candra is in Aśleṣā, and the expired Nāḍīkā is 56. Multiplying 56 by 27, the product is 1512, divided by 60 gives the remainder 12. Counting 12 Tārās from Aśleṣā, we get 9 + 12 – 1 = 20 = Pūrvāṣāṛhā. Dinendu is Pūrvāṣāṛhā. Again multiplying 56 (Nāḍīkā explored) by 60 and dividing it by 45, we get the quotient of 74. Dividing it by 4, we get the remainder of 2, which is South. Candra is in this direction. Likewise, the calculation must be made for Sūrya.

Jayanta: Thank you for clarifying this.

22.355. Having made the tabular statement as described in the above calculation, one must find whether Sūrya and Candra are in their compartments or in each other's interchanged If both Sūrya and Candra are in Candra's compartment, the person will get a treasure in that place. If both Sūrya and Candra are in Sūrya's compartment, the same Salya will be noted. If it is otherwise, it means there is no Salya in that place.

22.356. If either Sūrya or Candra is in its compartment or both in their compartments, the Salya regarding treasure must be calculated. If it is otherwise, it means there is no Salya. Even if Candra is in its own house but dṛṣṭied by a Krūra, the person will not get the treasure despite the fact of his having that desirable Salya.

22.357. If it is a Pūrṇacandra, the treasure will have mudras (gold coins), and if it is a partial Candra, the treasure will be meagre; if Candra is dṛṣṭied by the Graha, the native of the treasure will be of nine kinds (Navanidhi).

22.358. If Candra, arrived at by calculation, is dṛṣṭied by Sūrya, the treasure will be gold. But this Candra is dṛṣṭied by Candra at the time of Praśna, the treasure will be silver or pearl; if Candra is dṛṣṭied by Maṅgala, the treasure will be copper; if dṛṣṭied by Budha, it will be brass; if by Guru, the treasure will be gems; if by Śukra, it will be bronze; if by Śani it will be iron; if by Rāhu it will be lead; and if by Ketu it will be tin.

22.359. If Candra is dṛṣṭied by two or more Grahas, the treasure also will be of a mixed character; if no Graha dṛṣṭies Candra, the treasure too will be nothing. But if all Grahas aspect Candra, the treasure will be very large.

22.360. If Candra is in Saumyarāśi, there will be a gain of treasure. But if it is in a Krūrarāśi, there will be no gain, say those experts in this Śāstra of Salya.

22.361. If Candra is in Sūrya's Rāśi, the treasure will be in a golden vessel; if Candra is in Svarāśi, the vessel will be of silver or pearl; if in Maṅgala' Rāśi, it will be a copper vessel; if in Budha's Rāśi, the vessel will be of bronze; if in Guru's Rāśi it will be stone vessel; if in Śukra's Rāśi, it will be a mud pot, if in Śani's Rāśi it will be an iron vessel.

22.362. The size of the plot of ground where the treasure is found can be determined by the "Añśas" (strength) in Candra's Rāśi or by the strength of Raśmis in the Grahas in that Rāśi. If Candra is in a Nīca Añśa, the treasure will be underwater.

22.363. If Candra is in its Sva/Ucca Rāśi/Añśa, the treasure will be found easily in the upper layer. If Candra is in Uccāñśa, the treasure will be in still higher layers; and if Candra is in Rāśisandhi, the treasure will be inside a wall.

22.364. The 16 kinds of Salyas are determined according to the strength of the compartment in which Candra dwells. The Ṣadvargas of Candra give added strength, and the number obtained by ordinary reckoning is increased tenfold.

22.365. Of this tenfold increase, the first increase is related to the Graha concerned; the 2nd to the face; the 3rd to the Graha; the 4th to the guardian of the field (Kṣetrapala); the 5th to the divine mothers; the 6th to the bright luminous Devatās; the 7th to the terrifying Devatās; the 8th to Rudra; the 9th to Yakṣa; and the 10th to the Nāgas.

22.366. For the 1st increase, a Homa must be done; for the 2nd increase, the Nārāyaṇa Bali must be performed; in the 3rd, an ordinary sacrifice must be done; in the 4th increase, meat and wine must be offered; in the 5th increase, a big sacrifice must be made. यहे होमः प्रकर्तव्यो सुखे नारायणो बलिः । क्षेत्रपाले सुरां मांसं मातृकायां महाबलिः ॥३६६॥

22.367. In the 6th increase regarding luminous Devatās, the worship of lights must be performed; in the 7th, the worship of the frightful Devatās must be done; in the 8th, one must recite the mantras of Rudra; in the 9th, the Yakṣas must be appeased by appropriate measures. दीपेशे दीपजा पूजा भीषणे भोषणार्चनम् । रुद्रे च रुद्रजो जाप्यो यक्षे यक्षादिशान्तयः ॥३६७॥

22.368. In the 10th increase, worship to the Sarpa Devatās associated with the lord of the elementals (Gananātha) must be performed. In every kind of worship, prayer to wealth-giving elementals is also to be offered. नागे नागग्रहाः पूज्या गणनाथेन संयुताः । लक्ष्मीधरदितत्वानि सर्वकार्येषु पूजयेत् ॥३६८॥

22.369. By doing such rituals, even the impossible kinds of work can be accomplished. Undoubtedly people respect those who have obtained treasure. एवं कृते विधाने हि निरसाध्योपि सिद्ध्यति ॥ निधिप्राप्त्या नरा लोके वन्दनीया न संशयः ॥३६९॥

22.370-372. The length and breadth of the reckoned place must first be determined. By multiplying one by the other and dividing the product by 20, the quotient obtained is called *aratni* (अरत्नि). The remainder must be multiplied by nine and the product is called *nirisantāna* (र्निरिसन्तान). Multiplying this again by nine and dividing it by 20, the quotient is to be left out, and the remainder must be taken as Aṅgula. This is called *ratni prādeśaṃ aṃgulaṃ* (रत्नि प्रादेशं अंगुलं). This is the method by which the exact place of the treasure inside the earth in terms of Aratni and Aṅgula is determined. शङ्कास्थलस्य विस्तारायामावन्योन्यताडितौ । विंशत्यापहृतं शेषमरत्निरिति कीर्तितम् ॥३७०॥ रत्निं गुणित्वा नवभि र्निरिसन्तानमुच्यते । तत्प्रदेशं गुणित्वायै हृत्वा विंशतिभिर्यदि ॥३७१॥ शिष्टं अंगुलं एवोक्तं रत्नि प्रादेशं अंगुलं । एवं क्रमेण रत्न्याद्यं अगाधं कथयेदघः ॥३७२॥

22.373. If Krūras are in the Kendras, the ascertained Salya cannot be found. But if Saumyas are in the Kendras, the Salya will be found there. But if Saumyas and Krūras are in the Kendras, one can only predict that the Salya is there.

22.374-375. If Sūrya dṛṣṭies, a Kendra prediction is about Devatās. Suppose Maṅgala dṛṣṭies the Kendra one that refers to Brahmarākṣasa. If both Maṅgala and Candra are in a Kendra, and it happens to be the trough of a Tārā belonging to Maṅgala, one can find in the earth only an ant hill. If Guru and Candra are in a Kendra and it happens to be a trough of a Tārā belonging to Guru, one can find in the earth either gold or the bones of a cow or man.

22.376. If Rāhu is in Udaya/Āruṛha Kendra and it happens to be the trough of a Tārā belonging to Rāhu, one must predict the unearthing of an ant hill with a light nearby.

22.377. If Saumyas in a Kendra are dṛṣṭied by strong Krūras, one can predict a Salya (bone) in that place.

22.378. If Krūras are in Kendras, there is no doubt that in that place there will be Piśācas, Yakṣas or Devatās. In accordance with the number of Raśmis of the Grahas will be these Piśācas or Devatās down deep in the earth. देवयक्षपिशाचाद्यास्तत्र तिष्ठन्त्यसंशयम् । ग्रहांशुसङ्ख्यया तेषां खातमानं वदेत्सुधीः ॥३७८॥

22.379-381. If Maṅgala and Budha are in the trough of a Tārā belonging to Budha there will be found a "Salya" associated with Budha. If Śukra and Candra are in a Kendra which is the trough of a Tārā belonging to Śukra, there will be found silver or white stone. Sūrya, Candra, Maṅgala, Budha, Guru, Śukra, Śani, Rāhu and Ketu are respectively having 5, 6, 8, 5, 1¼ , 1¼, 1½, 2 and 12 Raśmis. In terms of these Raśmis, one must dig deep in the earth to find the Salya. चन्द्रे बुधेन संयुक्ते बुधनक्षत्रकोष्ठगे । स्वशल्यं विद्यते तत्र केन्द्रे शुक्रेन्दुसंयुते ॥३७९॥ शुक्रस्थितर्क्षगे कोष्ठे रौप्यं श्वेतशिलापिवा । पञ्चषडसुभूतानि सपादैकं तथैव च ॥३८०॥ सार्घरूपाक्षिरवयः सूर्यादीनां करास्स्मृताः । शल्यागाधमनेनैव करेण कथयेत्सुधीः ॥३८१॥

23. ON WELLS

Ācārya: Kūpa Praśna is a specialised field of Praśna, in which the specific location of water is found so that a well can be dug. Finding groundwater for drinking and sanitation has been a human need since antiquity. That required the development of this specialised field of Praśna.

Sunidhi: I suppose through this method, one can find where to dig a well to harvest ground water. Is that right?

Ācārya: That is right, Sunidhi. Searching for water in aquifers below the earth's surface requires painstaking effort to pump it. This must be done with the utmost care and precision to dig or drill wells in the best possible places and avoid expensive, discouraging failures.

Sunidhi: This means this method is still useful in today's world.

Ācārya: This is indeed very useful. Given the growing and vital importance of water and soil resources worldwide, as well as their scarcity, there is a great of doing everything possible to improve the finding, management and preservation of these essential and fragile resources.

Groundwater is usually good-quality water. As it is often buried at significant depths, it is highly advisable to locate it as precisely as possible and assess its quantity and quality before undertaking costly drilling work.

Finding groundwater becomes even more important in regions prone to severe droughts. Aquifers are natural underground reservoirs capable of supplying large quantities of drinking water during the dry season when rivers are likely to dry up.

Sunidhi: Aren't there modern scientific methods for determining this?

Ācārya: Yes, there are scientific methods available. One of them involves Hydro-geophysics. Geophysical methods can help with detecting underground aquifers. There is also an analysis of satellite photos or proton magnetic resonance investigations.

This involves studying the soil's physical and electrical properties. The aquifers are most often trapped between rock layers. All rocks conduct a certain amount of electricity. Still, their conductivity and resistivity vary according to their type: compact rock, dry rock, fractured rock, wet rock, permeable structures or impermeable ones. A material's electrical resistivity is its capacity to oppose the flow of electric current.

These methods are thus based on the capacity of the soil or rock to conduct electricity and the measurement of their conductivity or resistivity. The aquifer's type, size and quality are deduced and specified with a high probability from these measurements.

Sunidhi: If such advanced methods are available, why must one employ Praśna to do the job?

Ācārya: Praśna is reliable and is less time and effort-consuming than modern methods. Also, the method is mostly in the planes. This method is difficult to implement in mountainous regions due to the great depths involved.

Besides, even the Praśna method is scientific. It is just that we cannot decipher the governing principles behind this science. With the advancement of science, it should be able to identify the alignment of heavenly events and worldly affairs. One of the important outcomes of a scientific method is the consistency and reliability of the outcome. It must be scientific if the Praśna methods can consistently lead to an outcome.

Sunidhi: That makes sense, Guruji!

Ācārya: Below are the principles of identifying the potential place to dig for water well. However, I do not intend to cover it here since I have covered it in great detail in the Praśna 2nd volume (Book 23B). You must refer to that for the details of a special Cakra called the Candragupti Cakra.

Sunidhi: Noted, Guruji.

23.382-386. Now I will tell you the calculations about digging wells. Draw five lines across and 8 vertically (per śloka 22.346), forming 38 compartments. The Tārās must be filled up, considering Praśna's Tārā as the first. If the Praśna is in the morning, the compartments of the East must face forward; if the Praśna is made at noon, the compartments of the South must face forward; if the Praśna is made in the evening, the compartments of the West must face forward; if it is made after mid-night the compartments of the North must face forward.

23.387-388. If the Praśna is made at ***Noon***, leave out two compartments in the Southeast, and from the third, starting with ***Maghā,*** fill up the rest. If the Praśna is made in the ***Evening***, leave out two compartments in the Southwest and from the third, starting with ***Anurādhā***, fill up the rest. If the Praśna is made at ***Midnight***, leave out the first two compartments in the Northeast and from the third, starting with ***Dhaniṣṭhā***, fill up the rest.

23.389. The length of half a day must be divided among 7 Tārās starting from Kṛttikā, and they must be filled up in the compartments. Suppose a day is 29.75 Ghaṭis, then half a day is 14.875. If this is divided by 7, we get for each Tārā 2.125 Ghaṭis. If a Praśna is made in the first 2.125 Ghaṭis from 6:00 am, we must consider the Tārā as Kṛttikā. Similarly, we ascertain the 7 Tārās ruling the Praśna between 6:00 am to 12 Noon.

23.389-390. In a similar manner, from 12 Noon to 6:00 pm, the 7 Tārās from Maghā to Viśākhā rule. From 6:00 pm to 12 midnight, the 7 Tārās Anurādhā to Dhaniṣṭhā rule. From midnight to 6:00 am, the 7 Tārās from Śatabhiṣā to Bharaṇī rule.

Further at Praśna, one must determine the Tārā of the day according to the Pañcāṅga, and fix it up in the compartment, starting from Anurādhā if it is night from 6 to 12 and from Dhaniṣṭhā if it is morning from 12 midnight to 6 am. That compartment is called the house of Candra's Tārā.

23.391-393. Having constructed this, where Candra is situated, it must be noted that it is a watery place. If the compartment happens to have a Tārā associated with Śukra, one must predict that the place is watery. If the Tārā happens to be associated with Guru, one can predict the finding of gold there.

Tulā, Vṛṣabha, Karka, Kumbha, Vṛścika and Makara are Sajala. If the Tārā happens to rise in any one of the Rāśis, water is available in that place. If, in that place, Candra and Śukra are posited, a great volume of water is available.

23.394. A little water can be predicted if that Udayarāśi belongs to the Budha group. But if Śani or Sūrya dṛṣṭies the above Rāśis, there will be no water. If Rāhu dṛṣṭies them, there will be water.

23.395. If the Chatrarāśi is above the Udaya and Āruṛha Rāśis and is dṛṣṭied by a Jalatattva Graha or associated with it, water will be found at a deep level. But if an Urdhvamukhi Graha is in that Rāśi, the water can be found at a higher level.

Notes: The Grahas in the six Rāśis from Sūrya are Urdhvamukhi. The Grahas in the remaining six Rāśis (7H-12H) are Adhomukhi.

23.396. If Krūras are found either above or below Udaya, Āruṛha and Chatra, there will be no water there. But if a Krūra is in 4H from Udaya or Āruṛha, water will be found at a deep level.

23.397. Some Jyotiṣīs predict that a river will flow in that place after 7 or 1 year. Water availability must be determined by ascertaining Sajala or Nirjala Grahas.

23.398. Good potable water is available if Candra or Guru is in a Kendra. If Śukra and Candra are in a Kendra, water will be plenty, even if it is mountainous.

23.399. If Candra and Budha are in a Kendra, old salt water is available there. If Candra is in a Kendra to the Āruṛha and is dṛṣṭied by Pariveṣa or other Aprakāśa Grahas, water is at a deep level.

23.400. The depth in which water will be available is determined by counting the Raśmis of the Grahas detailed above. If Budha and Śukra are associated and posited in a Kendra, the water will be salty.

23.401. Water will be at a middle level (neither too high nor too low) if Budha is in his Svarāśi. If Guru is with Rāhu, granite stones will be in the middle level.

23.402. If Rāhu is with Śukra and Candra, there is a gush of water at a deep level. If Sūrya or Pariveṣa is there in Dhanu, the water is salty. If Śani is with Rāhu, water is available at a middle level.

23.403-404. The kind of soil a place would be where one wants to dig a well is determined thus. If Sūrya is there, the soil would be barren with saline content; the Krūras - Śani and Maṅgala indicate a soil where only thorns and brambles can grow. Guru indicates coconut, dates and areca nut groves; Śukra indicates plantain and creeper-growing expanse; Budha points to jackfruit-growing soil; Rāhu and Ketu indicate anthills.

23.405. If Śani or Rāhu is in Udaya, where one wants to dig a well, one can only meet with termites, snakes and insects. If Lagna Rāśi is dṛṣṭied by Lagneśa, the place where the well is being dug is owned by the person; but if it is either dṛṣṭied by or associated with other Grahas, the place belongs to someone else.

Kūpa Cakra - 6 am to 12 noon

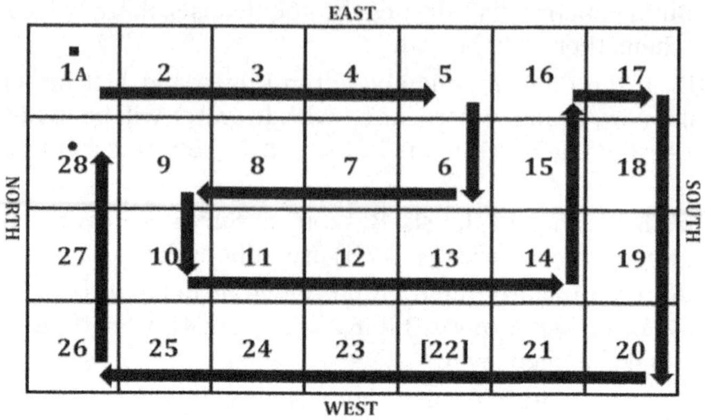

Kūpa Cakra - 6 pm to 12 midnight

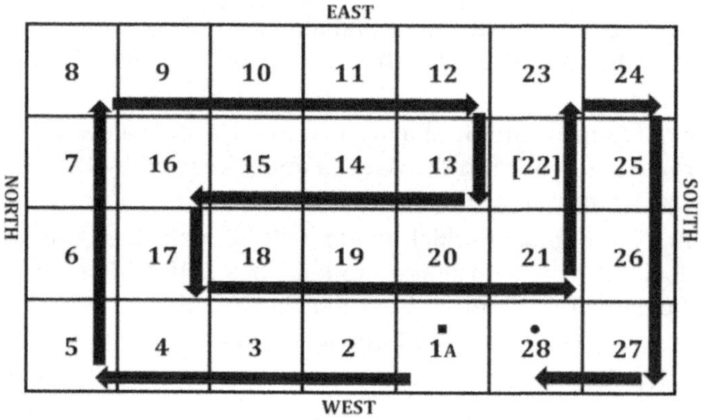

Jayanta: Guruji, I kindly request you to provide a high-level overview of this interesting Cakra. We will read up on the details in the book you mentioned.

Ācārya: Alright, let us do that.

Rain irrigates crops and replenishes waterbodies, whereas Kūpa helps quench thirst. Therefore, both are crucial for sustaining humans, animals, plants, and the world. After having studied the Varṣā Praśna, the next we should study is the Kūpa Praśna, which deals with the water in the well.

Jayanta: So, should we also study the Varṣā Praśna in this context?

Ācārya: When it comes to drinking water, studying rains is important. In a year of less rain, the demand for groundwater increases.

Jayanta: Noted, Guruji!

Ācārya: The Praśna about digging a well is called a Kūpa Praśna. Kūpa traditionally means well but can be extended to any underground waterbody, aquifer, or spring.

What we studied in the chapter on Varṣā Praśna, some of those principles also apply to Kūpa Praśna, mainly the concept of Sajala/Nirjala classification of the Rāśis/Grahas.

The Kūpa Praśna specifically addresses whether water can be found when a well is dug in a place. When someone wants to dig a well, this chapter shall guide us. I will use Praśnamārga as the basis for delineating the principles of Kūpa Praśna.

Jayanta: Noted, Guruji!

Ācārya: Ācārya Harihara starts by stating the months, which is good for digging well. It depends on the moisture level in the group. It cannot be dug in a Varṣā Ṛtu because of obvious reasons. Digging is not recommended in the summer, as the soil is too hard and dry. The best time to dig is when the soil is somewhat moist, and rain is absent.

Jayanta: So, it means we should start examining the soil quality before digging.

Ācārya: That is right. Ācārya Harihara states that according to some, the best time for digging wells is four months from Makara; according to some others, it should be done in the month of Mīna and 3 months succeeding it.

Jayanta: The Rāśis are not related to seasons in Niryāṇa Cakra. Isn't it?

Ācārya: Yes! This should be interpreted as Sāyana Māsa because only from that Cakra can we determine the season and the best time for digging.

Karka and Siṅha denote the Varṣā Ṛtu, and it takes about 4 months for the groundwater to be fully replenished and the soil is moist enough to commence digging.

The four months Kanyā to Dhanu in which the groundwater replenishment happens. Therefore, it should be the four months after that, i.e., from Makara to Meṣa, in which the digging must happen. They correspond to Śiśira (winter) and Vasanta spring).

While some scholars believe that the good time for digging is Mīna to Mithuna, which includes the 2 months of Summer, i.e., Vṛṣabha and Mithuna, and once it hits Mithuna, Varṣā Ṛtu starts. Therefore, Mīna to Mithuna is riskier.

I think digging should happen from Makara to Meṣa Māsa. Also, if the digging starts in summer (Vṛṣabha or Mithuna), it isn't easy to decipher the water depth from the soil moisture level.

One should decipher the right place for digging by examining the snake hills, trees, grasses, and certain fruits. The quality of certain fruit tells us whether the water is deep below in the ground or is at a shallow level.

Praśnamārga:

26.1. In this chapter, I shall be detailing 'Kūpa Praśna', explaining whether water can be had if a well is dug at a specified place.

26.2. According to some, the best time for digging wells is four months from Makara; others believe it should be done in the month of Mīna and 3 months succeeding it.

26.3. By scrutiny of snake hills, trees, grass, and certain fruits and by Kūpa Praśna, whether a water layer can be discovered in a certain spot can be known beforehand. The time for examining it has been given in the last śloka. The time must be such that there should be no difficulty in testing the nature of the soil.

Jayanta: Guruji, what are the Yogas in the Praśna Kuṇḍalī that indicate that the water can be found in the land for which the Praśna is put?

Ācārya: Rāhu is an important Graha to reckon with in this Praśna because he is the Kāraka for deep crevices and wells. Candra is important because the Praśna is about water, of which he is the Kāraka.

In the Praśna Kuṇḍalī, if the Lagna is Cara (water is moving underground) and is occupied by Rāhu and Candra, water shall be found in the selected spot.

Likewise, in the Kuṇḍalī, the presence of Sūrya in 10H and Bṛhaspati in 4H also favour an affirmative response.

Candra in the Lagna, which may or may not be a Cara Rāśi but is a Sajala Rāśi, indicates water in the selected spot.

If a Krūra is in 4H (Pātāla, nadir, depth) and Candra joins the Lagna, water shall be found when the digging is carried out to a great depth (Krūra in 4th = deeper).

Praśnamārga:

26.7. Whether there is water underground is to be ascertained from the following yogas, based on the Praśna time.

26.8. If the Lagna is a Cara Rāśi and Rāhu and Candra join it, there shall be water in the selected spot. There shall be water when Sūrya occupies the 10th, and Bṛhaspati occupies 4H.

26.9. There shall be water When Candra occupies the Lagna in a Sajala Rāśi. When a Krūra is in 4H, and Candra joins the Lagna, there shall be underground water.

Jayanta: So, we must examine the Yogas first to ensure water can be underground in the specified land.

Ācārya: We must do that before any further examination is undertaken. The Sajala Rāśis are Karka, Makara and Mīna, and among them, Mīna has the largest quantum of water, as an ocean symbolizes it.

When Candra is in Mīna and is dṛṣṭied by, say, Bṛhaspati and Śukra, water is certain to be found, even though the Āruṛha may be in Kanyā.

Jayanta: I suppose, Mithuna, Siṅha and Kanyā are Nirjala Rāśis, and they do not show water.

Ācārya: Yes, the Nirjala Rāśis normally do not indicate the presence of water. But if Āruṛha is in Kanyā, and the Lagna is strongly disposed in Mīna and dṛṣṭied by Śukra/Bṛhaspati, the indications of Āruṛha in Kanyā is overridden.

Jayanta: How about a strong influence of Śukra/Candra (Sajala Grahas on Āruṛha in a Nirjala Rāśi?

Ācārya: Water is also promised when the Āruṛha is in Kanyā but is hemmed between Śukra and Candra.

Several other yogas are mentioned, which I believe can independently indicate the presence of water.

In this regard, we must recall that Vṛṣabha, Dhanu and Kumbha are Ardhajala, and, Meṣa, Tulā and Vṛścika are Pādajala. Makara is Sajala, like Karka and Mīna; therefore, Lagna rising in Makara can indicate the presence of water.

Likewise, Śukra in Tulā, Bṛhaspati in Mīna, Candra in Karka/Mithuna, and Budha conjunct Rāhu in the same Rāśi indicate the presence of water in the selected spot. Budha is Pṛthvībhūta, and Rāhu digging underground. Their conjunction indicates that when the earth, the desired objective or the Praśna (finding of water) is fulfilled.

If the yogas are seen jointly in Kuṇḍalī, then it is nearly impossible to find a Kuṇḍalī where all these yogas are present. Therefore, they must be considered individually.

Praśnamārga:

26.10. (1) If Candra is in Mīna, dṛṣṭied by Bṛhaspati, or (2) Śukra and Āruṛha in Kanyā; (3) if Kanyā being Āruṛha is hemmed in between Candra and Śukra, water shall be discovered.

26.11. (4) If Makara rises, (5) Śukra is in Tulā, (6) Bṛhaspati is in Mīna, and (7) Candra is in Karka, (8) or Budha and Rāhu combine in the same Rāśi and (9) Candra is in Mithuna, there shall be water in the selected spot.

Jayanta: Dhanyavād, for clarifying this!

Ācārya: There is an old well buried underground, when either Śukra or Candra is Ucca and is dṛṣṭied by a Nīca Graha. The Ucca avasthā of the Sajala Grahas indicate an abundance of water, but the dṛṣṭi of the Nīcagraha indicate that the water is present deep within the ground.

Likewise, when the Āruṛha/Udaya is in Vṛṣabha with Ucca Candra. The presence of Ucca Candra in the Lagna denotes abundant water. Still, Vṛṣabha Rāśi denotes something that is deep below the ground because of Candra's dṛṣṭi on Vṛścika, which denotes a place that is buried deep underground.

We noticed previously that Cara Rāśi in the Lagna denotes the presence of water. Now, the case of Sthira Rāśi is narrated here. If the Lagna is in a Sthira Rāśi and is occupied by Śukra and Śani, then the water is available but is meagre.

If candra is in Siṅha (Nirjala and Sthira), but the Āruṛha is in a Sajala Rāśi, the result is somewhere in between, i.e., water is found but is meagre. When Āruṛha is in Mīna, then water is likely to be present even though Candra is in Kanyā (normally no water) or Bṛhaspati is in Mithuna (again, normally no water).

Praśnamārga:

26.12. (10) If Śukra and Candra are Ucca and dṛṣṭied by Nīca Grahas or the (11) Āruṛha or the Lagna is Vṛṣabha occupied by Candra, there is an old well buried underground.

26.13. (12) When Lagna is a Sthira Rāśi occupied by Śukra and Śani or (12) Candra is in Siṅha and Āruṛha is a Sajala Rāśi, there shall be only some water in the well.

26.14. (13) When Āruṛha is Mīna, Candra is in Kanyā, and Bṛhaspati occupies Mithuna, there shall be water. Thus, we have 13 yogas, besides two given in ślokas 13 and 14. Indications of having an old well are also given.

Jayanta: What are the Yogas for the absence of underground water?

Ācārya: Now, the yogas that indicate an absence of water are stated. When Candra is in Vṛṣabha, the presence of water in a deep underground well is indicated because of Candra's dṛṣṭi on Vṛścika.

We have already seen this yoga mentioned before. But, if this Candra is dṛṣṭied by Rāhu from Vṛścika, there is the digging of the well, but the water cannot be found. The act of digging the well can be seen from the presence of Rāhu in Vṛścika and his aspect on Candra in Vṛṣabha.

26.15. There shall be no water in the well dug if Candra is in Vṛṣabha and Rāhu is in Vṛścika.

Jayanta: What is next, Guruji?

Ācārya: Now, we shall learn how to find the direction in which the well should be dug, which should be done after ascertaining that the water is present following the previous yogas and the steps delineated before.

Jayanta: Guruji, kindly elaborate on the direction of the digging.

Ācārya: Firstly, the direction of the digging should be known from the body parts touched by the Pṛcchaka. In this context, the human body is divided into 3 zones, each denoting a corner direction.

They are (1) Southwest: left side of the body, (2) Northeast: Above the neck, (3) Northwest: Anywhere else, i.e., right side and below the neck. Notice that the Southeastern direction is ruled out.

If the Pṛcchaka touches a bony or raised part, such as the skull, forehead, nose tip, fingers, elbow, knee etc., they do not indicate water, as they symbolize mountains and plateaus.

The depressed parts of the body, such as eyes, mouth, crotch, anus etc., denote waterbodies because they symbolize the depressed places on earth. A fleshy spot indicates water in a muddy spot; a forehead denotes a rocky place.

Likewise, other body parts have specific meanings. For instance, the anus denotes a place where the water is stagnant and bereft of oxygen, thus not fit for drinking.

After examining these general Rāśis and yogas, if one concludes that there is water, then a ***Candragupti Cakra*** will be drawn and the direction determined.

26.16. From the above yogas, indications and other sources of information, if you conclude that water is available, then the direction where the well is to be dug can be known from the following.

26.17. If, at the time of Praśna, the Pṛcchaka feels the left side of his body, it means water can be located in the south-west; any organ above the neck in the north-east; the right side of his body and any organ below the neck, north-west.

26.18. If he touches any bony spot in his body, no water can be found; other spots of his body are favourable for getting water. A fleshy spot indicates water in a muddy spot; a forehead denotes a rocky place.

Ācārya: Now, the method of determining the direction using **Candragupti Cakra** is mentioned here.

Jayanta: Guruji, what is Candragupti Cakra?

Ācārya: It is a special Cakra used to determine where water is located.

Jayanta: Kindly elaborate more.

Ācārya: The method of drawing this Cakra involves 8 vertical and 5 horizontal lines. This gives rise to 7 * 4 = 28 compartments. In this Cakra, commencing from the 1st square (top left corner), enter numbers 1 to 5 horizontally, then 6 vertically down below; and 7, 8 and 9 horizontally towards the left; under 9, mark 10 and horizontally 11, 12, 13 and 14 towards the right; above 14 mark 15 and then 16.

From the last square to 16, mark the regular order from 17th to 28th. This Cakra is useful for determining the direction of digging.

26.19. After examining these general Rāśis and yogas, if one concludes that there is water, then a **Candragupti Cakra** will be drawn and the direction determined.

26.20-23. One should seat comfortably facing the east if the Praśna Rekha and the diagram (Cakra) are to be drawn from the morning till noon; south from noon to Sūryāsta; west from Sūryāsta to midnight; and north from midnight to next Sūryodaya.

Ācārya: The diagram of the Cakra is given here.

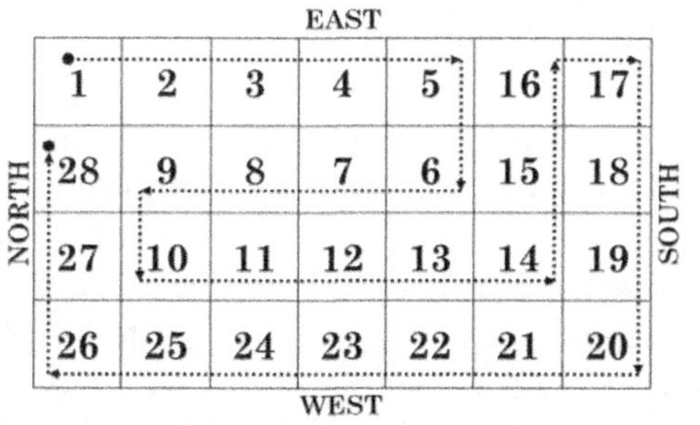

Jayanta: I suppose we assign 28 Nakṣatras in this Cakra.

Ācārya: Indeed! There are 28 Nakṣatras which are allotted to 60 Ghaṭis in a day. This means each Nakṣatra is 60/28 = 15/7 = 2.143 Ghaṭis or 51.4 min approx.

The counting starts from Aśvinī at the beginning of the day (Sūryodaya) and moves in the Nakṣatra order switching a nakshatra every 15/7 Ghaṭi (one-twenty-eighth of a day).

The Dinarkṣa Nakṣatra is the Nakṣatra prevailing that is mapped to the Ghaṭi in which the Praśna is put. This is derived by dividing the time elapsed from Sūryodaya to the Praśna's time by 15/7 and then rounding up the quotient.

Jayanta: Kindly give an example.

Ācārya: Suppose on a day, the Sūryodaya is at 05:20 (5.33), and the Praśna was put at 15:44 (15.73) in the afternoon.

The Praśna Iśtakāla is 15.73 – 5.33 = 10.4 hrs = 10.4 * 2.5 = 26 Ghaṭis.

The Dinarkṣa is 26 * 7/15 = 12.13, which should be rounded "up" to 13th Nakṣatra, Hastā. Therefore, the Dinarkṣa for the Praśna is Hastā, and we should write 13 in the square number 1 and rearrange the numbers in the specified order.

Jayanta: It is clear now.

Ācārya: You can use another method, i.e., Iśtakāla/24 * 28. In this case, Dinarkṣa = 10.4/24 * 28 = 12.13.

Jayanta: So Dinarkṣa means the Iṣṭaghaṭi converted to Nakṣatras. Isn't it?

Ācārya: That is correct. Therefore, it is called Dinarkṣa, where Dina means day and Arkṣa means Nakṣatra.

Jayanta: What is next?

Ācārya: Next, we identify the Nakṣatras held by the Grahas. The Nakṣatra held by the Lagna is Udayarkṣa, and that by Candra is Candrarkṣa, and likewise, Sūryarkṣa, Maṅgalarkṣa, Budharkṣa, Gurvarkṣa, Śukrarkṣa, Śanyarkṣa, Rāhvarkṣa, Ketvarkṣa, are the Nakṣatras held by the Grahas.

Jayanta: Why is that needed?

Ācārya: We need to identify where the Nakṣatras of these Grahas are from Dinarkṣa and put them in the right compartment.

Jayanta: Kindly elaborate.

Ācārya: Suppose at the Praśna, Udayarkṣa is Bharaṇī (2) and Candrarkṣa is Punarvasu (7), Gurvarkṣa is Maghā (10) and Śukrarkṣa is Anurādhā (17).

Dinarkṣa 13 is in the first square; therefore, Udayarkṣa Bharaṇī is in 2-13+1 = -10 = -10 + 28 = 18. Candrarkṣa is 7-13+1 = -5 = 23.

We have counted Abhijit in between because of the 28-Nakṣatra scheme. Therefore, in this example, Dinarkṣa (13) is in compartment 1, Udayarkṣa (2) is in compartment 18 and Candrarkṣa compartment 23 (7). Like Lagna and Candra, the position of the other Grahas should also be found in this Cakra. Gurvarkṣa = 10-13+1 = -2 = 26, and Śukrarkṣa = 17-13+1 = 5.

Jayanta: What should we do by finding a Graha's compartment?

Ācārya: From the placement of the Grahas, we can identify the spot on the ground where the digging should be undertaken. Normally, the compartment containing Candra or Śukra indicates where water can be found.

Jayanta: Now it makes sense. Kindly continue.

Ācārya: When we look up Candrarkṣa (compartment 13), we notice that it is in the E5N2 direction, where the digging could be done.

Jayanta: What is E5N2 direction?

Ācārya: Look into the diagram

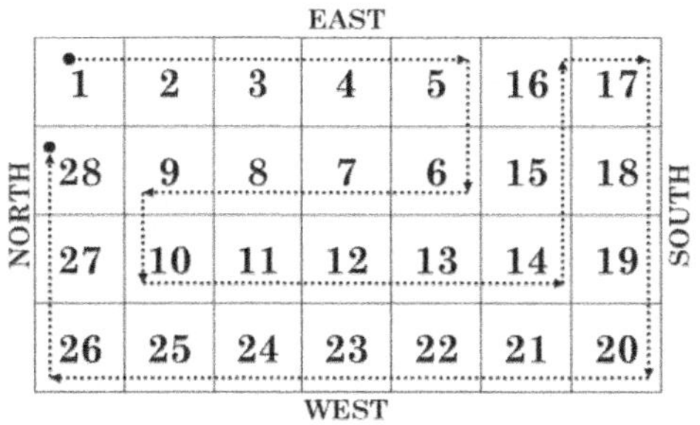

Compartment 13 is the 5th one from the left edge in the eastern direction and the 2nd one from the bottom edge in the northern direction. Therefore, it is named E5N2.

Jayanta: Now it makes sense.

Ācārya: Now let's see the variations of this Cakra based on the section of the day in which the Praśna is put.

Jayanta: Kindly elaborate, Guruji!

Ācārya: What we discussed so far requires some adjustment according to śloka 26.20-23.

In this method, we should divide a day into four zones, (1) forenoon, (2) afternoon, (3) night and (4) post-midnight.

(1) ***Forenoon*** is from Sūryodaya to midday, (2) ***Afternoon*** is midday to Sūryāsta, (3) ***Night*** is Sūryāsta to midnight, and (4) ***Post-midnight*** is midnight to next Sūryodaya.

Jayanta: Why must we do that?

Ācārya: Because there are four variations of the Cakra depending on the section of the day.

For the four sections of the day, the Cakras have four different orientations, as indicated in the diagrams. If the Praśna is put between Sūryodaya to Madhyānha, Cakra #1 is used.

If the Praśna is put from Madhyānha to Sūryāsta, the Cakra is to be turned clockwise (#2) so that the number 1 is aligned to the **Southeast** corner.

If the Praśna is put from Sūryāsta to Madhyarātri, the Cakra is to be turned clockwise again (#3) so that the number is aligned to the **Southwest** corner.

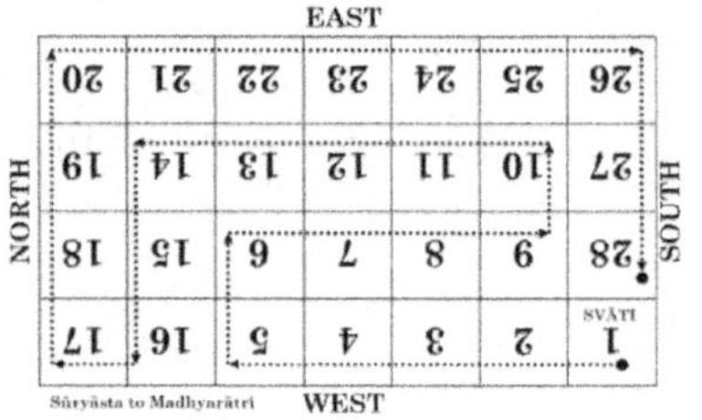

And lastly, if the Praśna is put between Madhyarātri and Sūryodaya, the Cakra is to be turned clockwise again (#4) so that the number 1 is aligned to the **Northwest** corner.

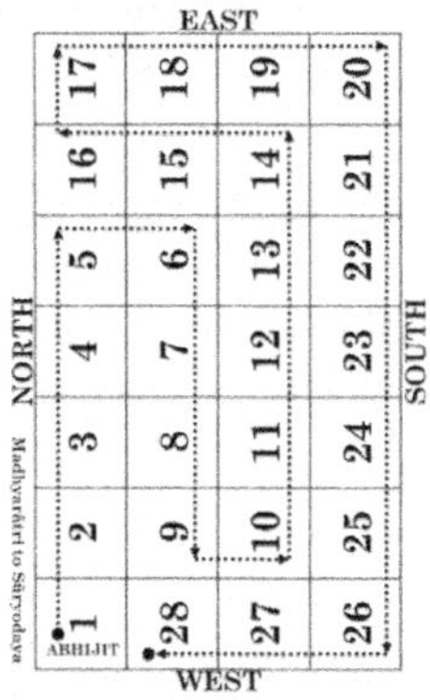

Jayanta: Dhanyavād, for clarifying this. Now it makes sense. It appears that the Cakra is rotated clockwise four times for the four sections of the day.

Ācārya: That is correct! Also, the different sections of the day correspond to different Dinarkṣa. The forenoon corresponds to Nakṣatras 1-7, afternoon 8-14, night 15-21 and midnight 22-28.

The 1st Nakṣatra of forenoon is 1 (Aśvinī), afternoon 8 (Puṣya), night 15 (Svāti) and midnight 22 (Abhijit). These are the starting point for counting the Dinarkṣa in the four time zones.

Jayanta: That makes sense. Kindly continue.

Ācārya: A day is to be divided into four sections depending on the time of Sūryodaya, Midday, Sūryāsta and Midnight.

We must note here that the astronomical noon, where Sūrya is straight up in the sky, is not always at 12:00 pm and depends on the coincidence of Sūrya with the Madhyalagna (MC). However, for practical purposes, we can assume it to be 12:00 pm.

Now, let us revisit our example. The duration of the forenoon is 12.00 – 5.33 = 6.67 hrs, and the afternoon is 18.00 – 12.00 = 6.00 hrs. In Ghaṭi, the forenoon and afternoon are 16.67 and 15 Ghaṭis.

The Praśna was put at 26 Ghaṭis from Sūryodaya; therefore, the Ghaṭis elapsed in the afternoon is 26 - 16.67 = 9.33 Ghaṭis. Since the Praśna is put in the afternoon, the counting must be from Puṣya (8). The duration of each Nakṣatra in the afternoon = afternoon / 7 = 15 / 7 = 2.143.

The afternoon Ghaṭis elapsed is 9.33/2.143 = 4.35 = 5th Nakṣatra from Puṣya, which is 8 + 5 – 1 = 12 (Uttarāphālgunī). The Dinarkṣa is 12, meaning we must put the 12th Nakṣatra in compartment 1 in the 2nd Cakra (afternoon).

At the Praśna, the Udayarkṣa is Bharaṇī (2), Candrarkṣa is Punarvasu (7), Gurvarkṣa is Maghā (10) and Śukrarkṣa is Anurādhā (17). Now, Candrarkṣa is in compartment 7-12+1 = -4 = 24. The 24th square in the 2nd diagram is on the upper side of the North, where the digging should be.

Notice that between the 2 calculations, after we have applied the corrections due to the sections of the day and re-oriented the Cakra, there is a slight change in the Dinarkṣa and the Candrarkṣa. Śrī Rāmakṛṣṇa Bhat also mentions the 2nd method in the "Essentials of Horary Astrology or Praśnapadavi".

Praśnamārga:

26.24-25. Dividing a day's duration, viz., 60 Ghaṭis by 28, each Nakṣatra gets 2 1/7 Ghaṭis. Dividing the time of Praśna in Ghaṭis 2 1/7, we get Dinarkṣa (दिनर्क्ष) counted from Aśvinī. The Nakṣatra indicated by Lagnasphuṭa at the Praśna is the udaya Nakṣatra.

26.26. The Dinarkṣa is to be inserted in the 1st square. Count in the order marked in the diagram till the Udayarkṣa.

26.27. Count from Udayarkṣa to Candrarkṣa according to the order of the diagram. The resulting square indicates the spot where the well must be dug. Just as in the case of Candra, the Nakṣatra held by other Grahas can also be considered.

Ācārya: This is only an introduction to the subject, and there are further details for which you need to refer to volume 23B.

Jayanta: Dhanyavād, Guruji, for explaining this important Cakra.

24. ON ARMIES

Jayanta: Guruji, teach us the principles of deciphering a war condition or Yuddha Praśna.

Ācārya: Yuddhapraśna is a crucial and integral part of Rāja Jyotiṣa, where a qualified Daivajña advises the King on invasion and protection of the borders.

The principles discussed here apply equally well in Muhurta Kuṇḍalī as well. Therefore, depending on the context, you apply them in Praśna or Muhūrta.

Jayanta: Isn't that true for all Praśnas?

Ācārya: Yes, that is generally true!

Jayanta: Kindly share the principles about his crucial subject.

Ācārya: When a country is invaded, one should cast a Muhūrta Kuṇḍalī at the moment when the news of the invasion is recorded. This tells us about the course of the war, its outcome, and whether any peace negotiations are possible.

The same can be seen in a Praśna by the King or a King's messenger.

Jayanta: Noted, Guruji!

Ācārya: In an invasion, the invading party is called *Yāyi*, and the defending party is called *Sthāyi*.

Jayanta: So *Yāyi* means aggressor, and *Sthāyi* means defender. Right?

Ācārya: Yes, that is right. According to Praśnatantra 3.39-40, 4H is the indicator of land (Kṣetra) and the land of the subject. This is also 10H from 7H (battle). Saumyas in the 4H cause the enemy to invade the land, while Krūras in this Bhāva cause their defeat and force them to retreat.

Kailāśa: Why does Saumyas in 4H cause the enemy to invade Guruji?

Ācārya: That is because 4H is the house of action for the enemy (7H).

Kailāśa: Guruji, still, it does not make sense. I thought Krūras in 4H should indicate that someone is trying to grab the land of the defender (*Sthāyi*).

Ācārya: Why not wait for some time? I hope that it will be clarified as we progress further.

Kailāśa: Sure, Guruji!

Ācārya: The Saumyas are Bṛhaspati, Budha and Śukra. The Krūras are Śani, Maṅgala, Rāhu and Ketu.

Sūrya and Candra are the Royal Grahas and are left out in determining invasion. When they occupy the 4H, the enemy does not invade, so the question of victory or defeat is ruled out.

Kailāśa: So what happens when Sūrya or Candra are in 4H?

Ācārya: When Sūrya-Candra are in 4H, and other indications of war are present, for instance, Krūras in 7H, it could mean that the fight is held remotely, i.e., cyber warfare.

Kailāśa: Ok, noted!

Ācārya: Both invasion and retreat are seen from 4H. For the enemy troop to invade and set up their barracks in the land of the defender (*Sthāyi*), 4H Rāśi must be hospitable.

Normally Saumyas in the 4H indicates invasion (and victory of aggressor), and Krūras, defeat. However, if the Grahas are in their Śatrurāśis, their (aggressor's) stay in this land is not prolonged.

If ***Saumyas*** are in 4H, in their ***Śatrurāśi***, the enemy troops (*Yāyi*) retreat after ***victory*** and if ***Krūras***, after ***defeat*** (Praśnatantra 3.36).

Kailāśa: So, we must check whether the Grahas in 4H are in good or bad dignity. Isn't it?

Ācārya: Yes, we must. Saumyas in 4H grants victory to the aggressor regardless of their dignity. But the battle does not last long if they are in low dignity. However, there is a caveat.

Kailāśa: What is it, Guruji?

Ācārya: The Sajala Rāśis (Karka, Mīna, Kumbha, Vṛścika) in 4H are not favourable towards the enemy troop (*Yāyi*), and they suffer defeat.

Kailāśa: Why so?

Ācārya: These Rāśis are gentle and are "not" conducive to the victory of the opposition (10H from 7H).

Kailāśa: How about Catuṣpāda Rāśis?

Ācārya: The Catuṣpada Rāśis denote brute force (physical prowess). When they occupy 4H, they denote obstacles caused by raw power (insurmountable obstacles).

Jayanta: The Catuṣpada Rāśis are those of Animals as their symbol, viz., Vṛṣabha, Siṅha, Dhanu 2H, Makara 2H

Ācārya: According to Praśnatantra 3.37, if Udaya is in one of the Catuṣpada Rāśis, the enemy troop retreats, facing an unsurmountable obstacle ahead.

There is also a special rule for Catuṣpāda Rāśi. According to Praśnatantra 3.38, the invader (*Yāyi*) retreats if Udaya or 4H is in Meṣa, Siṅha, Dhanu or Vṛṣabha (Catuṣpāda), regardless of being occupied by a Graha.

Kailāśa: Guruji, what are the sūtras of victory and defeat?

Ācārya: Krūras in the Lagna cause victory to the defender (*Sthāyi*). Krūras in the Lagna, in Catuṣpada Rāśis, certainly favours the *Sthāyi*.

Jayanta: You mentioned before that Saumyas in 4H cause victory to the aggressor (*Yāyi*). Isn't it?

Ācārya: That is true! In contrast, Krūra Rāśis/Grahas in 4H indicate defeat to the invader (*Yāyi*) and force them to retreat.

Sunidhi: What's next, Guruji?

Ācārya: Let us focus on Candra's Sūtra.

According to Praśnamārga 24.58, when Candra is in a Sthirarāśi and Udaya is in a Cara Rāśi/Añśa, the invader (*Yāyi*) comes soon to fight in strength.

Sunidhi: Why is this so?

Ācārya: Udaya in Cara Rāśi/Añśa affirms that the invasion happens since it indicates changes to the status quo.

Sunidhi: Then, what happens when it is reversed, i.e., Candra in a Cara and Udaya in a Sthira?

Ācārya: If Candra is in a Cararāśi and Udaya is in a Sthira Rāśi/Añśa, the enemy does not invade.

As mentioned, Cara Udaya indicates changes to the status quo, indicating an invasion.

On the other hand, Candra's position in Cara or Sthira Rāśi indicates their determination to fight. Candra in Sthira and Udaya in Cara indicates that the *Yāyi* fights with full determination.

Sunidhi: This makes sense now, Guruji!

Ācārya: According to Praśnamārga 24.60, when Candra is Sthira and Udaya is Cara, the invader (*Yāyi*) invades in strength. When Candra is Cara, and the Udaya is Sthira, the enemy, though well prepared, does not march for fighting.

Sunidhi: Guruji, we have already seen this before.

Ācārya: That is right. This is an important Sūtra and, therefore, re-emphasised.

Sunidhi: Noted, Guruji!

Ācārya: Let us focus on other elements of Candra Sūtra!

Sunidhi: Looking forward to it.

Ācārya: Sthira Udaya, Dvisva Candra and Budha, Bṛhaspati or Śukra is in 6H, the invader (*Yāyi*) is defeated (Praśnamārga 24.59).

Sunidhi: What is Sthira Udaya and Dvisva Candra?

Ācārya: Sthira Udaya means Udaya in Sthira Rāśi/Añśa. Dvisva Candra means Candra in Dvisva Rāśi/Añśa. Dvisva is the short form of Dvisvabhāva, and it also means Ubhaya.

Sunidhi: Got it.

Ācārya: According to Praśnamārga 24.61, Sthira Udaya and Dvisva Candra indicate that though the invader (*Yāyi*) may have come near, it returns without fighting.

Sunidhi: Why is this so?

Ācārya: Dvisva Candra indicates a state of dilemma. Sthira Udaya indicates that the invasion does not occur (no change in status quo).

Sunidhi: What happens when the reverse occurs?

Ācārya: Dvisva Udaya and Cara Candra indicate that the invader (*Yāyi*) enemy comes half the way but retreats without fighting.

Sunidhi: Kindly explain, Guruji!

Ācārya: Cara Candra indicates a demotivated army, and Dvisva Udaya indicates that the invader marches forth but returns before invading (quality of Dvisva).

Also, according to Praśnamārga 24.62, Cara Udaya and Dvisva Candra indicate that the invader (*Yāyi*) marches from two directions. But if Udaya is dṛṣṭied by Krūras, the enemy is defeated.

Sunidhi: What is the reasoning behind it?

Ācārya: Cara Udaya indicates invasion, and Dvisva Candra indicates an undecided stance (dilemma). Therefore, even though the *Yāyi* invades, they lack the determination to win.

Sunidhi: It makes sense now.

Ācārya: If, at such time, Udaya is Krūrayutidṛṣṭa, the enemy is defeated.

Jayanta: In a Yuddhapraśna, Krūras in the Lagna denote victory to the *Sthāyi*, and those in 7H denote victory to *Yāyi*!

Ācārya: If Krūras are in 5H/6H, the *Yāyi* retreats though he has proceeded half the distance. If Krūras are in 4H, the *Yāyi* is defeated in the fight (Praśnamārga 24.63).

Sunidhi: We have already seen that Krūras in 4H cause defeat to the invader. But why do Krūras in 5H/6H cause them to retreat?

Ācārya: That is because they are the next two Bhāvas of 4H. So, Krūras in 4H indicate the defeat of *Yāyi*, and their presence in the next two Bhāvas indicates their retreat!

Sunidhi: What if the invasion cannot be avoided?

Ācārya: When Krūras are in 1H, 2H, 3H, 5H, 6H and 12H, invasion happens, but when the Krūras are in 4H, invasion does not occur, or it becomes futile (Praśnamārga 24.64).

Sunidhi: Noted, Guruji!

Ācārya: When Sūrya and Candra are 4H, enemies do not invade. When Budha, Bṛhaspati and Śukra are in 4H, they certainly invade (Praśnamārga 24.65). When Catuṣpāda Rāśis, Meṣa, Vṛṣabha, Siṅha or Dhanu is in Udaya/4H and is not vacant, the enemy retreats without fighting (Praśnamārga 24.66).

Sunidhi: We have already seen these sūtras before.

Ācārya: Yes, we did. Let us examine the next principle!

Sthira Udaya with a Mandagati Graha Bṛhaspati/Śani indicates that the *Yāyi* does not invade. In contrast, Cara Udaya with Puruṣa Sūrya/Bṛhaspati indicates that the invasion occurs undoubtedly (Praśnamārga 24.67).

Jayanta: Sūrya in Cara Lagna indicate invasion as Krūras in 1H do so. This we have already learnt. What could be the reason Guru in Cara Lagna indicates invasion?

Ācārya: Guru in Lagna is Dikbali, and therefore, he supports Udaya. Udaya being Cara, indicates the invasion.

Jayanta: It makes sense!

Ācārya: When Bṛhaspati/Śukra is in 2H/3H, the invasion is swift and sudden (Praśnamārga 24.68), i.e., the enemy is at the gate without notice.

Jayanta: We have seen Krūras in 5H/6H make the enemies retreat. But in this case, Guru/Śukra in 2H/3H, i.e., the two Bhāvas preceding 4H, indicates a swift movement of the invader.

Ācārya: That is right. If Lagna is Cara, Guru/Śukra in 2H/3H indicates the fast manifestation of the due events.

Let us examine the last and most important principle of invasion and defence.

Kailāśa: Guruji, eagerly waiting for it!

Ācārya: The six Bhāvas commencing from 3H of the Praśnalagna stand for the defender (*Sthāyi*). The remaining six Bhāvas relate to the invaders (*Yāyi*).

The influences on 3H-8H indicate the position of the *Sthāyi* and those on 9H-2H about the position of invaders. Results, good or bad, to these Bhāvas, would reveal the good or bad of the party concerned.

Kailāśa: Noted, Guruji!

Daivajñavallabha:

Ācārya: Let me provide the sūtras from Ācārya Varāhamihira's Daivajñavallabha.

5.1. If Krūras are in 5H/6H the *Yāyi* retreats in between their way. When Krūras are in 4H, the *Yāyi*, even though he may have approached near, has his forces defeated and destroyed and returns disinterested.

5.2. If Vṛścika, Mīna or Karka (Jala) is in 4H and is dṛṣṭied by Saumyas, the *Yāyi* is defeated; if there is a Catuṣpāda Rāśi in 4H, the enemy who has come intending to conquer retreats.

5.3. If Cara Udaya contains a Saumya, it certainly causes more auspicious results for the invader (*Yāyi*). If Cara Udaya is with a Krūra, inauspicious results occur with the invader (*Yāyi*). If Sthira Udaya is with a Saumya, good results are produced certainly (to *Sthāyi*).

5.4. Sthira Candra and Cara Udaya indicate that the *Yāyi* certainly invades. But Cara Candra and Sthira Udaya indicate that the *Yāyi* does not invade.

5.5. Dvisva Candra and Sthira Udaya indicate that the Yāyi invades and retreats. In this Yoga, if Budha, Bṛhaspati and Śukra are in 6H, the enemy is destroyed.

5.6. Sthira Udaya with dṛṣṭi from Bṛhaspati and Śani indicates that either the *Yāyi* does not invade or it may not return after attacking. Krūras in 3H, 5H and 6H indicate that the *Yāyi* must be faced. Krūras in 4H indicates that the enemy certainly retreats (defeated).

5.7. Cara Candra and Dvisva Udaya indicate that the *Yāyi* comes halfway and then returns. Dvisva Candra and Cara Udaya indicate that the *Yāyi* comes with two armies. But if Udaya and Candra are dṛṣṭied by Krūras, the *Yāyi* is defeated.

5.8. If Candra and Sūrya are in 4H, the army of the *Yāyi* does not invade. But if Bṛhaspati, Budha and Śukra are 4H, the *Yāyi* invades soon.

5.9. If the Lagna or 4H is in a Catuṣpāda Rāśi, Siṅha, Meṣa, Dhanu and Vṛṣabha, devoid of a Graha, then *Yāyi* cannot stay (in *Sthāyi*'s land). This is certain.

5.10. Sthira Udaya with Sūrya or Bṛhaspati indicates that the *Yāyi* is quiet in their place (does not invade). But if the same Grahas are in Cara Udaya, *Yāyi* invades soon.

5.11. If Bṛhaspati and Śukra are in 2H/3H jointly or separately, the *Yāyi* invades soon. If 1L, 9L and 10L are in Sthirarāśis, the *Yāyi* never invades.

5.12. If there is no Graha between the Lagna and Candra, the *Yāyi* attack in as many days as indicated by the Rāśis occupied by Candra from Lagna.

[**Notes:** According to Bhātotpala, if a Graha is intervening between the Lagna and Candra, the enemy does not come.]

Ācārya: Here ends the principles from Daivajñavallabha.

Jayanta: Dhanyavād Guruji. We have already examined all of them at the beginning of this conversation, i.e., about an invasion of an army.

Jñānapradīpikā:

Ācārya: Let us focus on the principles of Jñānapradīpikā.

24.406. Now I shall describe the arrival of armies and the entry of the invader (*Yāyi*) into the country (*Sthāyi*'s land). He who knows Praśnaśāstra must predict the arrival of the *Yāyi* army if Udaya and Āruṛha are in a Cararāśi and Krūras are in 5H.

24.407. If the Udaya is in a Catuṣpāda or Dvipāda Rāśi and Lagneśa is Vakrī, the *Yāyi* army retreats.

24.408. The *Yāyi* army does not invade the country if Krūras are in 4H.

24.409. If Rāhu is in Udaya, Āruṛha or Chatra, or a Kendra, the *Yāyi* army will be far away, and it does not enter the town. It retreats midway.

24.410. If Āruṛha is in Kumbha, Karka, Vṛścika, or Mīna (Sajala), and 4H has a strong Graha, the *Yāyi* army retreats.

24.411. If Āruṛha is identical with a Cara Udaya and with yutidṛṣṭi from Maṅgala, Sūrya or Guru (Puruṣagrahas), the arrival of a big *Yāyi* army is expected.

24.412. If the Āruṛha Lord (Āruṛhapati), or the friend of Āruṛhapati is with or dṛṣṭied by an Uccagraha, the *Sthāyi* is victorious, and the *Yāyi* retreats after being defeated.

24.413. But there is a speciality in the case of Chatra, where the result will be the reverse of the above, i.e. if Chatra is strong, the *Yāyi* will be victorious. But if Āruṛha is strong, the *Yāyi* will be firm in his stand, i.e. the *Sthāyi* will be able to defeat the *Yāyi*.

24.414. If Āruṛhapati is Nīca, or with Krūrayutidṛṣṭi, the invader (*Yāyi)* captures the defender (*Sthāyi*). But if Chatra is in a similar situation, the reverse happens, i.e. the *Sthāyi* is victorious, and the *Yāyi* is defeated.

24.415. If a Saumya is in Udaya in the forenoon, the *Yāyi* succeeds. But in the evening (afternoon), if a Saumya is in Udaya, the *Sthāyi* succeeds.

24.416. If Chatra, Udaya or Āruṛha is fierce (owned by a Krūra) or with a Krūra, a prediction must be made that there will be a fierce battle imminent for the *Sthāyi*.

24.417. If Āruṛha is Pṛṣṭodayi with Krūrayutidṛṣṭi, a Krūra is in 10H, or Udaya is Catuṣpāda, conflict arises soon. If Āruṛha/Udaya is with Saumyadṛṣṭi, peace talks emerge between the warring parties.

24.418-419. If the six Rāśis from Udaya (1H-6H) have Saumyas, the *Sthāyi* is victorious. But if the six Rāśis from 7H (7H-12H) have Saumyas, the *Yāyi* is victorious. If the six Rāśis adjacent to Udaya (1H-6H) have Krūras, the *Sthāyi* is defeated. But if the six Rāśis from 7H (7H-12H) have Saumyas, the *Yāyi* is defeated. If both Krūras and Saumyas are present in these Rāśis, peace talks ensue between them. If strong Krūras are on either side of the Lagna (2H-12H, Pāpakartari), the two rival parties are of equal strength, i.e. both the *Yāyi* and the *Sthāyi* will have scored some successes.

24.420. The strength of the parties must be assessed thus: The strength of the six Rāśis from 4H of Udaya (4H-9H) determines the *Yāyi's* strength, while the remaining six Rāśis (10H-3H) beyond determines the *Sthāyi's* strength. Thus, a prediction is to be made from the relative strengths of the Grahas.

24.421. Now the effects of Grahas being in Udaya will be described: If at Praśna, Śani, Sūrya or Maṅgala is in Udaya, the *Sthāyi* (defender) is victorious. If Budha and Śukra are in Udaya, the *Sthāyi* is defeated. ग्रहोदये विशेषोऽस्ति शन्यर्काङ्गार कोदये । आगतस्य जयं ब्रूयात्स्थायिनो भङ्गमादिशेत् । बुधशुक्रोदये, यायी जयी चन्द्रगुरूदये ॥४२१॥

24.422. If Candra or Guru is in Udaya, the *Yāyi* (invader) is victorious. If Sūrya is in 5H, 6H, 11H or 12H, the *Yāyi* King returns to his kingdom after capturing women, wealth and property. पञ्चषड्लाभरिः फेषु तिग्मांशुः संस्थितो यदि । आगतः स्त्रीधनादीनि हृत्वा वस्तूनि गच्छति ॥४२२॥

24.423. If Śani is in 2H/10H from Udaya, there is intense battle. If Śukra is in 6H, there will be peace or settlement. द्वितीये दशमे सौरिर्यदि सेनासमागमः । यदि शुक्रः स्थितः षष्ठे योज्यं संधिर्भविष्यति ॥४२३॥

24.424. If Śukra is in 4H/5H, the *Yāyi* (invading King) gives away his women and property to the *Sthāyi* (defending King) and retreats defeated. चतुर्थे पञ्चमे शुक्रो यदि तिष्ठति तत्क्षणात् । स्त्रीधनादीनि वस्तूनि यायी दत्वा प्रयास्यति ॥४२४॥

24.425. If Śukra is in 7H, the *Sthāyi* is weak. If Maṅgala is anywhere except 9H, 8H, 7H and 3H, the *Sthāyi* fights bravely against the *Yāyi* and is victorious.

24.426. If Candra is in 4H/5H, the *Sthāyi* certainly becomes victorious. If Sūrya is in 3H/5H, there will be an intense fight.

24.427. If Sūrya is in a Mitrarāśi, there are peace talks (truce) between the parties. Otherwise, the *Sthāyi* is victorious. If Sūrya is in 4H, the *Sthāyi* will give away property to the *Yāyi*. If Sūrya is in 6H, the *Sthāyi* will die.

24.428. If Sūrya is 2H and Budha is 3H from Udaya, the *Sthāyi* is victorious. If it were the reverse, the *Yāyi* would be victorious.

24.429. If Sūrya and Budha are together (in 2H/3H), there will be an intense fight between the parties. If Budha is in 5H, the *Yāyi* gives away his property to the *Sthāyi*. But if Budha is in 2H/3H, the *Yāyi* becomes victorious.

24.430. If Budha is in 12H/11H (reverse of 2H/3H), the *Sthāyi* is victorious. If Sūrya is in 11H, the *Yāyi*'s women and relatives are killed in the battle. If Sūrya is in a Nīca/Śatru Rāśi (in 11H), the *Sthāyi* is defeated.

24.431. If Guru is in 5H, 3H or 12H from Udaya, the *Yāyi* is defeated. If Guru is in 2H, there are peace talks (truce) between the parties. If Guru is in 10H/ 11H, the *Yāyi* gives away his property.

24.432. If Sūrya and Candra are in Yugmarāśis, there is peace talks (truce) between the parties. If it were the reverse (in Ojarāśi), a battle ensues. If Candra is in 12H of Sūrya, there will be no war, says the Śāstra of Jñānapradīpikā. चन्द्रादित्यो समस्थाने संधिस्स्यात्तिष्ठतो यदि । विपरीते तु युद्धं स्याद्वानोर्द्वादशगे विधौ । तत्र युद्धं न भवति शास्त्रे ज्ञानप्रदीपके ॥४३२॥

24.433. If Candra/Udaya is in a Cararāśi, the *Yāyi* seeks peace. If it is the reverse (Sthira/Dvisva Rāśi), the effect will be reversed, i.e., no peace talks. [**Notes:** This principle applies only when the Praśna is about peace talks or truce.] चरराशिस्थिते चन्द्रे चरराश्युदयेपि वा । शत्रुरागत्य संधाता विपरीते विपर्ययः ॥४३३॥

24.434. If Candra is in an Yugmarāśi and Udaya is in a Sthirarāśi, the *Yāyi's* commander-in-chief comes halfway into the *Sthāyi's* kingdom and then retreats. युग्मराशिस्थिते चन्द्रे स्थिरराश्युदये तथा । अर्द्धराज्यं समागत्य सेनानीर्विनिवर्तते ॥४३४॥

24.435. If Candra is in Sūrya's domain (Siṅha, Kanyā, Tulā, Vṛścika, Dhanu and Makara), the *Sthāyi* is defeated. But if he is in the other six Rāśis i.e., Candra's domain (Karka to Kumbha), the *Yāyi* is defeated. Thus is prediction about success or defeat to the parties made by the position of the Grahas. [**Notes:** Candra in own domain favours the defender whereas in Sūrya's domain favours the aggressor.] सिह्मादिराशिषट्के तु स्थायिनो भङ्गदायकः । कर्कादिव्युत्क्रमात्षट्के यायिनश्चन्द्रमा स्थितः ।स्थायीयायीक्रमेणैवं ब्रूयाद्गहवशात्फलम् ॥४३५॥

25. ON TRAVEL

Jayanta: Guruji, let us focus on Yātrā Praśna.

Ācārya: Sure, let us examine the principles of Yātrā Praśna! The following principles are laid down by the author regarding this Praśna. It covers the outcome of the travel and the whereabouts of the traveller.

25.436. In the interest of all, I am now describing the auspicious time for travel. After properly examining the details about going, coming, gain, loss, good and bad, the Praśna must be answered. यात्राकाण्डं प्रवक्ष्यामि सर्वेषां हितलिप्सया । गमनागमनं चैव लाभालाभौ शुभाशुभम् । सर्वं विचार्यकथयेत्पृच्छतां शास्त्रवित्तमः ॥४३६॥

Kailāśa: Where do we start?

Ācārya: Let us examine the arrival of someone. In a Praśna, the arrival of a person is seen from the Graha aspecting Lagna.

Sunidhi: Why those aspecting Lagna and not in the Lagna?

Ācārya: The Graha aspecting Lagna indicate those who will be with the person in due course. One is subject to two kinds of influences. Intervention and advice.

When a Graha is in the Bhāva, it intervenes in the matters concerning the Bhāva. However, when a Graha aspects the Bhāva, it is in the advisory mode. Aspecting Graha indicates that the other person would meet a person in future (when the Graha reaches Lagna in due course).

Sunidhi: Alright! So, what do we know from the aspecting Graha?

25.437. If Grahas aspect their Mitrarāśis at Praśna, the arrival of friends must be predicted. Likewise, if Grahas aspect their Nīcarāśis, the arrival of lowly persons must be expected.

25.438. If Grahas aspect their Uccarāśis, the person's travel on official duty must be predicted.

Ācārya: Suppose Lagna is Vṛṣabha, and Śani dṛṣṭies it. Lagna is the native's place, and Lagneśa Śukra is the native. Śani is Śukra's Mitra, and therefore, Śani's dṛṣṭi on Lagna indicates a friend will arrive, and the characteristic of the friend is that of Śani, old and matured.

Sunidhi: What if Maṅgala dṛṣṭies?

Ācārya: Maṅgala is Śukra's Śatru (somewhat hostile), indicating that the person arriving will not be a friend but has differences in understanding.

Sunidhi: What if Lagna is Karka and Guru aspects it?

Ācārya: Guru is Lagneśa's Mitra, and he aspects his Uccarāśi. This means that the person is a well-to-do person. It can also mean that the person is on government duty.

Sunidhi: What if Guru is in Makara, Nīca?

Ācārya: This means that the person may not be doing well right now, even though he is well-to-do. But it is different if Guru aspects Karka from Mīna or Vṛścika. In that case, the person is doing well.

You should also examine the other characteristics of the Grahas and Rāśis.

Sunidhi: Such as?

Ācārya: That is what is explained in the next śloka.

25.439. If Puruṣa Grahas are in Ojarāśis, the travel is about some work with a man; and if Strī Grahas are in Yugmarāśis, the travel is in connection with a woman. Such events must be expected in other places too.

Ācārya: If the aspecting Graha are Puruṣagrahas is in an Ojarāśi, then the person is arriving in connection with a man. If Strīgrahas are in Yugmarāśis, then the person is arriving in connection with a woman. Similarly, the purpose for which the person is visiting can be known from the Rāśi and Bhāva held by the aspecting Graha.

Kailāśa: What if the person is about travelling?

Ācārya: In that case, examine Udaya and Āruṛha. If they are in Cararāśis, the travel is certain. The direction of travel, in that case, is known from the direction of Grahas aspecting them.

25.440. If Udaya and Āruṛha are Cara and are dṛṣṭied by several Grahas, travel will be in the direction of the respective Grahas.

Sunidhi: The direction of the Grahas are E Sūrya, S Maṅgala, W Śani, N Budha, SE Śukra, SW Rāhu, NW Candra, and NE Guru.

Ācārya: Indeed!

Kailāśa: When does the travel not occur?

25.441. If Udaya and Āruṛha are Sthira and Śani, Sūrya and Maṅgala are posited there or in 10H, neither arrival nor departure occurs. स्थिरराश्युदयारूढे शन्यर्काङ्गारकाः स्थिताः । अथवा दशमस्थाश्चेद्गमनागमने न च ॥४४१॥

Ācārya: Normally, the predominance of Sthira elements indicates that the travel does not occur. Besides Sthira Rāśis, the affliction of 10H by Krūras, Śani, Maṅgala, and Sūrya also indicate that the travel does not occur. It means neither someone is arriving nor the native is departing for somewhere.

Kailāśa: Why must Sūrya or Maṅgala in 10H indicate that the person is not moving anywhere? Aren't they Dikbala there?

Ācārya: Any of the 3 Grahas in Lagna (Udaya/Āruṛha) or 10H, which the Lagna in a Sthirarāśi indicate that the travel does not occur. The Sthirarāśi in Udaya/Āruṛha is an essential condition.

Kailāśa: But why the 3 Grahas?

Ācārya: Because they are Mandagati Grahas. Candra, Budha and Śukra are Śīghragati Grahas. Sūrya is Samagati, and the remaining is Mandagati.

Kailāśa: Then, why is Guru not included?

Ācārya: That is because Guru is a Saumya, and his presence in Kendra indicates assurance that the objective of the Praśna will be fulfilled.

25.442. If Śukra, Guru and Candra are in Cararāśis, travel takes place only in one's interest.

Ācārya: This śloka of the author clarifies that. If Udaya/Āruṛha is in a Cararāśi, and Śukra/Candra/Guru are in the Lagna or aspecting it, the travel occurs out of the person's interest. If Cararāśi in Lagna is afflicted, the person is compelled to travel.

Jayanta: Guruji, can you please clarify the following śloka, which states that travel does not occur in Śīrṣodayi Rāśi?

25.443. If Praśna is in connection with travel, if Udaya is Śīrṣodayi, there will be no travel, and if it is Pṛṣṭodayi, there will be travel, which will be beneficial. स्थितिप्रश्ने स्थिति ब्रूयान्मस्तकोदयराशिषु । पृष्ठोदयेषु गमनं क्रमेण शुभदं वदेत् ॥४४३॥

Ācārya: Good question Jayanta. I think that this relates to return. Śīrṣodayi Rāśi indicates an onward journey, whereas Pṛṣṭodayi Rāśi indicates the return to the place of origin. Therefore, if the Praśna is about whether the person who has gone out would return, Udaya/Āruṛha in a Pṛṣṭodayi Rāśi confirms that.

Jayanta: Guruji, it makes sense now. How about getting information from the unreachable person?

Ācārya: The next śloka clarifies that.

25.444. If a Puruṣa Graha is in 2H/3H from Udaya, a letter will come within three days; or a messenger will come from the person who has gone on travel. द्वितीये च तृतीये च तिष्ठन्ति यदि पुंग्रहाः । त्रिदिनात्पत्रिकायाति दूतो वा प्रेषितस्य च ॥४४४॥

Ācārya: If a Puruṣagraha is in 2H/3H from Udaya, it is expected to receive some information or message from the person who has gone out. In today's world, it can be a phone call or email.

Sunidhi: Guruji, why Puruṣagrahas? And why 2H/3H?

Ācārya: Puruṣagrahas are outgoing; they indicate going out to do something. Strīgrahas are homebound and indicate things which are done staying at home.

2H/3H are involved in communication and messages. 2H is speech, and 3H is communication. 2H indicates a phone call or an internet message, and 3H indicate a messenger (or a postman) carrying a message.

Kailāśa: How to decipher whether the person who has gone out will return soon?

25.445. If Candra, Budha or Śukra is in 1H, 2H, 3H, 10H or 11H, the man who has been sent out will return soon.

Ācārya: The faster Grahas are Candra/Budha/Śukra. If these Grahas are in Udaya, 2H/3H, or 10H/11H, the traveller will return soon. This is even more assured if Udaya is in a Cararāśi.

25.446. If Saumyas are in 4H/12H, a letter from the man who has gone out will come.

Ācārya: This is to be read in conjunction with 25.444. A Puruṣagraha in 2H/3H affirms that communication would arrive soon through a phone/email message or a messenger. Now, it is said that Saumyas in 4H/12H indicate the same.

Kailāśa: Why so, Guruji?

Ācārya: 4H/12H are part of Mokṣatrikoṇa and are associated with travelling out. They indicate one's comfort zone, as 4H/8H/12H are Trikoṇa to 4H (Sukha, comfort). Saumyas assure comfort and assurance in these places, provided they are not weak/afflicted.

25.447. If Krūras are in 6H/5H from Udaya, the man who has gone out will return with sickness.

Jayanta: Sometimes, the person is sick. How to know from Praśna?

Ācārya: If the Praśna is about a specific person who has gone out and their wellbeing, the Lagna of such Praśna represents that person. In that case, Krūras in 5H and 6H indicate sickness.

Jayanta: 6H is understandable since it is the Roga Bhāva. But why 5H?

Ācārya: 5H denotes one's future. Krūra in 5H indicates one is stuck due to stressful situations, including health troubles.

Krūras simultaneously in 5H, 6H and 7H indicate some serious sickness. Similarly, Krūras in 5H, 6H and 8H indicate a life-threatening condition.

Kailāśa: Regarding returning of the person, what other Yogas are there?

25.448. If Candra is in Dhanu, Vṛṣabha, Meṣa or Siṅha, the man of whom one is thinking will return soon. If Candra is in 4H, the man thought about will return.

Ācārya: According to the author, Candra in certain Rāśi and Bhāva indicate that the traveller will return soon. They are:

(1) Candra in Meṣa, Vṛṣabha, Siṅha and Dhanu.

(2) Candra in 4H

Kailāśa: What is so special about these Rāśis, Guruji?

Ācārya: They are Catuṣpāda Rāśis.

Kailāśa: Should we not include Makara also?

Ācārya: Makara and Mīna are Pakṣi Rāśis.

Kailāśa: Why are Catuṣpada Rāśis important?

Ācārya: Transports are of two kinds, water and land transports. Water transports are through ships and boats, whereas land transports are through vehicles. The vehicles indicate muscle power, like bulls, horses and elephants. Therefore, land transports are denoted by Catuṣpāda Rāśis.

Kailāśa: Makes sense, Guruji!

25.449. If Śukra, Guru, Candra and Budha are in their Svarāśis, travel will occur in the Grahas' direction.

Ācārya: When the Praśna indicates travel, the direction of travel is seen from the Grahas aspecting the Lagna. If several Grahas aspect the Lagna, the one in Svarāśi normally indicates the direction. Also, refer to ślokas 25.440 and 25.442.

Kailāśa: Can the principle be used for timing the travel?

25.450. When the Grahas reach their "Sva" Bhāvas, the fruits of travel must be told. The good and bad effects of travel must be predicted from the strength or weakness of the Grahas.

Ācārya: Śloka 25.449 states that three Śīghragati Grahas, Candra/Budha/Śukra or Guru in their Svarāśis indicate travel in their direction. Now, 25.450 states that when the Grahas are not in their Svarāśis, then the travel occurs when they reach their Svarāśis.

Kailāśa: How to know there is a danger to the traveller's life?

25.451. If Krūras are in 7H and 8H, the man who has gone on travel will be robbed of his property and may be killed.

Ācārya: For the traveller's well-being, one must examine 7H and 8H. If Saumyas are in these places, the person does well in his place. But if Krūras are in these places, there is a danger to the traveller's life.

In a Yātrā-Praśna, 7H is crucial to determine the traveller's return.

25.452. If a Krūra is in 6H, the man who has gone out will be imprisoned. If the Krūra is in a Sajala Rāśi, the travelling man will return home after a long time. The good and bad effects of travel must be predicted from the strength or weakness of the Grahas.

Ācārya: I have already explained that in a Praśna related to a traveller, Lagna denotes the traveller. If at the Praśna, 6H is afflicted, the traveller could be imprisoned.

According to 25.447, the person could also become sick. There should be equal Grahas in 2H-12H, 3H-11H, 4H-10H, 5H-9H, or 6H-8H for imprisonment. This cause equal Argalā and Virodhārgalā.

12H stands for jail/hospital. Therefore, if 6L is in 12H, the person may be hospitalized or imprisoned for a crime (6H).

26. ON RAINS

Jayanta: Guruji, shall we focus on predicting rains from Praśna now?

Ācārya: Yes, let us do it. The principles laid here can be applied to predicting rain through Varṣa, Māsa and Dina Kuṇḍalī also. These principles revolve around Sajala Rāśis and Grahas.

Jayanta: That makes sense. So, Sajala Rāśis are Tulā, Vṛṣabha, Karka, Kumbha, Vṛścika and Makara, and the Sajala Grahas are Śukra and Candra.

Ācārya: Indeed! They are endowed with Jala or water.

Karka, Makara and Mīna are **Sajala** Rāśis; **Vṛṣabha, Dhanu and Kumbha** are **Ardhajala** Rāśis; and, **Meṣa, Tulā are Vṛścika** are Pādajala Rāśis. **Mithuna, Siṅha and Kanyā** are **Nirjala** Rāśis.

Notice that Vṛścika is only Pādajala, even though it is a Jalatattva Rāśi. Furthermore, Makara is a Pṛthvītattva Rāśi, but it is Sajala because a swamp or a shallow river symbolizes it. The Ardhajala Rāśis has 50% water, and Pādajala Rāśis, 25% water.

Kailāśa: Who are Nirjala Grahas?

Ācārya: The Agni and Vāyu Tattva Grahas are Nirjala, i.e., Sūrya/Maṅgala, and Śani/Rāhu. They dry of water and, therefore, Nirjala. They are also called Śuṣka Grahas. Nirjala means no water and Śuṣka means dry.

Jayanta: That makes sense, Guruji!

26.453. If Udaya is in a Sajala Rāśi or dṛṣṭied by a Sajala Graha, the downpour of rain can be predicted. If it is otherwise, there will be no rainfall.

Ācārya: In a Praśna Kuṇḍalī if Udaya is in a Sajala Rāśi or with yutidṛṣṭi of Sajala Grahas (Śukra/Candra), we can expect rain.

Kailāśa: How to predict whether it will be heavy or light rain?

Ācārya: That depends on how much influence the Sajala Rāśis/Grahas have on Lagna. More influence indicates more rain. If there is a mixed influence of Sajala and Nirjala Rāśi/Grahas.

26.454-455. If Śukra or Candra is in a Sajala Rāśi, there will be he heavy downpour; and if Śukra or Candra is aspecting their Sva/Ucca Rāśis or posited in their Kendras, heavy downpour within three or four days can be predicted. If Śukra is Dikbali, the rain will fall on the same day the Praśna is made.

Ācārya: The following indicate heavy rain:

(1) Śukra/Candra in or aspecting Udaya in a Sajala Rāśi.

(2) Śukra/Candra in or aspecting their Sva/Ucca Rāśi in Udaya.

(3) Śukra/Candra in a Kendra, with Udaya being in a Sajala Rāśi.

(4) Śukra/Candra Dikbali in 4H with Udaya being in a Sajala Rāśi.

Sunidhi: How about Guru? He is not Nirjala. Does he indicate heavy rain?

26.456. If Śukra, Guru, and Candra are in Sajala Rāśis and aspect the Āruṛha or Udaya, there will be very heavy downpour.

Ācārya: Guru is Ākāśa Tattva. He is Sajala in a Sajala Rāśi. Therefore, he owns Mīna and attains Ucca in Karka, two Sajala Rāśis. If Guru dṛṣṭies the Lagna from a Sajala Rāśi, he indicates heavy rain. Guru in Udaya in Sajala Rāśi also guarantees the same.

Kailāśa: What are the other Yogas of heavy rainfall, Guruji?

26.457. If Chatra is Pṛṣṭodayi and is dṛṣṭied by a Pṛṣṭodayi Graha and at the same time the Pariveṣa (halo around Sūrya/Candra) is also seen, heavy rainfall is most likely.

Ācārya: According to the author, if Chatra is in a Pṛṣṭodayi Rāśi or has yutidṛṣṭi Pṛṣṭodayi Graha, and there is a halo around Sūrya/Candra, there is heavy Rain.

Kailāśa: I heard about Pṛṣṭodayi Rāśi. What are Pṛṣṭodayi Grahas?

Ācārya: Good question.

According to Jātakapārijāta 2.11., Sūrya, Maṅgala, Rāhu and Śani are Pṛṣṭodayi, Śukra, Candra and Budha are Śīrṣodayi, and only Guru is Ubhayodayi.

Kailāśa: So generally, the Krūras are Pṛṣṭodayi, Saumyas (except Guru) are Śīrṣodayi, and Guru is Ubhayodayi.

Ācārya: That is right. Pṛṣṭodayi Rāśi and Grahas are backwards looking as they want to go back to where they started. It is like Vakrī Graha, who is in reverse gear.

Kailāśa: Is that why one of Maṅgala's names is Vakra?

Ācārya: There is another reason for that – Maṅgala has high Ceṣṭābala. He is always eager to fight a war. Do you know that all Grahas become weak in a Śatrurāśi? But Maṅgala is different. He does not lose any strength in a Śatrurāśi. He revels in hostility and war.

Kailāśa: How do we know that Maṅgala does not lose strength in a Śatrurāśi? Is it written somewhere?

Ācārya: Indeed! Else, I would not have said so. Whatever I say is supported by the Śāstras. To understand that, do read Śatrukṣetra Haraṇa in Longevity computation methods.

Kailāśa: Dhanyavād, for clarifying this.

Jayanta: Let us focus on the Yogas for cyclones and tornadoes.

Kailāśa: Indeed!

26.458. If Śani, Maṅgala, Budha and Rāhu are in Kendra, there will be no rainfall, but a big windstorm will blow.

Ācārya: cyclones, tornadoes, hurricanes etc., occur when air (Vāyu) rushes in from the colder surface of the ocean (or sea) to fill the space created by hot air rising to the top of the land.

Jayanta: So, there is a heavy involvement of air besides water?

Ācārya: That is right. Normally, three things are involved:

(1) Hot air (Maṅgala) rises "up" on the land (Budha).

(2) Cold air (Śani/Rāhu) rushes in from the nearby ocean (Sajala Rāśis).

Therefore, the Yoga is formed when Śani, Maṅgala, Budha and Rāhu are in Kendra to Praśna Udaya (Āruṛha/Chatra). It can also have heavy rainfall after that if Sajala Grahas/Rāśis are also involved.

26.459. If Krūras in Kendras are in Saumyayuti, the rainfall will be little. If Rāhu and Śani are in Dhanu, there will be no rainfall. But if Saumyas are in Dhanu, there will be heavy rainfall.

Ācārya: Following up with the previous Yoga, with Śani, Maṅgala, Budha and Rāhu in Kendra, if they are subject to Saumyayuti, the tornado is also accompanied by little rainfall.

If Rāhu and Śani are in Dhanu (in a Kendra), there will be no rainfall, but there is a cyclone/tornado. If, however, in the Yoga, if Rāhu/Śani are elsewhere, and Dhanu has Saumyayuti, abundant rainfall is indicated after the tornado.

Commodity Prices:

Ācārya: The following are the principles of deciphering commodity prices in a Praśna!

Jayanta: Can we use them to decipher the prices of a commodity market?

Ācārya: Yes, we can! But these are only some principles. This requires a dedicated study of the market forces to decipher this. Argha Jyotiṣa deals with this!

Jayanta: What are the core principles of commodity pricing?

Ācārya: Each Rāśi and Nakṣatra governs a certain commodity. When the Rāśi is subject to Śubha influences, there is abundant growth or availability of those commodities. On the other hand, if there are Aśubha influences, the production or availability of those commodities declines.

Jayanta: Does that mean that when there is good production of certain commodities, people are well off?

Ācārya: According to market economics, when a commodity is abundant, the price declines, and the producer gets a lesser per unit price. It is the reverse when something becomes scarce, leading to a high price.

Let us see what the author states.

26.460. If Udaya is with a Uccagraha yutidṛṣṭi there will be an increase in prices of commodities. There will be fall in prices, if it is with yutidṛṣṭi of a Nīcagraha. उच्चेन युक्ते दृष्टे वा त्वर्घवृद्धिर्भविष्यति । नीचेन युक्ते दृष्टे वा स्यादर्घक्षय ईरितः ॥४६०॥

Ācārya: The author states that when Udaya is subject to a Uccagraha yutidṛṣṭi, the price increases and it decreases if the reverse occurs.

Jayanta: Isn't this contrary to what you mentioned before? If there is an abundance, the commodity price will decrease. Isn't it?

Ācārya: Yes, it is. But this Praśna is not about whether the commodity will be abundant or scarce. It is about whether someone would make good money from a commodity. So, it is focused on getting a good price from a commodity.

Jayanta: Now that makes sense, Guruji!

26.461. The prices will be moderate if Udaya is with yutidṛṣṭi of a Mitragraha or Lagneśa. If Udaya is in Saumyayuti, the prices will increase; if in Krūrayuti, the prices will fall.

Ācārya: The trader would get a moderate price in trading a commodity when a Mitragraha or Lagneśa has yutidṛṣṭi on Lagna. Similarly, Saumyayutidṛṣṭi indicates a good price, and Krūrayutidṛṣṭi not so good price.

27. ON ARRIVAL OF A SHIP

Ācārya: Let us now focus our attention on the arrival of ships.

Sunidhi: What is the use of this knowledge in today's world, Guruji?

Ācārya: Knowledge is useful in the right context. Sometimes ships travelling over long distances lose their way and become untraceable. It used to be more in ancient times, but it is still true today.

Even now, a lot of cargo is transported by ships, and we even have cruise ships which carry passengers.

Jayanta: You can check on the internet. Even in today's world, ships disappear.

Sunidhi: Alright, I will check.

Ācārya: Now, let us examine the principles of identifying whether the ship will return or reach its destination.

27.462. If Praśna is made about the arrival of ships, the method of answering is given below: If Udaya is in a Sajala Rāśi, and if Guru, Śukra, or Candra is in there, the arrival of ships must be stated. But if Krūras are in Udaya, no ship will arrive.

Kailāśa: Kindly narrate the principles, Guruji!

Ācārya: Firstly, let us examine the Sajala Rāśi and Grahas.

Sunidhi: Guruji, we have already learned about them before.

Ācārya: Indeed! The Sajala Rāśis are Tulā, Vṛṣabha, Karka, Kumbha, Vṛścika and Makara, and the Sajala Grahas are Śukra and Candra.

The principle is that when Udaya is in a Sajala Rāśi with yutidṛṣṭi of Śukra, Candra or Guru, the arrival of the ship can be expected.

Kailāśa: We are considering Sajala Rāśis and Grahas because it is about ship and water voyage. Besides, Udaya must be influenced by the Saumyas.

Jayanta: Two among them, Śukra, and Candra are Saumyas and also Sajala. Guru is Sajala in a Sajala Rāśi. Therefore the 3 Grahas are considered.

Kailāśa: So, if Udaya is in a Sajala Rāśi, but has Krūrayutidṛṣṭi, then the ship does not arrive?

Ācārya: It means that the ship has left the port but will not arrive. It may have been subject to a mishap and is stranded somewhere.

Sunidhi: Can we know if the ship is wrecked and sank?

27.463. If Krūras aspect Āruṛha or Chatra, the ship will sink. If Nīca/Śatru Grahas aspect the above Lagnas, damage to the ship must be predicted.

Ācārya: The author gives the Yoga to check that. Firstly, Krūra affliction to Udaya indicates that the ship is struck by a mishap. Secondly, if Krūrayutidṛṣṭi also afflicts Āruṛha or Chatra, the ship meets with a disaster and sinks.

If the Lagnas, Udaya, Āruṛha or Chatra has a Nīca/Śatru Graha, the ship is likely to be damaged, but it may not sink. For sinking, there must be Krūrayutidṛṣṭi.

Kailāśa: Guruji, can we examine the recent disaster of the Titan submersible, which imploded?

Ācārya: Let us do that. The dive operation began on 18 June at 9:30 am Newfoundland Daylight Time (NDT), or 12:00 UTC. For the first hour and a half of the descent, Titan communicated with Polar Prince every 15 minutes, but communication stopped after a recorded communication at 11:15 a.m. (13:45 UTC).

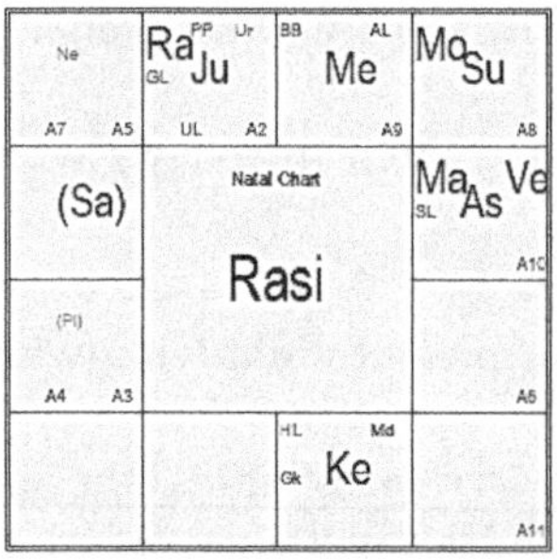

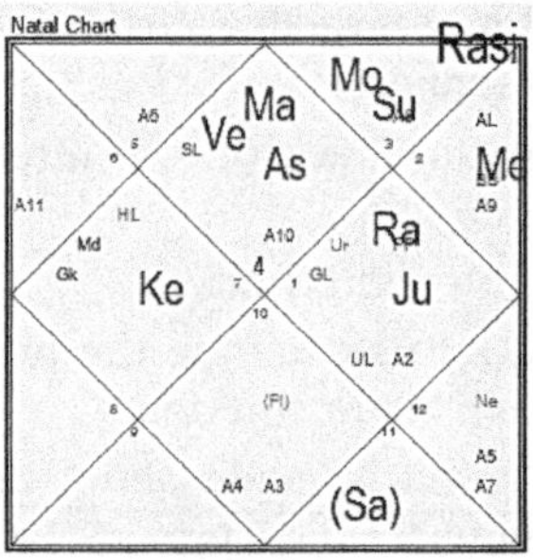

This is the Kuṇḍalī of the moment of launch, which is launched from a platform in the North Atlantic Ocean at 41°43′42″N 49°56′32″W. Udaya was in

Karka a Sajala Rāśi and with Śukra, a Sajala Graha. However, we immediately see some flaws in the launching moment.

(1) Lagna has Nīca Maṅgala indicating damage to the vehicle. There is affliction by a Krūra (Nīca Maṅgala). There is no Nīcabhaṅga of Maṅgala.

(2) Lagneśa Candra is in 12H (Vyāya, Trika), afflicted by Sūrya in Śukla Pratipada Tithi, Kiṁstughna Karaṇa (Sthira Karaṇa = danger).

(3) 10L (Kāryeśa) in Lagna, Nīca, also indicating that the submersible will meet with failure.

Titan's hull is believed to have collapsed due to enormous water pressure. The sub was built to withstand such pressure - and experts are trying to determine what went wrong.

Kailāśa: If the Praśna is about whether the ship has left the port, how to determine that?

Jayanta: The answer to the Praśna is in the next principle.

27.464. If Udaya is not Pṛṣṭodayi and dṛṣṭied by its lord, the ship will leave the country of destination. When Lagneśa is dṛṣṭied by a Graha, the ship will be sighted.

Ācārya: Pṛṣṭodayi Rāśi is backwards looking, and it brings someone to the point of origin. Therefore, if the ship leaves in a Pṛṣṭodayi Rāśi, it does not reach the destination and returns.

The same principle should apply to Praśna also. If Praśna Udaya is in a Pṛṣṭodayi Rāśi, it is inferred that the ship has not left its port. If it is in another Rāśi, it is on its way to the destination and will arrive when other Yogas are favourable.

Jayanta: Pṛṣṭodayi Rāśis are Meṣa, Vṛṣabha, Karka, Dhanu and Makara.

Ācārya: That is right!

Kailāśa: How about whether the ship will arrive soon or not?

Jayanta: That is answered in the next śloka.

27.465. If Udaya or Chatra is Cara, the ship will arrive soon. If Candra is in 4H/5H, the ship will arrive soon. If Śukra is in 2H/3H, the ship will arrive. Likewise, should other predictions be made after careful investigation?

Ācārya: We have already learned that Cara = movement, Sthira = steadiness, and Dvisva = movement with obstacles. The same principle is used here.

Jayanta: If Lagna is in a Cararāśi, the ship will arrive soon. Isn't it?

Ācārya: That is right. Besides, we should also examine Candra and Śukra. Candra in 4H or 5H indicates that the ship will arrive soon. Śukra in 11H from those places, i.e., 2H or 3H, indicate the same.

Kailāśa: What is the significance of those Bhāvas?

Ācārya: The four Bhāvas from the next house of Lagna are considered. 4H is Candra's Dikbala, but more than that, Lagna is in 9H/10H from Candra, which strengthens the Lagna. Besides, Saumyas in the Rāśis following the Lagna favours the Lagna, as Lagna would cross them in time (2hrs per Rāśi approx.).

28. ON ACHIEVEMENTS

Kailāśa: Guruji, kindly tell us how to decipher whether someone will be successful in their endeavour.

Ācārya: For that, we should examine the Yogas for Kāryasiddhi Praśna.

Sunidhi: What is Kāryasiddhi Praśna?

Jayanta: Kāryasiddhi Praśnas deal with the success or failure of something. Suppose you are applying for a job and wish to know whether you will succeed. Again, you wish to buy a house and want to know if you will succeed. All such Praśnas are called Kāryasiddhi Praśna.

Ācārya: Besides knowing success or failure, we can also predict when something will be successful using these principles.

Kailāśa: Dhanyavād Gurubhrāta, and Guruji. What are those principles?

Ācārya: The author of Jñānapradīpikā gives the following seven principles for them.

28.466-470. The time when the work will be accomplished is stated here. There are seven Yogas when work is accomplished: **(1)** When LL and 10L are in 10H; **(2)** when LL and 10L are in Lagna; **(3)** when Lagna is dṛṣṭied by LL or when 10L dṛṣṭies 10H; **(4)** when 10L is in Lagna and dṛṣṭies LL; **(5)** when LL is in 10H and dṛṣṭies 10L; **(6)** when LL dṛṣṭies 10H and 10L dṛṣṭies Udaya; and **(7)** when 10L dṛṣṭies LL and LL dṛṣṭies 10L. When Candra dṛṣṭies any of the above Yogas, the accomplishment of work is certain.

Kailāśa: What are the main pointers here, Guruji?

Ācārya: For job, success and honour, generally, 10H is involved. But for other matters, you can consider the appropriate Kāryabhāva, i.e., for business and travel, you should consider 7H; for financial gains, 11H and so on. The Lord of Kāryabhāva is called Kāryeśa.

Kailāśa: What is next?

Ācārya: There are three important rules here:

(1) The Lagneśa has yutidṛṣṭi with Lagna and Kāryeśa has yutidṛṣṭi with Kāryabhāva.

(2) The Lagneśa has yutidṛṣṭi with Kāryabhāva and Kāryeśa has yutidṛṣṭi with Lagna.

(3) The Lagneśa and Kāryeśa are in yutidṛṣṭi Sambandha.

Sunidhi: What is the role of Candra in these Yogas, Guruji?

Ācārya: Candra's yutidṛṣṭi on Lagna/Lagneśa, Kāryabhāva/Kāryeśa offers even more certainty to the success of the event.

Kailāśa: Dhanyavād, Guruji!

28.471. Suppose these Yogas are not available. Even then, when 10L transits Udaya, the achievement of the work must be predicted, says the Śāstra of Jñānapradīpikā.

Ācārya: The author states that suppose the Yogas are not present in the Praśna Kuṇḍalī, but instead, 10L transits Udaya shortly. Even then, the success of such an event can be expected.

Sunidhi: Are there any more such Yogas?

Ācārya: An event can also be timed when Kāryeśa has any Sambandha with Lagna, or Lagneśa has any Sambandha with Kāryabhāva, or Lagneśa and Kāryeśa have Sambandha. These can happen in Gocara.

Kailāśa: Should we also consider the strength of the Grahas in Gocara?

Ācārya: That we must do all the time. The results always depend on the dignity of the Grahas. Suppose Kāryeśa is transiting Lagna, and it is Ucca. Then it indicates a grand success. But instead, it is in Nīca/Śatru Rāśi/Añśa; then the success is limited.

Sunidhi: Should we also consider the Añśa transits?

Ācārya: Yes, we should always consider the Añśa transits, mainly Navāñśa. But if you have time, consider the Gocara through other Vargas. That is an advanced topic, and I intend to cover that in my Gocara Book.

28.472. If one carefully studies this Śāstra and gives his prediction after proper investigation, his words will not become untrue. This Śāstra of Praśna is an ornament to the world, provided it is applied rightly.

Ācārya: With this, let us conclude our discourse.

Om Tat Sat!

24.4 ABOUT "IN SEARCH OF JYOTIṢA"

The Book *"In Search of Jyotiṣa"* is a collection of 33 volumes containing several topics of Jyotiṣa, from beginning to advanced stages. This book focuses on retaining the authenticity of the subject as taught by the Maharṣis and the Ācāryas. I have retained the classical texts' originality while providing my thoughts, reflections, and interpretations. Jyotiṣa is vast, like a boundless ocean; therefore, mastering it in one's lifetime appears impossible. It is arduous to even go through each principle of Jyotiṣa, let alone master it. There are, however, a few who could attain a great deal of knowledge on this subject.

In my journey into the world of Jyotiṣa, which started in 1988, I studied numerous texts of the Maharṣis, Ācāryas and modern-day authors. However, I encountered challenges; firstly, not many authors have written, copiously sharing their experiences. Secondly, there are numerous contradictions, but few have explained how to reconcile or resolve them. **I have seen an attitude that "this is what my tradition and teacher teaches; therefore, the other teaching or interpretation must be incorrect".** Hardly many tried to reconcile the differences objectively. Among all authors, I hold Dr BV Raman on the highest pedestal for his yeoman service to the field of Jyotiṣa by writing several books on different topics explaining things in an easily understandable language.

Besides that, most books in the market are like an instruction manual or a coursebook, which instructs how to do this and do that. Several books are merely a narration of Jyotiṣa Yogas. **I always hoped that there were books that explained the "why" behind the Yogas.** For example, the classical texts state that when Candra is in Meṣa Rāśi, the person shall have such and such characteristics, but hardly anyone explains why that should be.

Hardly anyone explains the "Why" part of the equation, even among modern-day authors. **It always makes me curious about the "Why"; I reflected upon them and penned my thoughts.** I faced numerous challenges, but as time passed, the Yogas revealed themselves like a beam of sunshine in a dark cloud. I believe the blessings of my Guru, my Iṣṭadevatā, my parents, and countless others manifested in the form of this knowledge flowing through me.

Perhaps I am open-minded because I am not indoctrinated into any specific tradition from a young age. While receiving knowledge from a tradition is a fantastic way of learning it fast and furthering it, it makes one too attached to it and not question it. It is a blessing in disguise that I have to work hard to get something that one gets merely because one is born into a family or under some circumstances. It must be my Karma that I had to be born in a situation where I had to uncover the secrets on my own. It is also a blessing that I am not overly attached to a preconceived notion and am always ready to question myself, my understanding and my assumptions. **I do not outrightly reject a view and look for the truth behind it. The lack of preconceived notions helps me examine the thoughts and opinions of contradicting practitioners with an objective eye.**

The book "In Search of Jyotiṣa" is the outcome of the search for the divine principles that govern human lives and the lives of everything else, animate or inanimate. The idea that the same principles govern everything in the universe has always motivated me. This motivation pushed me to continue the journey without giving up. **I started penning down my thoughts on Jyotiṣa in 2004, and from 2012 onwards, it started taking the form of a Book.** I wrote two books before, which I never published, called the "Principles of Divination", a collection of principles from several classical texts. I didn't publish it because I did not want to publish another book of principles, Yogas and Sūtras.

"In Search of Jyotiṣa" took at least eight years, if not more, but it contained the gist of experiences of my studies spanning 33 years. I kept writing on several topics without realizing that it had become humongous. There are 33 volumes of the book containing a range of topics if not all. **I have also taken an unconventional approach to writing my thoughts on Lālkitāb. The focus has been to elucidate the principles.**

This book may not be a favourite among the exponents of Jyotiṣa, but my approach to Jyotiṣa is different. **I do not wish to decide what the readers should read or not.** I narrated my understanding and reflections hoping that someone would find it useful. **I do not belong to any specific tradition; therefore, I have no compulsion to follow any dictates. My Guru is Lord Śiva, and my tradition is that of a "Seeker".** I write on this subject with an open heart and mind, letting people choose what they wish to accept and what they do not.

I always believe that in my Kuṇḍalī, **Bṛhaspati's dṛṣṭi** on Dharmeśa Sūrya, Karmeśa Budha and Pañcameśa Maṅgala would keep in on the right track. I also believe that Ketu in the Trikoṇa to my Kārakāñśa and 2nd from Lagnāñśa would shower me with profound knowledge of this discipline. I do not wish to sound boastful, but I am a born Jyotiṣī and doing what I do best – sharing my reflections with the world! **I hope you find the journey into the world of Jyotiṣa equally engaging and enlightening. The list of 33 volumes of the book is as follows:**

Table 29: The 33 volumes

Book	Name	Content
Book 1	**Introduction to Jyotiṣa**	• The book introduces the discipline of Jyotiṣa. It covers the purpose of Jyotiṣa, its brief history, notable Jyotiṣīs, the current state, reflections on whether Jyotiṣa is a science, demonstrating how Jyotiṣa is a universal language. It covers thoughts and reflections on why Jyotiṣa work must, i.e., the philosophical basis of this subject, the scope of Jyotiṣa. There are important Yogas that make one a Jyotiṣī

Book	Name	Content
		and the fundamental building blocks of this subject. It covers the scope of the books in the series "In Search of Jyotish" and a brief introduction about me.
Book 2	**The Kārakatvas**	• This book covers in detail the entire domain of Graha Kārakatvas, Rāśi Kārakatvas and Bhāva Kārakatvas. There is a detailed deliberation on several topics of Kārakatvas, including the Dhātus, Doṣas, Grahas and avocations, Aprakāśa Grahas and Upagrahas and several others. • This book aims to provide a thorough grounding on the Kārakatvas of the Grahas, Rāśis and Bhāvas. This is a crucial step for those wishing to enter the Jyotiṣa world. • For a Seasoned Jyotiṣī, it should serve as a good reference book, and I believe they would benefit from the detailed deliberation of topics such as Dhātus and Doṣas, classification of matter into Dhātu Mūla Jīva.
Book 3	**Rāśi and Bhāva Phala**	• This book covers the results of Graha's placement in Rāśis and Bhāvas. When Grahas move through Rāśis, they give rise to specific results. The aura of the Graha intermingles with the Rāśis, and the Graha takes different forms. Even though every Graha has its innate nature, they undergo significant modifications depending on the Rāśis they occupy. • Like Lord Viṣṇu has 10 Avatāras, and in each of the Avatāras, Lord Viṣṇu appears significantly different; the Grahas also take 12 different forms when they occupy the 12 Rāśis. Analysing the results of a Graha in a Bhāva without considering its specific form is misleading. In this book, I have assigned a name to each of these forms of the Grahas, which could help readily understand the form. Besides this, the forms are also affected by the dṛṣṭi of the Grahas, which are also specified. Also, given why a Graha manifests certain kinds of results in a Rāśi, based on my years of reflections. I hoped to find it when I started my Jyotiṣa studies, but not much literature is available. • The book also covers the Bhāva effects of the Grahas, and the results are excerpted from several classical texts, including Bṛhajjātaka, Sārāvalī and Phaladīpikā. Also, given the results of Graha placement in different Bhāvas for the 12 different Lagnas, a total of 108 combinations. These are not exhaustive but can explain how Graha's Bhāvaphala changes for different Lagnas.
Book 4	**Strength and Bhāva Analysis**	• This chapter contains a detailed account of the computation of the strengths of Grahas, Rāśis and Bhāvas. A step-by-step computation of Ṣaḍbala is included in this chapter. Several topics, such as Ceṣṭā Bala, Yuddha Bala etc., are clarified with examples. In the Abdamāsadinahorā Bala, it is demonstrated how to find the Sṛṣṭi and Kali Ahargaṇa, based on which the Sāvana Varṣa Lord must be found. It is also explained what the basis of the Lordship is for Horā, Vāra, Māsa and Varṣa. • A detailed account of Rāśi and Bhāva Balas is also covered with worked-out examples. This dispels several doubts on the computation of the strength of various elements, viz.,

Book	Name	Content
		Graha, Rāśi and Bhāva. A detailed account of Graha yuddha is given, dispelling the doubts on when two Grahas must be considered in Grahayuddha and who is considered victorious. The ślokas support the arguments from Maharṣi Parāśara, Sūryasiddhānta, and Bṛhatsaṅhitā. • The second portion of the book contains a detailed account of how to judge a Bhāva methodically. The principles are adopted from Phaladīpikā Adhyāya 15 and are explained in great detail. This is followed by a detailed account of Bhāvanātha Bhāva Phala, covering the results of 12 Bhāveśas in 12 Bhāvas, a total of 144 combinations. I have given my thoughts and reflections on each of these topics, which I believe will dispel doubts in the mind of a seeker. A seasoned Jyotiṣī, I believe, will have a different perspective, which they find useful.
Book 5	**Janma**	• Janma means birth; therefore, this book covers almost everything that one must know on the subject of birth. It starts with the topic of deciphering birth circumstances from a Kuṇḍalī and an examination of Yogas contained in several classical texts, including Bṛhatparāśara, Bṛhajjātaka, Sārāvalī, Jātakatattva and others. There are several illustrations of the effects of Grahas on birth circumstances. • This contains the Yogas from Nāradapurāṇa regarding Śubha and Aśubha Janma, conditions of illegitimate birth, what is called Jāraja Yoga, and their annulation. The Niṣeka and Ādhāna Kuṇḍalī deal with the construction and interpretation of the conception chart, which is also called the pre-natal epoch. The Viyoni Janma chapter details non-human birth, such as animals, plants, birds etc., and how to decipher them. The principles of the naming chapter deal with naming a newborn child that is harmonious with the Kuṇḍalī. • The birth time rectification section provides a step-by-step method of rectifying a Kuṇḍalī with principles derived from several classical texts, including the Prāṇapada, Kunda, Janma Vighaṭika, Tattva and Antartattva methods. A few more principles and guidance are given to verify one's Lagna. A section is dedicated to the casting of a Kuṇḍalī from Praśna when the Kuṇḍalī is lost, and the birth time is completely unknown. Yet another section is dedicated to the effects due to birth in several time elements such as Bārhaspatya Varṣa, several Tithis, Vāras etc. These effects help in fine-tuning the results in a Kuṇḍalī. • The Lost Horoscopy section provides several methods of constructing a Kuṇḍalī from Praśna. This is called Naṣṭajātaka and is useful if the birth time is unknown or inaccurate.
Book 6	**Ariṣṭa**	• Ariṣṭas are the evil Yogas in a Kuṇḍalī. This starts with examining the 21 flaws in time in which birth, Muhūrta or Praśna yields troublesome results. Then, the Nakṣatra Ariṣṭa section covers the danger caused by being born in a certain Nakṣatra. Next, the Gaṇḍānta birth covers the

Book	Name	Content
		different Gaṇḍāntas. Then, it covers the topic such as Abhukta Mūla, Mūla Nivāsa, Mūlavṛkṣa and several other topics. Finally, the topic of Bālāriṣṭa is dealt with in great detail in a structured manner, starting with a robust foundation of the building blocks of such Yogas. These involve assessment of Kṣīṇacandra, afflictions to Candra Lagna, Udaya Lagna and several others. • There is a careful analysis of several Yogas that indicate danger to both the child, the mother, and, in some cases, the father. The Ariṣṭabhaṅga Yogas indicate the protection one has from the evils in a Kuṇḍalī. These protections work throughout one's lifetime; therefore, identifying them is vital. The Yogas, such as Bṛhaspati in dignity in a Kendra, work throughout life and protect the person from several evils. Similarly, Saumyas should be in Kendrakoṇas, and Krūras in Triṣaḍāyas are a great protective force.
Book 7	**Health and Longevity**	• This book is divided into four sections (1) Bodily characteristics, (2) Examination of longevity, (3) Cause and timing of death, and (4) Analysing diseases. Each of them covers significant areas. For instance, the bodily characteristics cover physical features, the predominant Guṇa of a person, the Varṇas or natural propensities, and the personality traits. The section on diseases thoroughly treats several diseases, including the brain, respiratory, eye, speech, etc.
Book 8	**The 12 Bhāvas**	• This book serves as an introduction to the 12 Bhāvas. Jyotiṣa is a vast subject, and each Bhāva comprises myriads of Yoga. It is nearly impossible to do an exhaustive treatment of each Bhāva in a book like this because each Bhāva deserves to be covered in a separate volume dedicated to the Bhāva. However, this book aims to cover the width of Jyotiṣa at the expense of depth. This book includes a high-level assessment of a few crucial Yogas of each Bhāva, those culled from Jyotiṣa classics Phaladīpikā and Sārāvalī. However, this is a compendium of Yogas contained in several classical texts, including Bṛhatparāśara, Jātakatattva, Saṅketa Nidhi, Suka Jātaka, and a few other important texts.
Book 9	**Nakṣatra**	• This book covers in detail what one should know about the Nakṣatras. This includes the Nakṣatra Devatās, their classification into seven classes, the Purāṇic lore, the Hoḍā or Avakahada Cakra, details of each Nakṣatra, including their symbol, Devatās etc. Tārās in the Nakṣatras, Nakṣatra and avocations, effects of Grahas and Bhāvanātha in the Nakṣatras, the Nakṣatra Puruṣa, Nakṣatra in the delineation of diseases, the blessing of Nakṣatras, usage of Nakṣatras in marital compatibility and a detailed delineation of birth in each Nakṣatra.
Book 10	**Crucial Building Blocks**	• This book covers several topics that are not yet covered, including how to write a Kuṇḍalī the traditional way, detailed deliberation on the construction of Bhāva Kuṇḍalī, including the opinions of several scholars, Maharṣis and Ācāryas, the Graha Avasthās, including

Book	Name	Content
		Bālādi, Jāgṛtādi, Dīptādi, Lajjitādi, Sayanādi and the Graha Samayas. • The section on the Aprakāśa Grahas and Upagrahas covers their computation and delineation in a Kuṇḍalī, the computation and usage of Prāṇapada, and deliberation on the Tattvas and Guṇas. • The section on Yogakārakas states the distinction between Auspicious vs Favourable, results due to ownership of a Bhāva, Yoga between Kendra-Koṇa Lords, Treatment of Rāhu and Ketu, The Kārakatvas of individual Bhāvanātha, and delineation of Yogakārakas for different Lagnas, that includes my reflections on the principles/Yogas presented by Ācārya Ramanuja, in Bhāvārtha Ratnākara.
Book 11	**Yogas**	• The book on Yoga covers the Yoga fundamentals, the Lagna Yogas, Candra Yogas, Sūrya Yogas, the Nābhasa Yogas, delineation of Paraspara Kārakas, Rājayogas of Maharṣi Parāśara and Ācārya Kalyāṇavarmā, and Rāja Sambandha Yoga, Rājabhaṅga Yoga, Adverse Yogas from classical texts such as Jātakapārijāta, Bṛhajjātaka and Horāsāra. It covers the controversial Yoga, the Kālasarpa Yoga and its several variations. There is an exhaustive treatment of the Pravrājya Yoga, and several other Yogas are excerpted from classical texts of Maharṣi Garga, Maharṣi Suka, Ācārya Mahādeva, and Ācārya Ramanuja. There is also coverage of the Dvigraha, Trigraha etc., Yogas.
Book 12	**Pañcāṅga and Muhurta**	• It covers the five elements of Pañcāṅga, including the Nakṣatra, the Vāra, the Tithi, the Karṇa and the Nityayogas. The section on Muhūrta elements covers the concept of 30 Muhūrtas, Sūrya's Saṅkrānti, the effects of Lagna, delineation of the portfolio owner of a year, such as the King of the year, minister of the year, lord of vegetation, lord of grains etc. There is a detailed treatment of the principles of Muhūrta, the Pañcāṅga Yogas, i.e., the special Yogas that are formed due to Vāra-Nakṣatra, Vāra-Tithi, Nakṣatra-Tithi etc. The special Nakṣatra Ghaṭis covers, the Viṣa, Uṣṇa, Amṛta Ghaṭis. There is a delineation of Ānandādi Yogas, the Samvatsara and Yugas, based on Bṛhaspati's mean motion, and the formation of adverse Yogas such as Ekārgala, Vaidhṛti, Krūrasaṅyuta etc. • The Muhūrta section deals with the principles of choosing important Muhūrtas, including the 16 Saṅskāras, travel, education, treatment of diseases, coronation, installing a Devatā etc.
Book 13	**Jyotish Siddhānta 1**	• This contains two sections, Modern Astronomy and Siddhāntika Astronomy. The Modern Astronomy section covers the measurement of time, the coordinate system, including equatorial and ecliptic coordinate systems, the transformation of coordinates, the computation of the mean and true position of Grahas as per the modern computation methods, coordinates of fixed stars, and examination of the concepts of obliquity and nutation. By studying this, one can determine the coordinates of Nakṣatras and Grahas per modern methods.

Book	Name	Content
		• The Siddhāntika Astronomy section starts with a deliberation of the classical and medieval astronomers, the Hindu Astronomy vis-à-vis others, the time and place of Sūryasiddhānta, the fundamentals, the mean places of Grahas, the true places of Grahas, the nine measures of times, notes on Indian calendars, and the 60 Jovian years. By studying this, one can compute the true places of Grahas using the Siddhāntika methods. I have also proposed some adjustments (Bīja corrections) of Sūryasiddhānta values to tally with the modern values.
Book 14	**Jyotish Siddhānta 2**	• This book has three sections: the Astronomical events, the Computation of Lagna, and Ayanāñśa. The Astronomical events section covers Grahayuti, Astāṅgata, Vakragati, Grahayuddha, and Grahaṇa. Each topic contains the astronomical computations and astrological delineation of these events. • The Computation of Lagna section deals with the method of determining the Lagna on a date and time based on the traditional Śaṅku Chāyā method as well as the modern method of using sidereal time. • The Ayanāñśa section covers the history of Ayanāñśa, the difference between the two zodiacs, Nirāyana and Sāyana, seven different methods of determining Ayanāñśas, including the method of Sūryasiddhānta libration, the IAU's method, from the length of a Tropical and Sidereal day, Nakṣatra Method and others. After that, I captured the important Ayanāñśas in vogue in today's world before delving into Ācārya Varāhamihira's Ayanāñśa and Sṛṣṭi Ayanāñśa.
Book 15	**Lagna Bhāva**	• This book dives deep into the topic of the Lagna Bhāva. This contains six sections, viz., What is Lagnabhāva, The nature of Lagna Rāśi, Birth in different Lagnas, Graha Lagna Phala, and Lagneśa Bhāvaphala. This is perhaps the most detailed treatment of this Bhāvas ever done by an astrological writer.
Book 16	**Special Lagnas**	• There are five sections of this book, viz., The Viśeṣa Lagna, Candralagna, The Āruṛhalagna, The Svāṃśa Lagna, and the Kāraka Lagna. This does an exhaustive treatment of various things delineated from these several Lagnas. The Viśeṣa Lagna section covers the Bhāva Lagna, the Horālagna, the Vighaṭika Lagna, the Varṇada Lagna, and the Prāṇapada Lagna.
Book 17	**Lagna Yogas**	• This is perhaps the most detailed delineation of the Lagna Yogas from several classical texts. There are twelve sections of this book, Lagna fundamentals, success in the homeland or abroad, judging three portions of life, dṛṣṭi Yogas, facial features, personality traits, health and diseases, madness, speech-related Yogas, fame, and fame renown, miscellaneous Yogas, and Yogas from other sources. Each of these sections has a detailed deliberation of the topic covered. For instance, the Lagna fundamentals contain Lagna Kārakatvas, strengths and weaknesses, body structure and complexion, physical felicity, and physical appearance. Similarly, success in the homeland or

Book	Name	Content
		abroad, the characteristics of the foreign land etc. This contains almost everything one needs to know about the Lagna Bhāva.
Book 18	**Aṣṭakavarga**	• This comprehensively covers the method of Aṣṭakavarga. There are eight sections viz., construction, the fundamentals, Rekhās and Karaṇas, Bhinnāṣṭakavarga, Samudāyāṣṭakavarga, Daśā application, Aṣṭakavarga Gocara, Kakṣyā, and Longevity estimation. This book is written after consulting several classical texts on this subject, including Bṛhatparāśara, Bṛhajjātaka, Sārāvalī, Phaladīpikā, Aṣṭakavarga Mahānibandha, Jātakapārijāta, Jātaka Deśamārga, and Praśnamārga. This book should be able to denounce several doubts, including whether Rāśi or Bhāva should be used for the construction of the Aṣṭakavarga, the Śodhanas etc. This book does an exhaustive treatment of almost all the topics of Aṣṭakavarga.
Book 19	**Important Methods and Tools**	• This book covers several topics, including Pācakādi Sambandha, Śrī Kālidāsa's Principles, Special chakras, Patāki Riṣṭa, Tripāpa Cakra, Bhṛgu's Paddhati, Pañcaka, Candra's special avasthās such as Candrakriyā etc., Miscellaneous tools such as Mṛtyubhāga, Bhṛgubindu etc., the Bādhaka and Strī Jātaka. • The special Cakra section contains esoteric diagrams, including Navatārā Cakra, Ghātaka Cakra, Dimbha Cakra, Nara Cakra, Graha Puruṣa Cakras, The Śatapada Cakra, the Kālānala Cakras, Yamadaṁṣṭrā Cakra, Trināḍī Cakra, Gaja and Aśva Cakras, Pañcasvara Cakra, Sannāḍī Cakra, Koṭa Cakra and Sanghatta Cakra. • The Bhṛgu Paddhati contains the translation of Bhṛgu Sūtra, Bhṛgu Saṅhitā, and Bhṛgu Saral Paddhati (BSP).
Book 20	**The Vargas**	• This covers several topics of Vargas or Subdivisions of a Rāśi. This includes delineation of the 16 Vargas of Maharṣi Parāśara, the principles of analysing Vargas, the Varga dignities, the variations of Vargas, such as Parivṛtti Vargas etc., the different kinds of Horās, Navāñśas, Dreṣkāṇas etc. This also contains the usage of individual Vargas for delineating a Kuṇḍalī. • It contains an examination of whether the Vargas can be used as Kuṇḍalīs and what the Śāstras say about it. Several dictums from the classical texts are given to clarify the views of the classical authors. • There are staunch believers of both schools of thought, those who do not accept the concept of Bhāva and dṛṣṭi in the Vargas, whereas there are those who support the view that Vargas should also be treated as Kuṇḍalīs. I do not wish to force anyone with what I believe; I only wish to present before the seekers what the different classical texts say on this topic to arrive at their conclusions.
Book 21	**Nakṣatra and Nāḍī Jyotiṣa**	• This book covers several facets of Nakṣatra and Nāḍī Jyotiṣa. The Nakṣatra Jyotiṣa delineates the core principles of the Mīna 1 Nāḍī, Mīna 2 Nāḍī, Kṛṣṇamūrti Paddhati (KP) and Iyer's Paddhati. Iyer's Paddhati is based on the

Book	Name	Content
		legendary Jyotiṣī Śrī HR Sheshadri Iyer, whose books, the New Techniques of Prediction 3 volumes are cornerstones of Jyotiṣa. • Śrī Iyer did not exclusively deal with the Nakṣatras. Still, his determination and usage of Yogī and Avayogi and the usage of Nakṣatra is pathbreaking, which is why it is included in this book dedicated to Nakṣatra and Nāḍī Jyotiṣa. I have covered in detail some abstruse concepts with worked-out examples, such as the Starter and Ruler for assessment of Viñśottarī Daśā. • The Nāḍī Jyotiṣa section covers the essential principles from Saptarṣi Nāḍī and Bhṛgu Nandi Nāḍī. Besides providing a synopsis of the genre of Nāḍī Jyotiṣa, there is a detailed exploration of topics such as the blending of Kārakatvas and how the blending is affected by the sequence of Grahas having yuti in a Rāśi. I am hoping that this book will provide wide coverage of topics from both Nakṣatra and Nāḍī Jyotiṣa that both beginners and advanced practitioners would find useful.
Book 22	**Jaimini Sūtra**	• This book introduces the subject of Jaimini Sūtra concisely to beginners. One who wishes to grasp the Sūtras quickly can find a systematic way of dealing with the subject. Jaimini Sūtra is complex and terse and requires years of Tapasyā to understand. I have given several examples to make the concept clearer. • It isn't easy to decipher and understand the profound meaning of a Sūtra without the guidance of a Guru. Therefore, this book does not intend to teach this complex subject; however, it presents a robust framework with apt translations to introduce this subject to an earnest seeker. One who wishes to pursue it further must study under a bonafide Guru.
Book 23	**Praśnaśāstra**	• In great detail, this book covers the subject of Horary Astrology, also called Praśna Śāstra. This is built upon the foundation of several classical texts, including Praśnamārga, Praśnatantra, Daivajña Vallabha, Kṛṣṇīyam, Ṣaṭpañcāśikā and others. The concepts are explained in great detail and with examples. This covers topics such as Nimittas, Aṣṭamaṅgala Praśna, Manomuṣṭi Praśna, Kāryasiddhi Praśna, Devapraśna, analysis of dreams, and some esoteric Cakras like Candragupti Cakra which is used to locate water underground. • There is an exhaustive treatment of Praśnas relating to the 12 Bhāvas. For instance, 2H Praśna deals with financial gains; 4H Praśna deals with Agriculture, cultivation, and leasing agreements. 6H deals with matters concerning diseases, employee-employer relationships etc. The treatment of each of these topics is detailed with copious notes and explanations.
Book 24	**Jinendramāla**	• Jinendramāla is an important Praśna text written by a Jain Monk, Upendrācārya. It has methods scantily found in other Praśna works, such as Praśnamārga. Concepts such as Chatra Rāśi, also called Kavippu, are explained in this

Book	Name	Content
		work. Besides that, the book explains the concept of Yamagraha, also called Jāmakkol or Sāmakkol. These are the special position of Grahas in a Kuṇḍalī, which is determined by dividing a day into Yāmas or Jāmams. The text gives the method of locating a treasure underground using Candragupti Cakra, explained in Praśnamārga in locating water underground. This method of Praśna is also called Jāmakkol Āruṛham and Sāmakkol Āruṛham and is widely used in southern India.
Book 25	**Svara Śāstra**	• Svaraśāstra is about breathing or Svara for regulating one's life or answering Praśna. The content of this book is based on the foundation laid by texts such as Praśnamārga, Svara Cintāmaṇi and Lord Śiva Svarodaya. The ślokas from these texts are examined in great detail and explained so that anyone with little or no knowledge of this subject can understand them. The Svara Śāstra has great usage in Horary; therefore, this is highly recommended for those who wish to attain mastery in Praśna.
Book 26	**Śrāpa and Puṇya Cakra**	• Śrāpas are curses that manifest as great evil in one's life. Maharṣi Parāśara details several kinds of Śrāpas that cause denial or loss of children and are called Sutakṣaya Śrāpa. This book explains all about such Śrāpas and the remedial measures that can be undertaken to reduce the effects of such Śrāpas. • The Puṇya Cakra is cast at the moment of death of an individual. From this Kuṇḍalī, the whereabouts of the person who has left his mortal frame can be deciphered. How long the person is wandering on the early plane, whether the person has attained peace after death, which spirit worlds, the person is guided to etc., can be known from this Kuṇḍalī.
Book 27	**Lālkitāb**	• Even though the Lālkitāb is not part of Vedic Astrology, it contains principles based on the same building blocks. The Kārakatvas for the Grahas, Bhāvas etc., are the same, but their application is different. Even though several practitioners of this text use this for prescribing several remedies that can be done relatively easily, there is more to this text than remedies. • This book is a storehouse of principles that are hardly found elsewhere. For instance, the text claims that when Rāhu is in the Lagna, Sūrya becomes negative, and the house occupied by such Sūrya is ruined. Before delineating the results, the text juxtaposes the Grahas in the Bhāvas to the Rāśis. Several unique delineations, such as Pucca Ghar, Andhe Graha, Sāthī Graha, etc., are explained to anyone who wishes to learn this text. Besides that, common remedies specified by the book are also stated. • Explained in the book, the concept of house Kuṇḍalī, i.e., the Kuṇḍalī of the house as well as Sāmudrika Śāstra, which includes corroborating the planetary positions in a Kuṇḍalī to the marks and Rāśis in one's Palm. This is an excellent text for those who wish to learn Astro palmistry.

Book	Name	Content
Book 28	Daśā system 1	• Daśās are crucial for timing events in Jyotiṣaśāstra. However, there are numerous Daśās besides the commonly used Viñśottarī Daśā. This book explains the 42 Daśā systems of Maharṣi Parāśara before delving deeper into Viñśottarī Daśā. A composite assessment of Daśā and Gocara follows this.
Book 29	Daśā system 2	• After covering the foundation of the Daśās and Viñśottarī Daśā in the Daśā System 1, this book covers several other Daśās. This includes Cara Daśā, Āyuṣa Daśās, Mūla Daśā, Yogini Daśā, Sudarśana Cakra Daśā, and other Daśās such as Kendrādi Rāśi Daśā and Dṛgdaśā. The Kendrādi Rāśi Daśā covers Lagna Kendrādi Rāśidaśā, Kāraka Kendrādi Rāśidaśā, and Sudaśā. The Sudaśā is used for timing wealth, and it commences from the Śrīlagna. • The Āyuṣa Daśās contain several Daśās related to longevity and death, and it covers the Daśās such as Niryāṇa Daśā, Brahmā Daśā, Śūladaśā, Niryāṇa Śūladaśā, Sthira Daśā, Navāñśa Daśā, and Maṇḍūka Daśā. The Maṇḍūka Daśā is specifically used along with a special Varga called the Rudrāñśa (D11). Some of these Daśās are also covered in the book on Jaiminīsūtra.
Book 30	Kālacakra Daśā	• The Kālacakra Daśā is a special Daśā that is based on both Rāśi and Nakṣatra. It is complex, and there are several opinions on the computation of this Daśā. I have explained the computation with detailed explanation and illustration, which would dispel doubts among the seekers. This Daśā uses a Varga called Navanavāñśa, which is a further subdivision of a Navāñśa into nine parts. Besides the Kālacakra Daśā, which is the most complex among all, also covered are the Kāla Daśā and Cakra Daśā.
Book 31	Other timing methods	• There are several other timing methods besides the Daśās and Gocaras. Covered in this book are the methods of Progression, Annual Horoscopy, and several other methods. The Progression section covers Rāśi Progression, Varga Progression, Daśā Progression, and Madhyagraha Progression. The Madhyagraha Progression is a special topic that cannot be found elsewhere because the concept of Madhyagraha or the mean Graha is not dealt with in a Jyotiṣa text. I have proposed this method based on my experience with Sūryasiddhānta. • The Annual Kuṇḍalī covers Varṣaphala, which is a Tājika Technique, and the Tithi Praveśa Cakra. The other timing methods contain the Bhāgyodaya Varṣa, which is used for timing the rise of fortune. Also covered are the techniques of Candra's Nakṣatra method, Hillaja's years, and Varṣa, Māsa and Dina Daśā.
Book 32	Gocara	• Gocara is the continuous movement of Grahas in the zodiac. This book covers several topics ranging from the common technique of Gocara of Grahas from Janmarāśi to Sarvatobhadra Cakra. • There are several other topics covered in this book, including the Gocara of Grahas over the Grahas and

Book	Name	Content
		Bhaveśas in the Janmakuṇḍalī. Besides this, the Nakṣatra Caraṇa Gocara is used for the precise timing of events. • The Niryāṇa Prakaraṇa covers the Gocara, which indicates life threat or death. The Gocara of Śani indicates the 2.5 years period in which death can occur. That of Bṛhaspati indicates the year of death, that of Sūrya, the month, and Candra, the day of death. These principles must be applied in yuti with the Daśā, such as Chidra Daśā, for accurately timing death.
Book 33	**Remedies**	• Remedies are an integral part of Jyotiṣa. Even though we are bound to face problems due to past-life Karmas, some remedies help us manage the pain and suffering. We have diseases, but we also have medicines and Āyurveda to cure them. Or at least make it more manageable. Like health troubles are caused by past life Karmas, other evils such as delay in marriage, frequent failures etc., are also caused by past life Karmas. • The presence of problems in one's life does not mean that one must suffer unconditionally. If that were so, why would Maharṣi Parāśara suggest remedies for Gaṇḍānta birth, Māraka Daśās etc.? Remedies do work, provided the right remedy is given, and the person is sincere in carrying out the remedy. If evil Karmas in the past give us problems in this life, the good Karmas also allow us to overcome them. • This book details several topics, including specific Parihāra Sthalams, temples and shrines meant for overcoming the evils of Grahas. This includes Mantras, Vratas, Gemstones, Donations, and Charity. Also included is the usage of music or Rāgas for therapy.

ॐ

Om Tat Sat

Made in United States
North Haven, CT
26 January 2024

47865679R00182